A Clinician's Guide to Binge Eating Disorder

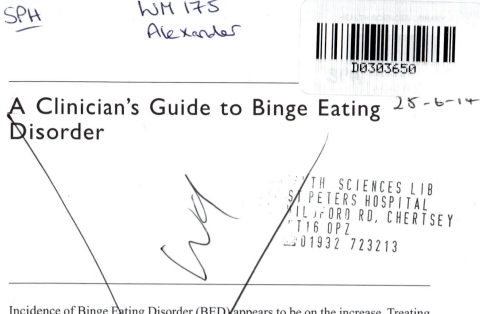

Incidence of Binge Eating Disorder (BED) appears to be on the increase. Treating it and overcoming it is all the more difficult, especially for those living in a culture that has an intense body image focus.

A Clinician's Guide to Binge Eating Disorder educates the reader about its triggers and behaviors, and describes steps to treat it and resume a full and productive life. Evidence-based research outcomes provide the framework and foundation for this book. First-person case studies bring application of this science to life to help close the gap between research and treatment/care, and the importance of clinicians developing a therapeutic relationship as a healing tool with their client is discussed, recognizing that medical and psychological dimensions are inextricably intertwined.

This book allays fear of the unknown, and explains the emotional chaos that can sweep in like a storm when, unintentionally, triggers are released. It provides practical steps and footholds for clinicians and researchers to help the patient take control of their life and look to a positive future.

June Alexander is an Australian writer and journalist with a particular focus on eating disorders.

Andrea B. Goldschmidt is Assistant Professor on the Eating Disorders Program at the University of Chicago.

Daniel Le Grange is Professor of Psychiatry in the Department of Psychiatry, and Director of the Eating Disorders Program at the University of Chicago.

A Clinician's Guide to Binge Eating Disorder

Edited by June Alexander,
Andrea B. Goldschmidt and
Daniel Le Grange

LONDON AND NEW YORK

First published 2013
by Routledge
27 Church Road, Hove, East Sussex BN3 2FA

Simultaneously published in the USA and Canada
by Routledge
711 Third Avenue, New York, NY 10017

Routledge is an imprint of the Taylor & Francis Group, an informa business

British Library Cataloguing in Publication Data
A catalogue record for this book is available from the British Library

Library of Congress Cataloging in Publication Data
A clinician's guide to binge eating disorder/edited by June Alexander, Andrea Goldschmidt, and Daniel Le Grange.

pages ; cm

Includes bibliographical references and index.

1. Compulsive eating--Psychological aspects. 2. Cognitive therapy. I. Alexander, June, 1950- editor of compilation. II. Goldschmidt, Andrea, editor of compilation. III. Le Grange, Daniel, editor of compilation.

RC552.C65C55 2013

616.85'26--dc23

2012034442

ISBN: 978-0-415-52717-0 (hbk)
ISBN: 978-0-415-52718-7 (pbk)
ISBN: 978-0-203-58599-3 (ebk)

Typeset in Times
by Fakenham Prepress Solutions, Fakenham, Norfolk NR21 8NN

MIX
Paper from
responsible sources
FSC
www.fsc.org   FSC® C004839

Printed and bound by CPI Group (UK) Ltd, Croydon, CR0 4YY

Contents

Contributors

Erin C. Accurso is a postdoctoral fellow with the Midwest Regional Postdoctoral Training Grant in Eating Disorders Research at the University of Chicago. She received her BA in psychology from Dartmouth College and her PhD in clinical psychology from the San Diego State University/University of California, San Diego Joint Doctoral Program in Clinical Psychology. Research interests include the treatment of eating disorders and overweight in youth, with the ultimate goal of greater dissemination and implementation of evidence-based practices in the community.

June Alexander developed anorexia nervosa at the age of 11 in 1962 and transitioned to bulimia nervosa. Her illness was not correctly diagnosed for 21 years. Her memoir, *A Girl Called Tim: Escape from an Eating Disorder Hell* (2011), chronicles the effect of eating disorders on her life. Other books by June on eating disorders include: *My Kid is Back: Empowering Parents to beat Anorexia Nervosa,* in collaboration with Professor Daniel Le Grange of the University of Chicago; *A Collaborative Approach to Eating Disorders,* with co-editor Professor Janet Treasure, of King's College, London; and *ED Says U said: Eating Disorder Translator,* co-authored with Cate Sangster, Melbourne. She also has co-authored with Professor Janet Treasure the 2nd Edition of *Anorexia Nervosa – Revovery Guide for Sufferers, Families and Friends* (Routledge 2013). June became passionate about raising awareness of BED upon meeting former sufferer and nowadvocate Chevese Turner (founder of the Binge Eating Disorder Association). People with BED, like sufferers of anorexia and bulimia, were experiencing isolation and stigma due to their illness being misunderstood. Discussion with Professor Le Grange about the need for education led to the creation of this textbook. June's blog and website link: www.junealexander.com

Myra Altman is a second-year graduate student in the clinical psychology program at Washington University in St Louis. She works with Dr Denise Wilfley in the Weight Management and Eating Disorders research lab. Her research interests include the prevention and treatment of eating and weight related disorders, and the public health and public policy implications of these issues.

Sarah E. Altman is a postdoctoral fellow with the Cleveland Center for Eating Disorders where she coordinates the Adult DBT Day Treatment/ Intensive Outpatient Program under the direction of Dr Lucene Wisniewski. She received her PhD in Clinical Psychology at the University of Illinois at Chicago after completing her pre-doctoral internship at West Virginia University in Morgantown. Research interests include the comorbidity of anxiety/OCD and eating disorders and psychophysiological correlates, as well as evaluation of treatments for multidiagnostic eating disorders.

Carrie Arnold is in recovery from anorexia and blogs daily at EDBites.com. Her most recent book is *Decoding Anorexia: How Breakthroughs in Science Offer Hope for Eating Disorders*, published by Routledge Press, 2012. She is an advisor to the advocacy organization FEAST (Families Empowered and Supporting the Treatment of Eating Disorders), and serves on the Board of Directors of the Eating Disorders Information Gateway. When not writing about eating disorders, Carrie writes on a variety of scientific and medical topics for magazines like *Scientific American*, *Psychology Today*, *Self*, and *Smithsonian*.

Judith Banker is founder and executive director of the Center for Eating Disorders, a non-profit support and outpatient treatment centre in Ann Arbor, Michigan established in 1983. She also serves as Lead Program Consultant to St Joseph Mercy Hospital Eating Disorder Recovery Program. Judith is a member of the Professional Advisory Panel of FEAST (Families Empowered and Supporting Eating Disorder Treatment) and the Advisory Board of the Academy for Eating Disorders (AED). The 2011 recipient of the AED Clinical Leadership Award, Judith lectures internationally on clinical treatment, in particular on the transtheoretical application of psychodynamic principles and techniques in eating disorder treatment and the integration of research with clinical experience. Her research and publications topics include research–practice integration, effective eating disorder treatment, and early identification and screening for eating disorders. Judith is Past President and a Fellow of the AED.

Kelly C. Berg is a postdoctoral fellow with the Midwest Regional Postdoctoral Training Program in Eating Disorders Research and the Director of Assessment for the Eating Disorders Research Program at the University of Minnesota. She received her PhD in Counseling Psychology at the University of Minnesota after completing her pre-doctoral internship at The University of Chicago Medical School. Research interests include assessment and diagnosis of eating disorders as well as the development of innovative treatments for reducing binge eating and compensatory behaviors.

Kerri Boutelle is an Associate Professor of Pediatrics and Psychiatry at University of California, San Diego. She completed her undergraduate degree in Food Science from Rutgers University, and completed her PhD in Clinical Psychology from the Illinois Institute of Technology. Dr Boutelle completed her pre-doctoral clinical internship at the University of Mississippi Medical Center and her postdoctoral fellowship in the Division of Epidemiology, University of Minnesota. She is an active member of the Academy for Eating Disorders, Eating Disorder Research Society, Obesity Society and the Association for Behavioral and Cognitive Therapies. She is Principal Investigator of numerous clinical trials evaluating behavioral treatments for binge eating disorder and obesity in children, adolescents and adults. Dr Boutelle is also active in training and supervision of psychology and medical students. Research interests include disseminating current behavioral treatment protocols for obesity, and new models of behavioral treatment for binge eating disorder and obesity.

Cynthia M. Bulik is Distinguished Professor of Eating Disorders, Department of Psychiatry University of North Carolina School of Medicine, Professor of Nutrition in the Gillings School of Global Public Health, and Director of the UNC Eating Disorders Program. She received her BA from the University of Notre Dame and her MA and PhD from the University of California at Berkeley. She completed internships and post-doctoral fellowships at the Western Psychiatric Institute and Clinic in Pittsburgh, PA. Research includes treatment, laboratory, animal, epidemiological, twin, and molecular genetic studies of eating disorders and body weight regulation. Dr Bulik has written more than 400 scientific papers and chapters on eating disorders, and is author of the books *Eating Disorders: Detection and Treatment, Runaway Eating, Crave: Why You Binge Eat and How To Stop, Abnormal Psychology* (Beidel, Bulik, Stanley), *The Woman in the Mirror* (2011), and *Midlife Eating Disorders* (2013, Walker).

Eunice Y. Chen is Assistant Professor of Psychology at Temple University. Her primary research interest is the etiology and treatment of people with eating and weight disorders. A focus of this work is on the development of psychosocial treatments for subgroups of people with eating disorders for whom standard treatments fail (e.g. non-responders to Cognitive Behavior Therapy as well as those with eating disorders and high negative affect and/or extensive co-morbidities). To this end Dr Chen has developed treatments for eating disorders utilizing dialectical behavior therapy and family based therapy. In addition, she is interested in the brain circuitry associated with eating disorders and how they are impacted by psychosocial treatment. As part of this work, Dr Chen runs a translational program utilizing functional magnetic resonance imaging, psychophysiological assessment and other behavioral neuroscience methods.

Scott Crow is Professor of Psychiatry at the University of Minnesota and Medical Director at the Emily Program. His research interests include causes, course and psychotherapeutic and pharmacologic treatment of eating disorders and obesity. Previously, he received a mid-career Independent Scientist

Award from NIMH focused on the treatment of eating disorders. He is a past President of the Academy for Eating Disorders. He is the Director of the Midwest Regional Postdoctoral Training Program in Disorders Research, as well as Director of the Disordered Eating/Assessment Core of the Minnesota Obesity Centre.

Michael J. Devlin is Professor of Clinical Psychiatry at Columbia University College of Physicians and Surgeons and Associate Director of the Eating Disorders Research Unit at New York State Psychiatric Institute. He is an active member of the Academy for Eating Disorders and a past president of that organization. He serves on the Editorial Board of the *International Journal of Eating Disorders* and *Eating Behaviors*. He is a member of the American Psychiatric Association Practice Guideline Work Group on Eating Disorders. In addition to research in eating disorders, he is active in medical student education and in training and supervision of psychiatry residents, particularly in cognitive behavioral therapy. Research interests include diagnosis and treatment of binge eating disorder, and psychological and behavioral aspects of weight regulation. Additional research relates to psychosocial, cognitive, and neuroendocrine outcomes in adults and adolescents undergoing bariatric surgery.

Scott Engel is a Research Scientist at the Neuropsychiatric Research Institute. He also is an Assistant Professor at the University of North Dakota School of Medicine and Health Sciences. Dr Engel received his doctoral degree from North Dakota State University in 2003 and worked at the Neuropsychiatric Research Institute as a post-doctoral fellow from 2003–2004. His primary research areas are in eating disorders, obesity, and bariatric surgery. He is particularly interested in the roles of cognitive and emotional variables in disordered eating and obesity. Much of Dr Engel's research involves the application of novel, technology-based methodologies to assess and intervene with these groups of patients. Most recently he has studied the development of alcohol use disorders in post-bariatric surgery patients.

Alison E. Field is Associate Professor of Pediatrics at Harvard Medical School and Associate Professor in the Department of Epidemiology at the Harvard School of Public Health where she co-directs Reproductive, Perinatal, and Pediatric Epidemiology. She received her BA in Psychology from the University of California, Berkeley and her ScD in Epidemiology from the Harvard School of Public Health. She is the co-founder and former co-director of the Growing Up Today Study, the largest prospective epidemiologic study of the development and consequences of disordered eating. Her research focus is on the modifiable causes and consequences of binge eating, purging, weight concerns, eating disorders, and obesity. She has written more than 100 scientific papers and book chapters on weight-related disorders.

Debra L. Franko is Professor in the Department of Counseling and Applied Educational Psychology at Northeastern University and serves as the Associate Dean for Faculty Affairs in the Bouvé College of Health Sciences. She is the Associate Director at the Harris Center for Eating Disorders at Massachusetts General Hospital and the Secretary of the Board of Directors of the Academy for Eating Disorders. She serves on the editorial boards of the *International Journal of Eating Disorders* and *Body Image: An International Journal of Research*. Dr Franko is a member of the Advisory Board for the Strategic Training Initiative for the Prevention of Eating Disorders based at the Harvard School of Public Health and Boston Children's Hospital. She has authored more than 100 peer-reviewed publications in the area of eating disorders, body image, and obesity.

Loren M. Gianini is a postdoctoral associate in the Program for Obesity, Weight, and Eating Research within the Yale University School of Medicine's Department of Psychiatry. She earned her PhD in clinical psychology from the University of New Mexico.

Andrea B. Goldschmidt, PhD, is an Assistant Professor in the Department of Psychiatry and Behavioral Neuroscience at The University of Chicago, where she fulfills research, clinical, and teaching responsibilities. She received her PhD in clinical psychology from Washington University in 2010. Her research interests concern the etiology, psychosocial correlates, and treatment of pediatric binge eating and obesity. This work includes the application of novel methodologies to study proximal triggers to aberrant eating in children. The ultimate goal of Dr Goldschmidt's research is to develop interventions for problematic eating in overweight and obese youth. Dr Goldschmidt's clinical interests include evidence-based treatments for eating disorders and obesity. She currently provides individual and family treatment for adolescents and young adults with eating and weight disorders. Dr Goldschmidt is also involved in several training activities, including supervising graduate-level externs and pre-doctoral interns in delivering assessments and interventions to eating- and weight-disordered individuals across the age spectrum.

Daniel Le Grange, PhD, is Professor of Psychiatry and Behavioral Neuroscience in the Department of Psychiatry, and Director of the Eating Disorders Program at The University of Chicago. Dr Le Grange has been devoting most of his career to the development and testing of treatments for eating disorders utilizing randomized controlled trials. His work expands across the eating disorder diagnostic spectrum (i.e., anorexia nervosa, bulimia nervosa, and eating disorders not otherwise specified).

Danuta (Dana) M. Gredysa is a PhD student in Clinical Psychology at Washington University in St Louis under the co-mentorship of Drs Tamara Hershey and Deanna Barch. She has worked under the mentorship of Dr Denise Wilfley on a large-scale family-based behavioral treatment study of obese children and adolescents. Her interdisciplinary research integrates clinical neuroscience and psychology to answer questions regarding how the brain and metabolic factors drive obesity-related behaviors, such as binge eating and impaired decision-making. In 2012, Ms Gredysa was awarded a National Institute on Drug Abuse (NIDA) training fellowship position (T32 Training Grant in Epidemiology, Services and Prevention Research) for her work in obesity, binge eating, and addiction, and received a National Science Foundation (NSF) graduate research fellowship honorable mention for her work on the relationships among neurophysiology, cognition, and goal-directed behaviors.

Lynn Grefe has served as president and CEO of the National Eating Disorders Association since 2003. She has led the creation and expansion of innovative programs to meet the needs of those seeking recovery, their families and friends. Recent accomplishments include the NEDA Navigators mentoring program; Loss Support Network; NEDA's Helpline, which serves in 14 languages; an ever-growing national conference; an interactive website for US teens, Proud2BMe.org in partnership with Rivierduien; and an annual "Proud" summit. Ms Grefe recently launched the expansion of the STAR program, to include federal advocacy through NEDA's Action Center. A published author and NEDA's national spokesperson, Ms Grefe's career has long centered on issues, advocacy, and solutions.

Andrea S. Hartmann, PhD is a postdoctoral research fellow at the Department of Psychiatry at Massachusetts General Hospital and Harvard Medical School in Boston, MA, USA. From 2008–2011, Dr Hartmann was a graduate student at Philipps University of Marburg, Germany. Her research focuses on etiological factors of eating disorders across the lifespan and body image disturbances across different disorders. In her PhD project, she investigated the maintenance of binge eating in children and adolescents. Dr Hartmann's current work examines joint etiological factors, including body image disturbances, in eating disorders and body dysmorphic disorder.

Phillipa Hay is Foundation Chair of Mental Health at University of Western Sydney, Adjunct Professor of Psychiatry at James Cook University, and Senior Consultant for Campbelltown Hospital, Australia. She has led research with specific aims to reduce community and individual burden from eating disorders. This includes analytic epidemiologic studies, treatments in eating disorders, and meta-analyses as well as primary research. She is a member of the expert panel for the 11th World Health Organisation revision of the ICD for Eating Disorders, a past-President of the Australian Academy for Eating Disorders, Deputy-Chair of the National Eating Disorders Collaboration, a current member of the scientific committee and conference committee of the International Academy for Eating Disorders (AED) and co-Chair of the AED Sisterhood and Chapters Committee. In addition to other editorial duties she is co-Editor-in-Chief of the *Journal of Eating Disorders*, www.jeatdisord.com.

Anja Hilbert is Professor of Behavioral Medicine at the University of Leipzig Medical Center, Germany, and Head of the Obesity Outpatient Research Unit. From 2010–2011 Dr Hilbert was an Associate Professor of Clinical Psychology and Psychotherapy at the Department of Psychology at the University of Fribourg, Switzerland, and before she was the leader of the interdisciplinary junior researchers group "Psychosocial, ethical, and legal implications of genetic research on obesity" at Philipps University of Marburg, Germany. In her work, Dr Hilbert adopts a developmental perspective to integrating basic research and clinical work on the treatment and prevention of binge eating disorder (BED) and obesity itself. Body image disturbance and its treatment is one of her research concentrations. Dr Hilbert is the Principal Investigator of numerous clinical research projects on binge eating disorder and obesity, and currently is the President of the German Eating Disorders Society.

Juliette M. Iacovino is a fourth-year Chancellor's Graduate Fellow in the Clinical Psychology Program at Washington University in St Louis. She graduated from Harvard University in 2009 with a Bachelor's Degree in Psychology. She has worked with Dr Denise Wilfley in the Weight Management and Eating Disorders Program at Washington University, and currently works with Dr Thomas Oltmanns on the St Louis Personality and Aging Network study. Her research interests include racial health disparities, treatment effectiveness, and improving access to mental health care among underserved populations.

Trisha M. Karr is an Assistant Professor of Psychology at Saint Mary's University in Winona, Minnesota. She completed a postdoctoral fellowship at the Neuropsychiatric Research Institute in Fargo, North Dakota, where she studied factors associated with body image, posttraumatic stress disorder, and physical activity. She obtained her doctoral degree in Developmental Psychology at Loyola University Chicago, and holds a Master's Degree in Clinical Psychology from Roosevelt University in Chicago.

Stephanie Knatz is a postdoctoral fellow at the University of California, San Diego, where she conducts research and clinical work in the areas of pediatric obesity and eating disorders. She specializes in family based treatments and behavioral parent management training for eating and weight issues. In addition to her clinical work, she is involved in developing and conducting novel treatments for both eating disorders and obesity.

Meghan E. Lovering is a doctoral student in the Department of Counseling and Applied Psychology at Northeastern University in Boston, Massachusetts. She earned her BA in psychology from Stonehill College in Easton, Massachusetts and MA in Counseling Psychology from Boston College in Chestnut Hill, Massachusetts. She currently works for the US Army Research Institute of Environmental Medicine as a research associate. In addition, she works for the Department of Counseling and Applied Psychology as a graduate assistant.

Her research interests include prevention of anxiety and eating disorders in college aged women.

Jennifer Madowitz is pursuing her doctorate at the San Diego State University/ University of California, San Diego Joint Doctoral Program in Clinical Psychology. Ms. Madowitz has worked with several disordered eating populations, including individuals with anorexia nervosa, bulimia nervosa, binge eating disorder, and obesity. Her current research interests include the development and assessment of successful interventions for obesity and eating disorders, as well as innovation of current therapies for underserved populations. Current research focus is on interventions that target the family and child.

Rachel Miller is a doctoral candidate in the Department of Medical and Clinical Psychology at the Uniformed Services University of the Health Sciences in Bethesda, Maryland. She is also a researcher in the Section on Growth and Obesity at the Eunice Kennedy Shriver National Institute of Child Health and Human Development, NIH. Ms Miller was a research assistant at the Obesity Research Center at St Luke's-Roosevelt Hospital, at Columbia University, and received her MA in Psychology from Teachers College, Columbia University. She has several peer-reviewed publications relating to eating pathology in youth and has presented her research at national and international conferences. Ms Miller's research interests include prevention programs for youth at risk for disordered eating, as well as physiological correlates of binge eating. Her Master's thesis examined the relationship between binge eating, cortisol, and metabolic dysfunction in youth.

James E. Mitchell is the NRI/Lee A. Christoferson MD Professor and Chairman of the Department of Clinical Neuroscience at the University of North Dakota School of Medicine and Health Sciences. He is also the Chester Fritz Distinguished University Professor at the University of North Dakota, and President and Scientific Director of the Neuropsychiatric Research Institute. Dr Mitchell's research has focused on eating disorders, obesity, and bariatric surgery.

Jonathan Mond is Associate Professor in the School of Medicine and Public Health at the University of Newcastle and the School of Sociology at the Australian National University. His research focuses on community-based studies of eating-disordered behavior, in particular, impairment in quality of life associated with eating-disordered behavior, public attitudes and beliefs concerning the nature and treatment of eating-disordered behavior and the use of epidemiological data in informing classification schemes for eating-disordered behavior. Dr Mond is Associate Editor of the *Journal of Eating Disorders* and *Journal of Mental Health* and has served on the Editorial Board of the *International Journal of Eating Disorders* since 2008. He has previously served on the Faculty of the Academy for Eating Disorders

Young Researcher Mentoring Program and International Conference on Eating Disorders Scientific Program Planning Committee and is a member of the Academy for Eating Disorders Research Practice Committee.

Robyn Osborn is a clinical health psychologist specializing in the behavioral and psychological aspects of weight management. She received a PhD in Medical and Clinical Psychology from the Uniformed Services University of the Health Sciences F. Edward Hébert School of Medicine and completed her internship at the Washington DC Veteran's Affairs Medical Center. With extensive training in cognitive behavioral therapy and interpersonal psychotherapy, her clinical focus is primarily on the treatment of emotional and binge eating with adults and adolescents. She has several peer-reviewed publications on weight management and health disparities. She is Assistant Director and Clinical Coordinator of the National Center for Weight and Wellness (NCWW) in Washington DC.

Amy Pershing is Executive Director of Pershing Turner Centers for Eating Disorders in Annapolis, MD, and Clinical Director of the Center for Eating Disorders in Ann Arbor, Michigan. Ms Pershing has pioneered a treatment approach for Binge Eating Disorder (BED) incorporating a variety of clinical paradigms, including Internal Family Systems (IFS), mindfulness strategies, and a range of somatic trauma techniques. In 1992, she developed "Bodywise™", a comprehensive treatment program for BED, the first of its kind in the nation. Ms Pershing offers training and supervision using this approach to clinicians treating BED nationwide. She lectures and writes extensively on the treatment of BED and her own recovery journey for professional and lay communities. She has been featured in the media speaking about BED treatment and recovery, relapse prevention, weight stigma, and intuitive eating and movement. Ms Pershing serves as President of the Binge Eating Disorder Association (BEDA).

Carol B. Peterson received her undergraduate degree from Yale University and her doctorate in Clinical Psychology from the University of Minnesota. She is a Research Associate/Assistant Professor in the Eating Disorders Research Program at the University of Minnesota, where her investigations have focused on the assessment, diagnosis, and treatment of bulimia nervosa, anorexia nervosa, binge eating disorder, and obesity. Dr Peterson has authored more than 80 articles and book chapters and has served as an investigator on several federally funded grants. She is also an adjunct assistant professor in the Department of Psychology at the University of Minnesota and has a part-time private practice in which she specializes in the treatment of eating disorders.

Debra L. Safer, Co-Director of the Stanford Adult Eating and Weight Disorders Clinic, obtained her MD from the University of California, San Francisco. She completed residency as well as a post-doctoral fellowship in eating disorder intervention research within the Department of Psychiatry and Behavioral Sciences at Stanford University. She was awarded an NIMH Career Development Award to conduct a clinical trial involving dialectical behavior therapy (DBT) as adapted for binge eating disorder (BED). Her clinical interests include working with patients with eating disorders and obesity, and she has been trained in evidence-based treatments such as CBT for BN/BED, DBT for BN/BED, Cognitive Remediation Therapy (CRT) for chronic anorexia, and Family-Based Therapy for adolescents with AN. In addition to her research focusing on clinical intervention trials for patients with eating disorders, other research interests include designing interventions for post-bariatric surgery patients.

Lisa Sanchez-Johnsen is a Visiting Associate Professor in the Department of Psychiatry and the Director of the Multicultural and Latino Health Research Program at the University of Illinois at Chicago. For 17 years she has conducted research and clinical work in the area of culturally competent health behavior, with a focus on weight and eating issues. She has funding through two separate NCI-R21 grants to examine culture constructs underlying diet, physical activity, and body image in Latina women and Latino men. She completed an NCI K01 award to develop a culture-based diet, physical activity, body image, and second-hand smoke intervention with overweight Latinas using a community participatory framework. She is active in national Latino and health organizations. She received the Presidential Latino Leadership Award from the American Psychological Association and the Distinguished Professional Early Career Award from the National Latino Psychological Association for her work in Latino health research.

Kay E. Segal is in private practice in Schaumburg, Illinois. Her clinical interests and areas of research include eating disorders, post-traumatic stress disorder, suicidality, non-suicidal self-injury, medical noncompliance, violence, and personality disorders. She has received extensive training in evidence-based treatments, including Dialectical Behavior Therapy, Prolonged Exposure Therapy, Motivational Interviewing, and Maudsley Family-Based Therapy. Dr Segal has prior experience developing and implementing a Dialectical Behavior Therapy program with court-mandated domestic batterers, as well as serving as the Senior Lead Clinician for the Kovler Diabetes Center Health and Wellness team. She also served as lead therapist in the Adult Eating and Weight Disorders Program at The University of Chicago, where she gained extensive experience developing innovative treatments for anorexia, bulimia, and binge-eating disorder. Dr Segal graduated from The Chicago School of Professional Psychology and completed her Postdoctoral training at The University of Chicago.

Heather Simonich earned her Master's Degree in Counseling Psychology from Ball State University in Muncie, Indiana. She is a Research Coordinator and Psychological Assessor at the Neuropsychiatric Research Institute in Fargo, North Dakota. She serves as the Project Coordinator for the Treatment Collaborative for Traumatized Youth and has received advanced training in evidence based practices for treating childhood trauma. She provides training and consultation to other clinicians interested in using these techniques. As a Licensed Professional Counselor she maintains a small clinical practice serving traumatized children and their families.

Kendrin R. Sonneville is a registered dietitian and behavioral scientist whose research interests include the intersection of eating disorders and obesity and the integrated prevention of weight-related disorders. Dr Sonneville received her ScD from Harvard School of Public Health and is an Instructor of Pediatrics at Harvard Medical School. Dr Sonneville works in the Division of Adolescent/Young Adult Medicine at Boston Children's Hospital, where she serves as the Director of Nutrition Training, Co-Director of the PREP weight management clinic, and Co-Director of the Strategic Training Initiative for the Prevention of Eating Disorders.

Anita Star is Senior Lecturer in Nutrition and Dietetics at the Griffith University School of Public in Queensland Australia. She is an Accredited Practicing Dietitian and has worked as a clinical dietitian in both obesity and eating disorders treatment facilities, including the Sydney Children's Hospital Mental Health Unit. Anita recently completed her PhD thesis entitled "Eating and weight problems in the community: prevalence, implications for mental health and community beliefs." Anita's clinical and research expertise is evident in a growing track record comprising eleven published peer review articles, five published abstracts of conference proceedings, one book chapter and several national and international conference presentations. Anita is a member of the Dietitians Association of Australia and the Australian and New Zealand Academy for Eating Disorders and in 2011 participated as a reference group member on the Dietitians Association of Australia Obesity Guideline committee.

Marian Tanofsky-Kraff is Associate Professor in the Department of Medical and Clinical Psychology at the Uniformed Services University of the Health Sciences in Bethesda, Maryland. She is also a Researcher in the Section on Growth and Obesity at the Eunice Kennedy Shriver National Institute of Child Health and Human Development, NIH. Prior to receiving her PhD in Clinical Psychology from the Catholic University of America, Dr Tanofsky-Kraff was a Research Associate at the Yale Center for Eating and Weight Disorders at Yale University. Her research program involves the intersection of obesity and eating disorders in pediatric samples and addresses questions about the risks, protective factors, maintenance, consequences, and prevention of childhood eating disturbance and excess adiposity, with a particular focus on loss of control eating. Dr Tanofsky-Kraff has extensive experience in the assessment of disordered eating patterns in youth, ranging from structured clinical interviewing to carrying out laboratory feeding paradigms. She also adapted interpersonal psychotherapy for the prevention of excess weight gain in adolescent girls at high risk for obesity and binge eating disorder. Dr Tanofsky-Kraff has published more than 70 empirical papers and chapters, has received research funding from multiple institutes, serves on several executive boards for eating disorders research, and is president (2012–2013) of the Eating Disorders Research Society.

Sara E. Trace is a Postdoctoral Fellow in Eating Disorders in the Department of Psychiatry at the University of North Carolina at Chapel Hill. Dr Trace's primary research interests focus on understanding genetic and biological risk factors for eating disorders. Dr Trace also provides group and individual therapy for individuals with eating disorders.

Chevese Turner is Founder and Chief Executive Officer, Binge Eating Disorder Association. A well-known advocate and speaker, Ms Turner founded the Binge Eating Disorder Association (BEDA) to bring recognition and resources to this most common eating disorder affecting more than 10 million people in the United States alone. She has extensive experience in non-profit operations and the intricacies of health care policy as a result of her leadership positions within several large charity organizations and the pharmaceutical industry. She contributes her skills and knowledge to building BEDA's support community and developing strategic partnerships amongst stakeholders. She is passionate about education and is committed to creating programming that will generate broad awareness and knowledge amongst treatment professionals to assure access to quality care for struggling individuals and their families. A graduate of Temple University in Philadelphia, where she received a BA in Political Science, Ms Turner is a past committeewoman to the City of Philadelphia's 21st ward and is a member of the Academy for Eating Disorders, the Eating Disorders Coalition, the International Association of Eating Disorder Professionals, and the Society for Non-Profit Professionals.

Anna Vannucci is a doctoral candidate in the Department of Medical and Clinical Psychology at the Uniformed Services University of the Health Sciences in Bethesda, Maryland. She is also an adjunct co-investigator in the Section on Growth and Obesity at the Eunice Kennedy Shriver National Institute of Child Health and Human Development, NIH. Prior to entering graduate school, Ms Vannucci was the recipient of a Fulbright Scholarship and worked as a research coordinator in the Department of Psychiatry at Washington University School of Medicine in St Louis, Missouri. Her primary research interests include the etiology and maintenance of disinhibited eating behaviors in youth and the development of early intervention programs for eating and weight disorders. Ms Vannucci has extensive experience in the assessment of disordered eating patterns and psychiatric comorbidity in youth. She is also trained to deliver interpersonal psychotherapy for the prevention of excess weight gain and in cognitive behavior therapy for the prevention of Type II diabetes in at-risk adolescent girls. Ms Vannucci has co-authored numerous empirical papers and chapters, been awarded several travel fellowships to present her research at scientific conferences, and is involved in the student organizations of professional eating disorder and psychology associations.

Heather L. Waldron graduated summa cum laude from Northwestern University in 2011, with majors in psychology and journalism. She is clinical lab supervisor for Dr Denise Wilfley at Washington University in St Louis, and plans to pursue a PhD in Clinical Psychology, studying treatments for eating and weight disorders.

B. Timothy Walsh is Ruane Professor of Pediatric Psychopharmacology in the Department of Psychiatry at the College of Physicians & Surgeons, Columbia University, and Director of the Division of Clinical Therapeutics at New York State Psychiatric Institute. Dr Walsh's research group has examined biological and psychological abnormalities which contribute to the development and perpetuation of disturbances in eating behavior, and investigated both psychological and pharmacological treatments for anorexia nervosa, bulimia nervosa, and binge eating disorder. Dr Walsh is a member of the DSM-5 Task Force and chairs the Eating Disorders Workgroup for DSM-5 and held the same positions for DSM-IV. He is a past president of the Academy for Eating Disorders, and of the Eating Disorders Research Society.

Jessica A. Weissman, studying for her MA, is interested in emotion dysregulation difficulties in disorders, including eating disorders and anxiety disorders, and behavioral treatments for these problems with a particular interest in mindfulness-based approaches. She was research coordinator in the Adult Eating and Weight Disorders Program in Psychiatry and Behavioral Neuroscience at the University of Chicago where she assisted with running and managing clinical trial studies examining behavioral treatments for adult women across the eating disorder spectrum.

Marney A. White is a clinical psychologist and an Assistant Professor of Psychiatry and of Epidemiology and Public Health (Chronic Diseases) at the Yale University School of Medicine. Her research focuses on binge eating disorder and the interaction of cigarette smoking with eating disorder symptomatology and weight problems.

Denise E. Wilfley is Professor of Psychiatry, Medicine, Pediatrics and Psychology and the Director of the Weight Management & Eating Disorders Program at Washington University School of Medicine in St Louis. She has been awarded more than $25 million from the NIH for a programmatic line of research examining the causes, prevention, and treatment of eating disorders and obesity among children, adolescents, and adults. She established the clinical significance of binge eating disorder, and has developed and tested novel interventions for recurrent binge eating and early intervention with eating disorders and obesity. She has published more than 150 articles in the eating disorders and obesity fields.

Stephen A. Wonderlich is Chester Fritz Distinguished Professor and Associate Chairperson in the Department of Clinical Neuroscience, University of North Dakota School of Medicine & Health Sciences. He is also Co-Director of the Eating Disorder and Weight Management Center and Director of Clinical Research for the Neuropsychiatric Research Institute. He has published widely in the literature. He currently sits on the Editorial Board for several professional journals, is a Past President of the Academy for Eating Disorders, and currently sits on the Eating Disorder Workgroup for DSM-5.

Foreword

Michael J. Devlin, Stephen A. Wonderlich, B. Timothy Walsh and James E. Mitchell

The following dialogue takes place in an eating disorders clinic at an academic medical center, circa 1990. The telephone rings.

Research Assistant:	Hello, Eating Disorders Treatment Research Program, RA speaking.
Caller:	Hello, this is C. I'm hoping you can help me with a problem I'm having with my eating. I've been looking desperately for some help, and no one seems to know what to do for me.
RA:	You've called the right place. What sort of problem are you having?
C:	Well, I'm ashamed to admit this, but just about every evening, I completely lose my resolve to eat well, and I end up eating way too much and all the wrong foods – two or three slices of cake, a big bag of chips, pizza, a whole pint of ice cream, you name it. It's making me miserable.
RA:	You're not alone. We get many calls from people with just this sort of problem. It's called binge eating. What do you do to compensate?
C:	I beg your pardon?
RA:	You know, what do you do to make up for overeating? Like, for example, some people vomit or use laxatives or water pills. What do you do?
C:	Uh … I don't do any of those things actually.
RA:	Really! Well that's OK, maybe you exercise a lot after binge eating or you completely stop eating for the next day until you feel you've burned off the excess calories?
C:	No, I don't do either of those things either. I just gain weight. Then I go on a diet for a while and drop weight. Then I lose control again and gain weight. I can't stand this. I now weigh 150 lbs and I'm only 5′2″ tall.
RA:	Well, the good news is, according to my DSM-III-R, you don't have bulimia nervosa. And based on your weight, you don't have anorexia nervosa either. That means you don't have an official eating disorder,

C: or at least not one that we have a name for. But I realize that you're
            looking for help. We don't have any programs that you'd be eligible
            for. But there's a great weight control program nearby – maybe
            you'd like to try that?

C: Been there, done that. Not helping. I've tried lots of weight control
            programs, and I do well for a while and then just blow it. I need
            something different.

RA: I'm really sorry. I don't think we have anything that fits what you
            have. But I'll keep my eyes open, and I'll call you back if I come
            across anything that might help. We seem to be receiving more and
            more calls from people with problems just like yours.

*

While not an actual recording, this dialogue is representative of the sorts of conversations that took place until recently when a person with what has come to be known as binge eating disorder (BED) reached out to an eating disorders program for help. In fact, the increasingly frequent experience of receiving calls for help from this hitherto under-recognized group, repeated across diverse programs in a variety of locations, was one of the key factors contributing to the recognition of BED as a syndrome. Combined with the experience of weight control programs that recognized the existence of binge eating as early as 1959 (Stunkard 1959) with a resurgence of interest in the 1980s (reviewed in Devlin et al. 1992), this led to the initial efforts to characterize and define the newly recognized disorder (Spitzer et al. 1992, 1993) culminating in its inclusion in the DSM-IV in Appendix B: Criteria Sets and Axes Provided for Further Study (American Psychiatric Association 2000).

BED has now been recognized as a provisional eating disorder for several years and has been recommended for inclusion in DSM-5 as a diagnostic category in its own right. Nonetheless, there continue to be a number of important questions regarding the fundamental nature of the disorder. Its name suggests that eating behavior, specifically binge eating, unaccompanied by the compensatory behaviors that characterize bulimia nervosa, lies at its core. Yet patients who present for treatment often display a cluster of symptoms along different dimensions including behavioral features (binge eating, frequent dieting), somatic features (weight gain leading to overweight or obesity, unstable weight), and psychological features (negative affect, body shape/weight overconcern), and, while the precise causal relationships among these features are far from clear, there are a number of potential relationships, illustrated in Figure F.1.

As the diagram suggests, the pattern of episodic overconsumption accompanied by a feeling of loss of control (LOC) may be profoundly distressing and may increase the individual's attention to and distress regarding weight and shape. In a reciprocal fashion, negative emotion, e.g. sadness, shame, or

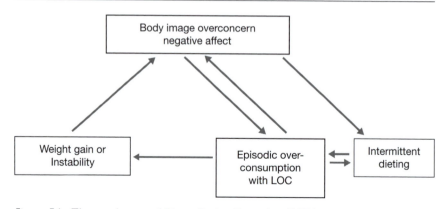

Figure F.1   The syndrome of Binge Eating Disorder (BED)

anxiety, which at various times may or may not be related to body image distress, can provoke binge eating. For many people, dieting represents an attempt to remedy this distress, but often fails to be sustained, leading to a resurgence of binge eating. Although not represented on the diagram, many would argue that dieting may additionally serve to amplify and sustain body image over-concern. Overconsumption may lead to weight gain, which in turn leads to intensified negative affect, particularly related to weight and shape, and promotes further binge eating.

While the general features of BED are relatively well established, important unanswered questions arise on closer examination. One such question relates to the "anatomy of a binge". BED is defined in DSM-IV-TR Appendix B in an identical fashion to the binge eating episode in bulimia nervosa (BN), with the two key features of ingesting an objectively large amount of food and experiencing a sense of lack of control. However, it is not clear that typical binge eating episodes in BED, which unlike binge eating episodes in BN are not punctuated by attempts at compensation via purging, exercise, or fasting, resemble typical binge eating episodes in BN. The relationships among negative emotion, cognitions regarding control or lack thereof, and actual and perceived amount consumed have yet to be fully elucidated. An important question for both BED and BN is whether the two defining features of an eating binge, i.e. objectively large amount of food and sense of lack of control, are equally important. For both disorders, it has been suggested that people who report only subjective eating binges, i.e. sense of lack of control without the consumption of an objectively large amount of food, in many ways resemble those who consume objectively large amounts of food during their eating binge (Wolfe *et al.* 2009). Despite this resemblance, it is possible that, particularly for people with BED who do not engage in compensatory behaviors, the outcome of recurrent objective binge eating may differ from that of subjective binge eating; specifically, objective binge eating may be more conducive to weight gain.

Beyond the question of whether binge size matters, the broader question of what exactly takes place during an eating binge is a more complex question than may initially be apparent. The complexities of assessment are ably reviewed in Chapter 9, and, upon careful review of the various methodologies that have been developed, it is clear that all have their limitations. Research methodologies, including laboratory studies, i.e. observed meals under instructions to engage in or avoid binge eating, and ecological momentary assessment (EMA), i.e. inter-mittent reporting via handheld computer, of real-life eating behavior and related experience, also have their limitations. It is apparent that, like the blind men and the elephant, only through ongoing study from a variety of vantage points, making use of different self-report, interview, laboratory, EMA, and perhaps other measures yet to be developed, will we be able to come to a full and accurate understanding of the nature and experience of the eating binge.

Another important question regarding BED concerns its relationship with obesity, reviewed in Chapter 1. Although obesity is not a criterion for the BED diagnosis, BED and obesity are often grouped together in the minds of patients and professionals alike, raising questions regarding the centrality of obesity or the potential for obesity in the diagnostic construct. For patients with both BED and obesity, the nature of the causal associations, if any, are unclear. In other words, it is theoretically possible that binge eating may contribute to the development of obesity, or be reinforced by a pattern of intermittent strict dieting, or both of the above. It is also possible that the genetic and environmental risk factors (see Chapter 3) that contribute to the risk for obesity and BED may be partially but not fully overlapping. Regardless of the theoretical relationship between BED and obesity, most people who present for treatment for BED are overweight or obese, and it may be important to take the presence of binge eating into account when initiating treatment for obesity, whether this involves behavioral weight loss (see Chapter 15), bariatric surgery (see Chapter 14), or other approaches.

During the past two decades, along with defining the central features of BED and developing reliable methods to assess these features, we have begun to learn about additional characteristics of those who suffer from this disorder. Given the intense and varied cultural meanings of food and body size and shape, it is not surprising that ethnicity and race may influence the risk for and particular expression of BED. These factors, including their interaction with age, gender, socioeconomic status, and other demographic features, are comprehensively presented in Chapter 2. One of the most consistently reported findings in the literature on BED is the increase in comorbid psychological symptoms, particu-larly in depression, in those with BED compared to otherwise similar individuals who do not binge eat (see Chapters 4 and 5). The multifaceted concept of body image disturbance is explored in Chapter 6, including its behavioral, perceptual, cognitive, and emotional components. It is of note that body image disturbance, so central to the experience of many who engage in binge eating, is not currently a BED diagnostic criterion, and questions regarding whether it should be regarded as part of the core construct of BED or simply as a frequently associated feature are the subject of ongoing investigation.

While a great deal is known about the many characteristics of BED, including behavioral, psychological, and medical dimensions, much less is known regarding its etiology and pathophysiology. The genetic and environmental contributions to BED, including heritability estimates, candidate genes, environmental risks, and gene-environment interactions, are summarized and discussed in Chapter 3. A particular and most unfortunate environmental factor that influences risk, not only for BED but also for a variety of disorders, is the experience of childhood trauma. The ways in which childhood trauma may both contribute to the risk for binge eating and affect a person's experience of binge eating are beginning to be characterized, and the growing literature on this topic is reviewed in Chapter 4. A very new area of investigation concerns the role of brain reward systems in initiating and maintaining a pattern of binge eating. The concept of binge eating or non-homeostatic eating leading to weight gain as phenomena akin to more classic substance use disorders is a fascinating and controversial one that has been the subject of recent cutting-edge research and discussion in the obesity literature (Marcus and Wildes 2009; Volkow and O'Brien 2007). In fact, a newly developed measure identifies more than one in two patients with BED as meeting criteria for "food addiction" (Davis *et al.* 2011), suggesting that this concept may be of particular relevance to binge eating.

As important as questions regarding diagnostic features and etiology of BED may be, the most immediately compelling questions, particularly for those who suffer from BED, involve treatment. Treatment, of course, rests on an under-standing of the causal factors that give rise to and, perhaps more importantly, maintain the disorder, and theories regarding initiating and maintaining factors are often inspired by analogies with related conditions. It is not surprising, given that BED is primarily characterized by a disorder of eating and that many patients who present for treatment of BED are overweight or obese, that treatments have largely derived from treatments for eating disorders, particularly BN, and for obesity. Psychological interventions including cognitive behavioral therapy (CBT), interpersonal therapy (IPT), dialectical behavior therapy (DBT) have shown great promise, and, as reviewed in Chapters 10 and 11, we are beginning to appreciate features that might allow the therapist to rationally select among these options. It is important to note that, in an age of escalating health care costs and diminishing resources, guided and pure self-help approaches have proven to be an effective and less costly alternative for some. As is the case for BN, medication may serve a useful adjunctive role for many patients with BED (Chapter 12).

While the person who called the eating disorders clinic for help in our opening example had tried weight control programs without success, there is in fact evidence that treatment approaches based on weight control treatment, including behavioral weight loss (Chapter 15) and bariatric surgery (Chapter 14), may be helpful for patients with BED who are overweight or obese and consider weight loss to be one of their goals. Our ever-increasing experience and knowledge base regarding BED has allowed these approaches to be tailored to manage the particular needs and problems of people with BED. Perhaps the most important example of an approach that re-conceptualizes the treatment based on the particular needs of individual patients with LOC eating and body image disturbance is intuitive eating and movement (IEM) reviewed in Chapter 16. However, regardless of the treatment approach, recognition of the ways in which treatment approaches evolve over time and in different contexts underscores the point that generalizations regarding various treatment approaches must be tempered by recognition of the ways in which the approach is operationalized in a particular setting with a particular patient population.

In considering not only the treatment but also the etiology and pathophysiology of BED, it is of course important to appreciate that children and adolescents are not simply small adults, but rather pose unique challenges in assessment and treatment. The important silver lining is that recognition and treatment at an early age may also present a unique opportunity to provide help in a way that creates particularly profound and long-lasting benefit. The challenges to assessment and treatment, i.e. the ways in which developmental stage must be taken into account when considering natural course of illness, assessment of eating, and management of what has come to be known as LOC eating, are reviewed in Chapter 13.

A final crucially important aspect of responding as a community to the psychological, emotional, medical, and economic costs of BED is, of course, prevention (Chapter 7). Furthering the science of prevention is productive only to the degree that advocacy for those who suffer from BED and their loved ones instills a collective will to eliminate BED from our worldwide community. Advocacy will fuel widespread recognition of the disorder, allocation of appropriate resources to its management, and implementation of effective prevention efforts. The prevention of illness turned on its head is, of course, the promotion of health, and BED presents an important challenge to us as scientists, physicians, therapists, family members, friends, citizens of the community, and people suffering from BED to consider the concept of health broadly, including medical, lifestyle, and psychological components such as self-acceptance and peace of mind. When BED was initially recognized, an important limiting factor in its management was the separation that existed between the research community on one hand, and clinicians and patients on the other. The recognition of the tremendous amount that we all can and must learn from one another has led to real progress in this regard, but important challenges remain (Chapters 17, 18, and Part Two, Introduction). Simply providing patients with information regarding the sciences of etiology, pathophysiology, treatment, and prevention is not only therapeutic in its own right (Chapter 8) but creates a dialogue that energizes and informs research.

So, nearly 20 years out from the initial recognition in 1994 of BED as a syndrome of interest that merited inclusion in DSM-IV, what do we now understand, and what challenges await us? The chapters in this volume, authored by scientists, clinicians, and advocates, represent the state of the field and, at the moment that BED is poised to gain official recognition as a diagnosis in the DSM-5, provide a roadmap for the years ahead.

References

American Psychiatric Association (2000) *Diagnostic and Statistical Manual of Mental Disorders (DSM-IV-TR)* (4th edn, text revision), Washington, DC: American Psychiatric Association.

Davis, C., Curtis, C., Levitan, R. D., Carter, J. C., Kaplan, A. S., and Kennedy, S. J. (2011) "Evidence that 'food addiction' is a valid phenotype of obesity", *Appetite* 57: 711–17.

Devlin, M. J., Walsh, B. T., Spitzer, R. L., and Hasin, D. (1992) "Is there another binge eating disorder?: a review of the literature on overeating in the absence of bulimia nervosa", *International Journal of Eating Disorders* 11: 333–40.

Marcus, M. D., and Wildes, J. E. (2009) "Obesity: is it a mental disorder?", *International Journal of Eating Disorders* 42: 739–53.

Spitzer, R. L., Devlin, M. J., Walsh, B. T., Hasin, D., Wing, R. R., Marcus, M. D., Stunkard, A. J., Wadden, T., Yanovski, S., Agras, S., Mitchell, J., and Nonas, C. (1992) "Binge eating disorder: a multisite field trial for the diagnostic criteria", *International Journal of Eating Disorders* 11: 191–203.

Spitzer, R. L., Yanovski, S., Wadden, T., Wing, R., Marcus, M. D., Stunkard, A., Devlin, M., Mitchell, J., and Hasin, D. (1993) "Binge eating disorder: its further validation in a multisite study", *International Journal of Eating Disorders* 13: 137–53.

Stunkard, A. J. (1959) "Eating patterns and obesity", *Psychiatric Quarterly* 33: 284–95.

Volkow, N. D., and O'Brien, C. P. (2007) "Issues for DSM-V: should obesity be included as a brain disorder?", *American Journal of Psychiatry* 164: 708–10.

Wolfe B. E., Baker C. W., Smith A. T., and Kelly-Weeder S. (2009) "Validity and utility of the current definition of binge eating", *International Journal of Eating Disorders* 42: 674–86.

Preface

A Clinician's Guide to Binge Eating Disorder brings science into everyday life by disseminating knowledge to where it is of greatest value and needed most – educating clinicians in the assessment, diagnosis, and treatment of people with binge eating disorder (BED).

Leading researchers, clinicians and advocates have collaborated to produce this benchmark work to coincide with the release in May 2013 of the DSM-5 that introduces binge eating disorder as a formal diagnosis. *A Clinician's Guide to Binge Eating Disorder* is one of the first textbooks to focus solely on BED, which is currently more commonly diagnosed than any other formally diagnosed eating disorder, and yet is only just now being understood.

The significance and implications of this historic achievement of a BED diagnosis is explained with a practical, expert approach. Evidence-based research outcomes provide the framework and foundation for this book. First-person case studies bring application of science to life to help close the gap between research and treatment/care. Descriptions of the suffering and stigma that people with BED experience provide insights into understanding the symptoms, often present since childhood, and life-changing treatments. This textbook for clinicians is about more than defining the illness and explaining how it is different from obesity and bulimia nervosa; it is about explaining the important role clinicians have in recognizing symptoms, and deciding what form of treatment is best. It is about more than food and diet: it is about behavior change; it is about recovery from BED. Perhaps most importantly, besides describing the application of evidence-based treatments, *A Clinician's Guide to Binge Eating Disorder* discusses the importance of clinicians developing a therapeutic relationship as a healing tool with their client. It acknowledges the important role of advocates in raising awareness and achieving change at all levels.

This book also acknowledges BED's entry into the wider field of eating disorders, a field where there is significant diagnostic overlap, and co-morbidity is often prevalent. For this reason, *A Clinician's Guide to Binge Eating Disorder* will be a valuable resource for everyone on the front line of diagnosing and treating eating disorders.

Part 1

The search for causes

Chapter 1

Binge eating disorder and obesity

Marney A. White and Loren M. Gianini

Case study

I didn't start out overweight. When I was a kid, I was maybe a little on the "thick" side, but I was healthy. I was really active until adolescence, when I started to put on weight. That was when I started buying lunch at high school – which really meant that I started eating fast food and snack pies sold in the cafeteria. I would get either pizza or a fried chicken sandwich or a hamburger, and polish it off with a package of cupcakes. My friends and I went straight to the nearby fast food joint on the way home, too, and we would get French fries and dip them in ranch dressing. I remember that: French fries every day after school. When we started driving to and from school, my eating really started to get out of control. I was babysitting a lot on weekends, and the families were always really nice and would leave treats – cookies and chips and things – and tell me to just help myself. And I would. It got to the point that I even started ordering out while I was babysitting. I would have a pizza delivered, and I would eat all of it. I felt terrible afterward, and ashamed, and I remember sneaking the pizza box into the neighbors' garbage can outside so that the family wouldn't know what I had done. It was terrible.

When I went away to college, the bingeing got worse. I was on the college meal plan, and they had a full range of healthy foods available, but they also had the soft-serve ice cream at every meal, and an entire table full of cookies right there as you were exiting the cafeteria. So of course I usually grabbed one (or more!) on the way out. The thing about college food was that I felt so deprived. The cafeteria was only open for a few hours around each meal time, which never seemed to match up with my schedule. So I never made it there in time for breakfast (they stopped serving at 10am), and by lunchtime I was really hungry. They had this policy where you couldn't take food "to go" – technically you weren't supposed to leave with food at all – and since I knew that I would not be able to get food again until the cafeteria reopened for dinner, I would sort of "store up" and eat more than I really wanted. I was afraid of going hungry later. By the time I finished college, I was probably 20 or 30 pounds overweight.

I started dieting right after college, but never could stick with anything for long. I've tried every diet, and sometimes I've lost five or ten pounds, but I always gain it right back. Every day, I start out by telling myself that "THIS is the day. I'll be good today. I can be good for a while." Most days I can even make it all day long without eating anything. But then I'm so hungry that I eat a lot of food at night. I get depressed afterward, and usually end up just giving up.

My doctors, for years, have been telling me to lose weight. I'm trying, but I can't lose it like everyone else can. I know that my health depends on it, and I really want to lose the weight! My doctors shake their heads and say: "You just need to eat less and exercise." Don't they know that's what I'm trying to do? I guess I'm just a defective person.

Jamie, age 48

This case study demonstrates several important themes in understanding patients who struggle with binge eating disorder (BED). Most notably, BED is frequently associated with substantial weight gain, which can lead to obesity and various physical and psychological health problems. This chapter will focus on complications that arise due to concurrent obesity in BED, and will describe treatment approaches for the obese patient with BED.

Obesity is one of the leading and costliest health problems in the United States (US) and worldwide. The National Health and Nutrition Examination Survey (2007–2008) estimated that 68 per cent of the US population is overweight and 34 per cent is obese (Flegal *et al.* 2010). National annual medical costs associated with obesity were estimated to be over $75 billion (about 6 per cent of medical expenditures) (Finkelstein *et al.* 2004) in 2004, and due to the increasing prevalence of obesity these estimates had nearly doubled to $147 billion annually by 2009 (Finkelstein *et al.* 2009). These financial estimates do not include the treatment of obesity itself, but rather are generated based on costs of treating obesity-associated diseases. Worldwide, rates of obesity have more than doubled in the past three decades (World Health Organization 2011).

Health complications associated with obesity and BED

Discussion of the clinical features and treatment of BED must also consider obesity, since many people who suffer from this illness are obese (American Psychiatric Association 2000). Binge eating is strongly associated with increased obesity (Spitzer *et al.* 1992; Telch *et al.* 1988). Consequently, the health risks associated with obesity are relevant to most individuals with BED. Both BED and obesity are associated with a variety of medical complications, including non-insulin dependent diabetes mellitus, hypertension, and heart disease (Bray 1998; Bulik and Reichborn-Kjennerud 2003). However, compared to their non-binge eating obese counterparts (non-binge-eating obese, or 'NBO'), people with BED experience *more* health problems (Hudson *et al.* 2007; Johnson *et al.*

2001; Kanter *et al.* 1992; Telch *et al.* 1988) and report greater dissatisfaction with their physical health (Bulik *et al.* 2002). Furthermore, compared to obese groups without binge eating, BED is associated with increased serious psychosocial problems and psychiatric difficulties (Grilo *et al.* 2001; White and Grilo 2006; Wilfley *et al.* 2000; Yanovski 1993).

The reasons for the elevations in medical problems are not fully understood, but point to binge eating behavior itself. Some research has found that BED is associated with increased risk of metabolic abnormalities, which may be attributed to the pattern of eating observed in BED. For example, eating large amounts of food in a discrete period of time (BED Diagnostic Criterion A1 in DSM-5) (American Psychiatric Association 2012) is associated with exaggerated insulin secretion, increased fasting glucose levels, decreased glucose tolerance, and elevated serum lipids (Jenkins *et al.* 1992; Taylor *et al.* 1999). Eating rapidly (Criterion B1) is associated with elevated serum lipids, higher waist–hip circumference ratio, and fatty liver in obese individuals (Kral *et al.* 2001). Irregular meal patterns, which are frequently observed in BED (Masheb and Grilo 2006; Masheb *et al.* 2011) and are described more below, are associated with the metabolic syndrome in the general population (Sierra-Johnson *et al.* 2008).

Epidemiology of obesity and BED

Lifetime rates of BED have been estimated at 2.8 per cent using DSM-IV-TR criteria (Hudson *et al.* 2007). The prevalence of BED is higher among obese adults (estimates range from 8 per cent to 28 per cent) (Hudson *et al.* 2007) and is much higher in most clinical settings, especially obesity-specific treatment facilities and clinics (Johnson *et al.* 2001; Wilfley *et al.* 2003). Estimated rates of significant problems with binge eating (although perhaps not meeting the full diagnostic threshold specified in DSM) are much higher, with binge eating reported in as many as 46 per cent of patients in weight control clinics (Marcus *et al.* 1985).

When looking at the demographic profiles of obese people with BED and obese people who do not binge eat, several differences emerge. On average, BED adults tend to be younger than NBO adults (Kolotkin *et al.* 2004). This difference may be especially pronounced among obese people presenting for treatment. Among obese treatment-seekers, women are about 1.5 times more likely to have BED than men, and this disparity is found in non-treatment seeking populations as well (Spitzer *et al.* 1992). Therefore, the gender difference in BED is much less pronounced than it is in anorexia nervosa or bulimia nervosa, wherein women are far more likely to carry these diagnoses than men. Interestingly, while women are more likely to have BED than men, rates of obesity are approximately equivalent in samples of men and women (Ogden *et al.* 2007). There are larger disparities in rates of obesity in different ethnic groups. Obesity is less prevalent in samples of non-Hispanic, white individuals than in ethnic minority populations such as Hispanic samples, and non-Hispanic, black samples (Flegal *et al.* 2010). Many published reports of obese people with BED do not have large enough samples of ethnic minority groups to assess for ethnic differences. Of the few studies that have assessed for ethnic differences in rates of BED, several studies have demonstrated equal prevalence rates among black and white obese adults (Smith *et al.* 1998; Striegel-Moore and Franko 2003). When considering sub-threshold binge eating, however, evidence suggests greater prevalence among non-white groups (Marques *et al.* 2011). BED is more prevalent among Latino/as than other ethnic/racial groups (Alegria *et al.* 2007) and is strongly associated with obesity in this ethnic group (Alegria *et al.* 2007; Marques *et al.* 2011).

Identification and diagnosis

As the clinical case demonstrates, physicians may not identify people with BED as having the disorder (Crow *et al.* 2004; Mond *et al.* 2010). This is unfortunate, since BED is associated with increased health service utilization (Johnson *et al.* 2001). Moreover, as described above, people with BED are also more likely to suffer from various medical complications. Whereas patients' primary care physicians may focus on their weight and inform them that weight loss is a health priority, the chaotic and out-of-control nature of the eating itself is unlikely to be addressed. Binge eating poses a significant obstacle to weight loss efforts and, when this issue is ignored, efforts to diet are unlikely to be successful. Critically, people suffering from BED may not realize that treatment is available, and their physicians may not provide adequate referrals.

Psychological functioning in BED

We turn now to discuss psychological functioning in obese people suffering with BED. Most notably, in comparison to obese people who do not binge eat, adults with BED tend to exhibit higher levels of *eating disorder-specific pathology* in addition to more non-eating-related psychopathology. Compared to their NBO counterparts, adults with BED are more concerned about their weight and shape, and more preoccupied with their eating (Grilo and White 2011; Marcus *et al.* 1988). This pattern is also found in obese treatment-seeking children and adolescents (Decaluwé *et al.* 2003). Adults with BED report a greater discrepancy between their current and ideal body size than NBO (Striegel-Moore *et al.*1998). There is also a significant subset of BED adults who overvalue their shape and weight, meaning that shape and weight are important aspects by which they evaluate their self-worth. As observed in bulimia nervosa and anorexia nervosa, when overvaluation is present, patients will value their body shape and weight even more than other central aspects of their life, such as career or school, family, and relationships. If their weight and shape are not where they would like them to be, they feel as though they are a "bad person", or, like Jamie, they may feel as though something is wrong with them and that they are "defective". Although not a formal diagnostic criterion in BED, this overvaluation of shape and weight is present among many patients, and has prognostic value in treatment. The subgroup of BED adults with overvaluation of body shape and weight has high levels of eating disorder pathology, including bouts of disinhibited eating, unhealthy forms of dietary restraint (i.e., overly and unrealistically restrictive), and binge eating itself (Grilo *et al.* 2008). Compared to NBO groups and BED groups with lower levels of overvaluation of shape/weight, this high overvaluation subgroup also exhibits higher levels of depressive symptomatology (Grilo *et al.* 2010).

On average, adults with BED report higher depression, lower quality of life, and lower self-esteem than NBO adults (de Zwaan *et al.* 2002; Isnard *et al.* 2003). Much like Jamie, they may feel depressed about their eating, shape, and repeated failed attempts to lose weight. In general, patients with BED tend to be more concerned with rejection and feeling unworthy as compared to NBO (Nauta *et al.* 2000). Additionally, binge eating obese adults have higher rates of Axis I comorbid psychopathology than NBO (Fontenelle *et al.* 2003). In particular, they are more likely to suffer from major depression, and, to a lesser extent, anxiety disorders (Fowler and Bulik 1997). In terms of Axis II diagnoses, some evidence suggests that people with BED have significantly higher rates of all personality disorder diagnoses, particularly borderline personality disorder and avoidant personality disorder (Telch and Stice 1998; Yanovski *et al.* 1993).

Eating patterns

In addition to psychological comorbidity, BED and NBO differ in other important ways that are relevant for clinical interventions. Evidence suggests that BED and NBO adults differ in their eating patterns. Several studies have shown that BED adults consume more calories per day than NBO adults (Engel *et al.* 2009; Raymond *et al.* 2003) and this difference is driven primarily by the high number of calories that are consumed on days when people with BED binge eat as compared to non-binge days. On days when people with BED binge, they eat significantly more fat (as opposed to carbohydrates or protein) than they do on non-binge days and compared to NBO adults (Raymond *et al.* 2003). Binge eating itself is more likely to occur during the midday or evening meal, and many binge episodes occur in restaurants (Allison and Timmerman 2007). Compared to NBO, people with BED eat more snacks, engage in more frequent nibbling or picking episodes, are more likely to eat two of the same meal (e.g., will eat two entire dinners on a single day), and have more nocturnal eating episodes (i.e., when they go to bed and then get up out of bed to eat) (Masheb *et al.* 2011). Furthermore, the number of binge episodes is inversely related to the number of meals consumed, meaning that people with BED frequently skip meals, which may itself make them vulnerable to binge episodes.

Overall, eating patterns in BED are chaotic, marked by irregular meals and snacking. These chaotic meal patterns are especially relevant for treatment, and one of the initial goals of treatment is to regulate eating by initiating a regular pattern of three meals and two or three snacks per day. Research supports the behavioral intervention of implementing a regular meal pattern: among BED adults there is some evidence suggesting that greater frequency of breakfast and lunch (i.e., eating these meals regularly, as indicated in behavioral treatments for BED and obesity) is associated with lower BMI (Masheb and Grilo 2006). Finally, compared to obese people who do not binge eat, obese patients with BED eat more throughout the day, even when not counting binge episodes (Allison *et al.* 2005).

Dieting history and current strategies

Many BED and NBO adults have attempted to diet to lose weight. Like Jamie, the majority of BED adults are overweight before the onset of their dieting or binge eating behavior (Reas and Grilo 2007). BED adults are more likely to become overweight and begin dieting earlier, lose more weight during dieting attempts, and experience greater weight fluctuations than NBO adults (Mussell *et al.* 1996). BED adults are also more likely to have engaged in dangerous dieting practices, such as self-induced vomiting and using diet pills (Mussell *et al.* 1996). Therefore, during assessment and treatment, full evaluation should occur of patients' dieting and weight loss histories, including any extreme weight loss measures or purgative/compensatory behaviors.

Treatment of obesity and binge eating

Given the significant overlap between BED, being overweight and obesity, and the health consequences of excess weight, it is important to address both the binge eating and excess weight during treatment. While the distress of binge eating itself may motivate patients to seek treatment, frequently patients also greatly desire weight loss as a treatment goal (Reas *et al.* 2004). Effective treatments for the reduction of binge eating have been identified; however, there remains a need to identify treatments to reduce weight in BED (Wilson *et al.* 2007). Cognitive Behavioral Therapy (CBT) is the best-established treatment for reducing binge eating (Grilo and Masheb 2005; Wilson *et al.* 2007), but it does not produce weight loss (Brownley *et al.* 2007; Grilo, Masheb and Salant 2005; Grilo, Masheb and Wilson 2005). Therefore, many obese patients with BED may benefit from Behavioral Weight Loss (BWL) interventions (Gladis *et al.* 1998). BWL treatment is widely used to treat obesity, including binge eating, via moderate caloric restriction, improved nutrition, and increased physical activity (Wadden *et al.* 2004).

Recent findings suggest that BWL may be a viable alternative to CBT for the treatment of binge eating, and may be superior to CBT for promoting weight loss (Grilo *et al.* 2011). It is important to note that BWL treatments typically do not address binge eating specifically, or include any supplemental components to address the BED diagnosis. Rather, standard, manualized BWL treatments, for example *The LEARN Program for Weight Management* (Brownell 2000), are effective at reducing binge eating and promoting weight loss even in the absence of specific treatment components to address binge eating. Importantly, BWL treatments, which emphasize moderate caloric restriction and *slow and gradual* weight loss, do not lead to a worsening of binge eating. Therefore clinicians working with patients with BED can effectively administer BWL treatments without concern that "dieting" for weight loss will lead to a worsening of eating disorder symptoms.

As described, the irregular and disorganized quality of eating is a distinguishing clinical feature in BED patients and is considered to play a major role in promoting binge eating (Masheb and Grilo 2006). A primary treatment goal of behavioral weight loss is to change eating behavior directly, to reduce disorganization and to produce a more regular eating pattern. In addition, the treatment prescribes moderate caloric restriction (1200–1500 kcals/day). That BWL is a treatment alternative to CBT is important because unlike CBT, which requires specialist training, BWL is easily administered and disseminated (Wilson *et al.* 2007).

Medications

Pharmacotherapy for BED is reviewed thoroughly in Chapter 12. Interested readers might also refer to a review and meta-analysis by Reas and Grilo (2008). In summary, medications do not offer significant advantage over CBT in reducing binge eating. Combining medications with CBT or BWL also does not provide a distinct advantage over CBT or BWL treatment alone. A few medications promote weight loss in the short term, but weight loss is modest and does not persist in the long term.

Conclusion

As with our case study, Jamie, patients with BED often struggle with obesity as well. With some frequency, patients with BED are repeating a frustrating cycle of strict dieting, followed by periods of binge eating. Weight loss efforts are often short lived and, when successful, are followed by periods of weight regain. This takes an enormous toll on mood and overall self-esteem. Tragically and too often, patients struggling with BED do not find the treatment resources or referrals they need. Their physicians tell them that they "just need to diet and exercise more". Unfortunately, this well-intentioned message only contributes to the desperation felt by these patients, and may exacerbate the problem. Overly strict dieting, marked by skipped meals or attempts to go all day without eating, likely serves to make people more vulnerable to binge eating. Whether the treatment emphasis is on the elimination of binge eating, or on achieving weight loss, treatment for people suffering from BED and obesity must first focus on the *regulation* of eating throughout the day. Given the challenges faced by obese patients with BED, it is recommended that physicians assess for binge eating among their obese patients so that they can refer them to the most appropriate types of treatment.

References

Alegria, M, Woo, M., Cao, Z., Torres, M., Meng, X., and Striegel-Moore R. (2007) "Prevalence and correlates of eating disorders in Latinos in the United States", *International Journal of Eating Disorders* 40 Suppl: S15–21.

Allison, K. C., Grilo, C. M., Masheb, R. M., and Stunkard, A. J. (2005) "Binge eating disorder and night eating syndrome: a comparative study of disordered eating" *Journal of Consulting and Clinical Psychology* 73: 1107–15.

Allison, S., and Timmerman, G. M. (2007) "Anatomy of a binge: food environment and characteristics of nonpurge binge episodes", *Eating Behaviors* 8: 31–8.

American Psychiatric Association (2012) *DSM-5 Proposed Diagnostic Criteria for Binge Eating Disorder.* Online. Available: http://www.dsm5.org/ProposedRevisions/Pages/proposedrevision.aspx?rid =372# (accessed 1 April 2012).

American Psychiatric Association (2000) *Diagnostic and Statistical Manual of Mental Disorders (DSM-IV-TR)* (4th edn, text revision), Washington, DC: American Psychiatric Association.

Bray, G. A. (1998) *Contemporary Diagnosis and Management of Obesity,* Newtown, PA: Handbooks in Health Care Co.

Brownell, K. (2000) *The Learn Program for Weight Management 2000*, Dallas, TX: American Health Pub Co.

Brownley, K. A., Berkman, N. D., Sedway, J. A., Lohr, K. N., and Bulik, C. M. (2007) "Binge eating disorder treatment: a systematic review of randomized controlled trials", *International Journal of Eating Disorders* 40: 337–48.

Bulik, C. M., and Reichborn-Kjennerud, T. (2003) "morbidity in binge eating disorder", *International Journal of Eating Disorders* 34 Suppl: S39–46.

Bulik, C. M., Sullivan, P. F., and Kendler, K. S. (2002) "Medical and psychiatric comorbidity in obese women with and without binge eating", *International Journal of Eating Disorders* 32: 72–8.

Crow, S. J., Peterson, C. B., Levine, A. S., Thuras, P., and Mitchell, J. E. (2004) "A survey of binge eating and obesity treatment practices among primary care providers", *International Journal of Eating Disorders* 35: 348–53.

Decaluwé, V., Braet, C., and Fairburn, C. G. (2003) "Binge eating in obese children and adolescents", *International Journal of Eating Disorders* 33: 78–84.

Engel, S. G., Kahler, K. A., Lystad, C., Crosby, R. D., Simonich, H., Wonderlich, S., Peterson, C. B., and Mitchell, J. E. (2009) "Eating behavior in obese BED, obese non-BED, and non-obese control participants: a naturalistic study", *Behaviour Research and Therapy* 47: 897–900.

Finkelstein, E. A., Fiebelkorn, I. C., and Wang, G. (2004) "State-level estimates of annual medical expenditures attributable to obesity", *Obesity Research* 12: 18–24.

Finkelstein, E.A., Trogdon, J., Cohen, J., and Dietz, W. (2009) "Annual medical spending attributable to obesity: payer-and service-specific estimates", *Health Affairs* 28: 822–31.

Flegal, K. M., Carroll, M. D., Ogden, C. L., and Curtin, L. R. (2010) "Prevalence and trends in obesity among US adults, 1999–2008", *Journal of the American Medical Association* 303: 235–41.

Fontenelle, L. F., Mendlowicz, M. V., Bezerra de Menezes, G., Papelbaum, M., Freitas, S. R., Godoy-Matos, A., Coutinho, W., and Appolinario, J. C. (2003) "Psychiatric comorbidity in a Brazilian sample of patients with binge-eating disorder", *Psychiatry Research* 119: 189–94.

Fowler, S., and Bulik, C. M. (1997) "Family environment and psychiatric history in women with binge-eating disorder and obese controls", *Behaviour Change* 14: 106–12.

Gladis, M. M., Wadden, T. A., Vogt, R., Foster, G., Kuehnel, R. H., and Bartlett, S. J. (1998) "Behavioral treatment of obese binge eaters: do they need different care?", *Journal of Psychosomatic Research* 44: 375–84.

Grilo, C. M., Hrabosky, J. I., White, M. A., Allison, K. C., Stunkard, A. J., and Masheb, R. M. (2008) "Overvaluation of shape and weight in binge eating disorder and overweight controls: refinement of a diagnostic construct", *Journal of Abnormal Psychology* 117: 414–19.

Grilo, C. M., and Masheb, R. M. (2005) "A randomized controlled comparison of guided self-help cognitive behavioral therapy and behavioral weight loss for binge eating disorder", *Behaviour Research and Therapy* 43: 1509–25.

Grilo, C. M., Masheb, R. M., and Salant, S. L. (2005) "Cognitive behavioral therapy guided self-help and orlistat for the treatment of binge eating disorder: a randomized, double-blind, placebo-controlled trial", *Biological Psychiatry* 57: 1193–201.

Grilo, C. M., Masheb, R. M., and White, M. A. (2010) "Significance of overvaluation of shape/weight in binge-eating disorder: comparative study with overweight and bulimia nervosa", *Obesity* 18: 499–504.

Grilo, C. M., Masheb, R. M., and Wilson, G. T. (2005) "Efficacy of cognitive behavioral therapy and fluoxetine for the treatment of binge eating disorder: a randomized double-blind placebo-controlled comparison", *Biological Psychiatry* 57: 301–9.

Grilo, C. M., Masheb, R. M., and Wilson, G. T. (2001) "Subtyping binge eating disorder", *Journal of Consulting and Clinical Psychology* 69: 1066–72.

Grilo, C. M., Masheb, R. M., Wilson, G. T., Gueorguieva, R., and White, M. A. (2011) "Cognitive-behavioral therapy, behavioral weight loss, and sequential treatment for obese patients with binge-eating disorder: a randomized controlled trial", *Journal of Consulting and Clinical Psychology* 79: 675–85.

Grilo, C. M., and White, M. A. (2011) "A controlled evaluation of the distress criterion for binge eating disorder", *Journal of Consulting and Clinical Psychology* 79: 509–14.

Hudson, J. I., Hiripi, E., Pope, H. G., and Kessler, R. C. (2007)"The prevalence and correlates of eating disorders in the National Comorbidity Survey Replication", *Biological Psychiatry* 61: 348–58.

Isnard, P., Michel, G., Frelut, M-L., Vila, G., Falissard, B., Naja, W., Navarro, J., and Mouren-Simeoni, M. C. (2003) "Binge eating and psychopathology in severely obese adolescents", *International Journal of Eating Disorders* 34: 235–43.

Jenkins, D. J., Ocana, A., Jenkins, A. L., Wolever, T. M., Vuksan, V., Katzman, L., Hollands, M., Greenberg, G., Corey, P., Patten, R., Wong, G., and Josse, R. G. (1992) "Metabolic advantages of spreading the nutrient load: effects of increased meal frequency in non-insulin-dependent diabetes", *American Journal of Clinical Nutrition* 55: 461–7.

Johnson, J. G., Spitzer, R. L., and Williams, J. B. W. (2001) "Health problems, impairment and illnesses associated with bulimia nervosa and binge eating disorder among primary care and obstetric gynaecology patients", *Psychological Medicine* 31: 1455–66.

Kanter, R. A., Williams, B. E., and Cummings, C. (1992) "Personal and parental alcohol abuse, and victimization in obese binge eaters and nonbingeing obese", *Addictive Behaviors* 17: 439–45.

Kolotkin, R. L., Westman, E. C., Ostbye, T., Crosby, R. D., Eisenson, H., and Binks, M. (2004) "Does binge eating disorder impact weight-related quality of life?", *Obesity Research* 12: 999–1005.

Kral, J. G., Buckley, M. C., Kissileff, H. R., and Schaffner, F. (2001) "Metabolic correlates of eating behavior in severe obesity", *International Journal of Obesity and Related Metabolic Disorders* 25: 258–64.

Marcus, M. D., Wing, R. R., and Hopkins, J. (1988) "Obese binge eaters: affect, cognitions, and response to behavioral weight control", *Journal of Consulting and Clinical Psychology* 56: 433–9.

Marcus, M. D., Wing, R. R., and Lamparski, D. M. (1985) "Binge eating and dietary restraint in obese patients", *Addictive Behaviors* 10: 163–8.

Marques, L., Alegria, M., Becker, A. E., Chen, C. N., Fang, A., Chosak, A., and Diniz, J. B. (2011) "Comparative prevalence, correlates of impairment, and service utilization for eating disorders across US ethnic groups: implications for reducing ethnic disparities in health care access for eating disorders", *International Journal of Eating Disorders* 44: 412–20.

Masheb, R. M., and Grilo, C. M. (2006) "Eating patterns and breakfast consumption in obese patients with binge eating disorder", *Behaviour Research and Therapy* 44: 1545–53.

Masheb, R. M., Grilo, C. M., and White, M. A. (2011) "An examination of eating patterns in community women with bulimia nervosa and binge eating disorder", *International Journal of Eating Disorders* 44: 618–24.

Mond, J. M., Myers, T. C., Crosby, R. D., Hay, P. J., and Mitchell, J. E. (2010) "Bulimic eating disorders in primary care: hidden morbidity still?", *Journal of Clinical Psychology in Medical Settings* 17: 56–63.

Mussell, M. P., Mitchell, J. E., de Zwaan, M., Crosby, R. D., Seim, H. C., and Crow, S. J. (1996) "Clinical characteristics associated with binge eating in obese females: a descriptive study", *International Journal of Obesity and Related Metabolic Disorders* 20: 324–31.

Nauta, H., Hospers, H. J., Jansen, A., and Kok, G. (2000) "Cognitions in obese binge eaters and obese non-binge eaters" *Cognitive Therapy and Research* 24: 521–31.

Ogden, C. L., Yanovski, S. Z., Carroll, M. D., and Flegal, K. M. (2007) "The epidemiology of obesity", *Gastroenterology* 132: 2087–102.

Raymond, N. C., Neumeyer, B., Warren, C., Lee, S. S., and Peterson, C. B. (2003) "Energy intake patterns in obese women with binge eating disorder", *Obesity Research* 11: 869–79.

Reas, D. L., and Grilo, C. M. (2008) "Review and meta-analysis of pharmacotherapy for binge-eating disorder", *Obesity* 16: 2024–38.

Reas, D. L., and Grilo, C. M. (2007) "Timing and sequence of the onset of overweight, dieting, and binge eating in overweight patients with binge eating disorders", *International Journal of Eating Disorders* 40: 165–70.

Reas, D. L., Masheb, R. M., and Grilo, C. M. (2004) "Appearance vs. health reasons for seeking treatment among obese patients with binge eating disorder", *Obesity Research* 12: 758–60.

Sierra-Johnson, J., Unden, A. L., Linestrand, M., Rosell, M., Sjogren, P., Kolak, M., De Faire, U., Fisher, R. M., and Hellenius, M. L. (2008) "Eating meals irregularly: a novel environmental risk factor for the metabolic syndrome", *Obesity* 16: 1302–7.

Smith, D. E., Marcus, M. D., Lewis, C. E., Fitzgibbon, M. L., and Schreiner, P. (1998) "Prevalence of binge eating disorder, obesity, and depression in a biracial cohort of young adults", *Annals of Behavioral Medicine* 20: 227–32.

Spitzer, R. L., Devlin, M., Walsh, B. T., Hasin, D., Wing, R., Marcus, M., Stunkard, A., Wadden, T., Yanovski, S., Agras, S., Mitchell, J., and Nonas, C. (1992) "Binge eating disorder: a multisite field trial of the diagnostic criteria", *International Journal of Eating Disorders* 11: 191–203.

Striegel-Moore, R. H., and Franko, D. L. (2003) "Epidemiology of binge eating disorder", *International Journal of Eating Disorders* 34 Suppl: S19–29.

Striegel-Moore, R. H., Wilson, G. T., Wilfley, D. E., Elder, K. A., and Brownell, K. D. (1998) "Binge eating in an obese community sample", *International Journal of Eating Disorders* 23: 27–37.

Taylor, A. E., Hubbard, J., and Anderson, E. J. (1999) "Impact of binge eating on metabolic and leptin dynamics in normal young women", *Journal of Clinical Endocrinology and Metabolism* 84: 428–34.

Telch, C. F., Agras, W. S., and Rossiter, E. M. (1988) "Binge eating increases with increasing adiposity", *International Journal of Eating Disorders* 7: 115–19.

Telch, C. F., and Stice, E. (1998) "Psychiatric comorbidity in women with binge eating disorder: prevalence rates from a non-treatment-seeking sample", *Journal of Consulting and Clinical Psychology* 66: 768–76.

Wadden, T. A., Butryn, M. L., and Byrne, K. J. (2004) "Efficacy of lifestyle modification for long-term weight control", *Obesity Research* 12 Suppl: S151–62.

White, M. A., and Grilo, C. M. (2006) "Psychiatric comorbidity in binge-eating disorder as a function of smoking history", *Journal of Clinical Psychiatry* 67: 594–9.

Wilfley, D. E., Friedman, M. A., Dounchis, J. Z., Stein, R. I., Welch, R. R., and Ball, S. A. (2000) "Comorbid psychopathology in binge eating disorder: relation to eating disorder severity at baseline and following treatment", *Journal of Consulting and Clinical Psychology* 68: 641–9.

Wilfley, D. E., Wilson, G. T., and Agras, W. S. (2003) "The clinical significance of binge eating disorder", *International Journal of Eating Disorders* 34 Suppl: S96–106.

Wilson, G. T., Grilo, C. M., and Vitousek, K. M. (2007) "Psychological treatment of eating disorders", *American Psychologist* 62: 199–216.

World Health Organization (2011) "Obesity and overweight" (Fact sheet no. 311). Online. Available: http//www.who.int/mediacentre/factsheets/fs311/en/ (accessed 27 March 2012).

Yanovski, S. (1993) "Binge eating disorder: current knowledge and future directions", *Obesity Research* 1: 306–24.

Yanovski, S. Z., Nelson, J. E., Dubbert, B. K., and Spitzer, R. L. (1993) "Association of binge eating disorder and psychiatric comorbidity in obese subjects", *American Journal of Psychiatry* 150: 1472–9.

de Zwaan, M., Lancaster, K. L., Mitchell, J. E., Howell, L. M., Monson, N., Roerig, J. L., and Crosby, R. D. (2002) "Health-related quality of life in morbidly obese patients: effect of gastric bypass surgery", *Obesity Surgery* 12: 773–80.

Chapter 2

Ethnicity, race and binge eating disorder

Debra L. Franko, Meghan E. Lovering and Heather Thompson-Brenner

Case study

I am a 24-year-old Latina woman who recently graduated from college with a degree in biology. I am the eldest of four children and have always felt much pressure to succeed academically. I began binge eating once a month at age 16 to help cope with the stress from school and feelings of isolation. I felt out of control during these episodes, eating eat any junk food I could find, alone in my bedroom. After binging, I felt incredibly embarrassed looking at all the food wrappers and hid them under my bed in an old trunk, a gift from my grandmother. I gained 30 pounds during my junior and senior year of high school and, feeling very depressed and isolated, I missed out on important events like the prom. I have tried many times to lose weight, but have never been able to stick with it. I have a good relationship with my parents but struggle with them at times because they think that I look fine even though I don't feel that way. These days I am distracted by my body size and shape and my constant urges to binge, which often intensify during stressful periods. My binge eating is at the point where it is not only affecting my personal life, but my career as well.

Felicia

Introduction to ethnicity and binge eating disorder

Binge eating disorder (BED), first introduced as a diagnostic concept in the DSM-IV, is characterized by recurrent, uncontrollable eating with little or no compensatory behavior (American Psychiatric Association 1994). BED is the most commonly diagnosed eating disorder (ED) (Greenberg *et al.* 2005; Hudson *et al.* 2007) and is associated with serious distress and impairment (Grilo 2003). Unique among the eating disorders is that BED appears to be equally represented across racial/ethnic minority groups in the United States (Alegria *et al.* 2007; Marques *et al.* 2011), as evidenced by data documenting the high frequency of this disorder among African American, Asian, and Hispanic/

Latino Americans (Gayle *et al.* 2004; Mazzeo *et al.* 2005; Sanchez-Johnson *et al.* 2003; Striegel-Moore and Franko 2003). However, studies suggest that underrepresented minority groups are less likely to receive treatment for EDs than Caucasians, due to lower treatment-seeking among these groups and potential clinician bias against referring individuals of color with ED symptoms for treatment (Becker *et al.* 2003; Cachelin *et al.* 2001; Marques *et al.* 2011; Pike *et al.* 2001; Striegel-Moore and Franko 2003; Wilfley *et al.* 2001). Despite the significant numbers of racial/ethnic minorities with BED, basic information about eating disorder psychopathology and treatment response on individuals from underrepresented minority groups is limited (Gayle *et al.* 2004; Smolak and Striegel-Moore 2001; Striegel-Moore *et al.* 2003; Wilson 2007). This chapter will describe what is known about the prevalence, risk factors, and treatment of individuals with BED from racial/ethnic minority backgrounds. Additionally, the relationship between BED and obesity and both clinical and research implications will be highlighted.

Prevalence rates

Within the United States, research suggests that the demographic profile of individuals with BED is ethnically and racially more diverse than other EDs (Striegel-Moore and Franko 2003) and that rates of binge eating and levels of cognitive BED symptoms (e.g., shape and weight concerns) in African Americans and Hispanic/Latinos are comparable to, and sometimes higher than, that among Caucasians (Alegria *et al.* 2007; Fitzgibbon *et al.* 1998; Franko *et al.* 2011; Shaw *et al.* 2004; Striegel-Moore *et al.* 2000). Rates of BED may be as high as 33–48 per cent among obese individuals in ethnically/racially diverse populations (Latner *et al.* 2004; Mazzeo *et al.* 2005). A recent study by Marques *et al.* (2011) examined the lifetime and past year prevalence of BED, anorexia nervosa (AN), and bulimia nervous (BN) for United States ethnic minorities (Latino, Asian, African American) using pooled data from the National Institute of Mental Health Collaborative Psychiatric Epidemiological Studies. No significant differences in rates of BED were found among the groups, indicating that prevalence rates for BED are similar across non-Latino Whites, Latinos, Asians, and African Americans populations.

> I have an incredibly hard time sleeping at night and frequently lay awake thinking about my weight. Recently I have been experiencing a lot of back pain and fatigue, which keeps me from going to the gym or trying to exercise. I'm often tired and I'm having trouble concentrating at work. When I was younger I played a number of team sports, like soccer or volleyball, but I have not participated in anything like that in years. I tend to stay to myself these days, I don't want to go out with friends after work to "grab a bite," instead I much prefer to go home and eat by myself. Also, I frequently pass up going to family social events because I feel too

embarrassed by the way I look, even though my family is very important to me.

Felicia

Comorbidity

People with BED often also have other comorbid mental health issues, such as anxiety, mood, impulse-control, and substance abuse disorders (Hudson *et al.* 2007). Studying co-occurring disorders can contribute to our understanding of BED etiology and treatment (Grilo *et al.* 2009). However, few studies have examined comorbidity within BED among racially/ethnically diverse groups. One study indicated that Caucasian and African American women with BED show similar rates of co-morbid axis I disorders (Pike *et al.* 2001) and multiple studies have indicated that depression is a risk factor for BED across ethnic/racial groups (Fitzgibbon *et al.* 1998; Marcus *et al.* 2007; Reagan and Hersch 2005).

Impairment

A study by Alegria *et al.* (2007) examined functional impairment within the Latino community using data from the National Latino and Asian American Study (NLAAS). Latino participants with BED reported severe impairment with home management (8.7 per cent), ability to work (22.7 per cent), personal life (1.2 per cent), and social life (9.6 per cent), and nearly one quarter were found to report at least one area of impairment. Nicdao *et al.* (2007) also examined functional impairment among Asian Americans with BED using the NLAAS. Rates of severe impairment were higher for the Asians, relative to Latinos, with ability to work (24.7 per cent), personal life (40.3 per cent), social life (42.9 per cent), and any impairment (42.9 per cent), whereas home management (0 per cent) was not affected.

Within-group differences

A number of studies have examined the prevalence of BED within subgroups of racial/ethnic minorities. The National Survey of American Life and The National Latino and Asian American Study sampled Blacks, Latinos, and Asian Americans, providing a wealth of information on BED prevalence and its correlates among these groups (Alegria *et al.* 2007; Nicdao *et al.* 2007; Taylor *et al.* 2007). Taylor *et al.* (2007) examined the prevalence of BED within a sample of adult and adolescent African American and Caribbean blacks and found similar prevalence estimates in these two groups. Using in-home interviews with 5191 adults and 1170 adolescents using the National Survey of American Life (NSAL), 1.66 per cent of people in both groups were found to meet criteria for BED. An extensive study of Latino subgroups found similar rates of binge eating across Cuban, Puerto Rican, and Mexican immigrants and among groups differing by acculturation status (e.g., US nativity) (Alegria *et al.* 2007). Similarly, Nicdao *et al.* (2007) explored the prevalence of binge eating among Chinese, Filipino, Vietnamese, and "Other Asians", including Japanese, Korean, and Asian Indian immigrants, and found low rates of BED among the various sub-groups within the Asian community. Specifically, the rates for Chinese (1.19 per cent), Filipino (1.87 per cent), Vietnamese (0.10 per cent), and other Asian (0.71 per cent) individuals did not differ significantly from each other. Swanson *et al.* (2012) examined the prevalence of BED within the Mexican community, finding prevalence rates of 1.6 per cent for Mexicans living in Mexico compared to 2.2 per cent among Mexican–Americans, suggesting Western exposure and acculturation may be contributing factors to the development of BED.

Gender

Understanding how various demographic factors, such as gender, age, and body mass index (BMI), might contribute to or protect against the development of BED among ethnic groups is important. Taylor *et al.* (2007) found a higher frequency of BED in black women (2.36 per cent) than black men (0.78 per cent). The average age of onset for black women (23.14 years) and black men (21.35 years) differed significantly from AN groups, suggesting that BED has a later onset than some of the other eating disorders. A study examining gender differences in the Latino community similarly found higher rates of BED in women (2.31 per cent) than men (1.55 per cent) (Alegria *et al.* 2007). Within the Asian community, the lifetime prevalence of BED was found to be significantly higher for women than men (Nicdao *et al.* 2007). Specifically, Asian women were found to have a 12-month prevalence rate of 1.36 per cent and a lifetime prevalence rate of 2.67 per cent for BED, relative to Asian men with prevalence rates of 0.53 per cent and 1.35 per cent, respectively. Therefore, across the black, Latino, and Asian ethnic groups examined, BED occurs more commonly in women than men, which is similar to what is found in Caucasian samples. However, the rates of BED in men are higher than rates of AN or BN in men, suggesting that males represent a group at greater risk to develop BED than other eating disorders.

> The last time I went to my weight loss program they said my body mass index was 32, which I know is considered obese. I stay indoors in the summer, because I'm embarrassed by how I look. Frequently, I try to feel better by eating at least a half gallon of peanut butter ice cream, but afterwards I always feel guilty. I rarely see friends anymore because I don't want them to see how much weight I have gained.
>
> Felicia

Age and body mass index

Age and Body Mass Index (BMI) have also been examined as important demographic correlates in studies of BED. When looking at rates by age, black adults (1.66 per cent) were found to have a higher prevalence rate than black adolescents (0.28 per cent) over a 12-month period (Taylor *et al.* 2007). BED was found to be eight times more likely in Asians age 18–29 than in the older than 60 age group (Nicdao *et al.* 2007). Interestingly, within the Latino community, age estimates for BED were found to be the same for older (greater than 30) and younger (30 years or less) Latinos (OR = 0.84, CI = 0.55–1.30) (Alegria *et al.* 2007). Prevalence rates appear to vary by age across ethnic/racial groups.

Alegria *et al.* (2007) documented that in the Latino community, people with a BMI higher than 30 had a significantly higher risk of lifetime BED than those with a BMI between 18.5 and 30. Within the Asian community, people with a BMI of 30–39.9 were nearly five times more likely to have BED, and those with a BMI of greater than 40 to be nearly six times more likely to have BED (Nicdao *et al.* 2007). These data indicate a strong association between BED and BMI across racial and ethnic groups, similar again to that found in Caucasian samples.

Factors influencing development of BED in ethnic minority individuals

Research suggests exposure to certain factors increases the risk of BED as well as obesity (Fairburn *et al.* 1998; Grilo *et al.* 2009). A known risk factor for BED is dieting, which may occur as a result of binge eating as well as a precursor to binge eating (Dingemans *et al.* 2002; Howard and Porzelius 1999). Research studying family characteristics in relation to BED is limited; however, one study found BED subjects rated their family environment as less supportive and cohesive, and less permissive of direct expression of feelings than participants in the healthy control group (Dingemans *et al.* 2002; Hodges *et al.* 1998).

Epidemiological research suggests that the interplay among ethnicity, socio-economic status (SES), BMI, depression, and binge eating include complex interactions and must be understood together. Research points to socio-economic status variables as particularly central; however, the findings are somewhat inconsistent. One community study found that depression, lower family income, and higher percentage of life lived in "neighborhoods with an unhealthy environment" all increased the likelihood of binge eating, whereas obesity and race did not have a significant effect when other factors were controlled (Reagan and Hersch 2005). In an epidemiological study of black and white women, recurrent binge eaters in both ethnic groups were more likely than non-binge eaters to be in the lowest category of educational attainment and less likely to be college graduates (Striegel-Moore *et al.* 2000).

BED has also been found to be associated with lower educational attainment in a large study of Latinos (Alegria *et al.* 2007). Further, a community-based study found that financial strain (e.g., "difficulty paying for basics") was associated with ED symptoms, whereas more traditional measures of SES (e.g., education level) were not. However, when BMI, current and past depression, and childhood abuse were co-varied, financial strain was no longer significant (Marcus *et al.* 2007). In a study of white, black, and Hispanic women (Fitzgibbon *et al.* 1998), education, depression, and body image ideal (preferring a slimmer ideal) were all found to be significant covariates of binge eating. This study found education level to be a stronger predictor of binge eating symptoms among white women than it was among black or Hispanic women. BMI was only a significant predictor of BED severity for Hispanic women; however, depression was a predictor for both Hispanic and white women. This study suggests that the effects of education (a proxy for socio-economic status) may differ by ethnic group, and that the protective effect of higher socio-economic status maybe more relevant for white women than those from other racial and ethnic groups. This group of studies suggests a variety of correlates (e.g., depression, socioeconomic status) may raise the risk for BED in diverse groups; however, prospective studies are needed to determine whether they are truly risk factors or correlates.

While women of color in the United States tend to have higher BMI on average than white women, some research has demonstrated that women of color exhibit less body dissatisfaction and a greater range of body size acceptance (Fitzgibbon *et al.* 2000). Greater body satisfaction and more weight tolerant attitudes may be a protective factor against the development of some eating disorders; however, researchers speculate that these same attitudes may increase risk for binge eating and obesity due to the absence of motivation to avoid weight gain (Fitzgibbon 1998). Black treatment-seeking women with BED showed significantly lower rates of binge eating and higher cognitive ED symptoms than non-treatment-seeking individuals identified in the community through epidemiological research (Grilo *et al.* 2005). Treatment-seeking black women had a higher BMI as well, though this difference did not fully account for the observed differences in concern over shape and weight (Grilo *et al.* 2005). This research may support the idea that shape and weight concern – though distressing – may contribute to the motivation to limit binge eating and to seek treatment for binge eating.

A recent study by Grilo, White, and Masheb (2012) examined overvaluation of shape/weight in an ethnically diverse sample of obese patients with BED in a primary care setting and found the overvaluation of shape/weight group, relative to the non-overvaluation group, had significantly greater levels of eating disorder psychopathology and poorer psychological functioning as well as higher rates of anxiety disorders. It has been suggested that a negative correlation may exist between two dimensions of ED pathology, namely cognitive ED symptoms and binge eating frequency (Grilo *et al.* 2005). This research has influenced investigators to call for further studies that include all underrepresented minority groups (Franko *et al.* 2007; Gayle *et al.* 2004; Smolak and Striegel-Moore 2001).

I struggle trying to decide whether to tell my parents about my binge eating, because my mother believes curvy women are beautiful. The majority of women in my family embrace their curves, and yet I can't seem to accept this. I know I should love my body, but I want to be thinner. I feel a great deal of pressure to be thin like my co-workers or models.

Felicia

Previous research suggests that exposure to Western culture, where thin bodies and weight management are valued, plays a role in the development of BED (Becker *et al.* 2011; Swanson *et al.* 2012). A study by Chamorro and Flores-Ortiz (2000) found that of the five generations studied, second-generation women had the highest rate of disordered eating, suggesting acculturation may contribute to a preoccupation with slimness and decrease in defense against eating disorders. While this study did not focus on BED, but instead on disordered eating patterns, it is notable that Alegria *et al.* (2007) examined the prevalence of BED and BN in Latinos using nativity and number of parents born in the United States as factors, and found neither to be significant predictors of BED. Swanson and colleagues (2012) examined the effect of migration on BED within six Mexican groups of varying immigration status, while adjusting for age, sex, and depressive or anxiety disorders, and found the prevalence of BED was significantly elevated only in the group with two parents born in the United States, suggesting that while exposure to Western culture does have an impact on BED, it is a relatively slow assimilation that requires more than one generation of exposure. While Mexican immigrants and Mexican–Americans born in the United States to one foreign parent were not significantly different, there was a trend indicating higher risk for BED with increased exposure (Swanson *et al.* 2012). More research is needed to better understand the complex interactions between exposure to Western culture, SES, and BMI on the transitional period of immigration to examine the role of these variables in the development of BED.

Relationship between BED and obesity

The relationship between BED and obesity has been well studied and obesity has been found to be both a risk factor for and a result of BED among Caucasians, African Americans, and Hispanics/Latinos (Alegria *et al.* 2007; Striegel-Moore and Franko 2003; Telch *et al.* 1988). Obesity in BED is thought to result from a combination of the lack of dietary restraint and binge eating without compensatory behaviors (Grilo 2010; White *et al.* 2010).

Latinos with a BMI greater than 40 (Alegria *et al.* 2007) and Asian Americans with a BMI greater than 30 (Nicdao *et al.* 2007) have been found to have a significantly higher lifetime risk of BED. Participants in obesity treatment trials who binge eat have shown poor treatment outcome (Blaine and Rodman 2007; Burette *et al.* 2005; Green *et al.* 2004). Furthermore, there is a clear association between BED and obesity, with the prevalence of BED increasing with the degree of obesity (Dingemans *et al.* 2002). Research has shown obesity develops several years after the onset of BED (Haiman and Devlin 1999).

I have decided to come for treatment because I feel as if my eating is out of control. I am binge eating two to three times a week and this is greatly affecting my life. I feel I am on a downward spiral and, while scared to seek treatment, I know I need it.

Felicia

Treatment studies

Many people suffering from BED are not accurately diagnosed and few receive empirically validated treatments (White *et al.* 2010; Wilson *et al.* 2007). Until recently, the treatment of BED has not been studied in relation to race and ethnicity (Reagan and Hersch 2005), because of the severe underrepresentation of racial/ethnic minority individuals in clinical trials (Berkman *et al.* 2006; Franko *et al.* 2011). In the only study to date that has examined demographic and clinical characteristics of diverse individual people seeking treatment for BED in randomized clinical trials, African Americans reported higher body mass index (BMI) and associated dietary restraint at baseline, whereas Hispanic/Latinos individuals with BED were found to have greater shape and weight concerns relative to Caucasian individuals with BED (Franko *et al.* 2011).

Extensive reviews (NICE 2004; Wilson *et al.* 2007) have established cognitive behavioral therapy (CBT) as treatment of choice for BED; however, preliminary evidence regarding treatment length for BED has shown inconsistent results. Some studies suggest longer treatment length (sixteen sessions as opposed to eight sessions) improves the overall outcome of treatment (Eldredge *et al.* 1997; Schlup *et al.* 2010), whereas a recent study by Grilo *et al.* (2011) found that longer treatment was not significantly superior to a six-month treatment course. A study by Grilo, Masheb, and Crosby (2012) reported overvaluation of shape/weight to be a significant predictor of treatment outcome. However, to date there is no published study examining treatment outcome in diverse groups, and research in this area is critically needed.

Felicia's treatment

I have started treatment with a psychologist for my binge-eating problem. We talk about my thoughts and feelings surrounding my binge eating episodes. For homework, I am keeping track of how frequently I binge and we discuss it during therapy. Having someone to talk to about this problem has really helped me feel better, especially since I know I can't talk to my family about this problem. My therapist has helped me realize that this problem is common, especially among my community, and that I shouldn't feel embarrassed about it. I am really happy I took the steps to get help, and wish I hadn't waited so long.

Felicia

Felicia started CBT for her binge eating disorder and receives medication for her depression. Her therapist is sensitive to the conflicting pressures she feels from that Latino community to be curvy and the American ideal to be thin.

Implications: research and clinical

Although studies have documented prevalence rates and clinical correlates of BED in diverse groups, there is a great need for treatment research with racial and ethnic minorities. Studies are needed that address treatment response as well as both predictors and moderators of treatment. Future studies should utilize a combination of quantitative methods and qualitative methods to fully understand the complexities of BED in diverse groups.

It is important for practitioners to consider ethnicity and race when screening, diagnosing, and treating BED. Our current treatments generally do not consider factors such as low socio-economic status, acculturation and treatment accessibility issues. The issue of underutilization of treatment by diverse groups needs to be addressed by developing creative and innovative ideas for outreach. Future treatment programs focused on people from diverse backgrounds should recognize and address the stigma and lack of trust in health care providers that might be responsible for limited treatment seeking by people with BED.

References

Alegria, M., Woo, M., Cao, Z., Torres, M., Meng, X. L., and Striegel-Moore, R. (2007) 'Prevalence and correlates of eating disorders in Latinos in the United States', *International Journal of Eating Disorders* 40 Suppl: S15–21.

American Psychiatric Association (1994) *Diagnostic and statistical manual of mental disorders* (4th edn), Washington, DC: American Psychiatric Association.

Becker, A. E., Fay, K. E., Agnew-Blais, J., Khan, A. N., Striegel-Moore, R. H., and Gilman, S. E. (2011) 'Social network exposure and adolescent eating pathology in Fiji', *British Journal of Psychiatry* 198: 43–50.

Becker, A. E., Franko, D. L., Speck, A., and Herzog, D. B. (2003) 'Ethnicity and differential access to care for eating disorder symptoms', *International Journal of Eating Disorders* 33: 205–12.

Berkman, N., Bulik, C., Brownley, K., Lohr, K., Sedway, J., Rooks, A., and Gartlehner, G. (2006) 'Management of eating disorders', *Evidence Report Technology Assessment* 135: 1–166.

Blaine, B., and Rodman, J. (2007) 'Responses to weight loss treatment among obese individuals with and without BED: a matched-study meta-analysis', *Eating and Weight Disorders* 12: 54–60.

Busetto, L., Segato, G., De Luca, M., De Marchi, F., Foletto, M., Vianello, M., Valeri, M., Favretti, F., and Enzi, G. (2005) 'Weight loss and postoperative complications in morbidly obese patients with binge eating disorder treated by laparoscopic adjustable gastric banding', *Obes Surg* 15: 195–201.

Cachelin, F. M., Rebeck, R., Veisel, C., and Striegel-Moore, R. H. (2001) 'Barriers to treatment for eating disorders among ethnically diverse women', *International Journal of Eating Disorders* 30: 269–78.

Chamorro, R., and Flores-Ortiz, Y. (2000) 'Acculturation and disordered eating patterns among Mexican American women', *International Journal of Eating Disorders* 28: 125–9.

Dingemans, A. E., Bruna, M. J., and van Furth, E. F. (2002) 'Binge eating disorder: a review', *International Journal of Obesity* 26: 299–307.

Eldredge, K. L., Stewart Agras, W., Arnow, B., Telch, C. F., Bell, S., Castonguay, L., and Marnell, M. (1997) 'The effects of extending cognitive-behavioural therapy for binge eating disorder among initial treatment nonresponders', *International Journal of Eating Disorders* 21: 347–52.

Fairburn, C. G., Doll, H. A., Welch, S. L., Hay, P.J., Davies, B. A., and O'Connor, M. E. (1998) 'Risk factors for binge eating disorder: a community-based, case-control study', *Archives of General Psychiatry* 55: 425–32.

Fitzgibbon, M. L., Blackman, L. R., and Avellone, M. E. (2000) 'The relationship between body image discrepancy and body mass index across ethnic groups', *Obesity Research* 8: 582–9.

Fitzgibbon, M. L., Spring, B., Avellone, M. E., Blackman, L. R., Pingitore, R., and Stolley, M. R. (1998) 'Correlates of binge eating in Hispanic, black, and white women', *International Journal of Eating Disorders* 24: 43–52.

Franko, D. L., Becker, A. E., Thomas, J. J., and Herzog, D. B. (2007) 'Cross-ethnic differences in eating disorder symptoms and related distress', *International Journal of Eating Disorders* 40: 156–64.

Franko, D. L., Thompson-Brenner, H., Thompson, D. R., Boisseau, C. L., Davis, A., Forbush, M. A., Roehrig, J. P., Bryson, S., Bulik, C. M., Crow, S. J., Devin, M. J., Gorin, A. A., Grilo, C. M., Kristeller, J., Mitchell, J. E., Peterson, C., Safer, D., Striegel-Moore, R. H., Wilfley, D. E., and Wilson, G. T. (2011) 'Examining ethnic differences in binge eating disorder: the role of socioeconomic status and body mass index', presented at the International Conference for Eating Disorders, Miami, Florida, April.

Gayle, J. L., Fitzgibbon, M. L., and Martinovich, Z. (2004) 'A preliminary analysis of binge episodes: comparison of a treatment-seeking sample of Black and White women', *Eating Behaviors* 5: 303–13.

Green, A. E., Dymek-Valentine, M., Pytluk, S., Le Grange, D., and Alverdy, J. (2004) 'Psychosocial outcome of gastric bypass surgery for patients with and without binge eating', *Obesity Surgery* 14: 975–85.

Greenberg, I., Perna, F., Kaplan, M., and Sullivan, M. A. (2005) 'Behavioral and psychological factors in the assessment and treatment of obesity surgery patients', *Obesity Research* 13: 244–9.

Grilo, C. M. (2003) 'Binge eating disorder', in C. G. Fairburn and K. D. Brownell (eds) *Eating Disorders and Obesity* (pp. 179–92), New York: Guilford Press.

Grilo, C. M. (2010) 'What treatment research is needed for eating disorder not otherwise specified and binge eating disorder?', in C. M. Grilo and J. E. Mitchell (eds) *The Treatment of Eating Disorders: A Clinical Handbook* (pp. 554–68), New York: Guilford Press.

Grilo, C. M., Lozano, C., and Masheb, R. M. (2005) 'Ethnicity and sampling bias in binge eating disorder: black women who seek treatment have different characteristics than those who do not', *International Journal of Eating Disorders* 38: 257–62.

Grilo, C. M., Masheb, R. M., and Crosby, R. D. (2012) 'Predictors and moderators of response to cognitive behavioral therapy and medication for the treatment of binge eating disorder', *Journal of Consulting and Clinical Psychology* e-publication ahead of press: doi:10.1037/a002700.

Grilo, C. M., Masheb, R. M., Wilson, G. T., Gueorguieva, R., and White, M. A. (2011) 'Cognitive-behavioral therapy, behavioral weight loss, and sequential treatment for obese patients with binge-eating disorder: a randomized controlled trial', *Journal of Consulting and Clinical Psychology* 79: 675–85.

Grilo, C. M., White, M. A., and Masheb, R. M. (2009) 'DSM-IV psychiatric disorder comorbidity and its correlates in binge eating disorder', *International Journal of Eating Disorders* 42: 228–34.

Grilo, C. M., White, M. A., and Masheb, R. M. (2012) 'Significance of overvaluation of shape and weight in an ethnically diverse sample of obese patients with binge-eating disorder in primary care settings', *Behaviour Research and Therapy* 50: 298–303.

Haiman, C., and Devlin, M. J. (1999) 'Binge eating before the onset of dieting: a distinct subgroup of bulimia nervosa?', *International Journal of Eating Disorders* 25: 151–7.

Hodges, E. L., Cochrane, C. E., and Brewerton, T. D. (1998) 'Family characteristics of binge-eating disorder patients', *International Journal of Eating Disorders* 23: 145–51.

Howard, C. E., and Porzelius, L. K. (1999) 'The role of dieting in binge eating disorder: etiology and treatment implications', *Clinical Psychology Review* 19: 25–44.

Hudson, J. I., Hiripiri, E., Pope, H. G. Jr., and Kessler, R. C. (2007) 'The prevalence and correlates of eating disorders in the national comorbidity survey replication', *Biological Psychiatry* 61: 348–58.

Latner, J. D., Wetzler, S., Goodman, E. R., and Glinski, J. (2004) 'Gastric bypass in a low-income, inner-city population: eating disturbances and weight loss', *Obesity Research* 12: 956–61.

Marcus, M. D., Bromberger, J. T., Wei, H. L., Brown, C., and Kravitz, H. M. (2007) 'Prevalence and selected correlates of eating disorder symptoms among a multiethnic community sample of midlife women', *Annals of Behavioral Medicine* 33: 269–77.

Marques, L., Alegria, M., Becker, A. E., Chen, C. N., Fang, A., Chosak, A., and Diniz, J. B. (2011) 'Comparative prevalence, correlates of impairment, and service utilization for eating disorders across US ethnic groups: implications for reducing ethnic disparities in health care access for eating disorders', *International Journal of Eating Disorders* 44: 412–20.

Mazzeo, S. E., Saunders, R., and Mitchell, K. S. (2005) 'Binge eating among African American and Caucasian bariatric surgery candidates', *Eating Behaviors* 6: 189–96.

National Institute for Clinical Excellence (NICE) (2004) *Eating disorders: core interventions in the treatment and management of anorexia nervosa, bulimia nervosa, and related eating disorders: clinical guideline no. 9*, London: NICE. Online. Available: http://www.nice.org.uk/guidance/CG9 (accessed 20 February 2012).

Nicdao, E. G., Hong, S. H., and Takeuchi, D. T. (2007) 'Prevalence and correlates of eating disorders among Asian Americans: results of the National Latino and Asian American Study', *International Journal of Eating Disorders* 40: S22–6.

Pike, K. M., Dohm, F. A., Striegel-Moore, R. H., Wilfley, D. E., and Fairburn, C. G. (2001) 'A comparison of black and white women with binge eating disorder', *American Journal of Psychiatry* 158: 1455–60.

Reagan, P., and Hersch, J. (2005) 'Influence of race, gender, and socioeconomic status on binge eating frequency in a population-based sample', *International Journal of Eating Disorders* 38: 252–6.

Sanchez-Johnsen, L. A., Dymek, M., Alverdy, J., and Le Grange, D. (2003) 'Binge eating and eating-related cognitions and behavior in ethnically diverse obese women', *Obesity Research* 11: 1002–9.

Schlup, B., Meyer, A. H., and Munsch, S. (2010) 'A non-randomized direct comparison of cognitive-behavioral short- and long-term treatment for binge eating disorder', *Obesity Facts* 3: 261–6.

Shaw, H., Ramirez, L., Trost, A., Randall, P., and Stice, E. (2004) 'Body image and eating disturbances across ethnic groups: More similarities than differences', *Psychology of Addictive Behaviors* 18: 12–18.

Smolak, L., and Striegel-Moore, R. H. (2001) 'Challenging the myth of the golden girl: ethnicity and eating disorders', in R. Striegel-Moore and L. Smolak (eds) *Eating Disorders: Innovative Directions in Research and Practice* (pp. 111–32), Washington, DC: American Psychological Association.

Striegel-Moore, R. H., Dohm, F. A., Kraemer, H. C., Taylor, C. B., Daniels, S., Crawford, P. B., and Schreiber, G. B. (2003) 'Eating disorders in white and black women', *American Journal of Psychiatry* 160: 1326–31.

Striegel-Moore, R. H., and Franko, D. L. (2003) 'Epidemiology of binge eating disorder', *International Journal of Eating Disorders* 34: S19–29.

Striegel-Moore, R. H., Wilfley, D. E., Pike, K. M., Dohm, F. A., and Fairburn, C. G. (2000) 'Recurrent binge eating in black American women', *Archives of Family Medicine* 9: 83–7.

Swanson, S. A., Saito, N., Borges, G., Benjet, C., Aguilar-Gaxiola, S., Medina-Mora, M. E., and Breslau, J. (2012) 'Changes in binge eating and binge eating disorder associated with migration from Mexico to the US', *Journal of Psychiatric Research* 46: 31–7.

Taylor, J. Y., Caldwell, C. H., Baser, R. E., Faison, N., and Jackson, J. S. (2007) 'Prevalence of eating disorders among Blacks in the National Survey of American Life', *International Journal of Eating Disorders* 40: S10–14.

Telch, C. F., Agras, W. S., and Rossiter, E. M. (1988) 'Binge eating increases with increasing adiposity', *International Journal of Eating Disorders* 7: 115–19.

White, M. A., Grilo, C. M., O'Malley, S. S., and Potenza, M. N. (2010) 'Clinical case discussion: binge eating disorder, obesity and tobacco smoking', *Journal of Addiction Medicine* 4: 11–19.

Wilfley, D. E., Pike, K. M., Dohm, F. A., Striegel-Moore, R. H., and Fairburn, C. G. (2001) 'Bias in binge eating disorder: how representative are recruited clinic samples?', *Journal of Consulting and Clinical Psychology* 69: 383–8.

Wilson, G. T. (2007) 'Binge eating disorder: preliminary results from a multisite trial', presented at Boston University Clinical Psychology Program.

Wilson, G. T., Grilo, C. M., and Vitousek, K. (2007) 'Psychological treatments for eating disorders', *American Psychologist* 62: 199–216.

Chapter 3

The genetics of binge eating disorder

Cynthia M. Bulik and Sara E. Trace

Case study

After my divorce I was devastated. I was having trouble sleeping and seemed to be crying all the time. A friend recommended I see a therapist, so I called for an appointment. During the initial consultation, the therapist asked about everything that was going on for me. She also asked about things I had experienced in my life and similar problems other family members might have experienced as well. Although I had never been treated for a mental illness, my mother was depressed a lot when I was a kid, and I remembered her making monthly trips to "a special doctor" – although we never knew who that doctor was. My mother used to say she was sad all the time because of her weight. Her weight went up and down a lot during my childhood. She would sit at the kitchen table paging through magazines looking for the latest new diet. She was always dieting, so imagine my surprise when I found her alone in her room surrounded by chips, cake, and candy bars. She was horrified that I saw her in that situation, and broke down in tears. The therapist asked about my own eating behaviors and patterns. Although I generally consider myself to be healthy (I don't drink or smoke and I go for walks with my dog every day), I described frustrations with my weight and how I thought, in addition to my divorce, that being heavy was making me depressed. When I went to my primary care doctor last week, she said my BMI was in the obese range. I broke down in tears and when I got home, despite my best attempts not to, I ate a pint of Ben and Jerry's. My weight had inched up throughout my adult life and since my divorce I gained 15 lbs (over 2 months). I told the therapist that, like my mother, I tried to stay away from fattening foods and carbohydrates, but once a week or so my willpower collapsed and I would run through the fast food drive-in, order enough food to feed a family of four, and eat it all before I got out of the car. During those driving and eating episodes, I felt completely out of control and ashamed that I didn't have more willpower. I have no idea how I avoided an accident. After hearing this story, my therapist mentioned BED. I had heard of the more common eating disorders like anorexia nervosa and bulimia nervosa, but this was the first I had heard about BED. To be honest, I couldn't believe there was a name for what I was experiencing! The therapist explained that my description of both my mother and me sounded like binge eating. She said it was not uncommon for these things to run in families and that genetic factors might be involved. She has helped me completely rewrite my own script about what was going on. I had thought I was a bad person who had no willpower, but now I have a better understanding of what this is, and I have hope that it is treatable. I have kept seeing my therapist and we have worked on both depression and BED. I have also used my experience to help educate my adult children about BED. My son has always been a "stress eater," so I let him know about my BED and the successes I have had with treatment.

Jill

Introduction

The role of genetic factors in the development of eating disorders, including binge eating disorder (BED), has become increasingly clear over the past decade (Fowler and Bulik 1997; Helder and Collier 2011; Javaras *et al.* 2008). Although environmental factors, including exposure to negative comments about shape and weight (Fairburn *et al.* 1998; Pike *et al.* 2006), weight-based teasing (Libbey *et al.* 2008; Thompson *et al.* 1995), and portion distortion (Schwartz and Byrd-Bredbenner 2006; Steenhuis and Vermeer 2009) likely contribute to the development of BED, in order to truly understand the causes of BED, we need to embrace complexity, and consider both biological and environmental factors in tandem. This includes the application of multimodal treatment interventions that address both biological and environmental vulnerabilities to which an individual is exposed.

Clinicians, families, and patients alike are frequently curious about the role of genetics in the development of eating disorders. It is not uncommon for patients or family members to say, "I have heard or read online that eating disorders are genetic", or "Have we found the gene for binge eating yet?" While it is true that genetic factors are involved in disordered eating, the media can grossly oversimplify the causes of complex disorders such as BED, leading to widespread misunderstanding. Providing patients and their family members with accurate and yet digestible information regarding the genetics of eating disorders is important in weaving scientific findings into the process of change. As clinicians, under-standing how to best facilitate these conversations with patients is a critical first step. The purpose of this chapter is to provide the clinician with the information necessary to understand and explain genetics research. Specifically, this chapter will discuss the latest scientific findings related to the genetics of BED couched within a clinical context.

Family studies

It is not unusual for patients to report an eating disorder or eating disorder symptoms among their family members. Even more common in a clinical setting, patients often discuss a family member's unusual eating behaviors. These disordered eating behaviors or eating disorders may go undetected in family members, appearing to transmit silently from generation to generation. Understanding family members' dynamics around food can open the door towards helping a patient understand her or his own eating behaviors. For example, in the case illustrated at the beginning of this chapter, Jill came to treatment for depression following a divorce; however, during the course of a thorough clinical assessment, she reported her mother's eating problems, which shed light on her own struggles. Like most people in this society, victimized by the media and the diet industry's message that overweight is a reflection of personal failure, Jill believed her symptoms were a reflection of her lack of willpower. Informing Jill that BED was a legitimate eating disorder with genetic and environmental underpinnings marked the first step in her recovery.

The family study design is typically the first step in assessing the heritability of a particular disorder or diagnosis. The primary aim of the family study is just as the name implies – to determine whether a disease or disorder runs in families. In the family study design, patterns of familial aggregation of the disorder are most frequently examined among the patient's first-degree relatives (including parents, children, and siblings) and compared to either 1) the risk of the disorder in the population or 2) the risk of the disorder in first-degree family members of similar individuals without the disorder. For example, a statistically increased risk of BED in first-degree relatives of people with BED compared to the population at large would demonstrate that the trait is familial (i.e., is more likely to occur in family members of a person with BED than family members of people without BED).

Family studies of BED largely suggest that the disorder runs in families. In one of the first family studies of BED, Fowler and Bulik (1997) found that significantly more obese adult women (n = 20) with a provisional diagnosis of Diagnostic and Statistical Manual of Mental Disorders (American Psychiatric Association 1994) BED reported having at least one first-degree relative who also had BED compared to obese adult women without BED (n = 20). A second large direct-interview family study by Hudson et al. (2006) also examined aggregation of BED within families. Overweight or obese probands with BED (n = 150) and without BED (n = 150), along with half of their first-degree relatives, were interviewed. BED was found to aggregate strongly in families, independent of obesity. Similarly, Lilenfeld et al. (2008) assessed the prevalence of comorbid psychopathology (including BED) in 283 first-degree relatives of non-treatment seeking individuals with (n = 31) and without BED (n = 32). Increased rates of BED in first-degree family members of individuals with BED were found compared to those without BED.

Although the aforementioned studies uniformly suggest that BED is familial, one family study (Lee *et al.* 1999), reported contradictory findings. Lee *et al.* compared obese treatment-seeking individuals with BED (n = 32) and without BED (n = 23) on a number of variables including eating disorders among first-degree family members. No significant differences were found in lifetime history of BED between the two groups. So, although the majority of investigations suggest that BED is familial, findings have not been entirely consistent.

Family studies are an important first step towards examining the genetics of a particular disorder or trait. However, one limitation of family studies is that they only provide information about *whether* a trait runs in families, not *why* a trait runs in families. Concretely, family studies cannot determine the extent to which something is passed down genetically, or transmitted by interpersonal processes like social modeling. Twin studies, in contrast, allow the researcher to parse out sources of familial contribution, at least to an extent.

Twin studies

Twin studies allow researchers to examine familial components of disordered eating by comparing rates of eating problems among monozygotic (MZ; identical or paternal) and dizygotic (DZ; non-identical or fraternal) twin pairs. MZ twins are generally assumed to share 100 per cent of their genetic material. DZ twins, on the other hand, share on average 50 per cent of their genetic makeup (like brothers and sisters). Although these numbers are not precisely true, it is fair to say that MZ twins are considerably more similar genetically than DZ twins. Variance in susceptibility to a disorder can be divided into additive genetic factors, shared environmental factors, and unique environmental factors. Additive genetic effects refer to the cumulative effects of many genes, each of which has a small to moderate contribution. Because MZ twins share ~100 per cent and DZ twins share ~50 per cent of their genetic makeup on average, genetic effects are believed to be operative when MZ twin correlations are approximately twice as strong as the DZ twin correlations.

Shared environmental influences reflect environmental influences that both members of a twin pair are exposed to regardless of whether they are MZ or DZ, and those influences are believed to make twins more similar. Shared environmental factors are inferred when MZ and DZ correlations are approximately equal or when the DZ correlation is larger than half the MZ twin correlation. Unique environmental effects, including measurement error, reflect environmental influences to which only one member of a twin pair is exposed. This type of environmental influence is believed to contribute to dissimilarity of twins. Unique environmental influences are identified when MZ twin correlations are less than 1.00 or when MZ and DZ twin pairs are not significantly correlated on the variables of interest.

Using these three factors, we are able to estimate the heritability of a disorder – or the extent to which genetic factors contribute to liability. What many people fail to realize is that there is not one specific heritability for a given trait. You cannot, for example, say that *the* heritability of binge eating is "X". Heritability is an estimate that is specific to a given population at a specific point in time, and can be influenced by a number of factors including the prevalence of the disorder and the number of MZ and DZ twin pairs where both twins have the disorder.

To date, two twin studies have estimated the heritability of the *DSM-IV-TR* (American Psychiatric Association 2000) diagnosis of BED and findings have been comparable (Javaras *et al.* 2008; Mitchell *et al.* 2010). In the first investigation, Javaras *et al.* (2008) estimated the heritability of men and women with BED in two samples (one from the USA and one from Norway) using structural equation modeling. In both samples, BED aggregated in families. Heritability was estimated at 45 per cent in the USA sample and 39 per cent in the Norwegian sample. In the second investigation, using female twins from the USA, Mitchell *et al.* (2010) also found that BED was moderately heritable. They reported that 45 per cent liability to BED was due to additive genetic effects.

Several prior investigations have also examined the heritability of specific components of BED. Reichborn-Kjennerud *et al.* (2004) examined the heritability of binge eating without compensatory behaviors in male and female Norwegian twins. However, they did not assess for *DSM-IV-TR* (American Psychiatric Association 2000) BED criteria B and C (concerning behavioral aspects of binge eating and attitude towards binge eating). The heritability of binge eating was 39 per cent and 48 per cent for men and women, respectively. With the exception of one investigation by Wade *at al.* (2008), where heritability was reported to be between 8 and 17 per cent, studies examining the heritability of binge eating have typically reported estimates above 40 per cent (Bulik *et al.* 1998; Bulik *et al.* 2003; Klump *et al.* 2002; Root *et al.* 2010; Slane *et al.* in press; Sullivan *et al.* 1998). Taken together, results of twin studies suggest that both BED and the component behavior of binge eating are moderately heritable. Unfortunately, twin studies are unable to provide information regarding which specific genes contribute to liability and how they function.

Genetic studies

The purpose of molecular genetics studies is to drill down biologically to provide greater clarity regarding which genes or chromosomal regions influence risk. The human genome is large, containing between 20,000 and 25,000 genes (Stein 2004). Locating the specific gene or genes that influence a disease or trait can be difficult, akin to finding a needle in a haystack. Linkage analyses and case control association studies, including genomewide association studies (GWAS), are frequently used molecular genetic analytic approaches.

Linkage studies identify regions of the genome that house genes that predispose or protect from a disorder or trait. They allow us to narrow the search from the entire human genome to specific regions. Molecular genetic designs that do not focus on one specific genes or set of genes include linkage analyses and GWAS.

Linkage has not yet been conducted for BED; however, it has shown limited success in mapping genetic factors associated with other complex diseases and is not currently the method of choice.

Association studies examine the relationship between a genetic variant and a trait. If the variant and trait are correlated there is said to be an association between the two. Association studies that involve a single gene or set of genes that have a hypothesized association with the trait under study are called candidate gene approaches. Until recently, association studies typically focused on single genes or several preselected genes. The typical pattern was an initial positive finding, followed by several non-replications. This finding was partly due to scientists vastly underestimating sample size requirements, and partly due to investigators across many fields focusing on the same handful of genes.

New technological developments have enabled genomewide approaches (GWAS) that examine 300,000 to 1,000,000 genetic markers scattered across the genome, comparing individuals with the trait (cases) to those without the trait (controls). GWAS represents an unbiased search of the human genome and has had remarkable success as a genetic discovery tool (Corvin *et al.* 2010).

To date, only candidate gene association studies have been conducted in BED – the field has not yet progressed to conduct a GWAS on BED. These studies have primarily examined neurotransmitter systems or genetic variants implicated in eating and obesity, including the serotonin and dopamine systems. Findings from these investigations will be briefly reviewed.

Serotonin

Serotonin is a neurotransmitter that influences a wide range of functions at the biological, physiological, and behavioral level, including eating behavior (Blundell 1992; Steiger 2004). Both animal and human studies have found that increases in serotonin can result in reduced eating, and that decreases in serotonin can prompt increased eating (Blundell 1986). In people both acutely ill and recovered from bulimia nervosa, an eating disorder characterized by binge eating and compensatory behaviors, a correlation has been observed between binge eating and impaired serotonin functioning (Jimerson *et al.* 1992; Kaye *et al.* 1990; Monteleone *et al.* 1998). The serotonin transporter (5HTT) protein plays an important role in determining how much serotonin is available for the brain to use. Variation has been found in the human 5-HTT gene (*5HTTLPR*), a gene that has also been implicated in anorexia nervosa (Gorwood 2004), bulimia nervosa (Di Bella *et al.* 2000), affective disorders (Collier *et al.* 1996), and impulsivity (Lesch *et al.* 1996).

Hypothesizing that variants of the *5HTTLPR* gene may also be implicated in BED, a 2005 case-control study (Davis *et al.* 2007) assessed the association between *5HTTLPR* and BED. Seventy-seven female European American obese or non-obese women with BED and 61 normal weight European American females without BED were enrolled in the study. People with BED were found to have a higher frequency of one *5HTTLPR* variant (the L allele), which was associated with a moderate but significant risk for BED. This study was limited by a relatively small sample size, and results should be considered preliminary.

Dopamine

Dopamine is a neurotransmitter that plays a major role in the reward system of the brain (Wise and Rompre 1989). Dopamine is implicated in eating behavior and is specifically associated with the rewarding properties of food (Wise 2006). In BED, the function of dopamine transporter genes has been explored. DAT1 is a dopamine transporter gene that is over 64 kilobases (kb; Vandenbergh *et al.* 1992). A kb is a unit of measurement in molecular biology. In humans, the *DAT1* gene occurs with the greatest frequency in two forms, referred to as the 9- and 10-repeat forms (Vandenbergh *et al.* 1992). Researchers hypothesize that these variants in the DAT1 transporter might be implicated in diseases that involve dopamine dysregulation (Miller and Madras 2002).

Davis and colleagues (2007) examined the role of the *DAT1* gene in BED. They compared 32 people with BED and 46 people without BED on their response rating to seeing and tasting a "favorite snack food item." Methylphenidate, a dopamine transporter inhibitor, was given to both groups to determine if decreasing the amount of dopamine available to the brain differently influenced their response to seeing and tasting their favorite snack item. People with BED who had at least one copy of the 9-repeat form showed suppression of appetite relative to controls with the 9-repeat form and people (both with and without BED) who had only the 10-repeat form. The authors conclude that there are likely differences in the dopamine system (or possibly genes that interact with the dopamine system) in people with and without BED. Additional dopamine genes, including the D2 receptor gene, have also been explored for their role in BED (Davis *et al.* 2009). However, as with the DAT 1 gene, results remain in the preliminary stage and require replication.

Other genes

Additional genetic factors have also been explored for their potential role in BED, particularly those previously associated with obesity. One early candidate for BED was the melanoncortin 4 receptor gene (*MC4R*) (Branson *et al.* 2003). Melanocortins are pituitary peptide hormones. One area that the melanocortin 4 receptor is expressed is in the hypothalamic nuclei of the brain, an area involved in feeding behavior (Fan *et al.* 1997; Huszar *et al.* 1997). In a 2003 investigation, Branson *et al.* (2003) found a significant association between mutations of the *MC4R* gene and binge eating. However, this association has not been consistently replicated (Hebebrand *et al.* 2004; Lubrano-Berthelier *et al.* 2006). Positive associations have also been found between BED and genes for brain derived neurotrophic factor (BDNF) (Rosas-Vargas *et al.* 2011) and ghrelin (Monteleone *et al.* 2007). BDNF is known for its role in promoting neuronal outgrowth, differentiation, and repair as well as for modulating eating behavior (Lewin and Barde 1996; Lindsay *et al.* 1994). Specifically, the 196G/A (val66met) polymorphism of the BDNF gene has been associated with binge eating (Monteleone *et al.* 2006; Rosas-Vargas *et al.* 2011). The Leu72Met polymorphism of the ghrelin, a hormone involved in feeding behavior, has also been implicated in BED. Investigations exploring the role of additional genetic factors remain in their infancy and, along with genes implicated within the serotonin and dopamine neurotransmitter systems, require replication.

Summary and future directions

The role of genetic factors in eating disorders, including BED, is increasingly apparent (Fowler and Bulik 1997; Helder and Collier 2011; Javaras *et al.* 2008). Family and twin studies suggest that BED is familial yet, despite initial molecular genetics efforts, candidate gene studies have not clearly confirmed the involvement of any one gene or genetic pathway in BED. Recent advances in technology have provided new tools, such as GWAS, which allow researchers to scan nearly the entire genome for variants that may contribute to a trait or disease. In the future, conducting a large-scale GWAS in BED, including measures of obesity or other metabolic traits, may be our best hope at shedding light on potential genes or genetic pathways implicated in the disorder. The inclusion of BED in the *DSM-5* is an important first step towards standardizing the definition of BED and acknowledging it as a legitimate diagnosis so that large-scale samples, necessary to conduct a well-powered GWAS, can be established. Genetic research in eating disorders is a rapidly evolving field. Despite the promise of genetic studies, it is important to keep in mind that the aetiology of complex traits, such as BED, is likely to be multifactorial, involving many genes and many environmental influences. Having a solid understanding of the genetics underpinnings of BED requires a working knowledge of the ways in which genetic and environmental variables may act together to increase or decrease susceptibility to the disorder. The next section will review various types of genetic and environmental interplays frequently cited in the literature.

Genes and environment

One way in which genetic and environmental factors can interact is through gene–environment correlations. In essence, gene–environment correlations occur when a person is exposed to certain environmental factors because of his or her genetic makeup. In the past, spurious attributions have been made between eating disorder behaviors and environmental factors when in reality gene–environmental correlations may have been at play. There are three types of genetic–environment correlations: passive, evocative, and active (Bulik 2004; Mazzeo and Bulik 2008). Passive gene–environment correlations occur when there is an association between the genes a child inherits from his or her parents and the environment that he or she is raised in (unless adopted). In other words, passive gene–environment correlations occur when parents create home environments for their children that are influenced by their genetic makeup. For example, in the case described at the beginning of this chapter, Jill reported that her mother had experienced symptoms of BED while she was a child. In a scenario, Jill may have been the recipient of some genes that influenced her risk for BED, but she may also have been exposed to her mother's binge eating behaviors (which itself was influenced by her mother's genetic makeup). This intertwined risk has been referred to as a "double dose" of risk. Jill's son, who she describes as a "stress eater", may have also incurred a similar pattern of increased risk.

A second type of gene–environment correlation is evocative in nature. In this situation, a person's genetic makeup may actually evoke certain types of environmental factors. For example, a child who is hard-wired to have a voracious and insatiable appetite may scream and yell and demand food from his or her mother, leading to overfeeding and the use of food to reduce distress. This correlation then forms the basis of later use of food for emotion regulation.

The third type of gene–environment correlation is active, which occurs when a person with a genetic vulnerability to an eating disorder seeks out an environment that reinforces his or her belief system or behavior. For example, if a person with BED were employed as a restaurant critic, which involved eating rich meals on a nightly basis, this may exacerbate her or his BED symptoms. Essentially, an active gene–environment correlation occurs when a person is drawn to a high "risk situation" secondary to a genetic predisposition.

Another type of genetic and environmental interplay is a gene–environment interaction. In this scenario, an person's genetic makeup influences his or her vulnerability to environmental risk factors. For example, many people attend all-you-can eat-buffets or take vacations on cruises with 24-hour access to food. For most people, these experiences will not result in binge eating behaviors. However, for someone with a genetic propensity for BED, this "toxic food environment" may trigger a binge-eating episode or may contribute to the development or maintenance of BED. Gene–environment interactions occur when an individual is more vulnerable to the environment due to genetic factors.

Clinical implications

Understanding the interplay between genetic and environmental factors that contribute to BED is complex and different scenarios may involve more than one mechanism. It is common to hear professionals in the eating disorder field ask, "How does information about genetics change the way that we work with patients in the room?" It is a common misperception that in order for genetics research to be applicable clinically, we must first identify the genes responsible for the disorder. Although this is the ultimate goal, the application of genetics research to clinical practice is not contingent upon the success of this specific endeavor, which would be the equivalent of hitting a home run in a baseball game or a six in cricket. Rather, small scientific gains (like base hits or ones) can be meaningfully used within a clinical setting. The purpose of this section is to discuss ways that the clinician can introduce current knowledge of BED genetics into his or her work with patients and their families in order to enhance the therapeutic process and to help provide explanatory models to patients and their families that incorporate biology.

Working with the patient

Patients often take great measures to educate themselves about their illness and they commonly report spending hours reading about their condition on the Internet or at the library. In approaching a conversation about genetics with a patient who has BED, the first step is determining what information he or she has already acquired and whether this information is accurate. Patients will often say, "I saw on the news that eating disorders are genetic. Does that mean that they've found the gene for my problem?" Unfortunately, the media can grossly oversimplify the causes of complex disorders such as BED, leading to widespread misunderstanding. As clinicians it is our job to provide patients with accurate and understandable information. One response to this patient's statement might be along the lines of:

> I'm really glad you brought that up because there is a lot of buzz in the media right now on the genetics of eating disorders. Some of that information is helpful and accurate and some is a little misleading. The media is misleading in its use of language that implies that one gene exists for complex disorders (like eating disorders) and that we simply have to find the gene in order to cure the disorder. Unfortunately, we know that complex disorders are just as their name implies, complex. While it is true that there is likely a genetic basis for BED, the most probable scenario is that numerous genes contribute to the development of this disorder. In addition, these genetic factors interact with environmental factors, which may also increase or decrease an individual's vulnerability for BED.

Although providing patients with accurate information regarding the biological basis of their disorder is important, it is equally critical to highlight the significant role that environmental factors can play (which may increase or decrease genetic vulnerabilities). There has been concern within the mental health field that viewing one's mental illness as having a genetic component may prevent a patient from believing that recovery is possible or may lead him or her to feel that he or she is "a victim of their genes". It is critical to remind patients that although there is likely a biological basis to BED, they are not powerless in their recovery. Rather, having knowledge about the genetic underpinnings of BED can be empowering. This newly acquired awareness may encourage patients to make environmental changes that can tip the scales to compensate for biological vulnerabilities.

Specifically, the goal in therapy is to help the patient to maximize protective environmental factors and reduce unhealthy environmental exposures. An additional but equally important goal is to help patients develop strategies to minimize the triggering effects of unavoidable environmental factors. One example of this may be working with patients on the automatic thoughts related to dieting and the diet industry. In this society, it is nearly impossible to avoid the messages related to dieting and the "thin ideal". Helping patients understand how these unhealthy messages influence their thoughts and behaviors and how they can counter these "toxic messages" is critical. Oftentimes, as a result of these conversations, patients will come to realize that their binge eating episodes are triggered by something as simple as reading beauty magazines in the checkout line of the grocery store or attending an all-you-can-eat buffet. These conversations may increase awareness, allowing patients to make empowering decisions (like choosing a different type of magazine or restaurant).

Recognizing that there is a biological component to BED may also help patients defuse any self-blame or stigma that they have associated with their disorder. We tend to be more accepting and less blaming of patients with medical diseases (particularly when we do not believe the disease is a result of poor lifestyle choices) than psychiatric disorders. A substantial percentage of the public views individuals with mental illness as responsible for their disorder or disorders (Corrigan *et al.* 1999). Perhaps most notable for promoting a medical model for mental illness is the National Alliance on Mental Illness's slogan that "mental illness is a brain disease". Educating patients that BED is a medical disorder that they did not choose to have, like numerous other medical conditions, may diffuse self-stigma and self-blame.

Parents and family members

Providing accurate information for parents and family members regarding the biology of BED is also critical. Parents and family members frequently have a great deal of influence on a patient's views and beliefs about their disorder. As parents and family members are often exposed to the same misleading messages from the media regarding the genetics of eating disorders, it is important that these topics are discussed within a family therapy context or that psychoeducational materials are provided to family members. An added benefit to educating parents and family members about the genetic contribution to BED is that it may reduce misguided guilt and self-blame. Historically, in the case of children or adolescents, parents have been held responsible for their children's eating problems. Educating parents on genetics may reduce guilt based on these inaccurate stereotypes.

Understanding that there is a genetic component to the behavior may also help parents and family members to be more empathic with the patient, clarifying that the individual is not having symptoms out of resistance or stubbornness. When working with family members it is critical to address concerns that they may have about having caused the eating disorder. Reducing the blame on all sides of the equation can facilitate a cooperative team approach towards treatment. As part of this conversation, it is useful to have an open dialogue about helpful things that family members may be able to do (or avoid doing) to minimize environmental triggers. For example, a patient might request that there is no "fat talk" in the house or that meals are scheduled at regular intervals. In this way the patient and her or his family members can begin to work together collaboratively, setting the patient up for success in his or her eating disorder recovery.

Diagnosis and prevention

Some additional ways that information regarding the genetics of BED can be useful within a clinical setting are for diagnostic and prevention purposes. For example, in the case of Jill, understanding the familial nature of BED prompted the clinician to ask Jill about her own eating behaviours. A family history of disordered eating behaviour or unusual behaviour around food should alert the clinician to explore this topic with the patient. Similarly, awareness of the familial nature of the disorder can help patient remain appropriately vigilant for symptoms in their children. Although little research has been done specifically with BED, results from focus groups and clinical studies have found that parents with eating disorders are eager to learn how to best care for their children, particularly with regards to feeding and eating (Hodes 2000; Mazzeo *et al.* 2005) In the future, developing evidence-based parenting interventions for people with BED may reduce trans-generational transmission of this disorder.

Conclusions

With advances in modern technology, our understanding of the genetic mechanisms underlying complex diseases is rapidly evolving. Genes appear to play a role in BED, but they clearly do not act alone. The information that we do have can be used in clinically meaningful ways to inform our interactions with patients and their families. To bypass a discussion of the genetics of BED in a treatment setting would be to miss out on a critical conversation, which has the potential to be empowering for both the patient and family members and to improve understanding, empathy, and outcome.

References

American Psychiatric Association (1994) *Diagnostic and Statistical Manual of Mental Disorders* (4th edn), Washington, DC: American Psychiatric Press.
American Psychiatric Association (2000) *Diagnostic and Statistical Manual of Mental Disorders* (4th edn, text revision), Washington, DC: American Psychiatric Press.

Blundell, J. E. (1986) "Serotonin manipulations and the structure of feeding behaviour" *Appetite* 7: S39–56.

Blundell, J. E. (1992) "Serotonin and the biology of feeding", *Americal Journal of Clinical Nutrition* 55: S155–9.

Branson, R., Potoczna, N., Kral, J. G., Lentes, K. J., Hoehe, M. R., and Horber, F. F. (2003) "Binge eating as a major phenotype of melanocortin 4 receptor gene mutations", *New England Journal of Medicine* 348:1096–103.

Bulik, C. M. (2004) "Genetic and biological risk factors", in J. K. Thompson (ed.) *Handbook of Eating Disorders and Obesity* (pp. 3–16), Hoboken, NJ: John Wiley & Sons.

Bulik, C. M., Sullivan, P. F., and Kendler, K. S. (1998) "Heritability of binge-eating and broadly defined bulimia nervosa", *Biological Psychiatry* 44: 1210–18.

Bulik, C. M., Sullivan, P. F., and Kendler, K. S. (2003) "Genetic and environmental contributions to obesity and binge-eating", *International Journal of Eating Disorders* 33: 293–8.

Collier, D. A., Stober, G., Li, T., Heils, A., Catalano, M., Di Bella, D., Arranz, M. J., Murray, R. M., Vallada, H. P., Bengel, D., Muller, C. R., Roberts, G. W., Smeraldi, E., Kirov, G., Sham, P., and Lesch, K. P. (1996) "A novel functional polymorphism within the promoter of the serotonin transporter gene: possible role in susceptibility to affective disorders", *Molecular Psychiatry* 1: 453–60.

Corrigan, P. W., River, L. P., Lundin, R. K., Wasowski, K. U., Campion, J., Mathisen, J., Goldstein, H., Gagnon, C., Bergman, M., and Kubiak, M. A. (1999) "Predictors of participation in campaigns against mental illness stigma", *Journal of Nervous and Mental Disease* 187: 378–80.

Corvin, A., Craddock, N., and Sullivan, P. F. (2010) "Genome-wide association studies: a primer", *Psychological Medicine* 40: 1063–77.

Davis, C., Levitan, R. D., Kaplan, A. S., Carter, J., Reid, C., Curtis, C., Patte, K., and Kennedy, J. L. (2007) "Dopamine transporter gene (DAT1) associated with appetite suppression to methylphenidate in a case-control study of binge eating disorder", *Neuropsychopharmacology* 32: 2199–206.

Davis, C. A., Levitan, R. D., Reid, C., Carter, J. C., Kaplan, A. S., Patte, K. A., King, N., Curtis, C., and Kennedy, J. L. (2009) "Dopamine for 'wanting' and opioids for 'liking': a comparison of obese adults with and without binge eating", *Obesity* 17: 1220–25.

Di Bella, D. D., Catalano, M., Cavallini, M. C., Riboldi, C., and Bellodi, L. (2000) "Serotonin transporter linked polymorphic region in anorexia nervosa and bulimia nervosa", *Molecular Psychiatry* 5: 233–4.

Fairburn, C. G., Doll, H. A., Welch, S. L., Hay, P. J., Davies, B. A., and O'Connor, M. E. (1998) "Risk factors for binge eating disorder: a community-based, case-control study", *Archives of General Psychiatry* 55: 425–32.

Fan, W., Boston, B. A., Kesterson, R. A., Hruby, V. J., and Cone, R. D. (1997) "Role of melanocortinergic neurons in feeding and the agouti obesity syndrome", *Nature* 385: 165–8.

Fowler, S. J., and Bulik, C. M. (1997) "Family environment and psychiatric history in women with binge eating disorder and obese controls", *Behavior Change* 14: 106–12.

Gorwood, P. (2004) "Eating disorders, serotonin transporter polymorphisms and potential treatment response", *American Journal of Pharmacogenomics*, 4: 9–17.

Hebebrand, J., Geller, F., Dempfle, A., Heinzel-Gutenbrunner, M., Raab, M., Gerber, G., Wermter, A. K., Horro, F. F, Blundell, J., Schafer, H., Remschmidt, H., Herpertz, S., and

Hinney, A. (2004) "Binge-eating episodes are not characteristic of carriers of melano-cortin-4 receptor gene mutations", *Molecular Psychiatry* 9: 796–800.

Helder, S. G., and Collier, D. A. (2011) "The genetics of eating disorders", *Current Topics in Behavioral Neurosciences* 6: 157–75.

Hodes, M. (2000) "The children of mothers with eating disorders", in P. Reder, M. McClure and A. Jolly (eds) *Family Matters: Interfaces Between Child and Adult Mental Health* (pp. 107–21), New York: Routledge.

Hudson, J. I., Lalonde, J. K., Berry, J. M., Pindyck, L. J., Bulik, C. M., McElroy, S. L., Laird, N. M., Tsuang, M. T., Walsh, B. T., Rosenthal, N. R., and Pope, H. G. (2006) "Binge-eating disorder as a distinct familial phenotype in obese individuals", *Archives of General Psychiatry* 63: 313–19.

Huszar, D., Lynch, C. A., Fairchild-Huntress, V., Dunmore, J. H., Fang, Q., Berkemeier, L. R., Gu, W., Kesterson, R. A., Boston, B. A., Cone, R. D., Smith, F. J., Campfield, L. A., Burn, P., and Lee, F. (1997) "Targeted disruption of the melanocortin-4 receptor results in obesity in mice", *Cell* 88: 131–41.

Javaras, K. N., Laird, N. M., Reichborn-Kjennerud, T., Bulik, C. M., Pope, H. G., Jr., and Hudson, J. I. (2008) "Familiality and heritability of binge eating disorder: results of a case-control family study and a twin study", *International Journal of Eating Disorders* 41: 174–9.

Jimerson, D. C, Lesem, M. D, Kaye, W. H., and Brewerton, T. D. (1992) "Low serotonin and dopamine metabolite concentrations in cerebrospinal fluid from bulimic patients with frequent binge episodes", *Archives of General Psychiatry* 49: 132–8.

Kaye, W. H., Berrettini, W., Gwirtsman, H., and George, D. T. (1990) "Altered cerebro-spinal fluid neuropeptide Y and peptide YY immunoreactivity in anorexia and bulimia nervosa", *Archives of General Psychiatry* 47: 548–56.

Klump, K. L., McGue, M., and Iacono, W. G. (2002) "Genetic relationships between personality and eating attitudes and behaviours", *Journal of Abnormal Psychology* 111: 380–89.

Lee, Y. H, Abbott, D. W, Seim, H., Crosby, R. D, Monson, N., Burgard, M., and Mitchell, J. E. (1999) "Eating disorders and psychiatric disorders in the first-degree relatives of obese probands with binge eating disorder and obese non-binge eating disorder controls", *International Journal of Eating Disorders* 26: 322–32.

Lesch, K. P., Bengel, D., Heils, A., Sabol, S. Z., Greenberg, B. D., Petri, S., Benjamin, J., Muller, C. R., Hamer, D. H., and Murphy, D. L. (1996) "Association of anxiety-related traits with a polymorphism in the serotonin transporter gene regulatory region", *Science* 274: 1527–31.

Lewin, G. R., and Barde, Y. A. (1996) "Physiology of the neurotrophins", *Annual Review of Neuroscience* 19: 289–317.

Libbey, H. P., Story, M. T., Neumark-Sztainer, D. R., and Boutelle, K. N. (2008) "Teasing, disordered eating behaviours, and psychological morbidities among overweight adoles-cents", *Obesity* 16: S24–9.

Lilenfeld, L. R., Ringham, R., Kalarchian, M. A., and Marcus, M. D. (2008) "A family history study of binge-eating disorder", *Compr Psychiatry* 49: 247–54.

Lindsay, R. M., Wiegand, S. J., Altar, C. A., and DiStefano, P. S. (1994) "Neurotrophic factors: from molecule to man", *Trends in Neurosciences* 17: 182–90.

Lubrano-Berthelier, C., Dubern, B., Lacorte, J. M., Picard, F., Shapiro, A., Zhang, S., Bertrais, S., Hercberg, S., Basdevant, A., Clement, K., and Vaisse, C. (2006) "Melanocortin 4 receptor mutations in a large cohort of severely obese adults:

prevalence, functional classification, genotype-phenotype relationship, and lack of association with binge eating", *Journal of Clinical Endocrinology and Metabolism* 91: 1811–18.

Mazzeo, S. E., and Bulik, C. M. (2008) "Environmental and genetic risk factors for eating disorders: what the clinician needs to know", *Child and Adolescent Psychiatric Clinics of North America* 18: 67–82.

Mazzeo, S. E., Zucker, N. L., Gerke, C. K., Mitchell, K. S., and Bulik, C. M. (2005) "Parenting concerns of women with histories of eating disorders", *International Journal of Eating Disorders* 37: S77–9.

Miller, G. M., and Madras, B. K. (2002) "Polymorphisms in the 3′-untranslated region of human and monkey dopamine transporter genes affect reporter gene expression", *Molecular Psychiatry* 7: 44–55.

Mitchell, K. S., Neale, M. C., Bulik, C. M., Aggen, S. H., Kendler, K. S., and Mazzeo, S. E. (2010) "Binge eating disorder: a symptom-level investigation of genetic and environmental influences on liability", *Psychological Medicine* 40: 1899–1906.

Monteleone, P., Brambilla, F., Bortolotti, F., Ferraro, C., and Maj, M. (1998) "Plasma prolactin response to D-fenfluramine is blunted in bulimic patients with frequent binge episodes", *Psychological Medicine* 28: 975–83.

Monteleone, P., Tortorella, A., Castaldo, E., Di Filippo, C., and Maj, M. (2007) "The Leu72Met polymorphism of the ghrelin gene is significantly associated with binge eating disorder", *Psychiatric Genetics* 17: 13–16.

Monteleone, P., Zanardini, R., Tortorella, A., Gennarelli, M., Castaldo, E., Canestrelli, B., and Maj, M. (2006) "The 196G/A (val66met) polymorphism of the BDNF gene is significantly associated with binge eating behaviour in women with bulimia nervosa or binge eating disorder", *Neuroscience Letters* 406: 133–7.

Pike, K. M., Wilfley, D., Hilbert, A., Fairburn, C. G., Dohm, F. A., and Striegel-Moore, R. H. (2006) "Antecedent life events of binge-eating disorder", *Psychiatry Research* 142: 19–29.

Reichborn-Kjennerud T., Bulik C. M., Tambs K., and Harris J. R. (2004) "Genetic and environmental influences on binge eating in the absence of compensatory behaviors: a population-based twin study", *International Journal of Eating Disorders* 36: 307–14.

Root, T. L., Thornton, L. M., Lindroos, A. K., Stunkard, A. J., Lichtenstein, P., Pedersen, N. L., Rasmussen, F., and Bulik, C. M. (2010) "Shared and unique genetic and environmental influences on binge eating and night eating: a Swedish twin study", *Eating Behavior* 11: 92–8.

Rosas-Vargas, H., Martinez-Ezquerro, J. D., and Bienvenu, T. (2011) "Brain-derived neurotrophic factor, food intake regulation, and obesity", *Archives of Medical Research* 42: 482–94.

Schwartz, J., and Byrd-Bredbenner, C. (2006) "Portion distortion: typical portion sizes selected by young adults", *Journal of the American Dietetic Association* 106: 1412–18.

Slane, J. D., Burt, S. A., and Klump, K. L. (in press) "Bulimic behaviors and alcohol use: Shared genetic influences", *Behavior Genetics*.

Steenhuis, I. H., and Vermeer, W. M. (2009) "Portion size: review and framework for interventions", *International Journal of Behavioral Nutrition and Physical Activity* 6: 58–68.

Steiger, H. (2004) "Eating disorders and the serotonin connection: state, trait and developmental effects", *Journal of Psychiatry and Neuroscience* 29: 20–29.

Stein, L. D. (2004) "Human genome: end of the beginning", *Nature* 431: 915–16.

Sullivan, P. F., Bulik, C. M., and Kendler, K. S. (1998) "The genetic epidemiology of binging and vomiting", *British Journal of Psychiatry* 173: 75–9.

Thompson, J. K., Coovert, M. D., Richards, K. J., Johnson, S., and Cattarin, J. (1995) "Development of body image, eating disturbance, and general psychological functioning in female adolescents: covariance structure modeling and longitudinal investigations", *International Journal of Eating Disorders* 18: 221–36.

Vandenbergh, D. J., Persico, A. M., Hawkins, A. L., Griffin, C. A., Li, X., Jabs, E. W., and Uhl, G. R. (1992) "Human dopamine transporter gene (DAT1) maps to chromosome 5p15.3 and displays a VNTR", *Genomics* 14: 1104–6.

Wade, T. D., Trelor, S., and Martin, N. G. (2008) "Shared and unique risk factors between lifetime purging and objective binge eating: a twin study", *Psychological Medicine* 38: 1455–64.

Wise, R. A. (2006) "Role of brain dopamine in food reward and reinforcement", *Philosophical Transactions of the Royal Society London B Biological Sciences* 361: 1149–58.

Wise, R. A., and Rompre, P. P. (1989) "Brain dopamine and reward", *Annual Review of Psychology* 40: 191–225.

Chapter 4

Loss of control eating in children and adolescents

Risk factors, correlates and development

Andrea B. Goldschmidt, Kerri Boutelle
(with Stephanie Knatz and Jennifer Madowitz) and
Marian Tanofsky-Kraff

Case study

Twelve-year-old "Becky", from a multi-racial background, has initiated interpersonal psychotherapy for "emotional eating" and weight concerns. Becky lives at home with her nine-year-old brother and parents. Becky presented at the 95th age- and sex-specific BMI percentile, with recurrent loss of control eating episodes. She denies compensatory behaviors, and reports modest depression and anxiety symptoms. Weight-related teasing by her brother, together with occasional feelings of exclusion by her peers, often trigger negative mood and loss of control eating.

Becky's first loss of control eating episode occurred at age 10. Her brother had began to tease her about her weight and at the same time her mother had changed jobs, requiring Becky to take on more caretaking responsibilities for her brother. Over time, his behavior became more unruly, as he refused to abide by her rules, but the mother held Becky responsible and often blamed her. The stress of anticipating her mother's return from work often precipitated loss of control eating episodes in Becky. She often ate in secret, and felt guilty afterwards.

Besides her immediate family, Becky's social network includes two close friends and an aunt. Her relationship with her dad is somewhat distant due to his busy work schedule and lack of understanding regarding her weight struggles. She has a mostly positive relationship with her mother but feels anxious about discussing her eating and weight concerns with her – she fears her loss of weight control is disappointing her mother. Becky feels closest to a maternal aunt, who has also battled obesity, and feels comfortable discussing eating concerns with her. Becky has discussed her relationships with two close friends who live in the same neighborhood. The three girls used to spend quite a bit of time together, but recently Becky has started to feel excluded as the other two girls often visit with each other without inviting her along.

Becky's treatment is described in Chapter 13: Part II.

Introduction

Loss of control eating is one of the most commonly reported eating disorder behaviors among children and adolescents. Given its associations with adiposity, psychosocial impairments such as depression and anxiety symptoms, and the development of exacerbated obesity and full-syndrome eating disorders, this behavior is of considerable public health significance.

Loss of control (LOC) while eating refers to the sense that one cannot control what or how much one is eating (American Psychiatric Association 2000), and may or may not be accompanied by the consumption of unambiguously large amounts of food (i.e., binge eating). LOC eating is among the most commonly reported eating disorder behaviors in children and adolescents (Goldschmidt, Aspen et al. 2008). Youth reporting LOC eating often present with psychosocial impairments (Glasofer et al. 2006; Goldschmidt, Jones et al. 2008; Tanofsky-Kraff et al. 2004) as well as obesity and excess body fat (Tanofsky-Kraff et al. 2004). Moreover, pediatric LOC eating predicts the onset of full-syndrome eating disorders (Stice et al. 2009; Tanofsky-Kraff et al. 2011). LOC eating is therefore a clinically significant behavior with considerable public health implications. While LOC eating often develops in childhood, there is a paucity of research in pediatric populations. Therefore, it is important to develop a greater understanding of the nature of pediatric LOC eating to inform intervention efforts.

This chapter reviews the current literature concerning LOC eating, including binge eating, in youth. First, we will review the classification of LOC eating in youth, focusing on issues pertinent to the current diagnostic scheme. Next, we will describe the prevalence and distribution of LOC eating in children and adolescents. We will then provide an overview of the physical and psychosocial correlates of LOC eating. Finally, we will discuss the etiology and course of LOC eating in youth (assessment and treatment are covered in Chapter 9 and Chapter 13: Part II, respectively). References to the case presented above will be provided throughout this chapter.

Eating episodes involving LOC but *not* unambiguously large amounts of food are quite prevalent among youth relative to true binge eating involving large amounts of food, and are strongly associated with eating-related and general psychopathology. As such, these two types of episodes are typically considered distinct constructs in the literature. This chapter therefore will include research findings germane to both types of eating episodes. Moreover, since empirical studies have often included both children and adolescents, we will discuss research pertaining to youth across the age spectrum (ages 6 to 18 years).

Classification

There is significant inter- and intra-individual variability in terms of the subjective experience and size of aberrant eating episodes in youth (Shomaker et al. 2010). Accordingly, investigators have distinguished among three types of aberrant eating episodes: objective binge eating refers to the consumption of unambiguously large amounts of food accompanied by LOC; subjective binge eating refers to LOC eating episodes that are *not* unambiguously large but are considered large by the respondent; and objective overeating refers to the consumption of unambiguously large amounts of food in the absence of LOC (Fairburn and Cooper 1993). Currently, the *Diagnostic and Statistical Manual of Mental Disorders* – 4th edition, text revision (American Psychiatric Association 2000) requires the presence of objective binge eating at least twice a week, on average, for a duration of six months in order for a diagnosis of binge eating disorder (BED) to be made, thus excluding youth who report less-frequent objective binge eating, or who report recurrent subjective binge eating. In the upcoming DSM-5, it has been suggested to lower the frequency threshold of objective binge eating to once per week, but this would still exclude individuals reporting subjective binge episodes.

Approximately 1 per cent of youth meet DSM-IV-TR criteria for BED (Decaluwé and Braet 2003), yet a substantially larger proportion (approximately 10 per cent) report sub-threshold LOC eating (Johnson *et al.* 2002; Tanofsky-Kraff *et al.* 2004). This has prompted a call for youth-specific diagnostic criteria for binge eating-spectrum disorders (Marcus and Kalarchian 2003; Tanofsky-Kraff *et al.* 2008). Central to this dialogue is the issue of whether consumption of an "unambiguously large amount of food" is an appropriate criterion for children and adolescents. It is often difficult to determine whether an eating episode is unambiguously large due to children's unreliable recall (Burrows *et al.* 2010), and because of their differing nutritional needs. Some evidence suggests that LOC is a more salient aspect of binge eating than the amount of food consumed for children and adolescents (Goldschmidt, Jones *et al.* 2008; Shomaker *et al.* 2009), and reported LOC eating appears to predict obesity, increases in weight and body fat, and eating disorder onset even in the absence of unambiguously large amounts of food (Tanofsky-Kraff *et al.* 2006; Tanofsky-Kraff *et al.* 2009; Tanofsky-Kraff *et al.* 2011). Moreover, youth reporting LOC show distinct eating patterns in laboratory settings compared to their peers, including greater overall energy intake (Hilbert *et al.* 2010; Mirch *et al.* 2006) and greater consumption of snack and dessert foods (Tanofsky-Kraff *et al.* 2009). Therefore, accumulating evidence suggests that the experience of LOC is a critical aspect of binge eating in youth. However, further research is needed to determine whether pediatric LOC eating is qualitatively different from that observed in adults to inform the diagnostic scheme.

Prevalence and distribution

Approximately 10 per cent of community-based children and adolescents endorse LOC eating (Goossens *et al.* 2009; Johnson *et al.* 2002; Neumark-Sztainer *et al.* 2011; Tanofsky-Kraff *et al.* 2004), with rates as high as 30 per cent documented in overweight, treatment-seeking samples (Eddy *et al.* 2007; Glasofer *et al.* 2006;

Goossens *et al.* 2007). LOC eating appears to be equally distributed among boys and girls during childhood (Decaluwé and Braet 2003; Tanofsky-Kraff *et al.* 2005), although some studies suggest that during adolescence, girls may be more likely to endorse LOC eating than boys (Field *et al.* 2003; Neumark-Sztainer *et al.* 2011). The literature has been inconsistent regarding racial/ethnic differences in LOC eating: some studies report increased rates of LOC eating in Hispanic (Field *et al.* 1997a) and African–American (Johnson *et al.* 2002) relative to Caucasian youth, while others have found decreased or similar rates of LOC eating in these populations (Field *et al.* 1997b; French *et al.* 1997; Neumark-Sztainer, Croll *et al.* 2002; Shisslak *et al.* 2006). Given the racial/ethnic diversity seen in adult BED (Striegel-Moore and Franko 2003), additional clarity regarding racial/ethnic differences in pediatric LOC eating is needed.

Correlates

LOC eating is associated with many negative physical and psychosocial health outcomes. Perhaps most concerning is its strong association with overweight, which is a major public health concern given the variety of adverse medical outcomes with which it is related (Reilly *et al.* 2003). Overweight youth are more likely to report LOC eating than their non-overweight peers (Allen *et al.* 2008; Neumark-Sztainer, Story *et al.* 2002; Tanofsky-Kraff *et al.* 2004), and prospective studies indicate that such behaviors predict the onset of overweight (Stice *et al.* 1999; Stice *et al.* 2002) as well as increases in body weight and body fat (Field *et al.* 2003; Tanofsky-Kraff *et al.* 2006; Tanofsky-Kraff *et al.* 2009; Tanofsky-Kraff *et al.* in press). This association is evident in Becky from our case description, who presented at the 95th age- and sex-adjusted BMI percentile. One study that specifically examined binge eating in childhood found that such behavior may predict the onset of metabolic syndrome, a condition characterized by abdominal adiposity, impaired fasting glucose, and high triglycerides, cholesterol, and blood pressure, although this appears to be at least partially accounted for by initial BMI and BMI changes over time (Tanofsky-Kraff *et al.* in press). However, in this study, binge eating was associated with higher triglycerides at five-year follow-up, even after controlling for weight change over time. Further research is needed to determine the impact of LOC eating on other physical health outcomes.

   LOC eating is associated with a range of other psychosocial problems. Youth reporting this behavior evidence elevated levels of depression, anxiety, body dissatisfaction, and behavioral problems (Decaluwé and Braet 2003; Eddy *et al.* 2007; Glasofer *et al.* 2006; Goldschmidt, Jones *et al.* 2008; Goossens *et al.* 2007; Hilbert *et al.* 2009; Johnson *et al.* 1999; Tanofsky-Kraff *et al.* 2005), and decrements in self-esteem and social functioning (Elliott *et al.* 2010; Goossens, Braet, Bosmans *et al.* 2011). In adolescence, binge eating is further associated with substance abuse and suicidality (Ross and Ivis 1999; Zaitsoff and Grilo 2010). These largely consistent data suggest that LOC eating represents a significant public health concern even outside of associations with obesity.

Etiology

Two pathways to adult binge eating have been described. The first posits that binge eating develops in response to prolonged and rigid dietary restraint (Polivy and Herman 1985). According to some theorists, perceived lapses in restraint (e.g., breaking a dietary rule) are interpreted as failure to control one's eating, which leads to temporary abandonment of restraint and subsequent binge eating (Grilo and Shiffman 1994). Some prospective data suggest that dietary restraint predicts the onset of binge eating in childhood and adolescence (Allen *et al.* 2008; Field *et al.* 2008; Stice *et al.* 1998; Stice *et al.* 2002) and several cross-sectional studies have found a relation between dieting and LOC eating in youth (Decaluwé and Braet 2005; Field *et al.* 2003; Tanofsky-Kraff *et al.* 2004; Tanofsky-Kraff *et al.* 2005). Conversely, other investigators have reported no differences between overweight children with and without LOC eating problems in terms of self-reported dietary restraint (Decaluwé and Braet 2003; Decaluwé *et al.* 2003; Glasofer *et al.* 2006). Further, most children report initiating LOC eating prior to any dieting attempts (Tanofsky-Kraff *et al.* 2005) and most youth deny having restricted their food intake prior to an LOC eating episode (Tanofsky-Kraff, Goossens *et al.* 2007). Dieting alone appears to be an insufficient factor in explaining binge eating onset as most dieters never develop binge eating problems (e.g., Fairburn *et al.* 2005); it may be that dieting in conjunction with other psychosocial risk factors confers the greatest risk for LOC eating onset (Goldschmidt *et al.* in press). Future research should identify specific dieting behaviors associated with LOC eating, as moderate, supervised dieting has actually been shown to decrease such behaviors in adolescent girls (Stice *et al.* 2005; Stice *et al.* 2006). Further pediatric data is also needed to identify dieters at highest risk for the onset of LOC eating.

An alternative hypothesis ascribes binge eating to the experience of negative affect. Theorists posit that eating provides a distraction from external stressors (Heatherton and Baumeister 1991) or that eating enables a "trade-off", whereby aversive emotions preceding binge eating (e.g., loneliness) are replaced by less-aversive emotions thereafter (e.g., regret) (Kenardy *et al.* 1996). Prospective studies indicate that negative affect precedes and predicts binge eating in youth (Stice and Agras 1998; Stice *et al.* 1998), and cross-sectional data suggest a more proximal relationship whereby children with LOC eating problems eat *in response to* negative affect (Tanofsky-Kraff, Goossens *et al.* 2007; Tanofsky-Kraff, Theim *et al.* 2007). Indeed, Becky from our case description reported that the stress of taking care of her brother often precipitated her LOC eating episodes. Investigations of the relation between mood and LOC eating in "real time" (e.g., using laboratory feeding paradigms or ecological momentary assessment) have produced mixed results, with some data demonstrating that low mood predicts a greater likelihood of reporting LOC while eating (Goldschmidt *et al.* 2011) and others showing limited support for negative mood as a precipitant to LOC (Hilbert *et al.* 2009; Hilbert *et al.* 2010). It is possible that the relation between negative mood and LOC eating occurs over a more distal time period (e.g., negative mood earlier in the day triggers LOC eating several hours later), thus impeding efforts to capture this relation in a momentary fashion. Indeed, children with LOC eating problems frequently report coping with negative mood by "giving up" or "perseverating" (i.e., ruminating) (Czaja *et al.* 2009); this combination of avoidance and rumination may result in a delayed reaction to the event that initially precipitated negative mood. Alternatively, children may not be aware of their mood state prior to eating, as supported by reports of "numbing out" during LOC episodes (Tanofsky-Kraff, Goossens *et al.* 2007).

Several investigators have attempted to account for both dietary restraint and negative affect in explaining the occurrence of binge eating. The dual pathway and cognitive behavioral models are two such models. While both implicate dietary restraint and negative affect as direct antecedents to binge eating, they differ in terms of the critical feature postulated to promote these precipitants: while the dual pathway model holds *body dissatisfaction* as the central construct (Stice and Agras 1998), the cognitive–behavioral model proposes that *low self-esteem* is the core feature that eventually leads to binge eating. Both models have received some support in the pediatric literature (Decaluwé and Braet 2005; Goossens *et al.* 2010; Stice 2001). Some investigators have expanded on affect regulation theories to propose specific affectively laden antecedents to LOC eating behaviors. For example, interpersonal events (Elliott *et al.* 2010; Tanofsky-Kraff, Wilfley *et al.* 2007), such as negative familial interactions (Czaja *et al.* 2011), have been suggested as precipitants to negative mood which then triggers LOC eating.

The cue reactivity model of binge eating, which is based on learning theory, posits that exposure to food cues elicits cravings, thereby enhancing the likelihood of binge eating (Jansen 1998). Although no research has examined cue reactivity in children with LOC eating, overweight children tend to be more responsive to food cues than their normal-weight peers (Aspen *et al.* 2012), which may translate to overeating (Jansen *et al.* 2003). Future research should investigate the applicability of this model to pediatric LOC eating.

In terms of other risk factors, appearance-related concerns appear to be a relevant marker for LOC eating onset in youth (Field *et al.* 2008; Stice *et al.* 2002). These concerns purportedly arise from societal pressures to attain the "thin ideal", and may manifest in dieting attempts that precipitate LOC eating, consistent with Restraint Theory (Polivy and Herman 1985). Dieting has been found to explain the relation between shape and weight concerns and LOC eating in cross-sectional studies (Decaluwé and Braet 2005), but prospective data are needed to confirm these findings. Since overweight youth are theoretically farther from the thin ideal than their normal-weight peers, this could explain why LOC eating is more prevalent in overweight youth. Relatedly, a history of negative weight-related comments from peers or family has been found to predict LOC eating onset in youth (Field *et al.* 2008; Haines *et al.* 2006), possibly because LOC eating serves as a way to cope with consequent negative affect (Suisman *et al.* 2008). In further support of the affect regulation model, Allen and colleagues (2008) found that emotional eating predicts the onset of LOC eating over one-year follow-up; it remains to be seen whether disinhibited eating more generally (e.g., eating in the absence of hunger) promotes the development of LOC eating as well (Zocca *et al.* 2011), which, taken together, could suggest a pathway whereby aberrant eating becomes more pathological over time.

Course

The natural course of LOC eating in children appears quite variable. Some studies have found that for most youth these problems remit over time (Allen *et al.* 2008; Stice *et al.* 2009), while others report that LOC eating generally persists without treatment (Neumark-Sztainer *et al.* 2011; Tanofsky-Kraff *et al.* 2011). LOC eating in childhood shows longitudinal associations with eating-related and general psychopathology, and children with persistent LOC eating appear to have the worst psychological outcomes (Goossens, Braet, Verbeken *et al.* 2011; Tanofsky-Kraff *et al.* 2011). Perhaps most alarming, sub-threshold LOC eating in childhood tends to develop into partial- or full-syndrome BED (Stice *et al.* 2009; Tanofsky-Kraff *et al.* 2011), highlighting the need for early identification and treatment.

Conclusion

Loss of control eating is a prevalent problem with important public health impli-cations. Youth endorsing this behavior are at risk for a variety of negative health outcomes, including obesity and partial- and full-syndrome eating disorders. Despite advances in understanding LOC eating, there is a relative paucity of research in pediatric populations. Future research should elucidate mechanisms involved in the onset of LOC eating in order to inform prevention and treatment interventions. Moreover, clarification of the most appropriate methods for classifying disorders involving LOC in youth is needed to assist these youth in accessing treatment. Clinicians and researchers should work in conjunction to increase public awareness of these problems and to further clarify the nature of these phenomena in youth.

References

Allen, K. L., Byrne, S. M., La Puma, M., McLean, N., and Davis, E. A. (2008) "The onset and course of binge eating in 8- to 13-year-old healthy weight, overweight and obese children", *Eating Behaviors* 9: 438–46.

American Psychiatric Association (2000) *Diagnostic and Statistical Manual of Mental Disorders (DSM-IV-TR)* (4th edn, text revision), Washington, DC: American Psychiatric Association.

Aspen, V. A., Stein, R. I., and Wilfley, D. E. (2012) "An exploration of salivation patterns in normal weight and obese children", *Appetite* 58: 539–42.

Burrows, T. L., Martin, R. J., and Collins, C. E. (2010) "A systematic review of the validity of dietary assessment methods in children when compared with the method of doubly labeled water", *Journal of the American Dietetic Association* 110: 1501–10.

Czaja, J., Hartmann, A. S., Rief, W., and Hilbert, A. (2011) "Mealtime family interactions in home environments of children with loss of control eating", *Appetite* 56: 587–93.

Czaja, J., Rief, W., and Hilbert, A. (2009) "Emotion regulation and binge eating in children", *International Journal of Eating Disorders* 42: 356–62.

Decaluwé, V., and Braet, C. (2003) "Prevalence of binge-eating disorder in obese children and adolescents seeking weight-loss treatment", *International Journal of Obesity and Related Metabolic Disorders* 27: 404–9.

Decaluwé, V., and Braet, C. (2005) "The cognitive behavioural model for eating disorders: a direct evaluation in children and adolescents with obesity", *Eating Behaviors* 6: 211–20.

Decaluwé, V., Braet, C., and Fairburn, C. G. (2003) "Binge eating in obese children and adolescents", *International Journal of Eating Disorders* 33: 78–84.

Eddy, K. T., Tanofsky-Kraff, M., Thompson-Brenner, H., Herzog, D. B., Brown, T. A., and Ludwig, D. S. (2007) "Eating disorder pathology among overweight treatment-seeking youth: Clinical correlates and cross-sectional risk modeling", *Behaviour Research and Therapy* 45: 2360–71.

Elliott, C. A., Tanofsky-Kraff, M., Shomaker, L. B., Columbo, K. M., Wolkoff, L. E., Ranzenhofer, L. M., and Yanovski, J. A. (2010) "An examination of the interpersonal model of loss of control eating in children and adolescents", *Behaviour Research and Therapy* 48: 424–8.

Fairburn, C. G., and Cooper, Z. (1993) "The Eating Disorder Examination (12th edn)", in C. G. Fairburn and G. T. Wilson (eds) *Binge Eating: Nature, Assessment, and Treatment*, New York: Guilford Press.

Fairburn, C. G., Cooper, Z., Doll, H. A., and Davies, B. A. (2005) "Identifying dieters who will develop an eating disorder: a prospective, population-based study", *American Journal of Psychiatry* 162: 2249–55.

Field, A. E., Austin, S. B., Taylor, C. B., Malspeis, S., Rosner, B., Rockett, H. R., Gillman, M. W., and Colditz, G. A. (2003) "Relation between dieting and weight change among preadolescents and adolescents", *Pediatrics* 112: 900–906.

Field, A. E., Colditz, G. A., and Peterson, K. E. (1997a) "Racial differences in bulimic behaviors among high school females", *Annals of the New York Academy of Sciences* 817: 359–60.

Field, A. E., Colditz, G. A., and Peterson, K. E. (1997b) "Racial/ethnic and gender differences in concern with weight and in bulimic behaviors among adolescents", *Obesity Research* 5: 447–54.

Field, A. E., Javaras, K. M., Aneja, P., Kitos, N., Camargo, C. A., Jr., Taylor, C. B., and Laird, N. M. (2008) "Family, peer, and media predictors of becoming eating disordered", *Archives of Pediatrics & Adolescent Medicine* 162: 574–9.

French, S. A., Story, M., Neumark-Sztainer, D., Downes, B., Resnick, M., and Blum, R. (1997) "Ethnic differences in psychosocial and health behavior correlates of dieting, purging, and binge eating in a population-based sample of adolescent females", *International Journal of Eating Disorders* 22: 315–22.

Glasofer, D. R., Tanofsky-Kraff, M., Eddy, K. T., Yanovski, S. Z., Theim, K. R., Mirch,

M. C., Ghorbani, S., Ranzenhofer, L. M., Haaga, D., and Yanovski, J. A. (2006) "Binge eating in overweight treatment-seeking adolescents", *Journal of Pediatric Psychology* 32: 95–105.

Goldschmidt, A. B., Aspen, V. P., Sinton, M. M., Tanofsky-Kraff, M., and Wilfley, D. E. (2008) "Disordered eating attitudes and behaviors in overweight youth", *Obesity* 16: 257–64.

Goldschmidt, A. B., Jones, M., Manwaring, J. L., Luce, K. H., Osborne, M. I., Cunning, D., Taylor, K. L., Doyle, A. C., Wilfley, D. E., and Taylor, C. B. (2008) "The clinical significance of loss of control over eating in overweight adolescents", *International Journal of Eating Disorders* 41: 153–8.

Goldschmidt, A. B., Tanofsky-Kraff, M., and Wilfley, D. E. (2011) "A laboratory-based study of mood and binge eating behavior in overweight children", *Eating Behaviors* 21: 37–43.

Goldschmidt, A. B., Wall, M., Loth, K. M., Le Grange, D., and Neumark-Sztainer, D. (in press) "Which dieters are at risk for the onset of binge eating? A prospective study of adolescents and young adults", *Journal of Adolescent Health*.

Goossens, L., Braet, C., and Decaluwé, V. (2007) "Loss of control over eating in obese youngsters", *Behaviour Research and Therapy* 45: 1–9.

Goossens, L., Soenens, B., and Braet, C. (2009) "Prevalence and characteristics of binge eating in an adolescent community sample", *Journal of Clinical Child and Adolescent Psychology* 38: 342–53.

Goossens, L., Braet, C., and Bosmans, G. (2010) "Relations of dietary restraint and depressive symptomatology to loss of control over eating in overweight youngsters", *European Child & Adolescent Psychiatry* 19: 587–96.

Goossens, L., Braet, C., Bosmans, G., and Decaluwé, V. (2011) "Loss of control over eating in pre-adolescent youth: the role of attachment and self-esteem", *Eating Behaviors* 12: 289–95.

Goossens, L., Braet, C., Verbeken, S., Decaluwé, V., and Bosmans, G. (2011) "Long-term outcome of pediatric eating pathology and predictors for the onset of loss of control over eating following weight-loss treatment", *International Journal of Eating Disorders* 44: 397–405.

Grilo, C. M., and Shiffman, S. (1994) "Longitudinal investigation of the abstinence violation effect in binge eaters", *Journal of Consulting and Clinical Psychology* 62: 611–19.

Haines, J., Neumark-Sztainer, D., Eisenberg, M. E., and Hannan, P. J. (2006) "Weight teasing and disordered eating behaviors in adolescents: longitudinal findings from Project EAT (Eating Among Teens)", *Pediatrics* 117: e209–15.

Heatherton, T. F., and Baumeister, R. F. (1991) "Binge eating as escape from self-awareness", *Psychology Bulletin* 110: 86–108.

Hilbert, A., Rief, W., Tuschen-Caffier, B., de Zwaan, M., and Czaja, J. (2009) "Loss of control eating and psychological maintenance in children: An ecological momentary assessment study", *Behaviour Research and Therapy* 47: 26–33.

Hilbert, A., Tuschen-Caffier, B., and Czaja, J. (2010) "Eating behavior and familial interactions of children with loss of control eating: a laboratory test meal study", *American Journal of Clinical Nutrition* 91: 510–18.

Jansen, A. (1998) "A learning model of binge eating: cue reactivity and cue exposure", *Behaviour Research and Therapy* 36: 257–72.

Jansen, A., Theunissen, N., Slechten, K., Nederkoorn, C., Boon, B., Mulkens, S., and

Roefs, A. (2003) "Overweight children overeat after exposure to food cues", *Eating Behaviors* 4: 197–209.

Johnson, W. G., Grieve, F. G., Adams, C. D., and Sandy, J. (1999) "Measuring binge eating in adolescents: adolescent and parent versions of the questionnaire of eating and weight patterns", *International Journal of Eating Disorders* 26: 301–14.

Johnson, W. G., Rohan, K. J., and Kirk, A. A. (2002) "Prevalence and correlates of binge eating in white and African American adolescents", *Eating Behaviors* 3: 179–89.

Kenardy, J., Arnow, B., and Agras, W. S. (1996) "The aversiveness of specific emotional states associated with binge-eating in obese subjects", *Australian and New Zealand Journal of Psychiatry* 30: 839–44.

Marcus, M. D., and Kalarchian, M. A. (2003) "Binge eating in children and adolescents", *International Journal of Eating Disorders* 34 Suppl: S47–57.

Mirch, M. C., McDuffie, J. R., Yanovski, S. Z., Schollnberger, M., Tanofsky-Kraff, M., Theim, K. R., Krakoff, J., and Yanovski, J. A. (2006) "Effects of binge eating on satiation, satiety, and energy intake of overweight children", *American Journal of Clinical Nutrition* 84: 732–8.

Neumark-Sztainer, D., Croll, J., Story, M., Hannan, P. J., French, S. A., and Perry, C. (2002) "Ethnic/racial differences in weight-related concerns and behaviors among adolescent girls and boys: findings from Project EAT", *Journal of Psychosomatic Research* 53: 963–74.

Neumark-Sztainer, D., Story, M., Hannan, P. J., Perry, C. L., and Irving, L. M. (2002) "Weight-related concerns and behaviors among overweight and nonoverweight adolescents: implications for preventing weight-related disorders", *Archives of Pediatrics & Adolescent Medicine* 156: 171–8.

Neumark-Sztainer, D., Wall, M., Larson, N. I., Eisenberg, M. E., and Loth, K. (2011) "Dieting and disordered eating behaviors from adolescence to young adulthood: findings from a 10-year longitudinal study", *Journal of the American Dietetic Association* 111: 1004–11.

Polivy, J., and Herman, C. P. (1985) "Dieting and binging: a causal analysis", *American Psychologist* 40: 193–201.

Reilly, J. J., Methven, E., McDowell, Z. C., Hacking, B., Alexander, D., Stewart, L., and Kelnar, C. J. (2003) "Health consequences of obesity", *Archives of Disease in Childhood* 88: 748–52.

Ross, H. E., and Ivis, F. (1999) "Binge eating and substance use among male and female adolescents", *International Journal of Eating Disorders* 26: 245–60.

Shisslak, C. M., Mays, M. Z., Crago, M., Jirsak, J. K., Taitano, K., and Cagno, C. (2006) "Eating and weight control behaviors among middle school girls in relationship to body weight and ethnicity", *Journal of Adolescent Health* 38: 631–3.

Shomaker, L. B., Tanofsky-Kraff, M., Elliott, C., Wolkoff, L. E., Columbo, K. M., Ranzenhofer, L. M., Roza, C. A., Yanovski, S. Z., and Yanovski, J. A. (2009) "Salience of loss of control for pediatric binge episodes: does size really matter?", *International Journal of Eating Disorders* 43(8): 707–16.

Shomaker, L. B., Tanofsky-Kraff, M., Savastano, D. M., Kozlosky, M., Columbo, K. M., Wolkoff, L. E., Zocca, J. M., Brady, S. M., Yanovski, S. Z., Crocker, M. K., Ali, A., and Yanovski, J. A. (2010) "Puberty and observed energy intake: boy, can they eat!", *American Journal of Clinical Nutrition* 92: 123–9.

Stice, E. (2001) "A prospective test of the dual-pathway model of bulimic pathology:

mediating effects of dieting and negative affect", *Journal of Abnormal Psychology* 110: 124–35.

Stice, E., and Agras, W. S. (1998) "Predicting onset and cessation bulimic behaviors during adolescence: a longitudinal grouping analysis", *Behavior Therapy* 29: 257–76

Stice, E., Cameron, R. P., Killen, J. D., Hayward, C., and Taylor, C. B. (1999) "Naturalistic weight-reduction efforts prospectively predict growth in relative weight and onset of obesity among female adolescents", *Journal of Consulting and Clinical Psychology* 67: 967–74.

Stice, E., Killen, J. D., Hayward, C., and Taylor, C. B. (1998) "Age of onset for binge eating and purging during late adolescence: a 4-year survival analysis", *Journal of Abnormal Psychology* 107: 671–5.

Stice, E., Marti, C. N., Shaw, H., and Jaconis, M. (2009) "An 8-year longitudinal study of the natural history of threshold, subthreshold, and partial eating disorders from a community sample of adolescents", *Journal of Abnormal Psychology* 118: 587–97.

Stice, E., Martinez, E. E., Presnell, K., and Groesz, L. M. (2006) "Relation of successful dietary restriction to change in bulimic symptoms: a prospective study of adolescent girls", *Health Psychology* 25: 274–81.

Stice, E., Presnell, K., Groesz, L., and Shaw, H. (2005) "Effects of a weight maintenance diet on bulimic symptoms in adolescent girls: an experimental test of the dietary restraint theory", *Health Psychology* 24: 402–12.

Stice, E., Presnell, K., and Spangler, D. (2002) "Risk factors for binge eating onset in adolescent girls: a 2-year prospective investigation", *Health Psychology* 21: 131–8.

Striegel-Moore, R. H., and Franko, D. L. (2003) "Epidemiology of binge eating disorder", *International Journal of Eating Disorders* 34 Suppl: S19–29.

Suisman, J. L., Slane, J. D., Burt, S. A., and Klump, K. L. (2008) "Negative affect as a mediator of the relationship between weight-based teasing and binge eating in adolescent girls", *Eating Behaviors* 9: 493–6.

Tanofsky-Kraff, M., Cohen, M. L., Yanovski, S. Z., Cox, C., Theim, K. R., Keil, M., Reynolds, J. C., and Yanovski, J. A. (2006) "A prospective study of psychological predictors of body fat gain among children at high risk for adult obesity", *Pediatrics* 117: 1203–9.

Tanofsky-Kraff, M., Faden, D., Yanovski, S. Z., Wilfley, D. E., and Yanovski, J. A. (2005) "The perceived onset of dieting and loss of control eating behaviors in overweight children", *International Journal of Eating Disorders* 38: 112–22.

Tanofsky-Kraff, M., Goossens, L., Eddy, K. T., Ringham, R., Goldschmidt, A., Yanovski, S. Z., Braet, C., Marcus, M. D., Wilfley, D. E., Olsen, C., and Yanovski, J. A. (2007) "A multisite investigation of binge eating behaviors in children and adolescents", *Journal of Consulting and Clinical Psychology* 75: 901–13.

Tanofsky-Kraff, M., Marcus, M. D., Yanovski, S. Z., and Yanovski, J. A. (2008) "Loss of control eating disorder in children age 12 years and younger: proposed research criteria", *Eating Behaviors* 9: 360–65.

Tanofsky-Kraff, M., McDuffie, J. R., Yanovski, S. Z., Kozlosky, M., Schvey, N. A., Shomaker, L. B., Salaita, C., and Yanovski, J. A. (2009) "Laboratory assessment of the food intake of children and adolescents with loss of control eating", *American Journal of Clinical Nutrition* 89: 738–45.

Tanofsky-Kraff, M., Shomaker, L. B., Olsen, C., Roza, C. A., Wolkoff, L. E., Columbo, K. M., Raciti, G., Zocca, J. M., Wilfley, D. E., Yanovski, S. Z., and Yanovski, J. A.

(2011) "A prospective study of pediatric loss of control eating and psychological outcomes", *Journal of Abnormal Psychology* 120(1): 108–18.

Tanofsky-Kraff, M., Shomaker, L. B., Stern, E. A., Miller, R., Sebring, N., Dellavalle, D., Yanovski, S. Z., Hubbard, V. S., and Yanovski, J. A. (in press) "Children's binge eating and development of metabolic syndrome", *International Journal of Obesity*.

Tanofsky-Kraff, M., Theim, K. R., Yanovski, S. Z., Bassett, A. M., Burns, N. P., Ranzenhofer, L. M., Glasofer, D. R., and Yanovski, J. A. (2007) "Validation of the Emotional Eating Scale adapted for use in children and adolescents (EES-C)", *International Journal of Eating Disorders* 40: 232–40.

Tanofsky-Kraff, M., Wilfley, D. E., Young, J. F., Mufson, L., Yanovski, S. Z., Glasofer, D. R., and Salaita, C. G. (2007) "Preventing excessive weight gain in adolescents: interpersonal psychotherapy for binge eating", *Obesity* 15: 1345–55.

Tanofsky-Kraff, M., Yanovski, S. Z., Schvey, N. A., Olsen, C. H., Gustafson, J., and Yanovski, J. A. (2009) "A prospective study of loss of control eating for body weight gain in children at high risk for adult obesity", *International Journal of Eating Disorders* 42: 26–30.

Tanofsky-Kraff, M., Yanovski, S. Z., Wilfley, D. E., Marmarosh, C., Morgan, C. M., and Yanovski, J. A. (2004) "Eating-disordered behaviors, body fat, and psychopathology in overweight and normal-weight children", *Journal of Consulting and Clinical Psychology* 72: 53–61.

Zaitsoff, S. L., and Grilo, C. M. (2010) "Eating disorder psychopathology as a marker of psychosocial distress and suicide risk in female and male adolescent psychiatric inpatients", *Comprehensive Psychiatry* 51: 142–50.

Zocca, J. M., Shomaker, L. B., Tanofsky-Kraff, M., Columbo, K. M., Raciti, G. R., Brady, S. M., Crocker, M. K., Ali, A. H., Matheson, B. E., Yanovski, S. Z., and Yanovski, J. A. (2011) "Links between mothers' and children's disinhibited eating and children's adiposity", *Appetite* 56: 324–31.

Chapter 5

Binge eating disorder, childhood trauma and psychiatric comorbidity

Trisha M. Karr, Heather Simonich and Stephen A. Wonderlich

Case study

I have tried countless diets over the years – some more successful than others. Regardless of my weight, I've always hated the way my body looks. The continual dieting is also accompanied by frequent binge eating. I also struggle with depression and have a history of drinking problems. I have had numerous relationship problems in my three marriages. I have gone to many therapists for help with my eating, but nothing has worked for me. As a child, my grandfather and an uncle sexually abused me, and I sometimes wonder if this trauma is connected to my eating problems. I have never told anyone and no one has ever really asked. I am not sure I will ever feel better.

Gina, 60

About 695,000 children within the United States (US) experience some form of child maltreatment in a given year (Administration for Children and Families 2010). This statistic is limited to cases reported to and investigated by child protective services and is therefore likely to be a gross underestimate. Early studies in the eating disorders suggested that prevalence rates of child maltreatment among eating disordered individuals were higher than those expected in the general population (Steiger and Zanko 1990; Vanderlinden *et al.* 1993). These observations led to a series of empirical studies over the past 20 years which examined the relationship between child abuse and eating disorders in research designs with rigorous measurement and adequate control groups. The general consensus of these studies has been that child maltreatment, particularly childhood sexual abuse (CSA), is associated with eating disorders, especially when there is a binge–purge component (Smolak and Levine 2007; Thompson and Wonderlich 2004; Wonderlich *et al.* 1997). Furthermore, as illustrated by Gina, one of the most consistent findings in this literature has been that eating disordered individuals who experienced childhood trauma display marked psychiatric comorbidity in the form of mood disorders, substance use disorders, anxiety disorders, and personality disorders

(Brewerton 2004; Kendler *et al.* 2000; Sansone and Sansone 2006; Thompson *et al.* 2003).

This chapter provides a brief overview of clinically relevant information about childhood trauma, which most commonly takes the form of child abuse and neglect. We will synthesize a small but growing body of research on the relationship of childhood trauma and binge eating disorder (BED). This overview will cover data examining the magnitude of the association between childhood trauma and BED, as well as particular correlates of childhood trauma in BED patients, such as marked psychiatric comorbidity and personality disturbances. Finally, we will provide a brief discussion of the clinical implications of a history of trauma in the overall treatment of BED patients.

Childhood trauma

Research since 1990 reveals a noteworthy association between child maltreatment and psychological dysfunction in adulthood (Briere and Jordan 2009; Kendler *et al.* 2000). The major types of child maltreatment associated with long-term negative outcomes include CSA, childhood neglect (CN), childhood physical abuse (CPA), and childhood emotional abuse (CEA). CSA is the most well-studied form of abuse and has been linked to numerous psychological and medical problems in adulthood (Kendall-Tackett *et al.* 1993; Wegman and Stetler 2009; Wilsnack *et al.* 1997).

Prevalence estimates of CSA have varied significantly across studies, but it is estimated that about 1 out of every 12 children in the US has experienced some form of sexual abuse before the age of 18 (Finkelhor *et al.* 2005). Given the secretive nature of sexual abuse and the likelihood that many cases go unreported, these rates may be under-estimations. Furthermore, definitions of childhood sexual abuse have varied across studies which often make interpretation of the prevalence rates difficult. For example, some investigators use a broad definition of CSA that includes observing sexual acts or indecent exposure by a stranger and others may use very specific definitions involving physical contact (e.g., sexual penetration). Research on CSA also relies heavily on retrospective, self-report data and is therefore subject to problems with selective recall and memory deterioration. Unfortunately, logistical and ethical issues prevent researchers from developing large prospective studies that would help to overcome many of these methodological shortcomings.

Although studied much less often than sexual abuse, childhood neglect is the most common form of maltreatment reported to child welfare authorities. In 2010, approximately 538,557 children from the US (78.3 per cent of all child maltreatment cases) were reported as being neglected (Administration for Children and Families 2010). Childhood neglect frequently goes unreported and, historically, has not been publicized as greatly as other types of abuse. Even professionals who work with children may underestimate the effects of childhood neglect despite recent findings that it may be just as detrimental to children's early brain development as sexual or physical abuse (De Bellis *et al.* 2009).

Childhood physical abuse is the second most common form of child maltreatment and legal definitions vary from state to state, but broadly defined CPA is any physical act by a caregiver that results in a child being injured. CPA is the only type of abuse reported more often by males than females (30 per cent vs. 20 per cent, respectively) in the general population (MacMillan *et al.* 1997). CPA has been linked to a variety of negative mental health outcomes in adulthood, such as post-traumatic stress disorder (PTSD), aggressive behavior, substance dependence, depression, poor communication skills, and lack of empathy toward others (Gershoff 2008). Importantly, childhood physical abuse is also associated with violent or criminal behavior as well as abusive behaviors in intimate relationships (Grogan-Kaylor 2004).

Childhood emotional abuse is infrequently reported and consequently prevalence rates are difficult to estimate. Nevertheless, some studies have shown that 15–20 per cent of adults in the general community report experiencing some form of CEA (Baker and Maiorino 2010). Several factors may contribute to the likelihood that this type of abuse goes unreported. First, it is difficult to determine what meets the threshold of emotional abuse and therefore mandated reporters may be reluctant to make a report to social services. Additionally, childhood emotional abuse is similar to childhood neglect in that the effects are often minimized. Finally, other forms of abuse that commonly co-occur (e.g., CPA) and are often thought to be more damaging, may overshadow CEA. However, researchers have found strong associations between CEA and numerous psychological problems in adulthood including eating disorders and body image disturbance (Allison *et al.* 2007; Brewerton 2007; Grilo and Masheb 2001; Wonderlich *et al.* 2007).

It is crucial to consider the effects of experiencing multiple forms of child maltreatment given that many children who experience one type of maltreatment will also be exposed to other traumatic life events. Exposure to multiple traumatic events appears to compound the effects of child abuse and therefore researchers since 2002 have begun to focus on "complex trauma". The term complex trauma describes children's exposure to multiple or prolonged traumatic events and the impact of this exposure on development. The exposure to trauma is often chronic, begins in early childhood, and typically occurs within the primary caregiving system (Cook *et al.* 2003). Exposure to these traumatic experiences in early childhood and the resulting loss of safety and consequent emotional dysregulation may set the stage for the development of various behavioral and psychological problems (e.g., eating disorders) during adolescence and adulthood. Recent research also suggests complex trauma may impact neurobiological development which may, in turn, modify risk for psychiatric conditions (McCrory *et al.* 2011).

Assessment of childhood trauma

As the link between childhood trauma and subsequent psychopathology is repeatedly demonstrated, the need for more reliable assessment methods is becoming increasingly important to further elucidate the exact nature of this relationship. Since the 1990s, the field has responded with the development of numerous measures for assessing childhood trauma. Assessment measures can be divided into three domains: 1) child vs. adult measures, 2) history of exposure (i.e., presence/absence) vs. impact of trauma (i.e., symptom measure), and 3) observer rated interviews vs. self-report questionnaires.

Obtaining adult retrospective accounts of various forms of childhood trauma is the most popular method of inquiring about maltreatment. The Childhood Trauma Questionnaire (CTQ) (Bernstein and Fink 1998) is a widely used self-report assessment that measures exposure to five types of trauma. Although the CTQ has excellent psychometric properties, trauma interviews may provide a better method of evaluation given that they allow the opportunity for interviewers to clarify information. Furthermore, the questionnaire is limited in that it does not assess certain types of childhood trauma (e.g., witnessing domestic or community violence). The Childhood Trauma Interview (CTI) (Fink *et al.* 1995) is a semi-structured interview that assesses seven types of traumatic experiences and includes a well-developed manual for the interviewer. Both of these measures have been used extensively to study the association between childhood trauma and various forms of psychopathology. However, both measures are limited by reliance on long-term retrospective recall and lack any measurement of the impact of trauma.

Instruments often assess the impact of experiencing traumatic events (e.g., Trauma Symptom Checklist for Children [Briere 1996]). The UCLA PTSD – Reaction Index (Pynoos *et al.* 1998) assesses both exposure to and the impact of trauma and has excellent psychometric properties. Although easily accessible and free to use, it relies heavily on PTSD traits as a measure of impact rather than a broader assessment of psychological symptoms. Overall, a wide variety of measures cover the full range of trauma in childhood and adolescence, but few have been designed for specific ages which may limit the ability to study child development. Furthermore, few measures are designed for very young or pre-school age children, which is a major limitation given that early identification and intervention is essential for the prevention of negative mental health outcomes in adolescence and adulthood.

Binge eating disorder and psychological trauma

Much of the early work addressing the relationship between child maltreatment in eating disorders focused on people with anorexia nervosa (AN), bulimia nervosa (BN), and variations of these two eating disorders. More recently, with growing interest in the concept of BED, there has been a parallel growth in the number of studies examining the relationship between child maltreatment and BED. Several early studies suggested that rates of childhood maltreatment were consistently higher in BED subjects than in control subjects (Dalle Grave et al. 1997; Grilo and Masheb 2001; Wonderlich et al. 2001). More recently, a number of studies have examined the child maltreatment–BED relationship and have used the CTQ to assess trauma. Interestingly, several studies have converged to suggest that approximately four out of five BED subjects score above clinical cutoffs on at least one of the types of child maltreatment measured in the CTQ (Allison et al. 2007; Grilo and Masheb 2001, 2002). For example, Grilo and Masheb (2001) found that more than two-thirds of BED participants reported childhood emotional neglect (CEN), nearly 50 per cent reported childhood physical neglect (CPN), and approximately 30 per cent reported CPA and CSA.

Because BED displays a strong relationship to obesity, it is interesting to consider the rates of child maltreatment in obese samples that may or may not display BED. For example, the Adverse Childhood Experiences (ACE) study (Felitti et al. 1998), which included 13,177 members of a Health Maintenance Organization (HMO), found that a history of child maltreatment was strongly linked to the risk of having a body mass index (BMI) > 40. Other studies have also found increased rates of child abuse in obese samples (Lissau and Sorensen 1994; Williamson et al. 2002). In a series of more recent studies, obese people who are candidates for bariatric surgery have also been examined in terms of their histories of childhood maltreatment. Using the CTQ, Grilo et al. (2005) found that 69 per cent of bariatric surgery candidates scored above the clinical cutoff on the CTQ, which is two to three times higher than normative values.

In a similar study, Grilo et al. (2006) also reported the same rate of child maltreatment (i.e., 69 per cent) in an obese surgery sample. This finding that approximately two-thirds of bariatric surgery candidates have a history of childhood maltreatment is intriguing, because it continues to be identified as an estimate of such maltreatment across several studies. For example Wildes et al. (2008) studied 230 bariatric surgery cases and reported 66 per cent had experienced one form of childhood maltreatment. In a study which relied on chart review for identification of child abuse, Clark et al. (2007) found that of 152 adults with morbid obesity who had bariatric surgery, 27 per cent had experienced sexual abuse, nine per cent adult sexual trauma, and 19 per cent physical abuse during either childhood or adulthood. It is unclear if a person may have experienced multiple forms of abuse in this study, therefore leaving the data somewhat difficult to interpret. However, it is noteworthy that this particular study assessed only three forms of abuse and still found a significant fraction of their sample had experienced some type of trauma. Supporting this basic idea that approximately two-thirds of obese persons experienced maltreatment, Sansone et al. (2008) reported that 63 per cent of their bariatric surgery candidates experienced at least one form of childhood abuse in the form of CPA, CPN, or CSA. Importantly, the estimates in this study were not based on the CTQ, but instead an interview which, given that it is consistent with the CTQ findings, provides some degree of concurrent validity of these assessments.

The above findings suggest that a significant fraction of patients with BED have substantial histories of child maltreatment and psychological trauma. Furthermore, other individuals who may experience binge eating, such as obese or overweight patients or individuals considering bariatric surgery, may also have significant histories of psychological trauma. Although documentation of an association between child maltreatment and binge eating related presentations is noteworthy, a more significant clinical focus may be to question how such traumatic experiences influence the clinical presentation of BED. For example, do persons with BED and histories of childhood trauma display more severe forms of this eating disorder? Alternatively, does the presence of childhood maltreatment predict high rates of psychiatric comorbidity, similar to the other eating disorders? Next, we will provide a brief overview of the impact of psychological trauma on the overall clinical presentation of BED.

Childhood maltreatment and binge eating disorder symptoms

Mixed findings have been shown in examinations of the impact of child maltreatment on core eating disorder symptoms (e.g., dieting behaviors, body dissatisfaction, BMI) among individuals with BED. For instance, among women with BED, dietary restraint has been associated with a history of CPN (Grilo and Masheb 2001), and an early age of dietary onset has been linked to CEN (Becker and Grilo 2011). Like Gina, those with BED who have experienced CSA or CEA frequently report body dissatisfaction (Dunkley et al. 2010; Grilo and Masheb 2001). However, neither the general experience of childhood maltreatment nor the specific types of maltreatment have been associated with current BMI among those with BED (Allison et al. 2007; Becker and Grilo 2011; Dalle Grave et al. 1997; Grilo et al. 2005; Grilo and Masheb 2001, 2002).

Psychiatric comorbidity and binge eating disorder

In general, numerous studies have shown that comorbid psychiatric disorders are common among individuals with BED, and have indicated that between 33-83 per cent of research participants have at least one additional diagnosis (Hudson et al. 2007; Peterson et al. 2005; Schulz and Laessle 2010; Specker et al. 1994; Telch and Stice 1998; Wilfley et al. 2000; Yanovksi et al. 1993). Similar to Gina, the most frequent diagnoses for participants with BED appear to be mood disorders, anxiety disorders, and substance use disorders. In regard to personality disorders, some studies have reported that personality disorders are more common among individuals with BED than obese controls (Specker et al. 1994; Telch and Stice 1998; Yanovski et al. 1993), whereas others have noted high rates of personality diagnoses, but no differences between obese samples with and without BED (Becker et al. 2010; Wilfley et al. 2000). Across studies, impulsive personality disorders, including borderline personality disorder (BPD) and histrionic personality disorder (HPD), as well as anxious, fearful personality disorders, including obsessive compulsive personality disorder (OCPD) and avoidant personality disorder (AVPD), appear to be the most prevalent personality diagnoses among individuals with BED. Indeed, Wilfley *et al.* (2000) found that the rates of OCPD and AVPD were twice as high among the BED group than a general psychiatric group. Furthermore, people with BED and OCPD or AVPD have reported higher rates of major depressive disorder (MDD), social phobia, post-traumatic stress disorder (PTSD), and generalized anxiety disorder (GAD) than participants without personality disorders (Becker *et al.* 2010; Wilfley *et al.* 2000). Therefore, comorbid psychiatric conditions appear to be typical characteristics of the majority of people with BED.

Psychiatric comorbidity, childhood maltreatment, and binge eating disorder

Given that there is evidence that trauma is related to a wide range of psychiatric problems (Johnson *et al.* 1999; Lobbestael *et al.* 2010), it may be that traumatized people with BED display increased psychiatric comorbidity. As noted in the case of Gina, the evidence suggests that, in general, a common clinical characteristic among traumatized people with BED is the presence of higher depression scores and lower self-esteem scores than in non-traumatized BED patients (Allison *et al.* 2007; Becker and Grilo 2011; Dunkley *et al.* 2010). Specific forms of psychiatric disturbance have also been associated with child maltreatment, for example CEA with dysthymia, CPA with substance use and depressive disorders, and CPN and CSA with PTSD (Becker and Grilo 2011). Currently, preliminary empirical evidence has shown associations between emotional abuse and personality pathology, including anxious–fearful personality disorders, especially AVPD (Grilo and Masheb 2002). It is possible that child maltreatment increases the likelihood of various psychiatric problems which often co-occur with BED, and may impact treatment strategies and effectiveness.

Binge eating disorder treatment: the influence of comorbidity and trauma

In general, comorbid psychopathology among people with BED, including symptoms of depression, anxiety, and personality disorders, has been associated with poor treatment outcomes (Masheb and Grilo 2008; Picot and Lilenfeld 2003; Schulz and Laessle 2010; Telch and Stice 1998; Wilfley *et al.* 2000). Compared to other people with BED, those with comorbid conditions are more likely to drop out of treatment, resume binge eating at one-year follow-up, and display a poorer treatment prognosis.

In regard to trauma, little is known about the impact of psychological trauma on BED treatment. There is evidence, however, that psychological trauma negatively impacts the treatment of disorders or conditions associated with BED. For example, among women suffering from bulimia nervosa (BN), those who had experienced childhood sexual abuse were at the greatest risk for treatment drop out and behavioral relapse (Rodriguez *et al.* 2005). Additionally, a history of CSA has been associated with an increased risk for psychiatric hospitalizations among bariatric surgery patients (Clark *et al.* 2007). Unfortunately, studies examining the predictive or moderating role of psychological trauma on BED treatment are not available. Given the clinical complexity often associated with histories of childhood trauma, however, clinicians must consider the role of developmental adversity in treatment outcomes from all eating disorders, including BED.

Conclusion – clinical implications of childhood trauma in the treatment of binge eating disorder

Given the paucity of empirical research examining the influence of childhood trauma on eating disorder treatment outcomes, very little can be said about evidence-based modifications of BED treatment for traumatized persons. The most reasonable strategy would seem to be to follow evidence based guidelines for all persons with BED, including those who are traumatized. However, experienced clinicians will know that BED patients with trauma histories, like Gina, may display clinical symptomatology which is not simply or easily addressed with available BED treatment protocols. Clinicians will need to make well-informed decisions about clinical issues such as comorbid substance use, post-traumatic stress disorder symptoms, extreme anxiety, and severe depression, including suicidal impulses and behaviors. As such complicating clinical situations arise, clinicians may need to go outside of the realm of eating disorder treatments to identify and deliver effective treatments for co-occurring problems. The adjunctive use of pharmacotherapy, exposure therapy, behavioral activation strategies, and other evidence-based interventions may need to be incorporated into BED treatment if traumatized persons display patterns of behavior which are not responsive to typical BED treatment.

References

Administration for Children and Families (2010) *Child Maltreatment 2009*, US Department of Health and Human Services: Children's Bureau. Online. Available: http://www.acf.hhs.gov/programs/cb/stats_research/index.htm#can (accessed 26 March 2012).

Allison, K. C., Grilo, C. M., Masheb, R. M., and Stunkard, A. J. (2007) "High self-reported rates of neglect and emotional abuse, by persons with binge eating disorder and night eating syndrome", *Behaviour Research and Therapy* 45: 2874–83.

Baker, A. J. L., and Maiorino, E. (2010) "Assessments of emotional abuse and neglect with the CTQ: issues and estimates", *Children and Youth Services Review* 32: 740–48.

Becker, D.F., and Grilo, C.M. (2011) "Childhood maltreatment in women with binge-eating disorder: associations with psychiatric comorbidity, psychological functioning, and eating pathology", *Eating and Weight Disorders* 16: e113–20.

Becker, D. F., Masheb, R. M., White, M. A., and Grilo, C. M. (2010) "Psychiatric, behavioral, and attitudinal correlates of avoidant and obsessive-compulsive personality pathology in patients with binge-eating disorder", *Comprehensive Psychiatry* 51: 531–7.

Bernstein, D., and Fink, P. (1998) *The Childhood Trauma Questionnaire: A Retrospective Self-Report, Manual*, San Antonio: Harcourt & Co.

Brewerton, T. D. (2004) "Eating disorders, victimization, and comorbidity: principles of treatment", in T. D. Brewerton (ed.), *Clinical Handbook of Eating Disorders: An Integrated Approach* (pp. 509–45), New York: Marcel Dekker.

Brewerton, T.D. (2007) "Eating disorders, trauma, and comorbidity: focus on PTSD", *Eating Disorders* 15: 285–304.

Briere, J. (1996) *Trauma Symptom Checklist for Children Professional Manual*, Odessa, FL: Psychological Assessment Resources.

Briere, J., and Jordan, C. E. (2009) "Childhood maltreatment, intervening variables, and adult psychological difficulties in women: an overview", *Trauma, Violence, & Abuse* 10: 375–88.

Clark, M. W., Hanna, B. K., Mai, J. L., Graszer, K. M., Krochta, J. G., McAlpine, D. E., Reading, S., Abu-Lebdeh, H. S., Jensen, M. D., and Sarr, M. G. (2007) "Sexual abuse survivors and psychiatric hospitalization after bariatric surgery", *Obesity Surgery* 17: 465–9.

Cook, A., Blaustein, M., Spinazzola, J., and van der Kolk, B. (eds) (2003) *Complex Trauma in Children and Adolescents*, National Child Traumatic Stress Network. Online. Available: http://www.nctsnet.org/nccts/nav.do?pid=typ_ct (accessed 26 March 2012).

Dalle Grave, R., Oliosi, M., Todisco, P., and Vanderlinden, J. (1997) "Self-reported traumatic experiences and dissociative symptoms in obese women with and without binge-eating disorder", *Eating Disorders* 5: 105–9.

De Bellis, M. D., Hooper, S. R., Spratt, E. G., and Woolley, D. P. (2009) "Neuropsychological findings in childhood neglect and their relationships to pediatric PTSD", *Journal of International Neuropsychological Society* 15: 868–78.

Dunkley, D. M., Masheb, R. M., and Grilo, C. M. (2010) "Childhood maltreatment, depressive symptoms, and body dissatisfaction in patients with binge eating disorder: the mediating role of self-criticism", *International Journal of Eating Disorders* 43: 274–81.

Felitti, V. J., Anda, R. F., Nordenberg, D., Williamson, D. F., Spitz, A. M., Edwards, V., Koss, M. P., and Marks, J. S. (1998) "Relationship of childhood abuse and household dysfunction to many of the leading causes of death in adults: the Adverse Childhood Experiences (ACE) Study", *American Journal of Preventative Medicine* 14: 245–58.

Fink, L. A., Bernstein, D., Hadelsman, L., Foote, J., and Lovejoy, M. (1995) "Initial reliability and validity of the childhood trauma interview", *American Journal of Psychiatry* 152: 1329–35.

Finkelhor, D., Ormrod, R., Turner, H., and Hambry, S. L. (2005) "The victimization of children and youth: a comprehensive, national survey", *Child Maltreatment* 10: 5–25.

Gershoff, E.T. (2008) *Report on Physical Punishment in the U.S.: What Research Tells Us About its Effects on Children*, Columbus, OH: Center for Effective Discipline. Online. Available: http://www.phoenixchildrens.com/PDFs/principles_and_practices-of_effective_discipline.pdf (accessed 26 March 2012).

Grilo, C. M., and Masheb, R. M. (2001) "Childhood psychological, physical, and sexual maltreatment in outpatients with binge eating disorder: frequency and associations with gender, obesity, and eating-related psychopathology", *Obesity Research* 9: 320–25.

Grilo, C. M., and Masheb, R. M. (2002) "Childhood maltreatment and personality disorders in adult patients with binge eating disorder", *Acta Psychiatrica Scandinavica* 106: 183–8.

Grilo, C. M., Masheb, R. M., Brody, M., Toth, C., Burke-Martindale, C. H., and Rothschild, B. S. (2005) "Childhood maltreatment in extremely obese male and female bariatric surgery candidates", *Obesity Research* 13: 123–30.

Grilo, C. M., White, M. A., Masheb, R. M., Rothschild, B. S., and Burke-Martindale, C. H. (2006) "Relation to childhood sexual abuse and other forms of maltreatment to 12-month postoperative outcomes in extremely obese gastric bypass patients", *Obesity Surgery* 16: 454–60.

Grogan-Kaylor, A. (2004) "The effect of corporal punishment on anti-social behavior in children", *Social Work Research* 28: 153–62.

Hudson, J. I., Hiripi, E., Pope, Jr, H. G., and Kessler, R. C. (2007) "The prevalence and correlates of eating disorders in the national comorbidity survey replication", *Biological Psychiatry* 61: 348–58.

Johnson, J. G., Cohen, P., Brown, J., Smailes, E. M., and Bernstein, D. P. (1999) "Childhood maltreatment increases risk for personality disorders during early adulthood", *Archives of General Psychiatry* 56: 600–606.

Kendall-Tackett, K. A., Williams, L. M., and Finkelhor, D. (1993) "Impact of sexual abuse on children: a review and synthesis of recent empirical studies", *Psychological Bulletin* 113: 164–80.

Kendler, K. S., Bulik, C. M., Silberg, J., Hettema, J. M., Myers, J., and Prescott, C. A. (2000) "Childhood sexual abuse and adult psychiatric and substance use disorders in women", *Archives of General Psychiatry* 57: 953–9.

Lissau, I., and Sorensen, T. I. A. (1994) "Parental neglect during childhood and increased risk of obesity in young adulthood", *Lancet* 343: 324–7.

Lobbestael, J., Arntz, A., and Bernstein, D. P. (2010) "Disentangling the relationship between different types of childhood maltreatment and personality disorders", *Journal of Personality Disorders* 24: 285–95.

MacMillan, H. L., Fleming, J. E., Trocmé, N., Boyle, M. H., Wong, M., Racine, Y. A., Beardslee, W. R., and Offord, D. R. (1997) "Prevalence of child physical and sexual abuse in the community: results from the Ontario Health Supplement", *Journal of the American Medical Association* 278: 131–5.

Masheb, R. M., and Grilo, C. M. (2008) "Examination of predictors and moderators for self-help treatments of binge-eating disorder", *Journal of Consulting and Clinical Psychology* 76: 900–904.

McCrory, E., De Brito, S. A., and Viding, E. (2011) "The impact of childhood maltreatment: a review of neurobiological and genetic factors", *Frontiers in Psychiatry* 2: 1–14.

Peterson, C. B., Miller, K. B., Crow, S. J., Thuras, P., and Mitchell, J. E. (2005) "Subtypes of binge eating disorder based on psychiatric history", *International Journal of Eating Disorders* 38: 273–6.

Picot, A. K., and Lilenfeld, L. R. R. (2003) "The relationship among binge severity, personality psychopathology, and body mass index", *International Journal of Eating Disorders* 34: 98–107.

Pynoos, R. S., Rodriguez, N., Steinberg, A., Stuber, M., and Frederick, C. (1998) *UCLA PTSD Reaction Index for DSM-IV*, Los Angeles, CA: UCLA Trauma Psychiatry Service.

Rodríguez, M., Pérez, V., and García, Y. (2005) "Impact of traumatic experiences and violent acts upon response to treatment of a sample of Colombian women with eating disorders", *International Journal of Eating Disorders* 37: 299–306.

Sansone, R. A. and Sansone, L. A. (2006) "Childhood trauma, personality disorders, and eating disorders", in R. A. Sansone and J. L. Levitt (eds), *Personality Disorders and Eating Disorders* (pp. 59–76), New York: Routledge.

Sansone, R. A., Schumacher, D., Wiederman, M. W., and Routsong-Weichers, L. (2008) "The prevalence of childhood trauma and parental caretaking quality among gastric surgery candidates", *Eating Disorders* 16: 117–27.

Schulz, S., and Laessle, R. G. (2010) "Associations of negative affect and eating behaviour in obese women with and without binge eating disorder", *Eating and Weight Disorders* 15: e287–93.

Smolak, L., and Levine, M. P. (2007) "Trauma, eating problems, and eating disorders, Part 1– 2007", in S. Wonderlich, J. E. Mitchell, M. de Zwaan, and H. Steiger (eds), *Annual Review of Eating Disorders* (pp. 113–23), Oxford: Radcliffe.

Specker, S., de Zwaan, M., Raymond, N., and Mitchell, J. (1994) "Psychopathology in subgroups of obese women with and without binge eating disorder", *Comprehensive Psychiatry* 35: 185–90.

Steiger, H., and Zanko, M. (1990) "Sexual traumata among eating-disordered, psychiatric, and normal female groups", *Journal of Interpersonal Violence* 5: 74–86.

Telch, C. F., and Stice, E. (1998) "Psychiatric comorbidity in women with binge eating disorder: prevalence rates from a non-treatment-seeking-sample", *Journal of Consulting and Clinical Psychology* 66: 768–76.

Thompson, K. M., Crosby, R. D., Wonderlich, S. A., Mitchell, J. E., Redlin, J., Demuth, G., Smyth, J., and Haseltine, B. (2003) "Psychopathology and sexual trauma in childhood and adulthood", *Journal of Traumatic Stress* 16: 35–8.

Thompson, K. M., and Wonderlich, S. A (2004) "Child sexual abuse and eating disorders", in J. K. Thompson (ed.) *Handbook on Eating Disorders and Obesity* (pp. 679–94), Hoboken, NJ: John Wiley & Sons.

Vanderlinden, J., Vandereycken, W., van Dyck, R., and Vertommen, H. (1993) "Dissociative experiences and trauma in eating disorders", *International Journal of Eating Disorders* 13: 187–93.

Wegman, H. L., and Stetler, C. (2009) "A meta-analytic review of the effects of childhood abuse on medical outcomes in adulthood" *Psychosomatic Medicine* 71: 805–12.

Wildes, J. E., Kalarchian, M. A., Marcus, M. D., Levine, M. D., and Courcoulas, A. P. (2008) "Childhood maltreatment and psychiatric morbidity in bariatric surgery candidates", *Obesity Surgery* 18: 306–13.

Wilfley, D. E., Friedman, M. A., Dounchis, J. Z., Stein, R. I., Welch, R. R., and Ball, S. A. (2000) "Comorbid psychopathology in binge eating disorder: relation to eating disorder severity at baseline and following treatment", *Journal of Consulting and Clinical Psychology* 68: 641–9.

Williamson, D. F., Thompson, T. J., Anda, R. F., Dieta, W.H., and Felitti, V. (2002) "Body weight and obesity in adults and self-reported abuse in childhood", *International Journal of Obesity* 26: 1075–82.

Wilsnack, S. A., Vogeltanz, N. D., Klassen, A. D., and Harris, T. R. (1997) "Childhood sexual abuse and women's substance abuse: national survey findings", *Journal of Studies on Alcohol* 58: 264–71.

Wonderlich, S. A., Brewerton, T. D., Jocic, Z., Dansky, B. S., and Abbott, D. W. (1997) "Relationship of childhood sexual abuse and eating disorders", *Journal of the American Academy of Child & Adolescent Psychiatry* 36: 1107–15.

Wonderlich, S. A., Crosby, R. D., Mitchell, J. E., Thompson, K. M., Redlin, J., Demuth, G.,

Smyth, J., and Haseltine, B. (2001) "Eating disturbance and sexual trauma in childhood and adulthood", *International Journal of Eating Disorders* 30: 401–12.

Wonderlich, S. A., Rosenfeldt, S., Crosby, R. D., Mitchell, J. E., Engel, S. G., Smyth, J., and Miltenberger, R. (2007) "The effects of childhood trauma on daily mood lability and comorbid psychopathology in bulimia nervosa", *Journal of Traumatic Stress* 20: 77–87.

Yanovski, S. Z., Nelson, J. E., Dubbert, B. K., and Spitzer, R. L. (1993) "Association of binge eating disorder and psychiatric comorbidity in obese subjects", *American Journal of Psychiatry* 150: 1472–9.

Chapter 6

Comorbidity and related considerations

Jonathan Mond, Anita Star and Phillipa Hay

Case study

I'm a 32-year-old secretary working at a solicitor's office. I've been overweight since adolescence, but in recent years this problem has increased to the point where I'm severely obese, with a BMI well in excess of 40 kg/^{m2}. Over the years, I've tried a number of diet and healthy eating plans, but have never been able to adhere to the recommendations for any length of time. I live alone, have a strained relationship with my family and have few friends that I feel I can rely on. Generally, my diet is regular in that I eat three meals a day and these meals contain a wide variety of foods. However, to help cope with my feelings of isolation, I "treat" myself with luxury foods such as chocolate, cheesecake, and ice-cream. Because this sort of eating is linked to my emotions, rather than level of hunger, it can occur at any time. When I get home from work I often go to the fridge for a small snack; trouble is, after eating the snack I'm unable to stop eating and continue to consume a large amount of food. For example, I may eat an apple, a slice of cheesecake, several biscuits, a peanut butter and jelly sandwich and drink several glasses of chocolate milk. Later in the evening I eat dinner and sometimes I'll lose control with this as well and eat the extra helping that I was planning to save for the next day. Guilt and sadness overwhelm me after eating like this and I despise my body shape. This is the first time I have told anyone about the way I feel or about my eating behavior. I have often thought about different ways to counteract the effects of binge eating, such as going without food for a couple of days, exercising really hard or taking laxatives, but I have never tried any of these things. Ideally, I would like to join a gym, but am terrified at the prospect of being exposed to ridicule or derision in the gym environment and in public more generally. Also, due to my chronic obesity, I am frequently short of breath and have chronic joint and back pain that makes even gentle exercise difficult. Yes, I have considered bariatric surgery, but my current BMI is too high to claim insurance coverage for this procedure. Aside from feeling powerless to improve my quality of life, I am becoming increasingly anxious around people due being alone so much. I know I need help to get my eating and emotional problems under control, but I don't have the strength to rake over my personal life with a therapist and, in any case, see being overweight as my primary problem.

Alison

Introduction

"Comorbidity" refers to physical or mental health problems that co-occur with a condition of interest. Like most mental disorders, binge eating disorder (BED) is associated with increased risk of other mental health problems, poor physical health, and stigma. However, the strongly aversive nature of uncontrolled binge eating and the strong association between BED and obesity are such that people with BED may be susceptible to high levels of both physical and mental health impairment.

In this chapter, we consider evidence concerning the nature and extent of comorbidity associated with BED. Rather than attempting to systematically review the relevant literature in any particular area, we highlight some aspects of BED comorbidity and related considerations that are not specifically addressed in other sections of this book and that may be of benefit in helping clinicians and other health professionals to understand the patients who present to them. The focus is on comorbidity associated with BED in adults, although many of the principles could be seen to apply to children and adolescents and adults alike.

This chapter is written from an epidemiological, rather than a clinical, perspective to reflect the primary interest and expertise of the first author. Elements of a sociological perspective also will be apparent. Our main goal is to introduce the epidemiological approach in addressing some of the issues raised when considering comorbidity associated with BED and with mental health problems more generally. In so doing we will facilitate the process of research-practice integration. However, there are implications for clinical practice and efforts will be made to highlight these when appropriate. We hope that readers whose interest is primarily clinical will bear with us.

Comorbidity from an epidemiological perspective

A basic tenet of the epidemiological approach to mental health problems is that the characteristics of community cases of people with mental health problems may be very different from those people who present with these problems to health services, particularly those presenting to mental health care (Williams *et al.* 1980). This is because various factors, other than the occurrence of symptoms, influence whether or not treatment is sought and, if treatment is sought, the type of treatment sought. These factors include variables particular to the illness, such as its severity; demographic variables such as age, gender and ethnicity;

socio-economic variables such as income and cultural values; environmental variables such as geographical location; and individual-level variables such as knowledge and beliefs about the nature and treatment of symptoms and perceived stigma associated with disclosure of symptoms or behaviors (Anderson and Newman 1973; Mond et al. 2007a).

Conclusions about the characteristics of people with bulimic-type eating disorders (namely, bulimia nervosa [BN], BED and variants of these disorders not meeting formal diagnostic criteria) based on treatment-seeking samples may be particularly problematic, given that many people with these disorders do not seek mental health care (Fairburn et al. 1996; Mond et al. 2007a; Wilfley et al. 2001). Further, there is good evidence that for people with bulimic-type eating disorders, like those with other mental health problems, the best predictors of whether specialist treatment is received are levels of distress and impairment in role functioning (Mond et al. 2007a, 2009). Since higher levels of comorbidity are strongly associated with distress and disability (Andrews et al. 2002), it is not surprising that the levels of comorbidity observed among individuals with BED receiving specialist treatment are high.

It also needs to be recognized that people with bulimic-type eating disorders are more likely to seek treatment for a problem or perceived problem with (over-) weight than for a problem with binge eating (Mond et al. 2007a). Even where treatment is sought specifically for a problem with eating, this may be more likely to be because of the perceived association between binge eating and body weight than the perceived effects of binge eating on quality of life, and more likely to be sought from a primary care practitioner than a mental health specialist. On the other hand, people with BED and variants of BED may be more likely than those with BN and variants of BN to present to health services, primary care at least, due to the combination of physical and mental health impairment. Primary care practitioners in particular need to aware of these patterns of service use (Hay et al. 2007; Mond, Myers et al. 2010).

Types and extent of comorbidity

Physical health impairment

As discussed in Chapter 1 of this volume, the most conspicuous comorbidity of BED is obesity. Findings from epidemiological studies suggest that approximately half to two-thirds of people meeting formal diagnostic criteria for BED meet the accepted criterion for obesity, namely, a body mass index (BMI, kg/m^2) of 30 or more (Hudson et al. 2007; Striegel-Moore et al. 2001). This figure is considerably higher than the prevalence of obesity in the general population, which in the USA and similar countries is approximately 25 to 30 per cent (Finucane et al. 2011).

Although evidence for adverse health consequences associated with overweight ($25.0 \leq BMI < 30.0$) and mild obesity ($30.0 \leq BMI < 35.0$) is not compelling, moderate ($35.0 \leq BMI < 40.0$) and severe obesity ($BMI \geq 40.0$) are associated with increased risk of a range of medical complications, including diabetes, heart disease, breathing difficulties, sleep problems, decreased mobility, and osteo-arthritic complaints, with the prevalence of these comorbidities increasing proportionally to the degree of overweight (Mond and Baune 2009). It is therefore significant that rates of severe obesity are markedly elevated among people with BED when compared with those of the general population (Hudson *et al.* 2007).

One interesting observation concerning the comorbidity between BED and obesity is that increases in the population prevalence of comorbid eating-disordered behavior and obesity appear to be outstripping increases in the prevalence of obesity or disordered eating alone. Findings from consecutive general population surveys conducted in the Australian population suggested that, between 1995 and 2005, the prevalence of binge eating increased from 3.1 per cent to 7.8 per cent, the prevalence of obesity increased from 11.4 per cent to 17.7 per cent and the prevalence of concomitant eating-disordered behavior (including binge eating, fasting and purging) and obesity increased from 1.0 per cent to 3.5 per cent (Darby *et al.* 2009; Hay *et al.* 2008).

Also of note in this research is that similarly pronounced increases in the prevalence of binge eating and other eating disorder behaviors were observed in men and women (Hay *et al.* 2008). However, as discussed below, the clinical significance of binge eating and other eating disorder behaviors is not as clear in men as it is in women.

Mental health impairment

As outlined in Chapter 4, BED is associated, in women at least, with increased risk of other mental health problems. Findings from epidemiological studies conducted in the USA suggest that as many as three out of four people meeting formal diagnostic criteria for BED have met criteria for another DSM diagnosis at some point in their lives (Hudson *et al.* 2007; Striegel-Moore *et al.* 2001). Anxiety and affective disorders are the most common of these comorbid mental health conditions, although rates of alcohol and substance abuse and behavioral problems are also elevated (Hudson *et al.* 2007; Striegel-Moore *et al.* 2001).

Further, these associations appear to be largely independent of the association between BED and body weight. Indeed, epidemiological studies have consistently shown that obesity is associated with little or no impairment in mental health in men and that impairment in mental health associated with obesity in women, where this occurs, is accounted for by the extreme concerns about weight or shape and/or eating-disordered behaviour that frequently co-occur with obesity (Mond *et al.* 2007b; Mond and Baune 2009).

The extensive comorbidity between eating-disordered behavior and other mental health problems has implications not only for clinical practice, in terms of which symptoms should be the focus of attention at which times, but also for public health practice, in terms of which problems should be the focus of health promotion efforts (Mond *et al.* 2004). Issues of the direction of the associations between symptoms of anxiety, depression, and eating-disordered behavior complicate this picture (Mond *et al.* 2004).

Whether the association between binge eating and mental health impairment is as strong in men as in women is unclear. Although findings from some early studies suggested that binge eating may be associated with comparatively low levels of distress in men, more recent studies suggest similarly high levels of distress and functional impairment in men as in women (Mond and Hay 2007; Striegel *et al.* 2012). Further research is needed to elucidate the correlates of binge eating and other eating disorder behaviors in men, including health service utilization. Even where high levels of distress and disability are observed, men may be particularly unlikely to seek treatment for a problem with eating due to lack of insight and/or perceived stigma associated with disclosure of eating disorder behaviors (Striegel *et al.* 2012).

The role of extreme weight or shape concerns or, in the language of the DSM, the "undue influence of weight or shape on self-evaluation" (American Psychiatric Association 1994), appears to be particularly important in accounting for mental health impairment associated with binge eating among people with BED and variants of BED. As many as one in two people with these conditions do not have extreme weight or shape concerns and evidence suggests that people in this subgroup may experience minimal distress and psycho-social impairment (Grilo *et al.* 2010; Mond, Hay *et al.* 2007). In contrast, people with these disorders who report extreme weight or shape concerns have very high levels of distress and disability (Grilo *et al.* 2010; Mond, Hay *et al.* 2007). Since distress and disability are strongly predictive of whether specialist treatment is received, people in this latter subgroup are likely to be over-represented in clinical samples.

What to do with this information poses an interesting dilemma for the architects of the proposed new diagnosis of BED (American Psychiatric Association 2012). On the one hand, the inclusion of the undue influence of weight or shape on self-evaluation among the diagnostic criteria for BED would seem appropriate since this would ensure that only people with "clinically significant" disorders are eligible for the diagnosis while also bringing diagnostic criteria for BED into line with those for anorexia nervosa and BN (American Psychiatric Association 1994, 2012; Fairburn *et al.* 2003). On the other hand, inclusion of the undue influence criteria among the diagnostic criteria for BED may mean that some people in need of treatment are excluded from receiving a diagnosis of BED and, perhaps, appropriate insurance coverage (Grilo *et al.* 2010). For this reason, some authorities have advocated a compromise position, namely, inclusion of undue influence as a specifier of illness severity rather than a diagnostic criterion (Grilo *et al.* 2010).

In our view, further community-based research is needed concerning the clinical significance of disorders characterized by recurrent binge eating (but not extreme weight-control behaviors) in the absence of extreme weight or shape concerns, before firm decisions can be made. Unfortunately, though, there may be a tendency to "study what we define" (Keel *et al.* 2001). Since there is currently no reference to the undue influence of weight or shape on self-evaluation in the DSM criteria – and proposed criteria – for BED, this construct may not be assessed in otherwise rigorous epidemiological studies.

The extent to which classification schemes for mental health problems should be informed by clinical considerations, as opposed to epidemiological data, is a vexing question (Fairburn and Beglin 1990; Williams *et al.* 1980). Since the DSM is intended primarily as an adjunct to clinical practice, it could be argued that priority should be given to findings from and implications for clinical practice (e.g. First *et al.* 2004). On the other hand, the influence of DSM extends well beyond clinical practice, so that the diagnostic criteria chosen for specific disorders exert a profound influence on the "mental health literacy" of primary care practitioners and the public (Rounsaville *et al.* 2002). To give just one example from the eating disorders field, the DSM distinction between purging and non-purging forms of BN may have been conducive to poor self-recognition of disordered eating and, in turn, low or inappropriate treatment-seeking, among people with BED and the non-purging form of BN (Mond, Rogers *et al.* 2006, Mond, Hay *et al.* 2006).

A second, related factor that needs to be considered when interpreting findings relating to mental health impairment associated with BED is that some degree of impairment may be embedded within the diagnostic criteria themselves. In both DSM-IV and in the proposed criteria for DSM-5, the diagnosis of BED requires that "marked distress regarding binge eating is present" (American Psychiatric Association 1994, 2012). So, if these criteria are adhered to in assigning diagnoses, high levels of distress associated with the diagnosis of BED are not surprising. Further, where the "marked distress" criterion is applied, and to the extent that binge eating in men is associated with comparatively low levels of distress, the prevalence of BED in men will necessarily be comparatively low. Whether it makes sense to include the occurrence of distress or disability among the criteria for specific diagnoses, or for mental disorders in general, is an equally vexing issue (Spitzer 1998).

Finally, with reference to the high levels of lifetime occurrence of anxiety and affective disorders among people with BED, it needs to be remembered that comorbidity between different mental health problems may reflect, in part, the way in which these problems are delineated in any given classification scheme at any given point in time (Maj 2005). Prior to the publication of the first standardized psychiatric nosology – the *Statistical Manual for the Use of Institutions for the Insane* – in 1918, authorities recognized only a handful of diagnoses and efforts to expand on this number were met with skepticism (Grob 1991). Eating disorders have been viewed, at one time or another, as variants of both anxiety and affective disorders (Hatsukami *et al.* 1984; Rothenberg 1986) and debate continues as to whether the separation of generalized anxiety disorder and major depressive disorder is tenable (Maj 2005).

None of these concerns detract from the fact that community cases of people with BED, or at least a substantial proportion of these cases, have very poor mental health. But they do indicate the limitations of classification schemes for mental health problems and of the evidence used to support these schemes (Mond 2012; Rounsaville et al. 2002). In addition, it will be apparent that in assessing the mental health of people with BED, scores on a continuous measure of impairment are likely to be more useful than information about the presence of absence of one or more comorbid diagnoses. As discussed next, one or more measures of quality of life may be particularly helpful in assessing the extent of impairment in different aspects of functioning and the impact of treatment on this impairment.

Impairment in quality of life

An important and increasingly recognized comorbidity of BED, other eating disorders, and mental health problems more generally, is impairment in quality of life. Whereas the assessment of other DSM diagnoses provides a formal indication of comorbidity, the assessment of quality of life provides a more tangible indication of the extent to which the symptoms of any given mental health problem(s) impact on a person's functioning in key aspects of his or her life. For this reason, improvement in quality of life is widely viewed as the ultimate end point of clinical intervention in psychiatry and medicine more generally (Coelho et al. 2005; Katschnig 2006).

Unfortunately, there is no agreed-upon definition of quality of life, let alone an agreed definition of impairment in quality of life, despite a proliferation of measures designed to measure this construct in recent years (Coelho et al. 2005; Katschnig 2006). However, two broad distinctions are helpful in introducing readers to this literature.

First, a distinction is often drawn between health-related quality of life, which refers to the perceived effects of a person's health on aspects of his or her daily functioning, and subjective quality of life, which refers to a person's subjective satisfaction with different facets of his or her life, including, but not limited to, his or her health (Coelho et al. 2005; Katschnig 2006). In practice, this distinction is one of degree rather than kind, since all quality of life measures are subjective to some extent (Frisch 1999).

An example of a widely used measure of health-related quality of life is the 36-item Medical Outcomes Study Short Form (SF-36) (Ware et al. 1994), whereas an example of a widely used measure of subjective quality of life is the brief World Health Organization Brief Quality of Life Assessment (WHOQOL-BREF) (WHOQOL Group 1998). The SF-36 is a 36-item, self-report measure, assesses the impact of health problems on functioning in eight domains (e.g. physical functioning, general health, social functioning, vitality), while also providing summary "physical health" and "mental health" scores (Ware et al. 1994). The WHOQOL-BREF, a 26-item self-report measure, yields scores on four domains relating to a person's subjective satisfaction with physical health, psychological health, social relationships and environment (WHOQOL Group 1998).

A second important distinction in quality of life assessment is that between generic measures of quality of life. Such measures assess a person's ability to function and/or his or her subjective well-being without reference to any specific symptoms or behaviors. There are also disease-specific measures, which assess the extent to which functioning in or satisfaction with different aspects of one's life may be affected by the specific symptoms or behaviors associated with a particular condition (Coelho *et al.* 2005; Engel *et al.* 2009). To date, much of the research addressing quality of life among people with eating disorders has employed generic quality of life measures, such as the Nottingham Health Profile, SF-36, the brief, 12-item version of SF-36 (SF-12) (Ware *et al.* 1996), and the WHOQOL-BREF (Jenkins *et al.* 2011). In recent years, however, a number eating-disorders-specific quality of life measures have been developed (Engel *et al.* 2009).

The putative advantage of disease-specific measures is that they are apt to be more sensitive to the improvements in quality of life that, it is hoped, accompany clinical interventions. A problem with these measures, however, is that they require the respondent to partition perceived impairment in different aspects of his or her functioning into that due to eating disorder symptoms and that due to other factors. Given the comorbidity of eating disorders with anxiety and affective disorders and medical problems, judgments of this kind may be problematic (Mond *et al.* 2004; Mond and Hay 2007). Therefore, for routine monitoring of quality of life outcomes, a combination of generic and disease-specific measures may be advisable.

Clinicians also need to be aware, when making use of different possible quality of life measures, of the potential for overlap with each other and with symptom measures. For example, measures of mental health impairment, such as the mental component summary scales of the SF-36 and SF-12, may be highly correlated with measures of anxiety and affective symptoms such as the Kessler Psychological Distress Scale (K-10) (Katschnig 2006; Mond *et al.* 2004). There are also high correlations between each of these measures and the psychological health subscale of the WHOQOL-BREF. Administering several highly correlated measures may be an unnecessary burden on respondents.

Available evidence suggests that community cases of people with BED have poorer quality of life than healthy people, although the nature and extent of this impairment has been found to be variable (Mond *et al.*, in press). In the US National Comorbidity Replication Study (Hudson *et al.* 2007), for example, most participants (62.6 per cent) who met DSM-IV criteria for a BED reported at least some degree of impairment in one or more domains of functioning (home, work, personal life, or social life). However, impairment among participants with a sub-threshold form of BED, which excluded the marked distress criterion, was less common (21.8 per cent), and severe impairment was relatively uncommon even among people meeting full DSM-IV criteria (18.5 per cent). There is a need for further research in both community and clinical samples to address impairment in quality of life among people with BED and variants of BED (Hay and Mond 2005; Jenkins *et al.* 2011).

Recent studies have also examined impairment in quality of life associated with specific eating disorder behaviors (Mond and Hay 2007; Mond, Rogers *et al.* 2011). One of the most consistent findings from this literature is that binge eating or, more specifically, loss of control over eating, is associated with marked impairment in quality of life independent of the occurrence of the extreme weight control behaviors characteristic of BN and variants of BN (Mond, Latner *et al.* 2010). Indeed, it was evidence of this kind that led to the inclusion of BED as a provisional diagnosis in DSM-IV (Wilfley *et al.* 2003). Further, in some studies, binge eating has been found to be stronger predictor of impairment than purging or other extreme weight-control behaviors (Hay 2003), although, in women at least, the occurrence of extreme concerns about weight or shape appears to be a stronger predictor of quality of life impairment than the occurrence of any particular eating disorder behavior (Mond and Hay 2007; Mond, Rogers *et al.* 2011).

As is the case for mental health impairment associated with BED, there is little in the way of evidence from community-based studies bearing on the issue of quality of life impairment associated with BED or variants of BED in men. It is reasonable to speculate that the impact of binge eating and other eating disorder behaviors on quality of life in men is increasing and findings from recent studies are consistent with this hypothesis (Mond and Hay 2007; Mond, van den Berg *et al.* 2011; Striegel *et al.* 2012). If future research confirms that both the prevalence of binge eating and its impact on quality of life are increasing in men, then the view that eating disorders are primarily a problem of women will be increasingly difficult to defend. Efforts then would be needed to address community mental health literacy in this regard (Mond, Hay *et al.* 2010; Mond and Arrighi 2011).

References

American Psychiatric Association (1994) *Diagnostic and Statistical Manual of Mental Disorders* (4th edn), Washington, DC: American Psychiatric Association.

American Psychiatric Association (2012) *DSM-5 Proposed Diagnostic Criteria for Binge Eating Disorder.* Online. Available: http://www.dsm5.org/ProposedRevisions/Pages/proposedrevision.aspx?rid =372# (accessed 15 April 2012).

Anderson, R., and Newman, J. (1973) "Societal and individual determinants of medical care utilization in the United States", *Milbank Memorial Fund Q* 51: 91–124.

Andrews, G., Slade, T, and Issakidis, C. (2002) "Deconstructing current comorbidity: data from the Australian National Survey of Mental Health and Well-Being", *British Journal of Psychiatry* 181: 306–14.

Coelho, R., Ramos, S., Prata, J., Bettencourt, P., Ferreira, A., and Cerqueira-Gomes, M. (2005) "Heart failure and health related quality of life", *Clinical Practice and Epidemiology in Mental Health* 1: 19.

Darby, A., Hay, P. J., Mond, J. M., and Quirk, F. (2009) "The rising prevalence of comorbid obesity and eating disorder behaviours from 1995 to 2005", *International Journal of Eating Disorders* 42: 104–8.

Engel, S. G., Adair, C. E., Las Hayas, C., and Abraham, S. (2009) "Health-related quality of life and eating disorders: a review and update", *International Journal of Eating Disorders* 42: 179–87.

Fairburn, C. G., and Beglin, S. J. (1990) "Studies of the epidemiology of bulimia nervosa", *American Journal of Psychiatry* 147: 401–8.

Fairburn, C. G., Cooper, Z., and Shafran, R. (2003) "Cognitive behaviour therapy for eating disorders: a 'transdiagnostic' theory and treatment", *Behaviour Research and Therapy* 41: 509–28.

Fairburn, C. G., Welch, S. L., Norman, P. A., O'Connor, M. E., and Doll, H. A. (1996) "Bias and bulimia nervosa: how typical are clinic cases?", *American Journal of Psychiatry* 153: 386–91.

Finucane, M. M., Stevens, G. A., Cowan, M. J., Goodarz, D., Lin, J. K., and Paciorek, C. J. (2011) "National, regional, and global trends in body-mass index since 1980: systematic analysis of health examination surveys and epidemiological studies with 960 country-years and 9·1 million participants", *Lancet* 377: 557–67.

First, M., Pincus, H., Levine, J., Williams, J., Ustun, B., and Peele, R. (2004) "Clinical utility as a criterion for revising psychiatric diagnoses", *American Journal of Psychiatry* 161: 946–54.

Frisch, M. B. (1999) "Quality of life assessment", in M. E. Maruish (ed.) *The Use of Psychological Testing for Treatment Planning and Outcomes Assessment* (2nd edn) (pp. 162–70), New Jersey: Lawrence Erlbaum Associates.

Grilo, C. M., Masheb, R. M., and White, M. A. (2010) "Significance of overvaluation of shape/weight in binge eating disorder: Comparative study with overweight and bulimia nervosa", *Obesity* 18: 499–504.

Grob, G. N. (1991) "Origins of DSM-I: a study in appearance and reality", *American Journal of Psychiatry* 148: 421–31.

Hatsukami, D. K., Mitchell, J. E., and Eckert, E. D. (1984) "Eating disorders: a variant of mood disorders?", *Psychiatric Clinics of North America* 7: 349–65.

Hay, P. (2003) "Quality of life and bulimic eating disorder behaviours: findings from a community-based sample", *International Journal of Eating Disorders* 33: 434–42.

Hay, P. J., Darby, A., and Mond, J. M. (2007) "Knowledge and beliefs about bulimia nervosa and its treatment: a comparative study of three disciplines", *Journal of Clinical Psychology in Medical Settings* 14: 59–68.

Hay, P. J, and Mond, J. M. (2005) "How to 'count the cost' and measure burden: a review of health-related quality of life in people with eating disorders", *Journal of Mental Health* 14: 539–52.

Hay, P. J, Mond, J. M., Darby, A., and Buttner P. (2008) "Eating disorder behaviours are increasing: findings from two sequential community surveys in South Australia", *PLoS ONE* 2: e1541.

Hudson, J. I., Hiripi, E., Pope, H. G., and Kessler, R. C. (2007) "The prevalence and corre-lates of eating disorders in the National Comorbidity Survey Replication", *Biological Psychiatry* 61: 348–58.

Jenkins, P. E., Hoste, R. R., Meyer, C., and Blissett, J. M. (2011) "Eating disorders and quality of life: a review of the literature", *Clinical Psychology Review* 31: 113–21.

Katschnig, H. (2006) "Quality of life in mental disorders: challenges for research and clinical practice", *World Psychiatry* 5: 139–45.

Keel, P. K., Mayer, S. A., and Harnden-Fischer, J. H. (2001) "Importance of size in defining binge eating episodes in bulimia nervosa", *International Journal of Eating Disorders* 29: 294–301.

Maj, M. (2005) "'Psychiatric comorbidity': an artifact of current diagnostic systems?", *British Journal of Psychiatry* 186: 182–4.

Mond, J. M. (2012) "A voice for all in mental health research", *Journal of Mental Health* 21: 1–3.

Mond, J. M, and Arrighi, A. (2011) "Gender differences in perceptions of the prevalence and severity of eating-disordered behaviour", *Early Intervention in Psychiatry* 5: 41–9.

Mond, J. M., and Baune, B. T. (2009) "Overweight, medical comorbidity and health-related quality of life in a community sample of women and men", *Obesity* 17: 1627–34.

Mond, J. M., and Hay, P. J. (2007) "Functional impairment associated with eating disorder behaviours in a community sample of women and men", *International Journal of Eating Disorders* 40: 391–8.

Mond, J. M., and Hay, P. J. (2008) "Public perceptions of binge eating and its treatment", *International Journal of Eating Disorders* 41: 419–26.

Mond, J. M., Hay, P. J., Paxton, S. J., Rodgers, B., Owen, C., Quirk, F., *et al.* (2010) "Eating disorders mental health literacy in low risk, high risk, and symptomatic women: implications for health promotion programs", *Eating Disorders: Journal of Treatment & Prevention* 18: 267–85.

Mond, J. M., Hay, P. J., Rodgers, B., Darby, A., Quirk, F., Buttner, P., *et al.* (2009) "When do women with eating disorders receive treatment for an eating problem? Findings from a prospective, community-based study", *Journal of Consulting and Clinical Psychology* 77: 835–44.

Mond, J. M., Hay P. J., Rodgers B., and Owen, C. (2007) "Binge eating with and without the 'undue influence of weight or shape on self-evaluation': implications for the diagnosis of binge eating disorder", *Behaviour Research and Therapy* 45: 929–38.

Mond, J. M., Hay, P. J., Rodgers, B., and Owen, C. (in press) "Quality of life impairment in a community sample of women with eating disorders", *Australian and New Zealand Journal of Psychiatry.*

Mond, J. M., Hay, P. J., Rodgers, B., Owen, C., and Beumont, P. J. V. (2005) "Assessing quality of life in eating disorder patients", *Quality of Life Research* 14: 171–8.

Mond, J. M., Hay, P. J., Rodgers, B., Owen, C., and Mitchell, J. E. (2006) "Correlates of the use of purging and non-purging methods of weight control in a community sample of women", *Australian and New Zealand Journal of Psychiatry* 40: 136–42.

Mond, J. M., Latner, J. D., Hay, P. J, Owen, C., Rodgers, B., and Owen, C. (2010) "Subjective vs objective bulimic episodes: another nail in the coffin of a problematic distinction", *Behaviors Research and Therapy* 48: 661–9.

Mond, J. M., Myers, T. C., Crosby, R. D., Hay, P. J., and Mitchell, J. E. (2010) "Eating disorders in primary care: hidden morbidity still?", *Journal of Clinical Psychology in Medical Settings* 17: 56–63.

Mond, J. M., Rodgers, B., Hay, P. J., Korten, A., Owen, C., and Beumont, P. J. V. (2004) "Disability associated with community cases of commonly occurring eating disorders", *Australian and New Zealand Journal of Psychiatry* 28: 246–51.

Mond, J. M., Rodgers, B., Hay, P. J., and Owen, C. (2006) "Self-recognition of disordered eating among women with bulimic-type eating disorders: a community-based study", *International Journal of Eating Disorders* 39: 747–53.

Mond, J. M., Rodgers, B., Hay, P. J., and Owen, C. (2007a) "Health service utilization for eating disorders: findings from a community-based study", *International Journal of Eating Disorders* 40: 399–409.

Mond, J. M., Rodgers, B., Hay, P. J., and Owen, C. (2007b) "Obesity and impairment in psycho-social functioning: the mediating role of eating-disordered behaviour", *Obesity* 15: 2769–79.

Mond, J. M., Rodgers, B., Hay, P. J., and Owen, C. (2011) "Mental health impairment associated with eating disorder features in a community sample of women", *Journal of Mental Health* 20: 456–66.

Mond, J. M., van den Berg, P., Boutelle, K., Neumark-Sztainer, D., and Hannan, P. J. (2011) "Obesity, body dissatisfaction, and psycho-social functioning in early and late adolescence: findings from the Project EAT Study", *Journal of Adolescent Health* 48: 373–8.

Rothenberg, A. (1986) "Eating disorder as a modern obsessive-compulsive syndrome", *Psychiatry* 49: 45–53.

Rounsaville, B., Alarcón, R., Andrews, G., Jackson, J., Kendell, R., and Kendler, K. (2002) "Basic nomenclature issues for DSM-V", in D. Kupfer, M. First and D. Regier (eds) *A Research Agenda for DSM-V* (pp. 1–29), Washington, DC: American Psychiatric Association.

Spitzer, R. L. (1998) "Diagnosis and need for treatment are not the same", *Archives of General Psychiatry* 55: 120.

Striegel, R. H., Bedrosian, R., Wang, C., and Schwartz, S. (2012) "Why men should be included in research on binge eating: results from a comparison of psychosocial impairment in men and women", *International Journal of Eating Disorders* 45: 233–40.

Striegel-Moore, R. H., Cachelin, F. M., Dohm, F. A., Pike, K. M., Wilfley, D. E., and Fairburn, C. G. (2001) "Comparison of binge eating disorder and bulimia nervosa in a community sample", *International Journal of Eating Disorders* 29: 157–65.

Ware, J. E., Kosinski, M., and Keller, S. D. (1996) "A 12-item short-form health survey: construction of scales and preliminary tests of reliability and validity", *Medical Care* 34: 220–33.

Ware, J. E., Kosinski, M., and Keller, S. D. (1994) *SF-36 Physical and Mental Health Summary Scales: A User's Manual*, Boston, MA: The Health Institute, New England Medical Center.

WHOQOL Group (1998) "Development of the World Health Organization WHOQOL-BREF Quality of Life Assessment", *Psychological Medicine* 28: 551–8.

Wilfley, D. E., Pike, K. M., Dohm, F. A., Striegel-Moore, R. H., and Fairburn, C. G. (2001) "Bias in binge eating disorder: how representative are recruited clinical samples", *Journal of Consulting and Clinical Psychology* 69: 383–8.

Wilfley, D. E., Wilson, G. T., and Agras, W. S. (2003) "The clinical significance of binge eating disorder", *International Journal of Eating Disorders* 34 Suppl.: S96–106.

Williams, P., Tarnapolsky, A., and Hand, D. (1980) "Case definition and case identification in psychiatric epidemiology: review and assessment", *Psychological Medicine* 10: 101–14.

Chapter 7

Body image disturbance

Anja Hilbert and Andrea S. Hartmann

Case study

Every time I come across any reflective surface, I see my body and am disgusted by how fat I am. My mood gets really bad and, if there is additional stress, I can't stop myself from buying candy and chocolates. Sometimes I even start devouring them on the way home, completely out of control. I feel deeply ashamed that I am not able to deal with frustration without food, so I try to eat it in secret. After such a binge, however, I feel even fatter and more disgusted with my body than before.

C., 37-year-old obese woman with BED

Definition of body image disturbance

The term "body image" is often used ambiguously. Head (Head and Holmes 1911) and Schilder (1923) first described body image as a somatosensory representation of one's own body and a mental image that one has about oneself, constructed by perceptual impressions. These early definitions already show that body image is a construct that cannot directly be observed, involving difficulties in operationalization.

Currently, body image is defined in a multidimensional way (Rosen 1990; Thompson 1990). Figure 7.1 illustrates the components of a disturbed body image. Regarding the cognitive–emotional component, people with body image disturbance are dissatisfied with their body and are overly concerned with their weight and shape. The feelings about weight and shape may even determine their self-esteem. Perceptually, they also overestimate their body size. Additionally, body image disturbance involves behaviors like body checking, e.g., pinching themselves and checking repeatedly if pants fit. As people with body image disturbance do not feel comfortable in their body, they also hide in loose-fitting cloth or by avoiding places such as the beach.

Body image disturbance itself is not listed as a separate disorder in the Diagnostic and Statistical Manual of Mental Disorders Fourth Edition (American Psychiatric Association 2000), but it is characteristic for several disorders. For

Body Image Disturbance		
Cognitive-Emotional	Perceptual	Behavioral
• Body dissatisfaction • Weight or shape concern • Importance of weight and shape for self-evaluation	• Perceptive representation of one's body	• Avoidance • Body checking • Masking

Figure 7.1 The three components of body image disturbance

anorexia nervosa (AN) and bulimia nervosa (BN), cognitive–emotional body image disturbance is part of the diagnostic criteria in DSM-IV-TR. For AN, despite underweight, an intense fear of gaining weight or becoming fat, and a disturbance in the way in which one's body weight or shape is experienced, or undue influence of body weight or shape on self-evaluation are required. Likewise, the BN criteria reflect the latter aspect of overvaluation of shape and weight.

In contrast, for BED, body image has not been included in the DSM-IV-TR provisional diagnostic criteria. For the DSM-5, various authors agree that overvaluation of shape and weight should be represented in the BED diagnostic criteria as a specifier (e.g., Goldschmidt *et al.* 2010; Grilo *et al.* 2010). However, so far the proposed DSM-5 criteria for BED do not include such a criterion or specifier (American Psychiatric Association 2012).

Body image disturbance is also a diagnostic criterion for body dysmorphic disorder (BDD). People with body dysmorphic disorder are excessively concerned about or preoccupied with one or more imaginary or small defects of their physical appearance, e.g., alterations of the face, skin, or hair. Most people with body dysmorphic disorder also engage in repetitive body checking or avoidance.

Current state of research

Cognitive emotional component

The cognitive emotional component of body image has received most research interest (Ahrberg *et al.* 2011). It incorporates attitudes, cognitions, and emotions regarding one's own appearance. Several studies reported higher body dissatisfaction in people with BED compared with obese people without BED (Hilbert *et al.* 2002; Mussell *et al.* 1996), while other studies did not (de Zwaan *et al.* 1994; Fichter *et al.* 1993). When compared to BN, several studies showed comparable body dissatisfaction in both disorders (Barry *et al.* 2003; Fichter *et al.* 1993). While the level of depression accounted for the level of body dissatisfaction (Mussell *et al.* 1996), findings with regard to body mass index (BMI, kg/m^2) are inconsistent (Barry *et al.* 2003; Fichter *et al.* 1993).

Other studies used the silhouette technique to measure body dissatisfaction according to which people were asked to identify which of a set of drawings of different body shapes and sizes was closest to their own body and which represented their ideal body. The discrepancy between these two silhouettes was used as indicator for body dissatisfaction. No differences were found between weight-matched patients with and without BED, but body dissatisfaction was greater in people with BED than in healthy non-weight matched controls (Legenbauer *et al.* 2011; Sorbara and Geliebter 2002). In summary, whether or not people with BED show greater body dissatisfaction than those without BED who have a similar BMI is unclear; only marginal differences may exist between BED and BN, but people with BED are more dissatisfied with their body than healthy normal-weight controls.

For weight and shape concerns, assessed by interview or self-report questionnaire, results are more conclusive. Several studies revealed higher weight and shape concern and greater overvaluation of shape and weight in overweight individuals with BED than in those without BED (e.g., Mussell *et al.* 1996). Further studies indicate that weight and shape concern is comparable to that in BN (Grilo *et al.* 2010; Hilbert and Tuschen-Caffier 2005), and independent of depression and BMI (Grilo *et al.* 2010; Hrabosky *et al.* 2007). In comparison to BN, however, overvaluation of shape and weight was not present in all people with BED (Grilo *et al.* 2010). In summary, significant weight and shape concerns and overvaluation of shape and weight suggest the presence of negative cognitive body-related and self-schemata in most people with BED.

Further evidence suggests that momentary or automatic thoughts are negative and body-related as well. For example, women with BED reported more negative body-related cognitions using a thoughts checklist when looking at themselves in a mirror than those without BED (Hilbert *et al.* 2002). When asked to "think aloud" in terms of a personal "body talk", women with BED and with BN showed a higher level of negative body-related cognitions than control women without an eating disorder, but women with BN showed a stronger increase of negative body-related cognitions during mirror exposure than control women (Hilbert and Tuschen-Caffier 2005). These findings corroborate the abovementioned results on a cognitive body image disturbance in BED.

Perceptual component

Various studies in AN and BN have focused on over- or under-estimation of body size, for example, using the silhouette technique or the photo distortion technique where patients are asked to adjust a distorted picture of themselves until it depicts the actual perceived body size. The evidence on an overestimation of body size in AN and BN is mixed, however (Cash and Deagle 1997), and estimates seem to depend on mood, general self-esteem, and the respective task. Therefore, there is considerable doubt that visual body size estimation is a purely perceptive concept. In BED, Sorbara and Geliebter (2002) found no difference between obese patients with and without BED using the silhouette technique. Employing the photo distortion technique, normal-weight controls underestimated their body size by seven per cent, obese participants without BED gave an accurate judgment, while obese patients with BED overestimated their body size by nine per cent (Legenbauer *et al.* 2011).

Behavioral component

Behaviors like body checking and avoidance were reported to be more common in patients with AN and BN than in healthy controls (Cash and Deagle 1997). Likewise, patients with BED showed substantial body-related checking and avoidance (Grilo *et al.* 2005; Reas *et al.* 2005). These behaviors speak for a disturbance in the behavioral component of body image in BED, although objective evidence is lacking.

Cognitive model of body image disturbance

Body image disturbance can become very self-destructive in the form of a self-perpetuating "negative body talk". Negative feelings and thoughts about appearance are overrepresented and are maintained by negative body-related behaviour. Figure 7.2 depicts a cognitive model (Hilbert 2000) to illustrate the self-perpetuating nature of body image disturbance.

Imagine an ambiguous situation that may provoke feelings of insecurity, for example a simple look from somebody crossing the road. A person with body image disturbance may perceive this situation selectively and automatically may

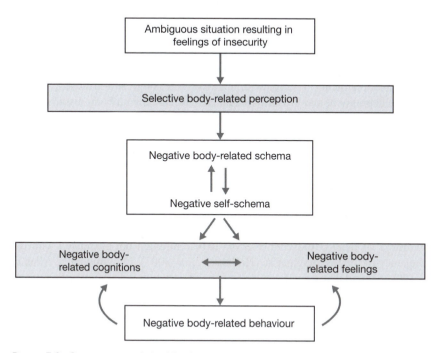

Figure 7.2 Cognitive model of body image disturbance (Hilbert, 2000)

focus on the body, with thoughts: 'Did the guy just look at me because I am fat?', and emotions such as insecurity or sadness may arise. These negative automatic thoughts may be elicited because thinking is guided by higher-level negative body-related and self-schemata. For example, generalized assumptions may include: "Only when you look good you are a valuable person." Body-related behaviour such as avoidance or checking may temporarily minimize negative thoughts and feelings, but in the long term negative body-related and self-schemata are reinforced, because corrective experiences that are not consistent with these schemata are not made. These cognitive and behavioral patterns can become part of everyday life, with body image disturbance as a heuristic to deal with any kind of ambiguous situation.

Development of body image disturbance

Body image disturbance develops against a background of the current societal thin-ideal and devaluation of overweight and obesity (Ata and Thompson 2010). Already children and adolescents pervasively face weight-related stigmatization and discrimination in many domains of everyday life (Puhl and Latner 2007), which in cross-sectional studies has been found to increase the risk for the development of body dissatisfaction in children and adolescents (Neumark-Sztainer *et al.* 2010; Shroff and Thompson 2004), adults (Shroff and Thompson 2004), and obese women with (Jackson *et al.* 2000) or without BED (Grilo *et al.* 1994). Longitudinal studies in adolescents have identified elevated body mass, pressure to be thin by peers, negative affect, parental support deficits, and dietary restraint as predictors of later body dissatisfaction (Bearman *et al.* 2006; Presnell *et al.* 2004). In BED, cross-sectional risk modeling has indicated that emotional or sexual maltreatment in childhood, childhood teasing, self-criticism, perfectionism, depression, and low self-esteem are associated with body dissatisfaction (Dunkley *et al.* 2010; Grilo and Masheb 2005). In sum, there is evidence for teasing experiences to be an etiological factor for body dissatisfaction. Other potential factors relating to BED need further investigation.

Body image disturbance as a risk factor

Body image disturbance is a well-established risk factor of eating disorders. A moderate level of overvaluation of shape and weight was cross-sectionally predictive of BED (Goldschmidt *et al.* 2010), although not associated with the frequency of binge eating per se (Hrabosky *et al.* 2007). Longitudinally, Allen *et al.* (2012) found that weight and shape concern in youth led to dieting behaviour, which in turn contributed to the development of binge eating. Overall, body image disturbance likely is a risk factor for the development of binge eating and BED, although further prospective evidence is desirable.

Body image disturbance as maintaining factor

> The biggest trigger for my binge eating is the disgust of my own fat body.
>
> G., 18-year-old overweight woman with BED

This statement illustrates that a negative body image can trigger binge eating in situations. In fact, body image disturbance plays a major role in the maintenance of BED:

> You know, my friends do not know about my problems with food. They see me as this upbeat, funny, outgoing person who likes to party. But for about one year I haven't been going out anymore. I don't like how everybody in the club can see my flabby arms and how my belly moves when I dance. But all the diets I tried did not work. I always come home hungry and eat whatever I find. Afterwards, I am angry with myself and feel ashamed. The next morning I try to start with dieting all over again, but this doesn't last long and I binge again ...
>
> G., 18-year-old overweight woman with BED

According to the cognitive behavioral model of BED (e.g., Hilbert and Tuschen-Caffier 2010) and the transdiagnostic model of eating disorders (Fairburn *et al.*

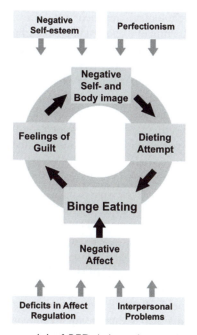

Figure 7.3 Maintenance model of BED (adapted according to Fairburn, Cooper and Shafran, 2003; Hilbert and Tuschen-Caffier, 2010)

2003), body image disturbance is part of the core pathology of eating disorders including BED. Figure 7.3 shows the vicious circle that patients with BED can end up in. A negative image of oneself and one's body, e.g., basing one's self-evaluation mainly on weight and shape, leads many patients to try to lose weight. These attempts often do not render the expected results. For example, if a person with BED decides to skip breakfast, they will be hungry at noon, and thereafter an episode of binge eating is more likely to occur, especially when in a negative mood. After this episode, the person likely will feel bad, angry, or guilty which will challenge his or her body image even further. Therefore, the next attempt to diet will follow and it often does not take long for the relapse to occur. This vicious circle can further be influenced by other factors integrated into the transdiagnostic model by Fairburn et al. (2003). Patients with high interpersonal problems, those who have difficulties in regulating their emotions, who have a very low global self-esteem, or high, perfectionist standards may be at further risk of recurrent binge eating.

Not only is body image disturbance a maintaining factor, but it is also predictive for treatment success as well as the course of the disorder (Fichter et al. 2008; Grilo et al. 2012; Hilbert et al. 2007), although not consistently (Castellini et al. 2011).

Treatment of body image disturbance

The state-of-the-art psychological treatment for BED is cognitive behavioral therapy (CBT). For the treatment of body image disturbance in eating disorders, transdiagnostic CBT primarily focuses on overvaluation of shape and weight (Fairburn 2008). Main elements are: identifying the overvaluation and its consequences, enhancing the importance of other domains for self-evaluation, addressing body checking and avoidance, addressing feeling fat, exploring the origins of overvaluation, and learning to control the eating disorder mindset. Therapeutic techniques used to target these elements are cognitive restructuring, psychoeducation, self-observation, and exposure in the case of avoidance. A meta-analysis over 38 studies indicated that both CBT and CBT self-help led to moderate, but significant reductions in shape and weight concern in the short term (Vocks et al. 2010).

Specific cognitive behavioral body image therapies have been developed for the treatment of body image disturbance. These therapies as described by Rosen (1990), Rosen et al. (1995), Cash (2008), and Vocks and Legenbauer (2010) are much more focused than general CBT on body image disturbance. Similar techniques as in CBT are used, but cognitive and behavioral techniques for body image disturbance seem to be more balanced. As for CBT, various patient groups, treatment settings and modalities are covered (e.g., eating disorders, obesity, high-risk populations; individual, group setting; treatment, self-help). Body image therapies have proven to be effective for the cognitive emotional component of body image disturbance in AN and BN, eating disorders not otherwise specified

(EDNOS), and obesity (Key *et al.* 2002; Nye and Cash 2006; Rosen *et al.* 1995; Vocks *et al.* 2008); however, without additive effects in behavioral weight loss treatment of obese individuals (Ramirez and Rosen 2001).

How cognitive behavioral body image therapy works

As an example, the 10-session cognitive behavioral body image therapy for AN and BN by Vocks and Legenbauer (2005) was initially developed for groups of patients with eating disorders, but can be used in individual context as well. At the outset, an individual model of the development and maintenance of body image disturbance is developed and psychoeducation on components of body image disturbance is provided. Dysfunctional body-related thoughts are identified and modified using various techniques of cognitive restructuring. Cognitive work is followed by exposure sessions including mirror and/or video feedback exposure tasks. Additional exposure and response prevention tasks can be applied in order to reduce body avoidance and checking behaviour and help transfer therapeutic gains into everyday life (e.g., going to the pool). Final sessions combine the enhancement of positive body-related activities and relapse prevention strategies. The authors underline the importance of between-session homework in order to elaborate the contents of each session.

Several studies evaluated specific behavioral body image interventions in BED. When comparing cognitive and emotional reactions of women with and without BED during a repeated mirror exposure (Hilbert *et al.* 2002), both groups reported significantly improved mood and appearance self-esteem as well as a reduced frequency of negative cognitions. The improvements were noted more during the second, rather than the first, exposure session. While these results provide evidence for the efficacy of body image exposure, a treatment study suggested that CBT group treatment including either a body exposure component or a cognitive restructuring component focusing on body image achieved the same substantial and stable improvements in cognitive emotional indicators of body image disturbance (Hilbert and Tuschen-Caffier 2004).

So far, exposure exercises have proven successful for the cognitive emotional component of the body image disturbance. No study has examined effects on the perceptual and the behavioral components in BED. In AN and BN, effects on perceptual indicators are inconsistent (Rushford and Ostermeyer 1997; Vocks *et al.* 2006), but behavioral indicators were consistently improved (Delinsky and Wilson 2006; Vocks *et al.* 2006).

Mirror and video exposure – a case example

During the first mirror exposure, patient G. was wearing normal street clothing. She was asked to describe all body parts from head to toe in a neutral way. To assist the patient, the therapist guided the exposure asking questions to elicit a non-judgmental description of each body part such as:

"How do your eyes look? Do you wear make-up on your eyes?" Particularly when confronted with her "problem areas" that she considered to be "fat" (e.g., her face, belly, hips, bottom, and thighs), G. engaged in negative descriptions and felt guilty, anxious, and sad. The therapist continued to ask for a realistic description of these negatively judged areas as well as positive aspects that the areas might have (e.g., her strong brown hair and her beautifully curved mouth), but also modeled descriptions such as: "You are overweight but I see your waist clearly, and in my opinion you propor-tions are good." Throughout the exposure, the therapist asked for the level of anxiety and tension, and ended the exercise only after a decreased level of both was reached. As homework, the patient was asked to conduct a mirror exposure in an exercise where she took a bath and afterwards applied body lotion, one means of reengaging in positive body-related activities. Repeated exposure in lighter clothing, summer clothing and swimming suit, in the next therapy sessions and as homework strengthened the more balanced perception of her body. Subsequently, patient G. and her therapist added a video exposure with a focus on body expression, posture, and movements. The patient was asked to imagine two different scenarios while being video-taped: a social situation where she usually feels insecure, and a situation with her family in which she feels good. In the video analysis with the therapist, G. was surprised to see that she looked much better when not obtaining the insecure posture and hiding herself but just being herself. The therapist also encouraged G. to identify and reduce other forms of camouflaging such as wearing loosely fitting dark clothes, checking such as pinching the fat on her hips, or asking for reassurance. She was advised to expose herself to the discomfort usually prompting negative body-related behaviour and to apply the techniques learned in the mirror exposure exercises. Patient G. reported to gain back more and more of her previous life, despite still being unhappy with her weight.

As the case of patient G. shows, mirror exposure is directly targeting all compo-nents of body image disturbance. From a cognitive perspective, the objective way of describing herself without slipping into negative self-depreciating remarks involves a reality check, and broadens the focus on all aspects (positive and negative) of the patient's body instead of a predominant focus on "problem areas", therefore facilitating cognitive restructuring. From a behavioral point of view, the body image exposure follows the typical anxiety reduction model by enabling habituation to feelings such as anxiety and disgust. However, it is still unclear which mechanism accounts for the efficacy of body image exposure.

Conclusion

Evidence suggests that body image disturbance is a core symptom of BED. In particular, disturbances in the cognitive emotional component of body image have been demonstrated. Therefore, people with BED experience significant weight and shape concerns as well as overvaluation of shape and weight that is partly related to overweight and depression. Preliminary evidence indicates that there might be a misperception of body size as well as body-related checking and avoidance behaviour.

Treatment of BED is not yet sufficiently successful. In order to further improve efficacy of psychological treatments, an inclusion of interventions from body image therapy might be promising, as they have proven to be helpful in AN, BN, EDNOS, and obesity, and, in preliminary studies, in BED.

With regard to the classification of BED, overvaluation of shape and weight has been considered a specifier rather than a diagnostic criterion in BED. Such a specifier would provide information on the severity of the disorder, without excluding people with BED who do not suffer from body image disturbance. Given the significance of body image disturbance as a maintaining factor for binge eating, as a predictor for treatment success, and as a risk factor for the development of eating disorder pathology, further examination of concept and treatment options for body image disturbance in BED is warranted.

Acknowledgment

Anja Hilbert was supported by grant 01EO1001 from the German Federal Ministry of Education and Research.

References

Ahrberg, M., Trojca, D., Nasrawi, N., and Vocks, S. (2011) "Body image disturbance in binge eating disorder: a review", *European Eating Disorders Review* epub ahead of print: doi: 10.1002/erv.1100.

Allen, K. L., Byrne, S. M., and McLean, N. J. (2012) "The dual-pathway and cognitive-behavioural models of binge eating: prospective evaluation and comparison", *European Child & Adolescent Psychiatry* 21: 51–62.

American Psychiatric Association (2000) *Diagnostic and Statistical Manual of Mental Disorders (DSM-IV-TR)* (4th edn, text revision), Washington, DC: American Psychiatric Association.

American Psychiatric Association (2012) *DSM-5 Proposed Diagnostic Criteria for Binge Eating Disorder.* Online. Available: http://www.dsm5.org/ProposedRevisions/Pages/proposedrevision.aspx?rid =372# (accessed 4 April 2012).

Ata, R. N., and Thompson, J. K. (2010) "Weight bias in the media: A review of recent research", *Obesity Facts* 3: 41–6.

Barry, D. T., Grilo, C. M., and Masheb, R. M. (2003) "Comparison of patients with bulimia nervosa, obese patients with binge eating disorder, and nonobese patients with binge eating disorder", *Journal of Nervous and Mental Disease* 191: 589–94.

Bearman, S. K., Martinez, E., Stice, E., and Presnell, K. (2006) "The skinny on body dissatisfaction: a longitudinal study of adolescent girls and boys", *Journal of Youth and Adolescence* 35: 217–29.

Cash, T. F. (2008) *The Body Image Workbook: An 8-Step Program for Learning to Like Your Looks* (2nd edn), Oakland, CA: New Harbinger Publications.

Cash, T. F., and Deagle, E. A. 3rd (1997) "The nature and extent of body-image disturbances in anorexia nervosa and bulimia nervosa: a meta-analysis", *International Journal of Eating Disorders* 22: 107–25.

Castellini, G., Lo Sauro, C., Mannucci, E., Ravaldi, C., Rotella, C. M., Faravelli, C., and Ricca, V. (2011) "Diagnostic crossover and outcome predictors in eating disorders according to DSM-IV and DSM-V proposed criteria: a 6-year follow-up study", *Psychosomatic Medicine* 73: 270–79.

de Zwaan, M., Mitchell, J. E., Seim, H. C., Specker, S. M., Pyle, R. L., Raymond, N. C., and Crosby, R. B. (1994) "Eating related and general psychopathology in obese females with binge eating disorder", *International Journal of Eating Disorders* 15: 43–52.

Delinsky, S. S., and Wilson, G. T. (2006) "Mirror exposure for the treatment of body image disturbance", *International Journal of Eating Disorders* 39: 108–16.

Dunkley, D. M., Masheb, R. M., and Grilo, C. M. (2010) "Childhood maltreatment, depressive symptoms, and body dissatisfaction in patients with binge eating disorder: the mediating role of self-criticism", *International Journal of Eating Disorders* 43: 274–81.

Fairburn, C. G. (2008) *Cognitive Behavior Therapy and Eating Disorders*, New York: Guilford Press.

Fairburn, C. G., Cooper, Z., and Shafran, R. (2003) "Cognitive behaviour therapy for eating disorders: a 'transdiagnostic' theory and treatment", *Behaviour Research and Therapy* 41: 509–28.

Fichter, M. M., Quadflieg, N., and Brandl, B. (1993) "Recurrent overeating: an empirical comparison of binge eating disorder, bulimia nervosa, and obesity", *International Journal of Eating Disorders* 14: 1–16.

Fichter, M. M., Quadflieg, N., and Hedlund, S. (2008) "Long-term course of binge eating disorder and bulimia nervosa: relevance for nosology and diagnostic criteria", *International Journal of Eating Disorders* 41: 577–86.

Goldschmidt, A. B., Hilbert, A., Manwaring, J. L., Wilfley, D. E., Pike, K. M., Fairburn, C. G., Dohm, F. A., and Striegel-Moore, R. H. (2010) "The significance of overvaluation of shape and weight in binge eating disorder", *Behaviour Research and Therapy* 48: 187–93.

Grilo, C. M., and Masheb, R. M. (2005) "Correlates of body image dissatisfaction in treatment-seeking men and women with binge eating disorder", *International Journal of Eating Disorders* 38: 162–6.

Grilo, C. M., Masheb, R. M., and Crosby, R. D. (2012) "Predictors and moderators of response to cognitive behavioral therapy and medication for the treatment of binge eating disorder", *Journal of Consulting and Clinical Psychology* epub ahead of print: doi: 10.1037/a0027001.

Grilo, C. M., Masheb, R. M., and White, M. A. (2010) "Significance of overvaluation of shape/weight in binge-eating disorder: comparative study with overweight and bulimia nervosa", *Obesity* 18: 499–504.

Grilo, C. M., Reas, D. L., Brody, M. L., Burke-Martindale, C. H., Rothschild, B. S., and Masheb, R. M. (2005) "Body checking and avoidance and the core features of eating disorders among obese men and women seeking bariatric surgery", *Behaviour Research and Therapy* 43: 629–37.

Grilo, C. M., Wilfley, D. E., Brownell, K. D., and Rodin, J. (1994) "Teasing, body image, and self-esteem in a clinical sample of obese women", *Addictive Behaviours* 19: 443–50.

Head, H., and Holmes, G. (2011) "Sensory disturbance from cerebral lesions", *Brain* 34: 102–254.

Hilbert, A., Saelens, B. E., Stein, R. I., Mockus, D. S., Welch, R. R., Matt, G. E., and Wilfley, D. E. (2007) "Pretreatment and process predictors of outcome in interpersonal and cognitive behavioral psychotherapy for binge eating disorder", *Journal of Consulting and Clinical Psychology* 75: 645–51.

Hilbert, A., and Tuschen-Caffier, B. (2004) "Body image interventions in cognitive-behavioural therapy of binge-eating disorder: a component analysis", *Behaviour Research and Therapy* 42: 1325–39.

Hilbert, A., and Tuschen-Caffier, B. (2005) "Body-related cognitions in binge-eating disorder and bulimia nervosa", *Journal of Social and Clinical Psychology* 24: 561–79.

Hilbert, A., and Tuschen-Caffier, B. (2010) *Essanfälle und Adipositas. Ein Manual zur kognitiv-behavioralen Therapie der Binge-Eating-Störungen*, Göttingen: Hogrefe.

Hilbert, A., Tuschen-Caffier, B., and Vogele, C. (2002) "Effects of prolonged and repeated body image exposure in binge-eating disorder", *Journal of Psychosomatic Research* 52: 137–44.

Hilbert, A. (2000) *Körperbild bei Frauen mit „Binge-Eating"-Störung* (Dissertation), Philipps University of Marburg, http://archiv.ub.uni-marburg.de/diss/z2000/0089/.

Hrabosky, J. I., Masheb, R. M., White, M. A., and Grilo, C. M. (2007) "Overvaluation of shape and weight in binge eating disorder", *Journal of Consulting and Clinical Psychology* 75: 175–80.

Jackson, T. D., Grilo, C. M., and Masheb, R. M. (2000) "Teasing history, onset of obesity, current eating disorder psychopathology, body dissatisfaction, and psychological functioning in binge eating disorder", *Obesity Research* 8: 451–8.

Key, A., George, C. L., Beattie, D., Stammers, K., Lacey, H., and Waller, G. (2002) "Body image treatment within an inpatient program for anorexia nervosa: the role of mirror exposure in the desensitization process", *International Journal of Eating Disorders* 31: 185–90.

Legenbauer, T., Vocks, S., Betz, S., Baguena Puigcerver, M. J., Benecke, A., Troje, N. F., and Ruddel, H. (2011) "Differences in the nature of body image disturbances between female obese individuals with versus without a comorbid binge eating disorder: an exploratory study including static and dynamic aspects of body image", *Behavior Modification* 35: 162–86.

Mussell, M. P., Peterson, C. B., Weller, C. L., Crosby, R. D., de Zwaan, M., and Mitchell, J. E. (1996) "Differences in body image and depression among obese women with and without binge eating disorder", *Obesity Research* 4: 431–9.

Neumark-Sztainer, D., Bauer, K. W., Friend, S., Hannan, P. J., Story, M., and Berge, J. M. (2010) "Family weight talk and dieting: how much do they matter for body dissatisfaction and disordered eating behaviors in adolescent girls?", *Journal of Adolescent Health* 47: 270–76.

Nye, S., and Cash, T. F. (2006) "Outcomes of manualized cognitive-behavioral body image therapy with eating disordered women treated in a private clinical practice", *Eating Disorders* 14: 31–40.

Presnell, K., Bearman, S., and Stice, E. (2004) "Risk factors for body dissatisfaction in adolescent boys and girls: a prospective study", *International Journal of Eating Disorders* 36: 389–401.

Puhl, R. M., and Latner, J. D. (2007) "Stigma, obesity, and the health of the nation's children", *Psychology Bulletin* 133: 557–80.

Ramirez, E. M., and Rosen, J. C. (2001) "A comparison of weight control and weight control plus body image therapy for obese men and women", *Journal of Consulting and Clinical Psychology* 69: 440–46.

Reas, D. L., Grilo, C. M., Masheb, R. M., and Wilson, G. T. (2005) "Body checking and avoidance in overweight patients with binge eating disorder", *International Journal of Eating Disorders* 37: 342–6.

Rosen, J. C. (1990) "Body image disturbance in eating disorders", in T. F. Cash and T. Pruzinsky (eds) *Body Images: Development, Deviance, and Change* (pp. 188–210), New York: Guilford Press.

Rosen, J. C., Orosan, P., and Reiter, J. (1995) "Cognitive behavior therapy for negative body image in obese women", *Behavior Therapy* 26: 25–42.

Rushford, N., and Ostermeyer, A. (1997) "Body image disturbances and their change with videofeedback in anorexia nervosa", *Behavior Research and Therapy* 35: 389–98.

Schilder, P. (1923) *Das Körperschema. Ein Beitrag zur Lehre vom Bewusstsein des eigenen Körpers*, Berlin: Springer.

Shroff, H., and Thompson, J. K. (2004) "Body image and eating disturbance in India: media and interpersonal influences", *International Journal of Eating Disorders* 35: 198–203.

Sorbara, M., and Geliebter, A. (2002) "Body image disturbance in obese outpatients before and after weight loss in relation to race, gender, binge eating, and age of onset of obesity", *International Journal of Eating Disorders* 31: 416–23.

Thompson, J. K. (1990) *Body Image Disturbance: Assessment and Treatment*, New York: Pergamon Press.

Vocks, S., Kosfelder, J., Wucherer, M., and Wachter, A. (2008) "Does habitual body avoidance and checking behavior influence the decrease of negative emotions during body exposure in eating disorders?", *Psychotherapy Research* 18: 412–19.

Vocks, S., and Legenbauer, T. (2005) *Körperbildtherapie bei Anorexia und Bulimia nervosa. Ein kognitiv-verhaltenstherapeutisches Behandlungsprogramm*, Göttingen: Hogrefe.

Vocks, S., and Legenbauer, T. (2010) *Körperbildtherapie bei Anorexia und Bulimia nervosa. Ein kognitiv-verhaltenstherapeutisches Behandlungsprogramm (2. überarbeitete Auflage)*, Göttingen: Hogrefe.

Vocks, S., Legenbauer, T., Troje, N., and Schulte, D. (2006) "Körperbildtherapie bei Essstörungen: Beeinflussung der perzeptiven, kognitiv-affektiven und behavioralen Körperbildkomponente". ["Body image therapy in eating disorders: Interaction of the perceptual, cognitive–affective and behavioral body image components"], *Zeitschrift Fur Klinische Psychologie Psychiatrie und Psychotherapie* 35: 286–95.

Vocks, S., Tuschen-Caffier, B., Pietrowsky, R., Rustenbach, S. J., Kersting, A., and Herpertz, S. (2010) "Meta-analysis of the effectiveness of psychological and pharmacological treatments for binge eating disorder", *International Journal of Eating Disorders* 43: 205–17.

Chapter 8

Why science matters

Carrie Arnold

When I began treatment for my eating disorder, I didn't know that science had a place in my therapist's office. My therapist's office held the therapist (obviously), me, a couch, and maybe a few bookshelves. None of the therapists I saw mentioned the research that supported their recommendations – not that I would have listened, anyway, not with my eating disorder firmly in charge. Science was for academia, for people in white lab coats. Strange things like Tukey's post-hoc test and ANOVA (Analysis of Variance) didn't seem to have anything to do with my recovery.

Except that it did. Some of the seemingly crazy things my therapist asked me to do – things like food logs and thought-restructuring worksheets – actually had a lot of research behind them saying that they helped with recovery. I didn't know that. Worksheets made me just roll my eyes, although I did keep freakishly accurate food logs. Some of the therapists that I saw seemed to pick their approach out of a hat, on a whim. They described their approach as "eclectic". I blindly trusted that these treatment providers were using the latest and best practices to help me recover.

Although I didn't suffer from BED, many of the thoughts and feelings that accompanied my eating disorder were eerily similar to many of the BED sufferers I have met. Many of the eating disorder symptoms I found distressing – the constant obsession with food, feelings of hopelessness, and loss of self-worth – were as much a result of the disorder as they were a cause of behaviors. Treat the eating disorder, I found, and the rest would follow. I have found similar things with other sufferers, irrespective of their actual diagnosis. Once their eating behaviors were better managed, they could better utilize the therapy to work on other, co-occurring conditions. Several decades of research supports these anecdotes.

In my advocacy work with eating disorder sufferers and their families, as well as my own personal journey to recovery after more than a decade with an eating disorder, I have learned that science can make the difference between someone receiving appropriate, intensive care and their being left to flounder for years. Of course, just because a treatment is backed by numerous scientific studies doesn't mean that it will work for every person, but it does mean that it's the best treatment we've got and provides a good starting point for most people.

Although psychology is a science, the idea of evidence-based treatment (or empirically supported treatment) isn't always received with open arms, and the eating disorder field is no exception. Not only does science help eating disorder treatment providers, an understanding of the latest research studies also helps patients. Most people with eating disorders aren't trained scientists, and therefore they need help in translating the often-arcane language of research journals into fodder for their everyday lives.

When someone with binge eating disorder (BED) presents for treatment, he or she often feel guilty and ashamed. The binge eating has probably resulted in weight gain. The person's eating behaviors feel out of control. He or she is filled with self-loathing and desperate to stop stuffing him or herself on a regular basis. Anxiety and depression frequently accompany BED, too. As a result, the patient feels isolation and despair.

Basic psychoeducation about the prevalence of BED and the common feelings that accompany binge eating can help to relieve some of those negative feelings. One in thirty-five Americans has BED (Bulik 2009). Over half of all people with BED have a mood disorder (Grilo et al. 2009). Out-of-control eating is actually a hallmark of a binge, which makes these feelings normal and even expected for someone with BED. Ditto for the weight gain. Knowing that lots of other people understand these tumultuous feelings can be a powerful tool against isolation and despair (Levine 2012).

This information is based on science. The white lab-coat-wearing crowd might not have done it, but it is science nonetheless. Statistics, however, don't treat BED. The science doesn't need to stop at psychoeducation. It should frame treatment recommendations and the course of care. It's easy to reject using science and randomized control trials as the basis for treatment because they sound so cold, clinical, and lack the important factors of warmth, caring, and the human touch. Just as statistics don't treat BED, science in and of itself doesn't treat BED, either. Psychologists, psychiatrists, dietitians, and others using this science, however, do.

Which is all well and good, people might say, but why should a BED sufferer actually care about science? Data wonks like yours truly may find p values inherently intriguing, but most people don't. As someone who writes about science for popular magazines and national newspapers, I have found that most people are interested in science – they just don't know it. They think they can't understand it, or that it's not for them. With a little bit of work, treatment providers can make the science of BED both interesting and accessible. It's about them, and most people find themselves to be an inherently important subject.

Science helps sufferers in a variety of ways.

Science provides hope

Studies show that most people with BED do recover (Wilson et al. 2010). They go on to live healthy, full lives without the compulsion to binge eat. It's not uncommon for eating disorder sufferers to feel that recovery is impossible and out of reach. Knowing that most people conquer BED can provide confidence in treatment and the recovery process.

Science provides reality

Alongside the hope for full recovery exists the tendency to relapse and return to old behaviors, especially in the early stages of recovery and under times of stress. If a patient knows to expect this, he or she can take measures to increase support at vulnerable times. As well, it can be easy to write off all of the progress made in recovery when someone slips or relapses. Yet most people who recover from BED have likely relapsed and come out the other side. In fact, some people have said that a relapse provided the most learning opportunities and ultimately pushed them towards recovery (McGowan 2010). This can help a patient reframe a relapse from the end of the world to a way to learn and move forward.

Many of the men and women I've spoken with who have sought treatment for BED say that one of their primary motivations for entering treatment for their eating disorder is weight loss. Although successful BED treatment often prevents further weight gain and may result in very modest weight loss, it generally doesn't result in the significant weight loss that patients often hope for (Blomquist *et al.* 2011). When this weight loss doesn't materialize, patients can become dissatisfied and leave treatment before their disorder is under control. Psychoeducation in the beginning phase of treatment using this research may help patients develop more realistic and attainable goals for treatment.

Science provides choices

Instead of simply accepting the type of therapy they're offered, or thinking that all types of therapy are created equal, science provides BED sufferers with options. Two types of therapy have been shown by different studies to be effective in the treatment of BED (Hilbert *et al.* 2012). Cognitive behavioral therapy (CBT) focuses on the maladaptive thinking patterns (cognitions) that drive a person's tendency to binge eat, and by changing this thinking, a person can change his or her behaviors. CBT typically uses such techniques as identifying irrational thoughts, known formally as cognitive distortions, and figuring out new ways to think about the situation. Many CBT therapists also ask BED patients to keep food logs to work on normalizing eating habits and tracking common emotions that may trigger binge eating (Fairburn 1995).

Interpersonal therapy (IPT) focuses on improving relationships and developing interpersonal skills. Originally developed for depression, IPT has been adapted to help treat a number of conditions, including post-traumatic stress disorder, bulimia nervosa, and BED (Weissman and Markowitz 1998). Like CBT, IPT has a strong focus on improving cognition and homework assignments. Depending on their needs and preferences, patients can choose between empirically supported therapies as they move through recovery. A therapist can also provide guidance towards the right treatment modality based on the patient's characteristics (Grilo *et al.* 2012).

Science can eliminate blame

In my own eating disorder treatment, I spent many years searching for the "why" of my disorder. My life became a veritable witch-hunt to find the people and events that caused my disorder. This blame game only served to alienate me from the people who could help me the most, and to leave me ultimately blaming myself for not being able to give up my eating disorder and recover. In the end, looking for blame helped no one, least of all myself.

Although much of the work on genetics and eating disorders has focused on anorexia and bulimia, scientists have begun to look more closely at binge eating. Studies have found that genetics plays a significant role in the likelihood that someone develops BED (Mitchell *et al.* 2010), and scientists have also discovered that puberty is an especially vulnerable time for the onset of binge eating, especially in females (Klump *et al.* 2011). Although researchers don't know exactly what causes BED, they do know that an eating disorder isn't anyone's fault. Instead of focusing on why someone may have developed an eating disorder, they can start to ask "now what?"

Science can provide a roadmap to recovery

No two BED recoveries will be identical because no two disorders are identical. Still, many recoveries are built on a similar foundation. One of the cornerstones of this foundation is eating regular meals, especially breakfast. To many people with BED, the thought of eating more seems antithetical to treatment – isn't the idea to eat less? Well, yes, but taking time for actual, sit-down meals can prevent the extreme hunger and blood sugar swings that lead to binge eating. This finding is so consistent that it has been identified in several large studies (Agras and Telch 1998; Arnow *et al.* 1992).

When scientists reviewed data from the National Weight Control Registry, which tracks information on people who have lost 30 or more pounds and kept it off for a minimum of a year, they found that 80 per cent of people in the registry ate breakfast every single day, and 90 per cent of the people at breakfast four or more days per week (Wyatt *et al.* 2002). In a separate study, researchers found that people who ate the largest portion of their daily calories at breakfast had the lowest BMIs (Purslow *et al.* 2008). Although the specific goal of BED treatment is a cessation in binge eating and not weight loss per se, this information can help patients see that eating breakfast and the normalization of eating habits won't lead to weight gain.

Science gives greater understanding

Many people with BED are told to snap out of it, or just stop eating. Of course, if it were that simple, books like this one wouldn't be necessary. But that doesn't stop friends, family, and co-workers from saying these things. Understanding the science of BED, and the biological factors that contribute to the disorder, can help reduce stigma and improve understanding of the disorder.

Researchers at the University of North Carolina, Chapel Hill asked a group of undergraduate nursing students to read one of two vignettes about a person with anorexia nervosa. One of the vignettes emphasized the biological nature of anorexia, whereas the other vignette emphasized sociocultural factors. The students that read the biological vignette were much less likely to blame the sufferer for their disorder. The researchers concluded that biological explanations for anorexia were a way to reduce the blame and shame surrounding the disorder (Crisafulli *et al.* 2008). Although this study didn't specifically look at BED, there's no reason to think that a similar approach to BED would have different results.

In the end, learning about science won't cure BED. It didn't cure my eating disorder, but it did give me a way forward. The hardest thing for me to overcome was the cycle of eating disorder symptoms. I would use eating disorder behaviors, feel guilty, lost, and hopeless, and then continue using behaviors as a way to alleviate these negative feelings. As well, my erratic eating habits fed the neuro-chemical chaos that drove me deeper into my disorder. To break this cycle, I needed to address my nutritional status first. At first, my therapy focused more on damage control, at identifying the factors that were keeping me from interrupting my symptoms. Then, as my eating disorder behaviors got more under control, I could address the depression, anxiety, perfectionism, and low self-esteem that fed my disorder.

References

Agras, W. S., and Telch, C. F. (1998) "The effects of caloric deprivation and negative affect on binge eating in obese binge-eating disordered women", *Behavior Therapy* 29: 491–503.

Arnow, B., Kenardy, J., and Agras, W. S. (1992) "Binge eating among the obese: a descriptive study", *Journal of Behavioral Medicine* 15: 155–70.

Blomquist, K. K., Barnes, R. D., White, M. A., Masheb, R. M., Morgan, P. T., and Grilo, C. M. (2011) "Exploring weight gain in year before treatment for binge eating disorder: a different context for interpreting limited weight losses in treatment studies", *International Journal of Eating Disorders* 44: 435–9.

Bulik, C. M. (2009) *Crave: Why You Binge Eat and How to Stop*, New York: Walker Books.

Crisafulli, M. A., Von, Holle, A., and Bulik, C. M. (2008) "Attitudes towards anorexia nervosa: the impact of framing on blame and stigma", *International Journal of Eating Disorders* 41: 333–9.

Fairburn, C. (1995) *Overcoming Binge Eating*, New York: The Guilford Press.

Grilo, C. M., Masheb, R. M., and Crosby, R. D. (2012) "Predictors and moderators of response to cognitive behavioral therapy and medication for the treatment of binge eating disorder", *Journal of Consulting and Clinical Psychology* DOI: 10.1037/a0027001.

Grilo, C. M., White, M. A., and Masheb, R. M. (2009) "DSM-IV psychiatric disorder comorbidity and its correlates in binge eating disorder", *International Journal of Eating Disorders* 42: 228–34.

Hilbert, A., Bishop, M. E., Stein, R. I., Tanofsky-Kraff, M., Swenson, A. K., Welch, R. R., and Wilfley, D. E. (2012) "Long-term efficacy of psychological treatments for binge eating disorder", *British Journal of Psychiatry* 200: 232–7.

Klump, K. L., Suisman, J. L., Culbert, K. M., Kashy, D. A., and Sisk, C. L. (2011) "Binge eating proneness emerges during puberty in female rats: a longitudinal study", *Journal of Abnormal Psychology* 120: 948–55.

Levine, M. P. (2012) "Loneliness and eating disorders", *Journal of Psychology* 146: 243–57.

McGowan, K. (2010) "The New Quitter". Online. Available: <http://www.psychologytoday.com/articles/201007/the-new-quitter> (accessed 22 May 2012).

Mitchell, K. S., Neale, M. C., Bulik, C. M., Aggen, S. H., Kendler, K. S., and Mazzeo, S. E. (2010) "Binge eating disorder: a symptom-level investigation of genetic and environmental influences on liability", *Psychological Medicine* 40: 1899–906.

Purslow, L. R., Sandhu, M. S., Forouhi, N., Young, E. H., Luben, R. N., Welch, A. A., *et al.* (2008) "Energy intake at breakfast and weight change: prospective study of 6,764 middle-aged men and women", *American Journal of Epidemiology* 167: 188–92.

Weissman, M. M., and Markowitz, J. C. (1998) "An overview of interpersonal psychotherapy", in J. Markowitz (ed.) *Interpersonal Psychotherapy (*pp. 1–33), Washington DC: American Psychiatric Press.

Wilson, G. T., Wilfley, D. E., Agras, W. S., and Bryson, S. W. (2010) "Psychological treatments of binge eating disorder", *Archives of General Psychiatry* 67: 94–101.

Wyatt, H. R., Grunwald, G. K., Mosca, C. L., Klem, M. L., Wing, R. R., and Hill, J. O. (2002) "Long-term weight loss and breakfast in subjects in the National Weight Control Registry", *Obesity Research* 10: 78–82.

Part 2

The search for solutions

Introduction

Closing the research–practice gap

Judith Banker

The field of eating disorders has acknowledged that its research findings are not regularly applied in clinical practice, and that the knowledge and observations of clinicians have little impact on the direction of research (Banker and Klump 2010; Mussell *et al.* 2000). While steps are being taken in the field to bridge research and practice, this endeavor is fraught with even greater levels of complexity in the assessment, diagnosis and treatment of people with binge eating disorder (BED).

Until the inclusion of BED in the DSM-5, people with BED were folded in to the nondescript diagnostic category of EDNOS. This category has been commonly excluded from research trials, yet it has been the most widely used clinical diagnosis (Walsh and Sysko 2009). Therefore, outside of several RCTS for BED since the late 1990s, clinicians treating people with BED have been compelled to rely primarily on their clinical expertise to develop treatments that borrow from the anorexia nervosa (AN), bulimia nervosa (BN), and obesity research literature. This chapter reviews the key findings from current eating disorder treatment research which apply specifically to BED and summarizes current popular BED treatment approaches developed and practiced by clinicians. Areas of overlap, division, and gaps in knowledge will be outlined. A "virtuous cycle" model for research–practice integration will be presented that is applicable for researchers and practitioners. Steps will be described that clinicians can take to participate in the cycle and therefore contribute to the knowledge base on BED treatments and influence BED treatment research directions.

A research–practice gap is endemic in fields with both applied and basic science components (Banker and Klump 2010: 460) and the field of eating disorders is no exception. The general dynamic goes something like this: those from the applied or praxis side of our field view research as irrelevant and unrealistic while those from the basic science side believe practice that is not based on research is not being done correctly. The forces that feed research–practice tensions are complex and varied, and include a combination of systemic, institutional, and relational factors (Banker and Klump 2009, 2010). As in any relationship, new, major developments accentuate the areas of disagreement or tension. While this is a challenge to the relationship, it is also, if managed effectively, an opportunity for growth and maturation. The inclusion of BED as an eating disorder diagnostic category in the DSM-5 certainly represents a major development in the field of eating disorders and therefore will inevitably aggravate pre-existing tensions in the field and perhaps trigger new ones. At the same time the inclusion of BED as an "official" eating disorder is a development that presents new opportunities for research and treatment, and for deepening our understanding of BED and of all eating disorders. To make the most of this time of unique opportunity for growth in our field it is essential that we respond proactively, with strategies in place to minimize tensions and to foster optimal collaboration, communication, and respect among key stakeholders.

Before outlining a model and strategies for how best to leverage ramifications of the inclusion of BED in the DSM-5 into a new level of research–practice integration, I will review the dynamics underlying the research–practice divide, specifically in the field of eating disorders, and describe steps that are already being implemented within the field to foster research–practice integration. An issue that captures the essence of the divide is the ongoing debate about the use of evidence-based treatments (EBTs) in eating disorder clinical care. Despite the fact that eating disorder treatment guidelines around the world recommend the use of evidence based therapies as the first line treatment of choice, research consistently shows limited utilization of these therapies by practitioners[1] (Mussell *et al.* 2000; von Ranson and Robinson 2006; Wilson 1998). With increasing support for the use of family-based therapy (FBT) in the treatment of adolescents with AN (Le Grange and Eisler 2009; Lock *et al.* 2001), and well-established research support for the use of cognitive behavioral therapy (CBT) and interpersonal psychotherapy (IPT) in the treatment of BN (Agras *et al.* 2000; Fairburn *et al.* 1993; McIntosh *et al.* 2000), one might expect to see these practices routinely implemented in clinical practice settings. Yet clinicians do not typically use these methods as their primary treatment approach (Arnow 1999; Crow *et al.* 1999). For example, one study reported that despite practice guideline recommendations for the use of CBT as a first-line treatment of choice for BN only 6.9 per cent of patients with BN are treated using CBT (Crow *et al.* 1999:39).

In fact, a minority of clinicians report that they adhere to a single theoretical approach in their treatment of patients with eating disorders. Instead most prefer to draw on a variety of treatments, reporting that manualized treatments are simply not practical for use in the treatment of patients with complex comorbidities and/or more severe, enduring symptoms, and, further, that little guidance is provided on how to adapt these treatments to meet the individualized needs of patients (Haas and Clopton 2003). Interestingly, however, clinicians do not appear to reject CBT out of hand. While most clinicians do not use the strict manualized form of CBT in their work with patients with eating disorders, they do regularly use CBT principles in their practice (Tobin *et al.* 2007; von Ranson and Robinson 2006). For example, regardless of their theoretical orientation, the majority of therapists regularly employ the following CBT-informed strategies in their treatments: teaching coping skills, psychoeducation about eating disorder symptoms and mental illness, suggestions of new behaviors to try, and requesting that patients keep records of important symptoms and behaviors (Tobin *et al.* 2007). Therefore, therapists are not entirely rejecting the utility of the content of manualized treatments like CBT, but rather the manualized form of delivery.

The problem with this, according to researchers, is that the manualized forms of EBTs are what have been tested repeatedly in research trials. It is the careful standardization of these treatment protocols that leads to the most reliable empirical findings. As therapists adapt EBTs to clinical practice, this standardization rapidly dissolves. The manual is discarded or perhaps used as a reference resource while strategies are selected and applied by the therapist in a manner that suits the therapist's purposes. The net result of this adaptation process is that the treatment intervention or approach ultimately utilized by the therapist bears little resemblance to the treatment protocol that garnered significant empirical findings. While clinicians argue the necessity of adapting EBTs to suit the exigencies of community-based treatment, researchers lament that when EBTs, so carefully studied under tightly controlled conditions in order to meet the highest scientific standards, are adapted by clinicians, they are actually "poorly delivered" in forms that have little or no evidence base (Shafran *et al.* 2009: 2). To promote the best practice of EBTs, researchers have focused on dissemination efforts by widely publishing treatment manuals (Agras and Apple 1997; Fairburn *et al.* 1993; Lock *et al.* 2001) and by calling for improved access to training and supervision in EBTs (Crow *et al.* 1999; Wilson 1998). As these attempts have reaped meager results, researchers posit that one factor perhaps contributing to the ongoing low utilization rate of ESTs is a reactionary attitude on the part of clinicians, a rigid adherence to familiar practices with a resistance to learning new treatments (Fairburn 2005). In response to these interpretations, clinicians state that they feel "under attack" and that their clinical wisdom and experience is being devalued (Banker and Klump 2010: 463). Clearly, this represents an impasse of seismic proportions.

One step toward bridging the gap in this instance is to target the study of the effectiveness of the adapted, integrated form of "treatment as usual" that appears to be widespread in community settings. The stalemate over the dissemination of ESTs in to clinical practice could shift if we had clear data comparing the effectiveness of ESTs adapted in "treatment as usual" to the efficacy of ESTs applied in their manualized forms. In addition, if in investigating the effectiveness of ESTs as implemented in community settings, it emerges that there is widespread uniformity in the way ESTs are incorporated in to and applied in an integrated treatment approach, we may learn more about the mechanisms of change or the essential aspects of ESTs that produce change.

In many fields the research–practice gap is defined as the time lag between the publication of new research findings and the application of these findings to practice (Demaerschalk 2004; Fain 2003). This definition presupposes a top-down, uni-directional knowledge flow. If we apply this definition of the gap to the dynamic in the field of eating disorders we would presume that the knowledge is generated in the research laboratory in the form of empirical findings or EBTs. The knowledge about EBTs is then transferred to practitioners via journal articles, books, conferences, and via other types of training settings. This is where the gap emerges. Despite a range of efforts by the research community to disseminate evidence-based treatments, clinicians are slow to access this knowledge or simply do not adopt it in their practice.

It is important to note that clinicians are not resisting new knowledge altogether. Rather, clinicians are enthusiastically pursuing new knowledge, albeit not from research trials. While researchers value the concrete, quantifiable, and highly controlled environment of the laboratory, in particular randomized controlled trials, clinicians value the wisdom and expertise gained from clinical observation and experience (Banker and Klump 2010). Therefore, clinicians continue to hone their skills and techniques, learning new ways to help patients and families. But they prefer to learn these new skills and approaches from other clinicians. So while researchers and clinicians share the goal of improving the lives of patients with eating disorders and their families, they pursue this goal on parallel, often non-intersecting tracks. Further, their parallel pursuits are carried on amid layers of mutual tension and mistrust. Clearly, this top-down, one-directional path to knowledge transfer, from laboratory to clinical practice, is not working. As it turns out, a rupture in this approach to knowledge transfer is more the rule than the exception. The Institute of Medicine (2001) estimates that the time between the discovery of an effective treatment and its incorporation into routine care is as long as 17 years.

It is against this backdrop that the diagnostic inclusion of BED comes in to play, bringing new and interesting challenges to this already complex dynamic in the field of eating disorders. The worlds of research and practice in the treatment, study, and prevention of BED have been striated for decades. Binge eating without accompanying compensatory behaviors was identified in the late 1950s as a common behavior in obese individuals (Stunkard 1959). However, the particular symptom constellation known as BED languished in diagnostic limbo since it was first identified in contemporary eating disorder literature in the early 1980s (Gormally *et al.* 1982; Marcus *et al.* 1985). Until its inclusion in the DSM-5, the diagnosis of BED was folded in to the diagnostic category of eating disorder not otherwise specified (EDNOS), a general diagnostic category that, due to its lack of specificity, has not commonly been the subject of empirical research. Ironically, however, since most cases of eating disorders did not fit neatly into the strict DSM-IV criteria for AN and BN, EDNOS has been by far the most widely used clinical diagnosis (Walsh and Sysko 2009). Therefore, since the beginning of our field, clinicians have been identifying and treating patients with symptoms of BED. Some referred to these symptoms as compulsive eating or emotional eating or binge eating. Treatments evolved, developed by clinicians and shared among clinicians, to address BED and accompanying comorbidities. In the 1970s and 1980s these treatments included behavior modification for habit change and/or weight loss, addiction models, and intuitive eating or the non-diet approaches described by authors like Susie Orbach (1978) and Geneen Roth (1982). Throughout this time and since, clinicians have drawn from their experience treating patients with AN and BN and have delivered treatments informed by CBT, dialectical behavior therapy (DBT), interpersonal therapy (IPT), and mindfulness training in their treatment of patients with BED. They have learned from their patients about the weight cycling that comes with efforts to lose weight through strict dieting. Clinicians have witnessed the weight stigma and intense shame that their patients endure inspiring them to develop the Health at Every Size (HAES) approach (Robison 2003) and to hone the approach to intuitive eating (Tribole 2003). Clinicians long ago recognized that trauma often underlies symptoms of binge eating and weight gain. They therefore have integrated approaches that target trauma, like long-term psychodynamic psychotherapy and eye movement desensitization and reprocessing (EMDR), and are drawn from principles of attachment theory and neurobiology in to their treatment of patients with BED.

Thousands of books have been written since the 1980s by clinicians and lay individuals about overcoming binge eating. As well, during this time, clinicians around the globe have conducted thousands of conference workshops, seminars, retreats, and other training sessions to teach other clinical professionals the best treatments for their patients who overeat. A US-based national organization, the Binge Eating Disorder Association (BEDA), was formed to "provide individuals who suffer from binge eating disorder with the recognition and resources they deserve to begin a safe journey toward a healthy recovery" (Binge Eating Disorder Association 2011). The interest and the dedication to treating people with BED is keen and longstanding within the clinical community and has evolved per force in the absence of significant guidance from the eating disorder research community.

As previously mentioned, BED treatment research has picked up momentum since the year 2000. Because of the overlap in binge eating behavior between BN and BED, investigators have looked to the BN literature to investigate their application to the treatment of people with BED, including psychological, pharmacological, and combination treatments. These studies have demonstrated the value of applying a range of empirically supported BN treatments to the treatment of BED, including CBT, IPT, DBT, and self-help treatments, as well as various pharmacological treatments applied in single treatment regimens and in combined psychological and pharmacological treatment regimens (Brownley *et al.* 2007; Hay *et al.* 2009; Reas and Grilo 2008; Vocks *et al.* 2010; Wonderlich *et al.* 2003). To date, CBT, guided self-help based on CBT (CBTgsh), and IPT demonstrate the strongest empirical support of the BED treatments tested in randomized controlled trials (RCTs), not only for the reduction of binge eating but also in the reduction of the associated symptoms of over-concern with eating, weight, and shape (Brownley *et al.* 2007; Fairburn 1995; Sysko and Walsh 2008; Vocks *et al.* 2010; Wilson *et al.* 2010), and depression (Wilson 2011). DBT shows promise but more studies are needed before a clear determination can be made as to its efficacy in the treatment of BED (Chen *et al.* 2008; Telch *et al.* 2000,

2001). None of these treatments has been shown to impact BMI in the long term (Wilson 2011).

Behavioral weight loss (BWL) has been investigated as a BED treatment for binge eaters with accompanying obesity. Behavioral interventions used in this form of treatment eschew strict dieting and a focus on an ideal weight goal in favor of promoting a healthy, balanced approach to eating, moderate and consistent dietary restraint, and an easily achieved and maintainable weight range (Wade and Watson 2012). BWL incorporating these CBT-based interventions, delivered in 20- to 30-week programs, have been shown to typically result in a weight loss of about 10 per cent of initial body weight. The ability to sustain this level of weight loss is linked to the ongoing practice of the behavioral techniques taught in the program (Wing and Hill 2001). The literature on pharmacotherapy treatments for BED indicates that certain medications can have short-term benefits in terms of remission of binge eating behavior and may enhance weight loss when combined with CBT and BWL (Munsch *et al.* 2007; Reas and Grilo 2008). In addition, important new knowledge about BED is being gained from research in areas including the treatment of children and adolescents with BED (Decaluwé *et al.* 2003; Marcus and Kalarchian 2003), the assessment of BED (Celio *et al.* 2004), the mutual impact and interaction of BED and bariatric surgery (Bocchieri- Ricciardi *et al.* 2006; Niego *et al.* 2007), and the role of abuse and trauma as risk factors for BED (Dunkley *et al.* 2010; Mitchell *et al.* 2012; Sachs-Ericsson *et al.* 2012)

The burgeoning research on BED treatment is a welcome and essential development. However, it is critical to keep in mind that throughout this time and the preceding years clinicians, faced with the responsibility of treating people with BED, including complex, enduring cases, borrowed and developed treatments and treatment philosophies based on AN and BN research, their own experience and observation, and by learning from their patients and their families, and from clinical peers and mentors. How do we begin to meld the knowledge developing on the BED research front and the body of knowledge that has grown from the study and experience of expert clinicians since the 1980s or earlier?

In order to promote the integration of the knowledge gained from the worlds of research and practice we must use consciously applied, proactive strategies grounded in an awareness of the causes and potential cures for research–practice tensions. Fortunately, the Academy for Eating Disorders (AED), a global professional association with a membership comprised of researchers, practitioners, prevention specialists, advocates, and other stakeholders, launched the AED Research–Practice Integration Initiative (Academy for Eating Disorders n.d.). Led by the AED Research–Practice Committee[2] (RPC), this initiative has outlined and continues to drive a strategic plan for fostering research–practice integration. In 2011, the RPC introduced a model for integration that offers a road map that can be applied to the challenges of bringing together the largely parallel pursuits of BED research and BED clinical treatment. If we consider the

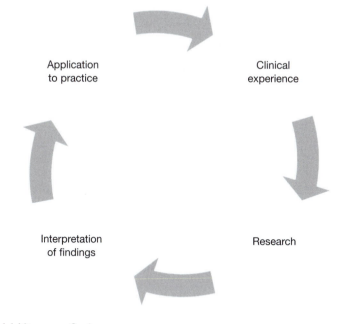

Figure I.1 Virtuous Cycle
(Developed by AED Research-Practice Committee 2011)

ongoing lackluster results from our attempts to disseminate research findings and improve clinical practice via a one-directional path of knowledge transfer from bench to bedside, we could say our field has been caught up in a vicious cycle. The AED Research–Practice Committee therefore developed a "virtuous cycle" model for research–practice integration (see Figure I.1) that addresses previous areas of contention and disagreement while promoting the involvement of all key stakeholders in enhancing the knowledge base in our field. Within this model no form or source of data or information has primacy. Clinical observation and experience, including the knowledge and experience of patients and carers, is as important as data from research laboratories. Knowledge can be introduced into the cycle at various entry-points but then becomes part of an iterative process of constant evaluation and improvement.

The viability of this model relies on three key principals drawn from the AED Research–Practice Integration Guidelines (Academy for Eating Disorders n.d.):

Scientific data and clinical observation, judgment and experience contribute to the knowledge base in our field.

Research evidence and evidence-based practice includes multiple types of evidence (e.g. efficacy, effectiveness, epidemiological, treatment utilization, etc.) drawn from a range of potential sources (e.g. laboratory and clinical settings, assessments, etc.); and evidence-based practice is not informed by randomized controlled trials alone, but rather multiple research designs (Levant 2006).

Improved communication, collegiality, and collaboration will be fostered by and will in turn help to create a universal language shared among research, clinical, advocacy, and lay stakeholders.

This Virtuous Cycle was created to provide a vision for bridging research and practice throughout the AED and the field of eating disorders. However, it holds similar promise as a model for connecting BED researchers, BED treatment and prevention professionals, and lay stakeholders. Through the use of the Virtuous Cycle the BED research community, in mutual collaboration and communication with BED treatment specialists and patient and carer experts, can learn about and test treatments as they are currently practiced in community settings and test research protocols in "real-life" treatment settings. Therefore, innovation and new developments in BED research and treatment can be built on common ground.

Certainly, the wheel of this cycle will turn slowly at first. At this time, for example, there are no well-worn natural entry points in to the cycle for clinical observation and experience. The writings and presentations of master clinicians primarily target the clinical and patient/carer community, not the academic research community. Similarly, researchers publish their findings in academic journals and interact professionally with academic colleagues or address clinicians in a one-way, didactic format, while presenting findings at meetings and conferences. The professional spheres and activities of clinicians and researchers simply take place in non-intersecting realms. Clinicians, however, can be instrumental in bridging these realms by creating an entry point for clinical wisdom and experience in the Virtuous Cycle that can have far-reaching impact on our understanding of BED and on developing the best BED treatments. Carving out this entry point can be achieved by following the steps outlined below to interface, collaborate, and communicate with like-minded members of the research community. Likewise, researchers who have the foresight to join clinicians in forging this entry point for dialogue and collaboration will benefit from the rich experience and observations of practitioners, gain access to significant pools of community-based treatment populations, and learn ways to improve the clinical relevance and thus the implementation of their research findings. Action:

• Join multidisciplinary professional groups or organizations. Many communities host informal, collegial meetings of researchers and clinicians specializing in eating disorder treatment. There are also organizations that create opportunities for clinicians and researchers to interface. The AED, for example, hosts a member listserv and member-lead special interest groups that promote interaction and discussion among members across disciplines and backgrounds. Talk and share ideas with researchers who are respectful of clinical expertise and wisdom.

- Develop a collaborative relationship with a research colleague so that you can formally test your treatments and theories and publish the results.
- Encourage your patients to take part in research protocols or collaborate with researchers who seek to test treatments in community settings.
- Find ways to access summaries or reviews of current BED treatment research findings (Banker and Klump 2010: 466). Share these findings and discuss them with colleagues.

Perhaps most importantly, BED treatment professionals who have a depth of experience should:

- Consider formally communicating their knowledge via case studies and/ or case experiments. This simple research format reaches not only clinicians, but also members of the BED research community and is eligible for submission to a number of highly regarded journals.

The case study uses a narrative, descriptive format focusing solely on the treatment of an individual patient or group of patients. It can also include the patient's perspective and the family's perspective. There are no comparison groups or experimental controls used, so no quantifiable data to present, only a detailed, intensive description of the treatment and the resulting change or lack of change (Kazdin 1981). Alternatively, the single case experiment or a case series experiment is a simple research method accessible to clinicians curious to test the effectiveness of their treatments. It is beyond the scope of this chapter to elaborate to any extent on the methodology of the case experiment, but suffice it to say that the process involves the use of easily administered standardized treatment outcome measurement tools. These tools are applied at the beginning and end of treatment and ideally at regular intervals throughout treatment, and draw conclusions based on the data gathered (Kazdin 1981). Examples of published case studies and case experiments as well as further information about how to write up and conduct case studies and case experiments, lists of journals that publish them, and lists of treatment outcome measurement tools that can be used are available at the Research–Practice Integration webpage at www.aedweb.org. Through the publication of case studies and case experiments, the treatments, theories, and observations of clinicians who have gained expertise and invaluable experience treating patients with BED will transfer into the realm of academic research and through sheer propinquity will begin to impact and inform the direction of other types of BED research.

The ongoing research–practice tension in the field of eating disorders has resulted in the loss of critical research findings and invaluable clinical wisdom and knowledge. This loss directly impacts the quality and relevance of our research and the effectiveness of our treatments. Ultimately it is our patients and their families who bear the brunt of this relational fiasco. With the guidelines created through the AED's Research–Practice Integration Initiative and the application of the Virtuous Cycle model for integration our field is taking steps to promote interaction and collaboration among researchers, practitioners, patients, and carers, and other key stakeholders. Enter the addition of BED as an eating disorder diagnostic category, carrying with it the decades of BED diagnosis and treatment experience of clinical professionals balanced against the more recent surge of BED treatment research findings. This imbalance can be mitigated and even used to advance our understanding of BED and all eating disorders, especially if practitioners use the tools of case studies and case experiments to communicate the experience and wisdom they have gained about BED aetiology, treatment, and prevention. Moreover, through the formation of researcher–clinician collaborations we can ensure that valuable clinical observations and critical research findings about BED are tested in the field and in the laboratory so that we can provide our patients with BED and their families with the highest quality treatment and research.

References

Academy for Eating Disorders (n.d.) "AED Research-Practice Initiative". Online. Available: http://www.aedweb.org/Research_Practice_Guidelines/2379.htm (accessed 11 April 2012).

Agras, W. S., and Apple, R. (1997) *Overcoming Eating Disorders: A Cognitive-Behavioral Treatment for Bulimia Nervosa and Binge-Eating Disorder: Therapist Guide*. Boulder CO: Graywind Publications.

Agras, W. S., Walsh, T., Fairburn, C. B., Wilson, B. T., and Kraemer, H. D. (2000) "A multicenter comparison of cognitive-behavioral therapy and interpersonal psychotherapy for bulimia nervosa", *Archives of General Psychiatry* 57: 459–66.

Arnow, B. A. (1999) "Why are empirically supported treatments for bulimia nervosa underutilized and what can we do about it?", *In Session: Psychotherapy in Practice* 55: 769–79.

Banker, J. D., and Klump, K. L. (2009) "Research and clinical practice: a dynamic tension in the eating disorder field!, in I. F. Dancyger and V. M. Fornari (eds) *Evidence-Based Treatments for Eating Disorders* (pp. 71–86), New York: Nova Science Publishers.

Banker, J. D., and Klump, K. L. (2010) "The research–practice gap: challenges and opportunities for the eating disorder treatment professional", in M. Maine, D. Bunnell and B. McGilley (eds) *Treatment of Eating Disorders: Bridging the Gap between Research and Practice* (pp. 459–77), London: Elsevier.

Binge Eating Disorder Association (2011) "About us". Online. Available http://www.bedaonline.com (accessed 11 April 2012).

Bocchieri-Ricciardi, L. E., Chen, E. Y., Munoz, D., Fischer, S., Dymek-Valentine, M., Alverdy, J. C., and Le Grange, D. (2006) "Pre-surgery binge eating status: effect on eating behavior and weight outcome after gastric bypass", *Obesity Surgery* 16: 1198–204.

Brownley, K. A., Berkman, N.D., Sedway, J. A., Lohr, K. N., and Bulik, C. M. (2007) "Binge eating disorder treatment: a systematic review of randomized controlled trials", *International Journal of Eating Disorders* 40: 337–48.

Celio, A. A., Wilfley, D. E., Crow, S. J., Mitchell, J., and Walsh, B. T. (2004) "A comparison of the binge eating scale, questionnaire for eating and weight patterns-revised, and eating disorder examination questionnaire with instructions with the eating disorder examination in the assessment of binge eating disorder and its symptoms", *International Journal of Eating Disorders* 36: 434–44.

Chen, E. Y., Matthews, L., Allen, C., Kuo, J. R., and Linehan, M. M. (2008) "Dialectical behavior therapy for clients with binge-eating disorder or bulimia nervosa and borderline personality disorder", *International Journal of Eating Disorders* 41: 505–12.

Crow, S. J., Mussell, M. P., Peterson, C. B., Knopke, A. J., and Mitchell, J. E. (1999) "Prior treatment received by patients with bulimia nervosa", *International Journal of Eating Disorders* 25: 39–44.

Decaluwé, V., Braet, C., and Fairburn, C. G. (2003) "Binge eating in obese children and adolescents", *International Journal of Eating Disorders* 33: 78–84.

Demaerschalk, B. M. (2004) "Evidence-based clinical practice education in cerebrovascular disease", *Stroke*: 35: 392–6.

Dunkley, D. M., Masheb, R. M., and Grilo, C. M. (2010) "Childhood maltreatment, depressive symptoms, and body dissatisfaction in patients with binge eating disorder: the mediating role of self-criticism". *International Journal of Eating Disorders* 43: 274–81.

Fain, J. (2003) *Reading, Understanding, and Applying Nursing Research: A Text and Workbook,* Philadelphia PA: F.A. Davis Co.

Fairburn, C. G. (2005) "Let data guide tx of eating disorders" (Guest Editorial), *Clinical Psychiatry News* 33(2): 7.

Fairburn, C. G. (1995) *Overcoming Binge Eating*, New York: Guilford Press.

Fairburn, C. G., Marcus, M. D., and Wilson, G. T. (1993) "Cognitive-behavioral therapy for binge eating and bulimia nervosa: a comprehensive treatment manual", in C. G. Fairburn and G. T. Wilson (eds) *Binge Eating: Nature, Assessment and Treatment* (pp. 361–404), New York: Guilford Press.

Gormally, J., Black, S., Daston, S., and Rardin, D. (1982) "The assessment of binge eating severity among obese persons", *Addictive Behaviors* 7: 47–55.

Haas, H. L., and Clopton, J. R. (2003) "Comparing clinical and research treatments for eating disorders", *International Journal of Eating Disorders* 33: 412–20.

Hay, P. P. J., Bacaltchuk, J., Stefano, S., and Kashyap, P. (2009) "Psychological treatments for bulimia nervosa and binging", *Cochrane Database Syst Rev* 3: CD000562. DOI: 10.1002/14651858.CD000562.pub2.

Institute of Medicine (2001) *Crossing the Quality Chasm: A New Health System for the 21st Century,* Washington DC: National Academy Press.

Kazdin, A. E. (1981) "Drawing valid inferences from case studies", *Journal of Consulting and Clinical Psychology* 49: 183–92.

Le Grange, D., and Eisler, I. (2009) "Family interventions in adolescent anorexia nervosa", *Child and Adolescent Psychiatry Clinics in North America* 18: 159–73.

Levant, R. F. (2006) "APA presidential task force report on evidence-based practice in psychology", *American Psychologisy* 61: 271–85.

Lock, J., Le Grange, D., Agras, W. S., and Dare, C. (2001) *Treatment Manual for Anorexia Nervosa: A Family-Based Approach*, New York: Guilford Press.

Marcus, M. D., and Kalarchian, M. A. (2003) "Binge eating in children and adolescents", *International Journal of Eating Disorders* 34: S45–57.

Marcus, M. D., Wing, R. R., and Lamparski, D. M. (1985) "Binge eating and dietary restraint in obese patients", *Addictive Behaviors* 10: 163–8.

McIntosh, V. V., Bulik, C. M., McKenzie, J. M., Luty, S. E., and Jordan, J. (2000) "Interpersonal psychotherapy for anorexia nervosa", *International Journal of Eating Disorders* 27: 125–39.

Mitchell, K. S., Mazzeo, S. E., Schlesinger, M. R., Brewerton, T. D., and Smith, B. N. (2012) "Comorbidity of partial and subthreshold PTSD among men and women with eating disorders in the National Comorbidity Survey-Replication Study", *International Journal of Eating Disorders* 45: 307–15.

Munsch, S., Biedert, E., Meyer, A., Michael, T., Schlup, B., Tuch, A., and Margraf, J. (2007) "A randomized comparison of cognitive behavioral therapy and behavioral weight loss treatment for individuals with binge eating disorder", *International Journal of Eating Disorders* 40: 102–13.

Mussell, M. P., Crosby, R. D., Crow, S. J., Knopke, A. J., Peterson, C. B., Wonderlich, S. A., and Mitchell, J. E. (2000) "Utilization of empirically supported psychotherapy treatments for individuals with eating disorders: A survey of psychologists", *International Journal of Eating Disorders* 27: 230–37.

Niego, S. H., Kofman, M. D., Weiss, J. J., and Geliebter, A. (2007) "Binge eating in the bariatric surgery population: a review of the literature", *International Journal of Eating Disorders* 40: 349–59.

Orbach, S. (1978) *Fat is a Feminist Issue*, London: Paddington Press.

Reas, D. L., and Grilo, C. M. (2008) "Review and meta-analysis of pharmacotherapy for binge-eating disorder", *Obesity* 16: 2024–38.

Robison, J. (2003) "Health at every size: antidote for the 'obesity epidemic'", *Healthy Weight Journal* 17: 4–7.

Roth, G. (1982) *Feeding the Hungry Heart: The Experience of Compulsive Eating,* Indianapolis IN: Bobbs-Merrill.

Sachs-Ericsson, N., Keel, P. K., Holland, L., Selby, E. A., Verona, E., Cougle, J., and Palmer, E. (2012) "Parental disorders, childhood abuse, and binge eating in a large community sample", *International Journal of Eating Disorders* 45: 316–25.

Shafran, R., Clark, D. M., Fairburn, C. G., Arntz, A., Barlow, D. H., Ehlers, A., Freeston, M., Garety, P. A., Hollon, S. D., Ost, L. G., Salkovskis, P. M., Williams, J. M. G., and Wilson, G. T. (2009) "Mind the gap: improving the dissemination of CBT", *Behavior Research and Therapy* 47: 902–9.

Stunkard, A. J. (1959) "Eating patterns and obesity", *Psychiatric Quarterly* 33: 284–95.

Sysko, R., and Walsh, B. T. (2008) "A critical evaluation of the efficacy of self-help interventions for the treatment of bulimia nervosa and binge-eating disorder", *International Journal of Eating Disorders* 41: 97–112.

Telch, C. F., Agras, W. S., and Linehan, M. (2001) "Dialectical behavior therapy for binge eating disorder", *Journal of Consulting and Clinical Psychology* 69: 1061–5.

Telch, C. F., Agras, W. S., and Linehan, M. (2000) "Group dialectical behavior therapy for binge-eating disorder: a preliminary uncontrolled trial'", *Behavior Therapy* 21: 569–82.

Tobin, D. L., Banker, J. D., Weisberg, L., and Bowers, W. (2007) "I know what you did last summer (and it was not CBT): a factor analytic model of international psychotherapeutic practice in the eating disorders", *International Journal of Eating Disorders* 40: 754–57.

Tribole, E. (2003) *Intuitive Eating: A Revolutionary Program that Works*, New York: St Martin's Press.

von Ranson, K.M., and Laverty, A.M. (2012) "Narrowing the psychotherapy research–practice gap", in J. Alexander and J. Treasure (eds) *A Collaborative Approach to Eating Disorders* (pp. 283–91), London: Routledge.

von Ranson, K. M., and Robinson, K. E. (2006) "Who is providing what type of psychotherapy to eating disorder clients? A survey", *International Journal of Eating Disorders* 39: 27–34.

Vocks, S., Tuschen-Caffier, B., Pietrowsky, R., Rustenbach, S. J., Kersting, A., and Herpertz, S. (2010) "Meta-analysis of the effectiveness of psychological and pharmacological treatments for binge eating disorder", *International Journal of Eating Disorders* 43: 205–17.

Wade, T. D., and Watson, H. J. (2012) "Psychotherapies in eating disorders" in J. Alexander and J. Treasure (eds) *A Collaborative Approach to Eating Disorders* (pp. 125–35), London: Routledge.

Walsh, B. T., and Sysko, R. (2009) "Broad categories for the diagnosis of eating disorders (BCD-ED): an alternative system for classification", *International Journal of Eating Disorders* 42: 754–64.

Wilson, G. T. (1998) "The clinical utility of randomized controlled trials", *International Journal of Eating Disorders* 24: 13–29.

Wilson, G. T. (2011) "Treatment of binge eating disorder", *Psychiatric Clinics of North America* 34: 773–83.

Wilson, G. T., Wilfley, D. E., Agras, W. S., and Bryson, S. W. (2010) "Psychological treatments of binge eating disorder", *Archives of General Psychiatry* 67: 94–101.

Wing, R. R., and Hill, J. O. (2001) "Successful weight loss maintenance", *Annual Review of Nutrition* 21: 323–41.

Wonderlich, S. A., de Zwaan, M., Mitchell, J. E., Peterson, C., and Crow, S. (2003) "Psychological and dietary treatments of binge eating disorder: conceptual implications", *International Journal of Eating Disorders* 34: S58–73.

Notes

1   To be sure, there are professionals in the field who might be dubbed researcher–clinicians or clinician–researchers. For ease of discussion, however, I refer to clinicians or practitioners and to researchers as two distinct camps of professional activity.
2   The 2011–2013 Members of the AED Research–Practice Committee include: Co-Chairs Howard Steiger and Dasha Nicholls, Co-Chair-in-training Wayne Bowers, Judith Banker, Anne Becker, Theresa Fassihi, Debbie Katzman, Isabel Krug, Michael Levine, Sloane Madden, Jonathan Mond, Laura Ratner, Dana Satir, and Christine Selby.

Chapter 9

Binge eating disorder assessment

Kelly C. Berg and Carol B. Peterson

Case study

I am a nurse manager at a local hospital, am married, and have two adolescent boys, ages 13 and 17. I'm seeking treatment for binge eating (BE), which occurs several times a week. As a child I would sneak food from my family's kitchen and hoard it in my bedroom. I would come home from school and binge in my room by myself. In typical episodes I would eat half a bag of brown sugar or a box of cookies. My BE has fluctuated in severity since childhood, with the worst periods occurring during college, my late twenties, and currently. My binge episodes usually occur in the evenings after dinner, when alone in the kitchen cleaning up and watching TV. In a typical BE episode I eat two pints of ice cream or 30 to 50 snack crackers and experience a sense of loss of control, particularly a feeling of being unable to resist eating the food that I know is in the kitchen. I have struggled with being overweight since adolescence and have made multiple attempts at weight loss, including structured programs and diet pills. My BMI has fluctuated from 24 to 36.5, based on measured height and weight, and it was 31.2 at the time of the evaluation.

Donna, a 52-year-old African American female

The accurate assessment and diagnosis of binge eating disorder (BED) can have enormous benefits for the process and outcome of treatment as well as clinical rapport (Peterson 2005). Assessment is the foundation of ongoing treatment because it can be used to inform diagnosis, identify treatment priorities, and measure treatment progress and outcome. Moreover, when psychosocial assessments are conducted effectively, the assessment process can facilitate trust, enhance clinical rapport, and reduce the likelihood of attrition (Peterson 2005). The use of structured assessment tools in conjunction with clinical interviews can improve the reliability of self-reported data and ensure that the assessment is comprehensive.

Overall, research suggests that BED is not restricted to any specific subgroup of clients based on age, gender, race, or ethnicity (e.g., Swanson *et al.* 2011), is not necessarily associated with weight status (e.g., Hudson *et al.* 2007), and is often overlooked in clinical and medical settings (e.g., Hudson *et al.* 2007; Swanson *et al.* 2011). As such, it is recommended that clinicians assess BED symptoms in all patients, regardless of their clinical or demographic characteristics. Accordingly, this chapter aims to provide guidelines for the assessment and diagnosis of BED that can be used by clinicians regardless of whether they specialize in eating or weight disorders. Topics include the following: a) diagnostic criteria for BED; b) tips for how to integrate BED assessment into a clinical interview; c) special considerations when assessing BED; and d) descriptions of several structured assessment tools that are widely used and potentially helpful in the assessment of BED symptoms.

Section I: Diagnostic criteria for binge eating disorder

The *Diagnostic and Statistical Manual of Mental Disorders*, 4th Edition, Text Revision (DSM-IV-TR) (American Psychiatric Association 2000) did not formally recognize BED as a full-threshold eating disorder (ED). Rather, the DSM-IV-TR included BED as an example of eating disorder not otherwise specified (EDNOS), a diagnosis that was assigned to individuals with clinically significant ED symptoms that did not meet criteria for either anorexia nervosa (AN) or bulimia nervosa (BN) (American Psychiatric Association 2000). However, the following specific criteria for BED were included in Appendix B of the DSM-IV-TR: a) BE, defined by the consumption of an unusually large amount of food accompanied by a sense of loss of control over eating; (b) the BE occurs, on average, twice per week for six months; c) the BE is accompanied by at least three associated features (e.g., eating more rapidly than normal, eating until uncomfortably full, eating large amounts of food when not physically hungry, eating alone because of feeling embarrassed about how much one is eating, and feeling disgusted, depressed, or guilty after eating); d) significant distress regarding BE; and e) the absence of AN and BN. It is important to note, however, that the purpose of these criteria was to encourage research on the validity of the syndrome rather than to diagnose patients in clinical practice.

With the publication of the fifth edition of the *DSM* (American Psychiatric Association 2012), several changes to the BED criteria must be noted. First, and most importantly, DSM-5 will include BED as a formal ED diagnosis. The DSM-5 criteria for BED are largely unchanged from those included in the appendix of DSM-IV-TR, including the fact that diagnoses of AN and BN "trump" BED. The exception is that the frequency and duration of BE will be reduced to once per week for three months. In sum, the diagnosis of BED requires the assessment of the following variables: a) presence and frequency of BE; b) the associated features of BE; and c) distress associated with BE. It is also generally useful to assess weight status and the presence and frequency of compensatory behaviors, as this information enables AN, BN, and potential medical co-morbidities to be ruled out.

Section II: Assessing binge eating disorder in a clinical interview

During clinical interviews, clinicians are required to obtain a comprehensive assessment while developing and maintaining rapport with the client, two goals that may, at times, be at odds with one another (Peterson 2005). Clinicians working in specialized ED clinics may choose to conduct a comprehensive assessment of BE with all patients; however, in general outpatient clinics, a comprehensive assessment of BED may not be necessary or feasible. Therefore, clinicians in general practice may choose to screen for BE and then follow up with a more comprehensive assessment if necessary.

Screening for binge eating

Questions used to screen for BED can be easily integrated into a clinical interview. Clinicians may find it easiest to transition slowly from relatively benign questions about eating patterns to more pointed questions about BE. Given that many clinicians already ask questions about sleep and eating patterns to assess patients' self-care as well as to assess potential mood disorder symptoms, these questions can provide a natural segue into a screen for BED. For example, general questions such as "What is your general eating pattern?" and "Do you ever skip meals?" can introduce the topic of eating behaviors without causing initial discomfort. At this point, clinicians can gently transition into more specific questions regarding BE, such as "Have you ever felt a sense of loss of control over your eating?" If a patient endorses BE or loss of control eating, additional probing is required to determine whether the patient meets DSM-5 criteria for BED. Although asking directly about the presence of BE may yield an affirmative response, the term "binge eating" is often defined differently by clients and patients than it is by clinicians (Beglin and Fairburn 1992). Asking about episodes of "overeating" or times when the patient believed that they had eaten too much at one time may yield more accurate responses with less confusion (Fairburn *et al.* 2008).

Making differential diagnoses

If BED is suspected, additional probing can be used to confirm a BED diagnosis. Of primary importance to differential diagnosis for BED is the presence and frequency of BE. As described above, BE is characterized by eating an unusually large amount of food and simultaneously experiencing a sense of loss of control over one's eating. Determining whether an amount of food is unusually large can be problematic. For example, most people would agree that a gallon of ice cream would be an unusually large amount of ice cream to eat in one sitting (Arikian *et al.* 2012). However, what if a patient reported eating cake and ice cream? Whether this amount of food would be considered unusually large would likely depend on a variety of factors such as the kind of cake, how many slices of cake, the size of the slices, how much ice cream, and perhaps the environmental context (e.g., at home on a typical day vs. at a holiday party). To further complicate the assessment of BE, research suggests that patient factors such as gender and BMI may impact whether an amount of food should be considered unusually large (Arikian *et al.* 2012). When assessing the amount of food consumed during BE episodes, it is generally helpful to elicit at least two specific examples of BE episodes and to obtain extensive detail about the type and quantity of food consumed as well as the context of the episode. In addition, it can be helpful to assess the extent to which these examples are "typical" of other BE episodes (Fairburn *et al.* 2008).

Loss of control can also be difficult to assess because it is a subjective feeling that may be experienced differently across patients. Although many patients may spontaneously endorse feeling as though their eating is out of their control, clinicians may find that for some patients, they will need to provide specific examples of how loss of control eating might feel. For example, the clinician could ask whether the patient felt that they could have stopped or resisted eating or whether their eating felt driven or compelled (Fairburn *et al.* 2008). Some patients may deny that their eating feels out of control because they report that their "binges" are planned in advance. However, loss of control eating can still be present in the context of a planned BE episode. Even in the cases of "planned" binges, patients will often indicate that they felt driven or compelled to carry out the binge, which reflects a sense of loss of control over their eating. In this case, the clinician can ask whether the patient felt as though they could have resisted going to the restaurant or if the patient felt as though they had to go, even if they did not really want to go. Additionally, the clinician can ascertain whether the patient could have stopped eating the food once they had started.

Once it has been established that a patient is experiencing BE episodes that are characterized by the consumption of a large amount of food and accompanied by a sense of lack of control, it is necessary to determine the frequency and duration of the episodes, the extent to which the BE episodes are characterized by the associated features of BE (e.g., eating until uncomfortably full), and whether there is significant distress regarding the BE. Additionally, it is important to rule out AN and BN, both of which "trump" a diagnosis of BED. AN can be ruled out by determining the patient's weight status, particularly the extent to which the individual is underweight. The DSM-IV-TR recommended that underweight be defined as less than 85 per cent of expected weight; however, the DSM-5 allows clinicians to exercise more clinical judgment in determining whether a patient is underweight. If a patient does not meet criteria for underweight, a diagnosis of AN can be ruled out. To diagnose BN, BE must be accompanied by the regular use of compensatory behaviors. Therefore, the absence of regular compensatory behaviors (i.e., self-induced vomiting, laxative misuse, diuretic misuse, fasting, or excessive exercise) would rule out BN. Importantly, although weight gain can be associated with regular BE, it also can indicate another medical (e.g., hypothyroidism) or psychiatric (e.g., depression) condition that may require treatment.

Questions about the onset and nature of symptoms as well as referral to a medical specialist can clarify whether weight gain is due to BED or other condition.

Case example

Donna:	My eating is just really out of control right now. It feels like every time I eat, I binge – especially at night.
Clinician:	It sounds like it feels as though the binge eating has taken over your life.
Donna:	That's right, it has.
Clinician:	Do you mind if I ask you some specific questions about your binge eating?
Donna:	No, go ahead.
Clinician:	Okay. First, I'd like you to think of a recent binge episode and describe exactly what you had to eat and how much of it you had.
Donna:	Does it matter when the binge happened?
Clinician:	If you can think of a more recent episode, perhaps one that occurred in the last month, that might be easier to remember.
Donna:	Well, I remember last night's episode. I was cleaning up after dinner and then just started eating the food that I was supposed to be putting away.
Clinician:	What types of food were you eating?
Donna:	I heated a frozen lasagna, made a salad and French bread. We had just eaten dinner. I wasn't hungry but kept eating the leftovers while cleaning up. I couldn't seem to stop myself.
Clinician:	So you had lasagna, salad, and French bread. Did you have anything else to eat?
Donna:	We also had dessert. We each had a bowl of ice cream after dinner.
Clinician:	Okay, so how much of the lasagna did you have for dinner?
Donna:	I had one square.
Clinician:	How big was the square? Can you estimate the size?
Donna:	It was probably 4″ x 4″. And then when I was cleaning up, I probably ate another square the same size.
Clinician:	What about salad?
Donna:	I think I had about a cup of salad. It was a Caesar salad.
Clinician:	Did you have any salad when you were cleaning up?
Donna:	No. It was gone.
Clinician:	And what about the bread?
Donna:	I ate a piece of bread at dinner and another one when I was cleaning up. They were slices of regular French bread, about three inches long.
Clinician:	And how much ice cream did you have?
Donna:	We each had a bowl of ice cream.
Clinician:	Do you have any idea how much ice cream was in each bowl?

Donna: Probably about 1.5 cups. And then I ate more when I was cleaning up. I ate the rest of the container. It was probably three or four more cups.

Clinician: And during this episode last night, did your eating feel out of control?

Donna: I actually felt sort of resigned. I knew what was going to happen. I knew that I was going to keep eating when I started cleaning up.

Clinician: Did it feel like you had a choice in the matter? Did you feel like you could have resisted eating more when you were cleaning up? Or did you feel like you were driven or compelled to keep eating?

Donna: No, it didn't feel like a choice. I felt I had to do it. Like with the ice cream, I had to eat it all until the container was empty. So I guess, yeah, I did feel like it was out of my control.

Clinician: That makes sense. And about how much time went by from the time you started eating dinner until you were done cleaning up?

Donna: About an hour and a half.

Clinician: You have done a great job describing that episode, especially the details of what you ate and how it felt. I really feel like I have a sense of what that was like for you. Now I'd like you to describe one more episode of binge eating. You can describe a similar episode or, if you're having different types of episodes, you could describe one of those. For example, if you have binge eating episodes at work, or during the day, or outside your home, it would be helpful to hear about those as well.

Section III: Special considerations for the assessment of binge eating disorder

All psychological assessment can be compromised by one or more biases (e.g., minimization, confusion regarding terminology; Schacter 1999). However, the assessment of BE and related symptoms can be especially challenging given the potential for inadvertent or deliberate minimization of symptoms and recall biases. In addition, special considerations may be warranted when assessing and diagnosing BED in children, adolescents, and culturally diverse groups.

Inadvertent or deliberate minimization

Patients with BED may minimize symptoms for a number of reasons. For example, some patients may inadvertently minimize symptoms because they misunderstand abstract constructs (e.g., loss of control) or because they have limited capacity for self-awareness. Confusion can often be avoided by providing concrete information about the symptoms being assessed (e.g., "By binge eating, I mean eating an amount of food that other people may consider unusually large and feeling as though you're unable to control what or how much you're eating";

First *et al.* 1995) and by obtaining detailed information whenever possible. In contrast, some patients may deliberately minimize symptom severity because of feelings of shame or an attachment to their BE (e.g., Vitousek *et al.* 1998). In such cases, accurate self-disclosure may be enhanced by conveying empathy, encouraging collaboration, avoiding criticism, and posing questions or statements in an open-ended format (Miller and Rollnick 2002). Additionally, patients may feel reassured when clinicians convey a matter of fact and accepting attitude towards topics that may be a source of shame (e.g., quantity or type of food consumed during a binge). Non-verbal signals can also affect minimization. For example, lengthy silences, hesitation, or facial cues can imply judgment, lack of expertise, or fear and should be avoided (Miller and Rollnick 2002; Vitousek *et al.* 1998).

Recall biases

Beyond minimization, information provided during a clinical interview can be influenced by a number of biases. For example, research has demonstrated that people with or without BED tend to underestimate their intake in both daily food records and retrospective recall. In addition, retrospective recall can be impacted by a person's current mood and behavior (Schacter 1999). Finally, research suggests that BE may function to reduce or mitigate negative affect (Smyth *et al.* 2007) and in the process, lead to symptoms of dissociation or cognitive narrowing (Heatherton and Baumeister 1991). As such, BE may be particularly difficult to recall accurately. To minimize recall biases, clinicians may choose to implement the timeline follow-back procedure (e.g., (Fairburn *et al.* 2008, Sobell *et al.* 1979), which orients participants to the past 12 weeks and then asks them to recall the frequency of behaviors during that period. In addition, asking detailed questions can reduce potential overgeneralization (e.g., "Are weekends any different than weekdays?"; Fairburn *et al.* 2008).

Assessment of binge eating with children and adolescents

Like Donna, other people with BED often report that their BE began in childhood or adolescence and that these episodes often occurred in secret. Indeed, recent epidemiological evidence suggests that BED is more common in children and adolescents than originally thought (e.g., Swanson *et al.* 2011). Although the symptom presentations of children and adolescents with BED are similar to those of adults with BED, two specific issues unique to the assessment of BE in children and adolescents can make assessment of BE particularly challenging in younger patients.

First, children and adolescents may have a particularly difficult time recalling the type and quantity of food consumed during BE episodes. In addition to using the timeline follow-back procedure and obtaining concrete examples as described above, clinicians may find it useful to provide pictures of food or plastic models of food to help younger clients arrive at more accurate estimates of the quantity and type of food consumed. Relatedly, the clinician's task of determining whether the amount of food consumed was "unusually large" may be especially problematic when assessing children and adolescents because nutritional requirements vary by age, gender, height, and developmental status (Tanofsky-Kraff *et al.* 2011).

Second, the criteria for BE includes "a sense of lack of control over eating during the episode", which can be difficult to assess among children and adolescents if their eating is largely controlled by their parent(s) or guardian(s). Furthermore, determining whether a child or adolescent has lost control of their eating requires cognitive skills (e.g., abstract reasoning, meta-cognition) that may not be fully developed in younger clients (Bravender *et al.* 2011). Using age-appropriate metaphors to describe loss of control can enhance comprehension. For example, the child version of the Eating Disorder Examination (see below) describes loss of control as a car rolling down a hill with no brakes. When assessing symptoms of BE in children and adolescents, consideration may also be given to parental reports and behavioral indicators (e.g., hoarding food, sneaking food).

Assessment of binge eating with diverse client groups

Assessing symptoms of BED in diverse client groups can also pose unique challenges because the cognitive and behavioral symptoms of BED need to be determined in the context of culturally normative experiences. Some types of overeating, for example, may be culturally normative and, as such, would not be indicative of BED (Becker 2011). Additionally, some culturally diverse patients and clients may misunderstand assessment questions that include concepts that are foreign in their culture (e.g., loss of control; Becker 2011). Assessments that overlook cultural differences in symptom presentations or language could lead to BED being under-diagnosed, over-diagnosed, or misdiagnosed. Asking open-ended questions, soliciting concrete examples, and clarifying abstract concepts can help ensure accurate assessment.

Section IV: structured assessment tools

When used in conjunction with unstructured clinical interviews, structured assessments can improve the reliability and scope of self-reported data (Anderson *et al.* 2004; Peterson 2005). In addition, structured assessment instruments can offer objective data regarding a patient's treatment progress and outcome, provide the opportunity to aggregate patient data for program evaluation, and improve communication between clinicians and across treatment centers.

Structured Interviews

Widely used in research, the Eating Disorder Examination (EDE) (Fairburn *et al.* 2008) is a clinician-administered interview that assesses cognitive and behavioral symptoms of EDs and is considered the most accurate and comprehensive ED assessment (Grilo 2005; Wilson 1993). The EDE can be used as either a dimensional assessment of symptom severity or as a diagnostic tool. Four subscale scores (i.e., Restraint, Eating Concern, Shape Concern, and Weight Concern) can be derived from the EDE and used to compare scores to normative data from community samples. The EDE also measures behavioral symptoms of EDs during the past three months, including the frequency of BE and compensatory behaviors. Psychometric data support the reliability and validity of the EDE (Berg *et al.* 2012) and research demonstrates that the EDE can be used to distinguish between overweight women with and without BED (Wilfley *et al.* 2000). Because the EDE is available in the public domain, the clinician can incorporate subscales or items in the context of initial or ongoing clinical evaluations (Fairburn *et al.* 2008).

Several questionnaires can be used in the context of clinical evaluations to enhance the assessment of BED symptoms. The Eating Disorder Examination-Questionnaire (EDE-Q) (Fairburn and Beglin 2008) is a self-report questionnaire that was derived from the EDE to provide a more time- and cost-efficient alternative to the interview version. A number of research investigations have supported the reliability and validity of the EDE-Q as well as its correlation with the EDE interview (e.g., Berg *et al.* 2012). Another self-report questionnaire, the Eating Disorder Diagnostic Scale (EDDS) (Stice *et al.* 2000), is a 22-item measure that can be used to derive ED diagnoses or as a dimensional measure of symptom severity. Psychometric data support the reliability and validity of the EDDS (e.g., *Stice et al.* 2000). Finally, the Binge Eating Scale (BES) (Gormally *et al.* 1982) is a 16-item self-report questionnaire used to measure the presence and severity of BE symptoms. BES scores can be used categorically to identify potential binge eaters and/or as an initial and ongoing measure of BE severity. Research has supported the reliability and the validity of the BES (Gormally *et al.* 1982) and suggests that the BED may be a useful screening instrument for BED (e.g., Greeno *et al.* 1995), provided that a follow-up assessment is used to confirm a BED diagnosis.

Conclusion

In summary, it is recommended that symptoms of BED are assessed in all patients presenting to treatment regardless of their clinical or demographic characteristics. When conducted effectively, assessment can determine the presence and severity of BED symptoms, enhance the clinical relationship, and inform treatment planning and outcome evaluation in BED. Screening for BED symptoms can be easily integrated into clinical interviews and when indicated, further assessment can be used to determine the presence and frequency of BE episodes. Assessment of co-occurring symptoms including distress about eating, weight status, and compensatory behaviors are essential for assigning an accurate diagnosis as they may indicate a different type of ED. Assessing BED can be particularly challenging in youth and culturally diverse populations given the complexity of some of the diagnostic concepts. The use of open-ended questions, collaborative clarification, concrete examples, and structured assessment tools can enhance the accuracy of assessment.

References

American Psychiatric Association (2000) *Diagnostic and Statistical Manual of Mental Disorders (DSM-IV-TR)* (4th edn, text revision), Washington, DC: American Psychiatric Association.

American Psychiatric Association (2012) *DSM-5 Proposed Diagnostic Criteria for Binge Eating Disorder.* Online. Available: http://www.dsm5.org/ProposedRevisions/Pages/proposedrevision.aspx?rid =372# (accessed 4 April 2012).

Anderson, D. A., Lundgren, J. D., Shapiro, J. R., and Paulosky, C. A. (2004) "Assessment of eating disorders: review and recommendations for clinical use", *Behavior Modification* 28: 763–82.

Arikian, A., Peterson, C. B., Swanson, S. A., Berg, K. C., Chartier, L., Durkin, N., and Crow, S. J. (2012) "Establishing thresholds for unusually large binge eating episodes", *International Journal of Eating Disorders* 45: 222–6.

Becker, A. E. (2011) "Culture and eating disorders classification", in R. H. Striegel-Moore, S. A. Wonderlich, B. T. Walsh and J. E. Mitchell (eds) *Developing an Evidence-Based Classification of Eating Disorders: Scientific Findings for DSM-5* (pp. 257–66), Arlington, VA: American Psychiatric Association.

Beglin, S. J., and Fairburn, C. G. (1992) "What is meant by the term 'binge'?", *American Journal of Psychiatry* 149: 123–4.

Berg, K. C., Peterson, C. B., Frazier, P., and Crow, S. J. (2012) "Psychometric evaluation of the Eating Disorder Examination and Eating Disorder Examination-Questionnaire: a systematic review of the literature", *International Journal of Eating Disorders* 45: 428–38.

Bravender, T. D., Bryant-Waugh, R., Herzog, D. B., Katzman, D., Kreipe, R. E., Lask, B., Le Grange, D., Lock, J. D., Loeb, K. L., Marcus, M. D., Madden, S., Nicholls, D., O'Toole, J. K., Pinhas, L., Rome, E., Sokol-Burger, M., Wallin, U., and Zucker, N. (2011) "Classification of eating disturbance in children and adolescents", in R. H. Striegel-Moore, S. A. Wonderlich, B. T. Walsh and J. E. Mitchell (eds) *Developing an Evidence-Based Classification of Eating Disorders: Scientific Findings for DSM-5* (pp. 167–84), Arlington, VA: American Psychiatric Association.

Fairburn, C. G., Cooper, Z., and O'Connor, M. (2008) "Eating disorder examination (16.0D)", in C. G. Fairburn (ed.) *Cognitive Behavior Therapy and Eating Disorders* (pp. 265–308), New York: Guilford Press.

First, M. B., Spitzer, R. L., Gibbon, M., and Williams, J. B. (1995) *Structured Clinical Interview for the DSM-IV Axis I Disorders – Patient Edition (SCID-I/P, Version 2),* New York: New York State Psychiatric Institute, Biometrics Research Department.

Gormally, J., Black, S., Daston, S., and Rardin, D. (1982) "The assessment of binge eating severity among obese persons", *Addictive Behaviors* 7: 47–55.

Greeno, C. G., Marcus, M. D., and Wing, R. R. (1995) "Diagnosis of binge eating disorder: discrepancies between a questionnaire and clinical interview", *International Journal of Eating Disorders* 17(2): 153–60.

Grilo, C. M. (2005) "Structured instruments", in J. E. Mitchell and C. B. Peterson (eds) *Assessment of Eating Disorders* (pp. 79–97), New York: Guilford Press.

Heatherton, T. F., and Baumeister, R. F. (1991) "Binge eating as escape from self-awareness", *Psychological Bulletin* 110: 86–108.

Hudson, J. I., Hiripi, E., Pope Jr., H. G., and Kessler, R. C. (2007) "The prevalence and correlates of eating disorders in the National Comorbidity Survey Replication", *Biological Psychiatry* 61(3): 348–58.

Miller, W. R., and Rollnick, S. (2002) *Motivational Interviewing* (2nd edn), New York: Guilford Press.

Peterson, C. B. (2005) "Conducting the Diagnostic Interview", in J. E. Mitchell and C. B. Peterson (eds) *Assessment of Eating Disorders* (pp. 32–58), New York: Guilford Press.

Schacter, D. L. (1999) "The seven sins of memory: insights from psychology and cognitive neuroscience", *American Psychologist* 54: 182–203.

Smyth, J. M., Wonderlich, S. A., Heron, K. E., Sliwinski, M. J., Crosby, R. D., Mitchell, J. E., and Engel, S. G. (2007) "Daily and momentary mood and stress are associated with binge eating and vomiting in bulimia nervosa patients in the natural environment", *Journal of Consulting and Clinical Psychology* 75: 629–38.

Sobell, L. C., Maisto, S. A., Sobell, M. B., and Cooper, A. M. (1979) "Reliability of alcohol abusers' self-reports of drinking behavior", *Behavious Research and Therapy* 17: 157–60.

Stice, E., Telch, C. F., and Rizvi, S. L. (2000) "Development and validation of the Eating Disorder Diagnostic Scale: a brief self-report measure of anorexia, bulimia, and binge-eating disorder", *Psychological Assessment* 12: 123–31.

Swanson, S. A., Crow, S. J., Le Grange, D., Swendsen, J., and Merikangas, K. R. (2011) "Prevalence and correlates of eating disorders in adolescents", *Archives of General Psychiatry* 68: 714–23.

Tanofsky-Kraff, M., Yanovski, S. Z., and Yanovski, J. A. (2011) "Loss of control over eating in children and adolescents", in R. H. Striegel-Moore, S. A. Wonderlich, B. T. Walsh, and J. E. Mitchell (eds) *Developing an Evidence-Based Classification of Eating Disorders: Scientific Findings for DSM-5* (pp. 221–36), Arlington, VA: American Psychiatric Association.

Vitousek, K., Watson, S., and Wilson, G. T. (1998) "Enhancing motivation for change in treatment-resistant eating disorders", *Clinical Psychology Review* 18: 391–420.

Wilfley, D. E., Schwartz, M. B., Spurrell, E. B., and Fairburn, C. G. (2000) "Using the Eating Disorder Examination to identify the specific psychopathology of binge eating disorder", *International Journal of Eating Disorders* 27(3): 259–69.

Wilson, G. T. (1993) "Assessment of binge eating", in C. G. Fairburn and G. T. Wilson (eds) *Binge Eating: Nature, Assessment, and Treatment* (12th edn), New York: Guilford Press.

Chapter 10

Dialectical behavior therapy for binge eating disorder

Kay E. Segal, Sarah E. Altman, Jessica A. Weissman, Debra L. Safer and Eunice Y. Chen

Case study

For years, I struggled with my weight, often fluctuating between starvation and binge-eating. This was only one of many problems I faced. I also self-injured, abused alcohol, ruined relationships, and even attempted suicide a few times in my younger years. Often the way I felt after a binge would cause me to cut myself as a punishment for losing control. My therapists usually gave up on me. My family often only made things worse, having been a source of physical and emotional abuse since childhood. At some point, I began to understand that all of these destructive ways to cope stemmed from my inability to manage my emotions; this made sense given my traumatic history. I was just trying to feel better or different, or to numb these terrible feelings.

Jennifer

Introduction

Dialectical Behavior Therapy (DBT) represents an example of one of the new-wave behavior therapies that integrate mindfulness practice into the treatment of Binge Eating Disorder (BED), e.g. acceptance commitment therapy (Lillis *et al.* 2011) and mindfulness-based cognitive therapy (Kristeller and Wolever 2010). DBT is an outpatient cognitive-behavioral therapy originally developed by Linehan (1993a, 1993b) for women with extreme emotion dysregulation and recurrent suicidal behavior i.e., borderline personality disorder (BPD). A comprehensive skills-based treatment, DBT integrates change-based behavioral strategies (e.g. problem-solving and contingency management) and crisis intervention with strategies derived from acceptance-based practices such as Zen and contemplation practice (e.g. mindfulness and validation). These strategies are integrated within a dialectical framework, emphasizing wholeness, interrelatedness, and process, and utilizing persuasive dialogue and the therapeutic relationship.

Since its inception, DBT has been modified to address a variety of problematic behaviors associated with emotion dysregulation, including eating disorders (EDs). This chapter describes the application of DBT for patients with BED and illustrates the course of therapy (including case examples and specific therapist guidelines) for two approaches: 1) a six month course of standard DBT modified for patients with BED who do not respond quickly to other treatments such as cognitive behavior therapy (CBT); and 2), a 20 session, two-hour weekly group therapy developed at Stanford University, the Stanford DBT Model for BED.

Rationale for the modification of DBT for BED

DBT was modified for BED patients for several reasons. Currently, about half of bulimia nervosa (BN) and BED patients (Fairburn and Brownell 2001) remain symptomatic after treatment with the most empirically supported ED treatments, that is, CBT and interpersonal psychotherapy (IPT). Predictors of poor outcome in standard treatments for BED or BN include co-occurring Cluster B Axis II disorders or impulsivity (Agras *et al.* 2000; Wilfley *et al.* 2000), and this co-occurrence increases risk for recurrent suicidal behavior more than the presence of Axis II disorders alone (Chen *et al.* 2009; Dulit *et al.* 1994). Given the empirical support for DBT's use within severe and chronic multi-diagnostic suicidal groups (see Lieb *et al.* 2004), modifying DBT for BED represents a viable option for eating disorder patients with comorbid disorders or those for whom existing treatments have failed. Indeed, to our knowledge, there have been seven open trials (Ben-Porath *et al.* 2009; Chen *et al.* 2008; Courbasson *et al.* 2011; Federici 2009; Kroger *et al.* 2010; Palmer *et al.* 2003; Salbach-Andrae *et al.* 2008) utilizing DBT for eating disorder groups selected for co-occurrence with other disorders. Chen *et al.* (2008) demonstrated that DBT for BED with co-occurring BPD reduced suicidal behavior and non-suicidal self-injury and binge eating, secondary eating disorder concerns, and co-existing non-eating disorder Axis I psychiatric disorders, as well as increased social functioning. Though results are promising, more randomized controlled trials are needed to establish the treatment efficacy for this patient group.

DBT also has been modified by a group at Stanford University for people with BED without co-occurring disorders (Safer *et al.* 2009).The Stanford DBT Model for BED has been supported through a case report (Telch 1997b), a small case-series (Telch *et al.* 2000), and two randomized controlled trials (Safer *et al.* 2010; Telch *et al.* 2001). Telch *et al.* (2001) reported that 8 per cent of women receiving the Stanford DBT Model for BED were abstinent from binge eating compared to 12.5 per cent of the wait-list controls at the end of the 20-week treatment study. These abstinence rates dropped over the six-month follow-up period to 56 per cent. In addition, as compared to wait-list control, DBT improved body image, eating concerns, and urges to eat when angry.

Similar promising findings were found using the Stanford DBT Model for BED when expanded to include both men and women and people on stable doses of psychotropic medication. When compared to an active supportive psychotherapy group, Safer *et al.* (2010) reported that while both groups improved substantially, DBT achieved results more quickly and had a significantly lower drop-out rate (4 per cent) compared to the active control (33 per cent). At post-treatment, abstinence rates were 64 per cent for DBT and 36 per cent for the comparison control; at the one-year follow-up, abstinence rates were 64 per cent (DBT) and 56 per cent (comparison control). BED participants with higher levels of baseline pathology (e.g., depressive symptoms) achieved significantly better outcomes when randomized to DBT than the comparison control (Robinson and Safer 2011) indicating that an emotion regulation-based approach may be particularly useful for those with psychiatric co-morbidity. In addition, higher percentages of participants in DBT-BED experienced a rapid response to treatment, which was a positive predictor of abstinence at both the end of treatment and at the one-year follow-up (Safer and Joyce 2011).

Aside from promising empirical data, DBT also offers an etiological framework for the development of ED behaviors through its utilization of the Biosocial Theory (Linehan 1993a, 1993b). According to the Biosocial Theory, dysfunctional behaviors such as binge eating are understood as the product of transactions, over time, between an individual with biologically based heightened emotional vulnerability and an invalidating environment. The invalidating environment may include specific invalidation of ED behaviors (e.g., "Why can't you just stop eating?"), weight-related teasing, or over-concern with weight by peers and family. DBT, unlike CBT or IPT, is uniquely based upon an affect regulation model. In DBT modified for BED, binge eating and other eating disorder behaviors are conceptualized as the result of attempts to regulate affect rather than directly from overly restrictive dieting and over-valuation of weight and shape (as in CBT) or as a result of difficulties with resolving interpersonal problems (as in IPT). Therefore eating disorder behaviors, in the absence of other more adaptive emotion regulation skills, may become negatively reinforced (i.e., as escape behaviors) or lead to secondary emotions such as shame or guilt that then prompt further dysfunctional (e.g., life-threatening and/or eating disorder) behaviors. In Jennifer's case, DBT's affect regulation model offered her a comprehensible explanation for her use of binge eating and restriction as ways to "numb" unwanted negative emotions and for how consequent shame from bingeing led to self-injury. Standard DBT treatment is designed to teach adaptive affect regulation skills and to target behaviors resulting from emotional dysregulation; therefore, a theoretical rationale exists for applying DBT to treating BED.

Utilizing standard DBT for patients with BED

Case study

I gained so much weight over the years that I finally stopped leaving my house altogether. Physically, it was difficult to get around and society did not work too hard to accommodate someone of my size. On the other hand, it was simply embarrassing to be seen by anyone, who looked at me in shock, disbelief or disgust. I felt so anxious and ashamed every time I went out in public that I ended up working from home, ordering my groceries, and cutting off all ties to family and friends. I stopped taking care of myself completely. Of course, this only added to my depression and thoughts of suicide. I would sit in my house alone and dream up ways I could die. Why not go ahead and binge? It was the one pleasure I still had and I was going to die anyway.

Mary

Structure of treatment

Standard DBT as utilized for patients with BED includes weekly individual sessions (including four pre-treatment sessions), 24 2-hour weekly group skills training sessions, regular meetings of the DBT consultation team and 24-hour phone consultation. See also Resources, at the end of this chapter, for obtaining complete descriptions of standard DBT.

Individual therapy sessions

In the pre-treatment stage, patients meet with their individual therapist and are oriented to the structure of treatment. During the orientation phase patients identify cues to problem behaviors, examine the pros and cons of these behaviors, and are taught several crisis survival skills. A crisis plan to prevent life-threatening and other dysfunctional behaviors is formulated. Patients commit to cease life-threatening behaviors, maintain regular treatment attendance, and stop binge eating.

At each DBT session, the patient is weighed and rates their urges (0 to 5) to commit suicide, quit therapy, binge eat, fast or restrict food, or engage in other target behavior. Daily food intake prior to session is assessed. The standard DBT diary card, modified to include assessment of ED urges/behaviors, is reviewed, skillful behavior is reinforced, and problem behaviors are noted.

Target hierarchy

Individual treatment sessions in DBT are organized around the highest-ranking (or highest-risk) target behavior engaged in that day or during the previous week, as indicated on the patient's diary card. The target hierarchy prioritizes these risks in order to effectively manage sessions. At the top of the hierarchy are 1) life-threatening behaviors (e.g., suicide ideation, non-suicidal self-injury). These are followed by: 2) therapy-interfering behaviors (e.g., patient/therapist missing or late to sessions, not completing homework, crisis-generating behavior within sessions); 3) quality-of-life-interfering behaviors (e.g., substance abuse, bingeing); and 4) behavioral skills. The principle-driven nature of DBT offers guidance for structuring a session, so that multiple problems – such as self-injury, missed sessions and binge eating – can be addressed. Additionally, DBT delineates protocols for managing suicidal behavior, and therapy-interfering behavior. In the case of Jennifer, life-threatening behaviors (self-injuring, suicidal ideation/plans) would be targeted first if they occurred, followed by any therapy-interfering behaviors in session or between session that led her therapists to "give up on her" and, finally, any quality-of-life behaviors, including binge eating, restriction, and/or problematic drinking.

Eating disorder behaviors are considered quality-of-life-interfering behaviors and are not specifically prioritized among the other quality-of-life targets. In deciding which quality-of-life target to treat, the clinician prioritizes patient problems that are immediate, easily solved, functionally related to higher priority targets such as life-threatening behavior, and that fit the patient's goals. For example, in the case of Mary, her BED and major depression were accompanied by complaints of difficulty maintaining relationships. As she describes, intense social anxiety led to her retreating alone to her apartment for hours. When binge eating was prioritized over social anxiety, her bingeing, anxiety, and depression did not improve and the patient increasingly disengaged from therapy. Frequent assessment via chain analysis throughout the course of treatment is required for determining the relationship between quality-of-life targets and life-threatening behaviors. Chain analysis revealed that Mary's social anxiety was functionally related to higher-order targets (i.e., social anxiety led to isolation, which led to increased depression, increased bingeing and, in turn, feeling suicidal) and she believed her bingeing occurred only as a result of her "social failure." When social anxiety was prioritized ahead of bingeing, Mary re-engaged in therapy and both behaviors improved.

Because overweight patients with BED often list weight loss as a quality-of-life goal, we recommend that clinicians establish realistic expectations about weight loss with patients early in treatment. This prevents later frustration with failure to lose unrealistic amounts of weight. Clinicians should help patients focus on specific achievable lifestyle changes (e.g., increasing social contact, not eating after 8pm) and the possible use of ancillary treatments such as walking groups. For instance, Mary was assigned social "homework" each week (e.g., sitting in a bookstore for thirty minutes, placing two phone calls a day, walking to meet a friend). Over time, her self-isolation decreased, her social competence and relationships improved and, as a result, she engaged in fewer eating disorder behaviors.

As in standard DBT, a chain analysis is completed with the target hierarchy as a guide (e.g. life-threatening behaviors/urges first, followed by therapy-interfering and/or quality-of-life interfering behaviors). If no target behaviors occurred, skills are taught or reinforced. It is important to balance chain analyses of problem behaviors with analyses of successes (i.e., "How did you make it through the whole weekend without bingeing?").

Chain analysis

Addressing multiple complex problems in one session is challenging but necessary. Chain analysis is a meticulous analysis of the topography, intensity, frequency, duration, antecedents, and consequences of a problem behavior. Repeated chain analyses of a problem behavior allow the clinician and patient to determine the cues, maintaining factors and function of a behavior, as well as structure, evaluate, improve, and individualize treatment. Once the clinician and patient have collaboratively established a solution and plan to prevent future problem behaviors, a number of commitment strategies (e.g. pros/cons and devil's advocate) can be utilized. A session may include: 1) identifying patterns applying to multiple behaviors and coaching patients to skillfully address these; 2) conducting a chain analysis on multiple target behaviors (e.g., a negative review at work led to a depressed mood, getting drunk, fighting with a boyfriend, bingeing, and a feeling of shame); and/or 3) focusing on multiple brief chain analyses, (e.g., asking "What would you have done differently to be more effective?" or "What skill could you have used instead?").

Group skills training

Like standard DBT for BPD, group skills training in standard DBT for BED targets the acquisition of new behavioral skills in a structured psycho-educational format and is divided into four modules: mindfulness, distress tolerance, emotion regulation, and interpersonal effectiveness. Mindfulness skills involve observation and description of thoughts and emotions, including taking control of where attention is focused. Acquisition of emotion regulation skills increases identification of emotions and how they operate, reduces vulnerability to negative emotions, and alters negative emotional states. The distress tolerance module provides skills to tolerate painful emotions or difficult situations without making them worse. Finally, interpersonal skills focus on validation, effective communication, maintaining positive relationships, and assertiveness.

Skills training is organized around the tension between acceptance and change and assumes that patients must learn to change their dysregulated emotional states and, simultaneously, tolerate and accept the presence of painful emotions without engaging in maladaptive behavioral responses. There is no module uniquely addressing eating disorder behaviors and only minor adaptations to the skills program are made (i.e., modeling the use of skills to prevent binge eating behaviors). For patients who also attempt to regulate their emotions through restriction or over-exercise, more adaptive alternatives (e.g., practicing progressive muscle relaxation) incompatible with binge eating are identified. For patients with poor body image, mindfulness exercises concerning eating and body awareness are utilized, including imagining themselves in a full-length mirror while noting any judgmental thoughts that may arise (e.g., "I look disgusting").

DBT therapist consultation team

DBT recognizes that therapists serving a challenging, multi-problem population require encouragement and a supportive environment. Part of the therapists' work involves that they practice skills themselves both to maintain their own wellbeing and improve outcomes for their patients. In addition to the standard consultation team practice, team members are trained in the identification and treatment of eating disorders (e.g., high-risk eating disorder behaviors, consequences of eating disorders behaviors and medical complications of eating disorders, including obesity and diabetes) and gain information regarding activity, weight, and healthy eating. Training may take the form of lectures, journal clubs, engaging a consultant, and workshops.

24-hour phone consultation

Like standard DBT, 24-hour telephone consultation provides emergency crisis intervention and disrupts potential reinforcement of problem behavior by contacting the therapist *before* engaging in the behavior. Additionally, skills coaching is provided for skill generalization and to repair patient-clinician relationships. Patients are advised to contact the therapist *before* engaging in the problem behavior for a 5- to 10-minute phone coaching session. However, patients contacting the therapist *after* engaging in the problem behavior must wait 24 hours following the behavior to receive phone coaching. Standard DBT for BED phone consultation limits for life-threatening behaviors are the same as standard DBT, although the time interval before the patient can call after engaging in binge eating is determined by examination of the patient's chain analysis, binge eating frequency, the degree of reinforcement experienced by clinician contact, and patient and clinician agreements. Phone consultation is used to help patients apply new skills in their real life and, therefore, this brief coaching is focused on the specific and current urge to engage in target behavior.

Ancillary treatment

Patients complete a medical evaluation and ongoing medical monitoring (e.g., regular assessment of electrolytes). Ancillary activities are also utilized for weight management or related medical issues (e.g., personal trainer, gym, specialist in diabetes) or for other psychological treatment (e.g., Alcoholics Anonymous, pharmacotherapy). Although ancillary providers are often accustomed to speaking with the clinician rather than patient, the "consultation-to-the-patient" case consultation strategy in DBT encourages patients to skillfully interact directly with ancillary treatment providers after being coached by the DBT therapist.

Dialectical strategies

Dialectical strategies target dichotomous thinking, behavior, and emotions to assist patients in finding balanced and synthesized responses to polarities (i.e., finding "the middle path" between love and hate, bingeing and restriction, all or nothing). Various dialectical strategies (e.g., metaphors, devil's advocate, cognitive restructuring) highlight continual change and validating a patient's intuitive wisdom. During pre-treatment, the concept of dialectical abstinence from objective binge eating is provided (see description to follow in the Stanford DBT model section). Secondary targets and dialectical dilemmas include "over-controlled eating" versus "out-of control objective binge eating", the vacillation between "extreme dieting" and "loss of control", with the synthesis involving engagement in neither extreme but eating in moderation. The dialectical dilemma of "no activity" versus "over-exercise" is often discussed with patients trying to lose weight and provides a synthesis that incorporates healthy activity into their lifestyle.

Validation strategies

In every DBT encounter with a patient, change strategies are balanced with acceptance strategies (e.g., validation). Validation strategies further strengthen commitment and include: listening in an interested fashion, reflecting accurately, articulating unstated thoughts and emotions, communicating how behaviors make sense given the patient's learning history or present situation, and being radically genuine (i.e., treating the patient as one would treat an equal).

Stylistic strategies

The stylistic strategies of DBT also balance acceptance and change. On the one hand, irreverent communication involves an outrageous, humorous, or blunt style which can be utilized when a clinician and patient become deadlocked and therapy becomes polarized. Alternatively, reciprocal communication involves interpersonal warmth, responsiveness to a patient's concerns and strategic self-disclosure.

Similar to standard DBT, the clinician attempts to validate the patient during every interaction, as appropriate, paying particular attention to the shame and guilt many eating disorder patients feel regarding their eating behavior, as well as demonstrating an understanding that, given the patient's experience, it makes sense they find ways to cope with emotional dysregulation (i.e., bingeing). To demonstrate a balance of acceptance and change, a clinician may say, "On the one hand, Mary, you feel really fearful when you're around people so it makes sense that you do things to help you feel better, like bingeing or working from home. On the other hand, those behaviors are getting in the way of having a life worth living, a life worth waking up for every morning. Let's work on finding new ways for you to feel better."

Utilizing the Stanford DBT Model for patients with BED

Case study

My family was large. It wasn't unusual for us to run out of food before my mother's next paycheck. I've often thought that had a big impact on my binging, since I overstock my cupboards, eat fast, and always clean my plate. My life is so busy with kids and a full-time job – most days I try to diet during the day just to make up for all the food the night before. I usually wait to binge until after my husband and kids fall asleep at night. Sometimes this is the only time I have during the day to just sit down, relax, and take time for myself. Food feels good in those moments. On the other hand, my clothes don't fit, my health has started to decline and I feel pretty terrible about my body and my lack of self-control.

Denise

The Stanford Model of DBT, initially developed by Telch (Safer *et al.* 2009; Telch 1997a, 1997b), is an adaptation of standard DBT targeting patients with primary symptoms of BED, as in Denise's case. People with active suicidal or self-injurious behaviors are referred to more comprehensive treatment, such as the standard DBT Model described above.

In the group-only DBT program modified for BED, treatment targets are the same as standard DBT, although most patients with a primary diagnosis of BED will spend most time in treatment targeting quality-of-life-interfering behaviors. These include: "Mindless Eating", or not attending to one's eating (e.g., eating popcorn while watching TV only to find one has finished the bowl without being aware); "Food Preoccupation", or having their thoughts/attention absorbed or focused on food to the point that functioning is adversely affected (e.g., inability to concentrate at work or school); "Capitulating", or giving up on their goals to cope skillfully with emotions and stop binge eating and, instead, acting as if coping with food is the only option; and "Apparently Irrelevant Behaviors", or behaviors that do not initially appear relevant to binge eating or are ones that patients convince themselves "do not matter" but which, on examination with the chain analysis, actually play an important role in relation to binge eating (e.g., buying extra dessert to have on hand "for tomorrow" may seem irrelevant but may lead to binge eating).

A distinctive feature of the Stanford Model is that it combines both individual and group functions of standard DBT into one two-hour group session (for BED). The Stanford Model includes a pre-treatment interview followed by 20 treatment sessions, which include further orientation, the Mindfulness, Emotion Regulation and Distress Tolerance skills modules, and review and relapse prevention.

Patients meet individually with one of the clinicians for 30–45 minutes of pre-treatment and are oriented to the DBT emotion regulation model of binge eating and the targets and expectations of group treatment. A commitment from the patient to stop binge eating is elicited and potential treatment-interfering behaviors are addressed.

The group format differs from standard DBT skills training groups. Homework review occurs in the first hour and incorporates discussion of patient diary cards, chain analyses, and practice of the prior week's skills, including description of specific successes/difficulties in applying the skills to replace targeted problem eating behaviors. The second half is devoted to skills instruction – teaching, practicing, and strengthening new skills and previously presented skills.

Sessions 1 and 2

A major task of Session 1 is to obtain a group commitment to stop binge eating. After initial introductions, clinicians create a groundswell of motivation and commitment from group members by flexibly utilizing the commitment strategies of standard DBT. In addition to this group commitment, other tasks of Session 1 are to orient group members to: 1) the emotion regulation model of binge eating; 2) the treatment targets and group agreements; 3) the biosocial model; and 4) the diary card and chain analysis.

In Session 2, after conducting homework review for the first half of the session (see above), clinicians introduce patients to the concept of dialectical abstinence, a concept originally developed in DBT for substance use disorders (DBT-SUD) (Linehan and Dimeff 1997). Dialectical abstinence is a synthesis of a 100 per cent commitment to abstinence and a 100 per cent commitment to relapse prevention strategies. Before a patient engages in binge eating, there is an unrelenting insistence on total abstinence. After a patient has engaged in binge eating, however, the emphasis is on radical acceptance, nonjudgmental problem solving and effective relapse prevention, followed by a speedy return to an unrelenting insistence on abstinence.

Sessions 3 to 5

Mindfulness skills are introduced Sessions 3 to 5 and reviewed in Session 12. These skills are the same as in standard DBT (e.g. "Wise Mind", the "What/How" Skills) except for an additional three: "Mindful Eating", "Urge Surfing", and "Alternate Rebellion". These latter skills, "Urge Surfing" and "Alternate Rebellion", have origins in earlier substance abuse work (Linehan and Dimeff 1997; Marlatt and Gordon 1985).

Mindful eating

Mindful eating, as opposed to mindless eating, is the experience of full participation in eating (i.e., observing and describing in one's mind the experience). It is eating with full awareness and attention (one-mindfully) but without self-consciousness or judgment.

Urge surfing

Urge surfing involves mindful, non-attached observation of urges to binge eat or eat mindlessly. Mindfulness skills teach acceptance of the reality that there are cues in the world that trigger urges to binge eat. Patients are taught how urges and cravings are classically conditioned responses that have been associated with a particular cue. Mindful urge surfing involves awareness without engaging in impulsive mood-dependent behavior and involves "letting go" or "detaching" from the object of the urge and "riding the wave" of the urge. In Denise's case, she was encouraged to practice urge surfing when she was alone after her children and husband went to bed.

Alternate rebellion

The aim of this skill is to satisfy the wish to rebel without destroying the overriding objective of stopping binge eating. The purpose is not to suppress or judge the rebellion but to find creative ways to rebel so as not to "cut off your nose to spite your face." In other words, this skill makes use of the mindfulness skill of being *effective*. Clinicians encourage patients to observe and label the urge to rebel, and then, if patients decide to act on the urge, to do so effectively. For example, a patient who feels judged by society for being obese might "rebel" by mindfully going to a restaurant and openly, unselfconsciously treating herself to a healthy and delicious bowl of soup.

Sessions 6 to 18

Emotion regulation skills taught in standard DBT are covered in Sessions 6 to 12, without any specific modifications for BED. Sessions 13 to 18 cover the distress tolerance skills of standard DBT. One additional skill, "Burning Bridges", has been borrowed from DBT-SUD (Linehan and Dimeff 1997). This radical acceptance skill involves patients accepting at the deepest and most radical level the idea that they are really not going to binge eat or mindlessly eat or abuse themselves with food ever again; in this way, they are burning the bridge to those behaviors. Patients accept that they will no longer block, deny or avoid reality with binge eating. Instead, they make a covenant from deep within to accept reality and their experiences.

Sessions 19 to 20

Relapse prevention begins with a review of the modules in Session 19. In addition, patients are asked to fill out a "Planning for the Future" worksheet for Session 20. In this worksheet, patients are asked to identify typical circumstances and emotions that previously triggered binge eating and to make specific plans for skills to use in such instances. In Session 20, each group member reviews her worksheet. Final goodbyes and perhaps a goodbye ritual (e.g., writing cards) are used to mark the end of treatment.

Throughout treatment, clinicians meet weekly with the treatment team to confer regarding the progress of treatment and adherence to DBT principles. Unlike standard DBT in which individual therapy and group skills therapy modes are discussed, only the group sessions are discussed. Patients are encouraged to call clinicians if they have questions during the week (e.g., checking on what homework was assigned); however, 24-hour telephone consultation as practiced in standard DBT is not used.

Resources

To be competent in the delivery of this modified treatment, familiarity with behavioral principles and of the standard DBT program is essential. Reading of Linehan's two manuals is recommended: *Cognitive-Behavioural Treatment of BPD* (Linehan 1993a), and the *Skills Training Manual for Treating BPD* (Linehan 1993b), and a manual, *Dialectical Behaviour Therapy for Binge Eating and Bulimia,* by Safer *et al.* (2009). Finally, for further training in DBT, readers are referred to Behavioural Tech. LLC (http://behaviouraltech.org/), a company focused on the dissemination of DBT and other empirically validated treatments.

References

Agras, W., Crow, S., Halmi, K., Mitchell, J. E., Wilson, G., and Kraemer, H. (2000) "Outcome predictors for the cognitive behaviour treatment of bulimia nervosa: data from a multisite study", *American Journal of Psychiatry* 157: 1302–8.

Ben-Porath, D. D., Wisniewski, L., and Warren, M. (2009) "Differential treatment response for eating disordered patients with and without a comorbid borderline personality diagnosis using a dialectical behaviour therapy (DBT)-informed approach", *Eating Disorders* 17: 225–41.

Chen, E. Y., Brown, M. Z., Harned, M. S., and Linehan, M. M. (2009) "A comparison of borderline personality disorder with and without eating disorders", *Psychiatry Research* 170: 86–90.

Chen, E. Y., Matthews, L., Allen, C., Kuo, J. R., and Linehan, M. M. (2008) "Dialectical behavior therapy for patients with binge-eating disorder or bulimia nervosa and borderline personality disorder", *International Journal of Eating Disorders* 41: 505–12.

Courbasson, C., Nishikawa, Y., and Dixon, L. (2011) "Outcome of dialectical behaviour therapy for concurrent eating and substance use disorders", *Clinical Psychology & Psychotherapy* doi: 10.1002/cpp.748.

Dulit, R. A., Fyer, M. R., Leon, A. C., Brodsky, B. S., and Frances, A. J. (1994) "Clinical correlates of self-mutilation in borderline personality disorder", *American Journal of Psychiatry* 151: 1305–11.

Fairburn, G., and Brownell, K. (2001) *Eating Disorders and Obesity*, New York: The Guilford Press.

Federici, A. (2009) "Effectiveness of a dialectical behaviour therapy skills group for the treatment of suicidal/self-injurious behaviour and eating disorder symptoms in patients with borderline personality disorder" (dissertation),York University, Canada.

Kristeller, J. L., and Wolever, R. Q. (2010) "Mindfulness-based eating awareness training for treating binge eating disorder: the conceptual foundation", *Eating Disorders* 19: 49–61.

Kroger, C., Schweiger, U., Sipos, V., Kliem, S., Arnold, R., Schunert, T., and Reinecker, H. (2010) "Dialectical behaviour therapy and an added cognitive behavioural treatment module for eating disorders in women with borderline personality disorder and anorexia nervosa or bulimia nervosa who failed to respond to previous treatments: an open trial with a 15-month follow-up", *Journal of Behavior Therapy and Experimental Psychiatry* 41: 381–8.

Lieb, K., Zanarini, M. C., Schmahl, C., Linehan, M. M., and Bohus, M. (2004) "Borderline personality disorder", *Lancet* 364: 453–61.

Lillis, J., Hayes, S. C., and Levin, M. E. (2011) "Binge eating and weight control: the role of experiential avoidance", *Behavior Modification* 35: 252–64.

Linehan, M. M. (1993a) *Cognitive-behavioural treatment of borderline personality disorder*, New York: The Guilford Press.

Linehan, M. M. (1993b) *Skills Training Manual for Treating Borderline Personality Disorder*, New York: The Guilford Press.

Linehan, M. M., and Dimeff, L.A (1997) *Dialectical behaviour Therapy Manual Of Treatment Interventions for Drug Abusers with Borderline Personality Disorder*, Seattle, WA: University of Washington Seattle.

Marlatt, G. A., and Gordon, J. R. (1985) *Relapse Prevention and Maintenance Strategies in the Treatment of Addictive Behaviours*, New York: The Guilford Press.

Palmer, R. L., Birchall, H., Damani, S., Gatward, N., McGrain, L., and Parker, L. (2003) "A dialectical behaviour therapy program for people with an eating disorder and borderline personality disorder – description and outcome", *International Journal of Eating Disorders* 33: 281–6.

Robinson, A. H., and Safer, D. L. (2011) "Moderators of dialectical behaviour therapy for binge eating disorder: results from a randomized controlled trial", *International Journal of Eating Disorders* doi: 10.1002/eat.20932 [e-pub ahead of print].

Safer, D. L., and Joyce, E. E. (2011) "Does rapid response to two group psychotherapies for binge eating disorder predict abstinence?" *Behavior Research and Therapy* 49: 339–45.

Safer, D. L., Robinson, A.H., and Jo, B. (2010) "Outcome from a randomized controlled trial of group therapy for binge eating disorder: comparing dialectical behaviour therapy adapted for binge eating to an active comparison group therapy", *Behavior Therapy* 41: 106–20.

Safer, D. L., Telch, C. F., Chen, E. Y., and Linehan, M. M. (2009) *Dialectical Behaviour Therapy for Binge Eating and Bulimia*, New York: The Guilford Press.

Salbach-Andrae, H., Bohnekamp, I., Pfeiffer, E., Lehmkuhl, U., and Miller, A. L. (2008)

"Dialectical behaviour therapy of anorexia and bulimia nervosa among adolescents: a case series", *Cognitive and Behavioral Practice* 15: 415–25.

Telch, C. F. (1997a) *Emotion Regulation Skills Training Treatment for Binge Eating Disorder: Therapist Manual* (unpublished manuscript), Stanford University.

Telch, C. F. (1997b) "Skills training treatment for adaptive affect regulation in a woman with binge-eating disorder", *International Journal of Eating Disorders* 22: 77–81.

Telch, C. F., Agras, W. S., and Linehan, M. M. (2001) "Dialectical behaviour therapy for binge eating disorder", *Journal of Consulting and Clinical Psychology* 69: 1061–5.

Telch, C. F., Agras, W. S., and Linehan, M. M. (2000) "Group dialectical behaviour therapy for binge-eating disorder: a preliminary, uncontrolled trial", *Behavior Therapy* 31: 569–82.

Wilfley, D. E., Friedmand, M. A., Dounchis, J. Z., Stein, R. I., Welch, R., and Ball, S. A. (2000) "Comorbid psychopathology in binge eating disorder: relation to eating disorder severity at baseline and following treatment', *Journal of Consulting and Clinical Psychology* 68(4): 641–9.

Chapter 11

Psychotherapy for binge eating disorder

Myra Altman, Denise E. Wilfley, Juliette M. Iacovino, Heather L. Waldron and Dana M. Gredysa

Introduction

BED is associated with significant functional impairment (Rieger *et al.* 2005), but prognosis is good with appropriate therapeutic intervention. Specialist treatments for BED, such as cognitive behavioral therapy (CBT) and interpersonal psychotherapy (IPT), which directly address binge eating and related psychopathology, are associated with robust short- and long-term binge abstinence rates. CBT and IPT have been found to produce superior outcomes as compared to pharmacotherapy (Devlin *et al.* 2005), and generalist treatments such as behavioral weight loss (BWL) (Grilo *et al.* 2011; Wilson *et al.* 2010) and supportive psychotherapy (Kenardy *et al.* 2002).

Cognitive behavioral therapy for BED

Case study

> Since childhood I have had a troubled relationship with food, and have binged for as long as I can remember. When growing up my relationship with my parents was incredibly dysfunctional and abusive. I think I began to equate food with love, and started to have an unhealthy relationship with food. I was quite chunky as a child, and got heavier as I got older. Because I kept gaining weight, I started dieting – counting calories, weight loss programs, even diet pills. I went on my first diet when 13 years old. I've been a "yo-yo" dieter pretty much ever since. I did once manage to lose 40 pounds, but could never keep the weight off. I'm still disgusted with the way I look, and the thought of someone else seeing my body makes me extremely uncomfortable, so I avoid bathing suits or shorts. At the moment I binge about four times a week, but every day I'm scared that I won't be able to control what I eat.
>
> Ellen

Rationale for modifying CBT for BED

The rationale of CBT for BED is based on the restraint model of binge eating. This model posits that problematic eating patterns and concerns about shape and weight result in extreme dietary restriction (Wilfley 2002). This promotes a dysfunctional pattern in which patients alternate between dietary restraint and binge eating (see Figure 11.1). The goal of CBT is to disrupt this "diet-binge cycle" by promoting healthier, more structured eating patterns (e.g., regular meals and snacks), improving shape and weight concerns, and encouraging the use of healthy weight-control behaviours (e.g., monitoring food intake and engaging in moderate dietary restraint). CBT encourages patients to normalize eating patterns by setting goals and using self-monitoring to develop flexible restraint and modify negative views of themselves, in order to reduce binge eating. Indeed, increases in flexible restraint and decreases in rigid restraint over the course of CBT guided self-help have been found to predict greater likelihood of abstinence post-treatment and at three months follow-up (Blomquist and Grilo 2011).

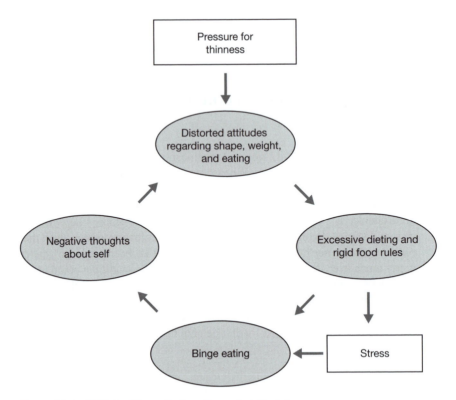

Figure 11.1 CBT for Binge Eating: Restraint Model

The evidence base for CBT for BED is well established, as it is the most well studied psychological treatment for BED (Wilson and Shafran 2005). More than a dozen randomized controlled trials have shown that both individual and group CBT are associated with significantly higher abstinence rates when compared with no treatment (Agras *et al.* 1997; Dingemans *et al.* 2007; Eldredge and Agras 1997; Gorin *et al.* 2003; Schlup *et al.* 2009; Telch *et al.* 1990; Wilfley *et al.* 1993), supportive therapy (Kenardy *et al.* 2002), and BWL treatment (Agras *et al.* 1994; Devlin *et al.* 2005; Devlin *et al.* 2007; Grilo and Masheb 2005; Grilo *et al.* 2011; Munsch *et al.* 2007). Randomized controlled trials of CBT conducted since 2007 show that 15 or more sessions can produce binge abstinence rates ranging from 44–84 per cent immediately post-treatment, and up to 52 per cent within 12 months after the discontinuation of treatment (Iacovino *et al.* in press). CBT-BED has also shown strong long-term recovery rates, with 52 per cent of participants remaining abstinent from binge eating four years post-treatment (Hilbert *et al.* 2012).

Implementing CBT for patients with BED

CBT for BED is a triphasic, focal psychotherapy that can be delivered in individual or group formats. In the initial phase (sessions 1–6), behavioral strategies (e.g., dietary self-monitoring) help patients identify and eliminate episodes of over-restriction and under-restriction, and encourage the normalization of eating patterns. During the intermediate phase (sessions 7–14), patients identify stressors that often lead to binge eating, and learn cognitive skills to counter negative thoughts that predispose an individual to binge eating. Additionally, cognitive restructuring helps patients challenge harsh stereotyped views of overweight and promotes the acceptance of diverse body sizes. In the termination phase (sessions 15–20), treatment gains are consolidated, relapse prevention techniques are discussed, and patients develop a lifestyle plan for continuing to manage weight and binge eating.

Initial phase

The initial phase of CBT consists of standard assessment and diagnosis of BED, establishment of treatment expectations and goals, and a focus on behavioral strategies. The patient is formally diagnosed and assured that BED is a known disorder with effective treatment options and a good prognosis. The format and expectations of treatment are then discussed. The clinician explains that the purpose of treatment is to eliminate excessive dietary restraint, normalize eating patterns and address negative thought processes that reinforce binge eating.

The clinician's main focus during the initial phase is utilizing behavioral strategies to help patients develop flexible restraint. Patients are encouraged to eat three planned meals and up to two snacks per day. Patients are also instructed to plan the inclusion of "forbidden" foods in their diet, as binge eating is often

Daily Food Record

(Week 1 of Treatment)

Name *Ellen*   Day *Tuesday*   Date *5/6/96*

Time Eating Began/ Time Eating Ended	Food Eaten (Please provide as much detail as possible. E.g. ingredients in combination of dishes	Quantity	Meal (M), Snack (S), or Binge (B)
7:15-7:30	Eggs English Muffin	2 1	M
9:00–9:15	Bacon, Egg and Cheese Breakfast Sandwich (McDonalds)	2	B
12:15-12:20	Apple	1	S
1:00-1:15	Tuna & Mayo English Muffin	3oz/1tbsp 1	M
5:15-5:20	Spaghetti	2 plates	B
7:30-7:45	Tuna & Mayo English Muffin	3oz/1tbsp 1	M

Exercise: *None*

Daily Food Record

(Week 19 of Treatment)

Name *Ellen*   Day *Monday*   Date *2/27/97*

Time Eating Began/ Time Eating Ended	Food Eaten (Please provide as much detail as possible. E.g. ingredients in combination of dishes	Quantity	Meal (M), Snack (S), or Binge (B)
7:00-7:15	Oatmeal Banana	1 cup 1	M
10:00-10:20	Bagel Cream Cheese	1 1 tbsp	S
1:00-1:20	Turkey Burger (Pattie and English Muffin) Carrots	1 1/2 cup	M
3:00-3:10	Apple	1	S
6:45-7:15	Chicken Baked Beans Coleslaw	1 breast 1 cup 1 cup	M

Exercise: *Walked for 30 minutes after work*

Figure 11.2 Daily food records: Week 1 and Week 19

triggered when these foods are consumed in an unplanned manner. The clinician stresses that moderation, rather than avoidance of certain foods, is most effective for weight management and binge prevention. Patients are told that rigid and perfectionistic rules about eating can lead to hunger, discouragement, and negative self-talk, which triggers binge eating and reinforces over-restriction (e.g., "If I were a better dieter, I wouldn't binge"). Flexible restraint is described as a more sustainable and realistic lifestyle plan that can lead to greater control over eating.

Development of flexible restraint is accomplished through self-monitoring and goal setting. Patients are expected to keep daily self-recorded food logs, which enables them to monitor the regularity and nutritional balance of their meals. Each week, patients can use these food logs to notice the unhelpful patterns in their eating that are linked to binge eating. For example, Ellen noticed that she often went five or more hours without eating, which usually triggered a binge later in the day. She was able to set the goal to include a healthy afternoon snack, like an apple, in these long periods without food to avoid bingeing. Ellen also wanted to establish a regular eating pattern of three meals and two snacks a day. These changes are clear when comparing Ellen's food logs at the beginning and end of treatment (see Figure 11.2). In this way, food logs help patients to make connections between over-restriction and binge eating within their own lives, and develop personal goals that are appropriate to their particular circumstances.

Additionally, patients are encouraged to eat a variety of foods in their meals. Eating substantial, well-balanced meals helps prevent bingeing. For example, Ellen and her clinician noticed that when Ellen ate meals with little food variety (e.g., eating only a Caesar salad for dinner), she usually binged shortly thereafter. To help patients identify healthy meals, clinicians can present a list of "sample meals", or examples of properly portioned, balanced meals and snacks.

Intermediate phase

Cognitive work begins in the intermediate phase of CBT. This phase includes identifying and increasing awareness of the specific thoughts that are associated with the dieting mentality and how these are linked to binge eating, as well as developing more adaptive ways of thinking.

During this phase, the clinician emphasizes that the way a person thinks about the events in his or her life can trigger a binge episode. People with BED tend to engage in negative, self-critical styles of thinking, which can promote low self-esteem, thus increasing vulnerability to binge eating. Cognitive restructuring techniques are utilized to help patients identify their negative thoughts and develop alternative thoughts to challenge them (see Table 11.1). For example, Ellen expressed that she did not think she would ever find anyone that accepted her the way she looked. These thoughts led to feelings of loneliness and often triggered binge eating. Through the use of cognitive restructuring techniques, Ellen was able to develop an alternative thought, "I am a good person, no matter

Table 11.1 Dysfunctional thought examples

Event	Automatic thoughts	Alternative thoughts
Ate a "forbidden" food	• I shouldn't have eaten that • I blew my diet so I might as well eat whatever I want	• I was craving sweets and it's okay to eat a little bit • I'm allowed to have dessert with my meals
Binged	• I gave in, it's hopeless • I'll never get better	• I only binged twice this week and before I was bingeing almost every day • I've made a lot of progress, but I'm still working on it
Feeling depressed or stressed	• Eating will make me feel better • I had such a tough day, I deserve to binge	• Eating when I'm sad usually makes me feel worse in the long term • I have lots of things I can do to relieve stress besides eating
Didn't binge all week/ Made weekly goal	• I deserve to comfort myself with a binge • I was "on" all week, so now I can be "off"	• Bingeing will only make me feel bad, instead I'll give myself the weekly reward I wrote down • Successfully sticking to my routine this week felt good, I'll try keep it up through the weekend
Feeling bad about shape/weight	• I'm not losing any weight, maybe I should stop eating any foods that have fat • I have to lose 5 pounds, I should stop eating breakfast	• I can plan to include some "forbidden" foods into my regular meals otherwise I am more likely to binge • I've been doing a good job of having regular meals and snacks, I will try to keep doing that because it's more healthy

how I look. If I accept myself, others will also." Alternative thoughts such as this one lead to more positive views of the self, removing the binge eating trigger and ultimately leading to a decrease in binge eating.

Another example of a negative automatic thought is patients blaming themselves excessively for not meeting unrealistic standards (e.g., completely cutting out "forbidden" foods, ceasing bingeing altogether, or losing a large amount of weight), which often leads to more binge eating. For example, after a

Mid-Treatment Evaluation – Please briefly answer the following questions	
1. Are you typically eating breakfast?	*Yes*
2. Are you typically eating 3 meals per day?	*Yes*
3. Do you tend to eat at regular time intervals? IF so what are these time intervals?	*Yes, 3–4 hours*
4. Do you tend to eat a wide variety of foods? What foods have you incorporated into your meal plan?	*Yes, all food groups*
5. Are you planning snacks into your mealtime?	*Yes*
6. Are you incorporating "forbidden foods" into your meal plan in a planned and controlled manner? How so?	*Yes, my binge foods (pasta and pizza) are included and planned*
7. Have you established a calorie and fat guideline and meal plan that is reasonable and flexible? If so, what have you done to accomplish this? And what calorie/fat range are you using?	*No on calories, but monitor fats*
8. Please answer the following questions related to your binge eating:	
a. Has the frequency of your binge eating changed? If so, how?	*Yes, lowered*
b. Has the overall quantity of food you eat during a binge changed? If so, how?	*Yes, less*
c. Have there been times when you've been able to stop yourself mid-binge? If so, how?	*Yes, throw away the rest of the food on my plate*
d. Have there been times when you have been able to delay a binge? If so, how?	*Yes, got busy doing something else or went to bed*
e. Have you been able to identify situations that are "high-risk" times for binge eating? If so, what are these situations?	*Yes, the combination of being tired and lonely make me vulnerable for a binge*
f. After having a binge, what strategies have you identified to cope with the binge?	*Tried not to be too hard on myself*
9. Please answer the following questions about exercise:	
a. What exercise activities are you planning into your schedule? How many days per week?	*Park in outer parking lots and walk, trying to join a walking group 1–2 days/week*
b. Are you increasing overall daily movement (i.e., lifestyle activity)?	*Just by parking farther away*

Figure 11.3 CBT mid-treatment evaluation

binge, Ellen reported thinking that: "It didn't seem worth it. I don't feel any better than before, so this food didn't comfort me. I am annoyed with myself for being so weak." Patients are instructed to verbalize challenges to these thoughts, as well as positive alternatives to negative self-talk. Ellen and her clinician worked together to formulate the following counter-thought: "I realize that I binged now, but overall, bingeing only one time this week is a huge improvement for me. I'm not weak, I have been putting in a lot of effort toward getting better … I will continue to make major gains." Patients are encouraged to practice positive self-talk outside of session and to notice how helpful it is in reducing over-restriction and binge eating.

During this phase, patients also work on generating and practicing alternative healthy strategies to cope with difficult situations. For example, through the use of thought records and food logs Ellen identified that binge eating was triggered by feelings of loneliness. She identified calling a friend on the phone, reading, or journaling as possible alternative coping strategies.

During the intermediate phase, patients also complete a mid-treatment evaluation that asks a variety of questions related to eating choices, patterns and behaviours, binge eating, physical activity, and cognitive processes (see Figure 11.3). This evaluation gives the patient and therapist the opportunity to evaluate the patient's progress, and to identify additional goal areas. One major goal of this evaluation is to highlight the importance of having multiple indices of success, rather focusing solely on weight loss as an indicator of progress. Therapists emphasize the importance of weight stabilization and moderate weight loss, and promote healthier attitudes concerning shape and weight, including the acceptance of diverse body sizes.

Termination phase

The final phase of treatment is the consolidation phase, which focuses on the concept of reasonable weight and relapse prevention. The clinician explains that a common, shared experience of people with BED is the past inability to maintain long-term weight change. The clinician emphasizes that specific skills can be developed to maintain weight changes over time.

The clinician discusses the concept of reasonable weight, which eschews the idea of having an unrealistic "goal" weight based on unattainable beauty ideals or height-weight tables. People with BED tend to think very rigidly about weight and weight loss, but one of the most damaging psychological experiences can be to fall short of a set-upon weight loss goal. Therefore, focusing on small, modest weight-loss goals or weight maintenance can lead to sustained changes, positive psychological effects, greater improvement in risk factors, and reduced likelihood of reactivating the diet–binge cycle.

During the termination phase, patients problem-solve any remaining issues and anticipate future problems. The termination phase culminates in the formulation of a lifestyle plan (see Figure 11.4). This plan helps patients avoid falling

Lifestyle Plan to Manage Binge Eating and Weight	
1 Eat 3 meals and 1-2 snacks a day, at regular intervals	**Perceived barriers:** Trips; weekends when I sleep in & there doesn't seem to be time **Personalized plan:** Take snacks in my purse; be aware and put in the effort to do it
2 Incorporate a variety of foods including "forbidden" foods:	**Perceived barriers:** Don't go to the store often enough **Personalized plan:** Incorporate it into my routine, e.g. shop every Monday night
3 Choose a nutritionally-balanced meal plan that includes heart-healthy foods:	**Perceived barriers:** Always working so no time **Personalized plan:** Cook different menu items on Sundays and freeze for the week
4 Monitor overall caloric levels (approx. 1500–2000 for women, and 2000–2500 for men) and amount of dietary fat (<30% of calories, or 50–67 grams for women, and 67–83 grams for men)	**Perceived barriers:** Just don't like to do it **Personalized plan:** Read labels for fat content, and pay more attention to calories
5 Maximize lifestyle physical activity:	**Perceived barriers:** Sometime feel tired and park close to building so I don't have to walk **Personalized plan:** Make commitment to myself to persevere
6 Schedule planned exercise regularly (305 times per week)	**Perceived barriers:** Don't want to – bad attitude **Personalized plan:** Plan it as a routine with friends so I won't not do it
7 Monitor mood, stress levels, and negative self-talk:	**Perceived barriers:** I tell myself I'm OK when I'm not **Personalized plan:** Write down how I'm feeling so I get in the habit of noticing when I'm not OK
8 Monitor high-risk situations and problem-solve accordingly:	**Perceived barriers:** Won't have a group to answer to so I will get careless and not do it **Personalized plan:** I will discuss my progress with my friends
9 Plan ways to take care of yourself and identify non-food-related rewards:	**Perceived barriers:** Won't want to spend the money **Personalized plan:** Remind myself how valuable I am and I am worth it. Flowers from farmers' market, manicure
10 Develop strategies for dealing with urges to binge, binge episodes, or overeating episodes:	**Perceived barriers:** I won't analyze the situation until it is too late **Personalized plan:** Keep records of my eating to make be conscious of what I am eating

Figure 11.4 Lifestyle Plan to Manage Binge Eating and Weight

back into a habit of out-of-control eating, by addressing approaches to calorie reduction, weekly weight monitoring, meal regularity, physical activity, creating a healthy food and eating environment, monitoring emotions and self-talk, asserting needs, and being receptive to support and praise from others.

The clinician also discusses how to conceptualize and prevent relapse. "Slips" are described in three stages: lapse, relapse, and collapse. A lapse involves a binge episode or two, in which the patient does not feel particularly out of control, or in immediate danger of repeated episodes. A relapse is a regular pattern of binge eating over a week or so, that involves some negative thinking and out-of-control feelings. A collapse is when a patient engages in sustained binge eating over a month or longer, and feels back at "square one." It is important to distinguish these "slips", as people with BED often engage in all or nothing thinking, and will feel as if they have "blown it" after just one binge episode, which can lead to feelings of ineffectiveness. Understanding the difference between lapse, relapse, and collapse can help patients to feel capable in dealing with these challenging post-treatment situations. For example, Ellen reported one binge episode towards the end of treatment. She was able to identify what triggered the episode, and develop strategies to avoid it happening in the future. Importantly, Ellen felt confident in her ability to cope with the lapse, and not allow it to lead to more binge episodes.

Interpersonal psychotherapy for BED

Case study

> I've been through years of dieting, and my weight has constantly fluctuated. I started binge eating when I was 15. Ever since then, I tend to eat more and gain weight when I'm in relationships, and I diet a lot when I'm single … I guess I've always done a good job of keeping people from knowing a lot about me. My boyfriend doesn't even know that I binge eat. I binge usually three times a week, but he has no idea. The other night I ordered three things from Taco Bell, and ate two in the car on the way home, so he only saw me eat one. But I hadn't eaten all day. I work in the salon from 7am to 7.30 at night and I'm overextending myself. But which customers am I going to tell I'm not going to do their hair? They all love me.
>
> Barb

Rationale for modifying IPT for BED

IPT has been applied to the treatment of BED based on a strong body of evidence demonstrating a consistent relationship between poor interpersonal functioning and eating disorders (Wilfley *et al.* 2005). People with eating disorders report past difficult social experiences, problematic family histories, and specific interpersonal stressors more often than people who do not have eating disorders

(Fairburn *et al.* 1998; Fairburn *et al.* 1997). Laboratory paradigms suggest that interpersonal distress may trigger overeating (Steiger *et al.* 1999; Tanofsky-Kraff *et al.* 2000), and potentially perpetuate binge eating.

The interpersonal model of binge eating (see Figure 11.5) posits that social problems create an environment in which binge eating develops and is maintained as a coping mechanism, serving to reduce negative affect in response to unfulfilling social interactions (Rieger *et al.* 2010). Binge eating may in turn worsen interpersonal problems by increasing social isolation and impeding fulfilling relationships, thereby maintaining the eating disorder (Rieger *et al.* 2010). People with BED often present with suppressed affect, so instead of expressing negative affect, they eat to cope. IPT helps these people acknowledge and express this painful affect, so that they can better manage negative feelings without turning to food. IPT also seeks to reduce binge-eating pathology by supporting the development of healthy interpersonal skills that can replace maladaptive behaviours and promote a positive self-image.

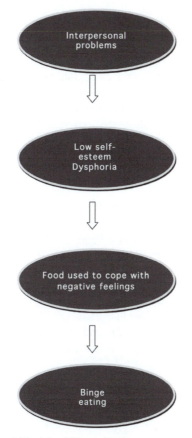

Figure 11.5 Interpersonal Model of Binge Eating

IPT is the only treatment that has shown comparable long-term outcomes to CBT. In the earliest such study, Wilfley and colleagues (1993) found that group IPT led to similar post-treatment abstinence rates as group CBT (Wilfley *et al.* 1993). A follow-up study by Wilfley and colleagues (2002) found that group CBT and IPT were associated with equivalent abstinence rates post-treatment, and at one-year and four-year follow-ups (Hilbert *et al.* 2012; Wilfley *et al.* 2002). Further, individual IPT was shown to be more effective than behavioral weight loss (BWL), and as effective as guided self-help CBT (CBTgsh) two years following treatment (Wilson *et al.* 2010). Notably, when compared to CBTgsh and BWL, IPT is associated with superior two-year abstinence rates among participants with lower baseline self-esteem, and greater body image disturbance, negative affect, and distress (Wilson *et al.* 2010). IPT has also been applied to the treatment of loss of control eating in adolescents, and has demonstrated greater efficacy than standard-of-care health education (Tanofsky-Kraff *et al.* 2009).

Implementing IPT for patients with BED

IPT is also a triphasic therapy with an active focus on specific target areas and goals. Like CBT, it can be delivered in an individual or group format. In a group format, patients can use the group as an interpersonal "laboratory", in which they can practice improved ways of communicating with others. Interpersonal psychotherapy focuses on problem resolution within four social domains: grief, interpersonal role disputes, role transitions, and interpersonal deficits. During each phase, clinicians utilize specific strategies, such as communication analysis (see Table 11.2), to help patients meet their goals. The therapeutic stance is warm, supportive, and empathetic. Throughout all phases of treatment, the clinician is an active advocate for the patient.

The initial phase (sessions 1–5) involves examining a patient's interpersonal and eating disorder history in order to identify the interpersonal problem area(s) associated with BED onset and maintenance. From this history, a detailed plan is formulated that specifies what problem area(s) are most relevant to the patient and how changes in interpersonal functioning can be achieved. The intermediate phase of treatment (sessions 6-15) focuses on illuminating connections between symptoms and interpersonal events during the week, and implementing strategies to help patients make changes in the identified problem areas. In the termination phase (sessions 16–20), patients evaluate and consolidate gains, detail plans for maintaining improvements, and outline any remaining work to be completed.

Table 11.2 IPT therapeutic strategies

General Therapeutic Strategies for Interpersonal Psychotherapy	
Therapeutic Strategy	Explanation
Exploratory questions	Using general, open ended questions to facilitate the free discussion of material. This is especially useful during the beginning of a session. Progressively more specific questioning should follow.
Encouraging affect	Assisting patients in (1) acknowledging and accepting painful emotions by allowing the patient to express them in therapy, and validating the feelings, (2) acting more constructively in relationships, by appropriately expressing or suppressing affect, and (3) drawing out suppressed affect.
Clarification	Having patient explain or simplify what they have previously communicated in order to (1) increase the patient's awareness about what they have said, and (2) draw awareness to contradictions that may have occurred in descriptions of interactions or situations.
Communication analysis	Asking patient to describe, in great detail, a recent interaction or argument with a significant other. The clinician can gain further information by using probe questions, like "What did you specifically say?" or "Thinking back to the interaction, did you send the message that you wanted to convey?"
Use of the therapeutic relationship	Exploring the patient's thoughts, feelings, expectations, and behavior in the therapeutic relationship, and relating these to the patient's characteristic way of behaving and/or feeling in other relationships.

Initial phase

The initial phase of IPT consists of standard assessment and diagnosis of BED, identification of interpersonal problem areas, and development of treatment goals. The clinician conducts a full assessment, including instruments such as the Emotional Eating Scale (Arnow et al. 1995), the Inventory of Interpersonal Problems (Horowitz et al. 1988), and the Eating Disorder Examination (Cooper and Fairburn 1987). The patient is then formally diagnosed with BED and assigned the "sick role". The diagnosis helps the patient understand that he or she has a known condition that can be treated, and the "sick role" relieves the patient of other responsibilities, granting permission to recover. This is especially helpful to patients who tend to set aside their own needs to care for and please others.

AGE	WEIGHT/EATING PROBLEM	RELATIONSHIPS	EVENTS/CIRCUMSTANCES	MOOD
5	Normal weight		Tonsils are removed	
6	Begins gaining weight			
14			Grandfather died	Feels sad at funeral but does not cry because she thinks it would be a sign of weakness
15	Concerns about weight; first binge; prescribed amphetamines to lose weight		Sister gets married, borrows money from parents, & files for bankruptcy with her husband	Perceives parents as being extremely disappointed in sister
16	Less concern about weight because "Paul's ex-wife was a lot heavier than me" but began binge eating	Meets Paul, 23, who works at a gas station	Does not tell parents about Paul given father's high profile job and position in the community	Comfortable in relationship; fearful of parents' disappointment; worries about their finding out
18	Binge eating when alone	Becomes engaged to Paul	Graduates from high school; goes to beauty school	
		Tells sisters, not parents	Abortion	
	Loses weight	Paul breaks off the engagement	Paul "steals" back the ring (seen on Paul's new girlfriend); throws herself into work as a secretary; is promoted repeatedly	
	More comfortable about weight ("Dean's wife was a lot heavier than me");	Meets Dean, who works as a salesman; Dean says he is separated from his wife who is pregnant		Does not feel guilty about the relationship
	Binge eating when alone ("food was my only friend when he was away"); never ate when with him.	Lies to family and friends, telling them that they got married	Moves to Chicago with Dean	Secrecy (wanting to be "perfect & not disappoint my parents"); homesick
		Spouse of coworker tells her Dean is cheating on her	Throws Dean out of the house; on his way out, Dean takes her ring from her jewelry box	
27	Binge eating as an outlet	Gets pregnant, marries Bob, an alcoholic, who is "cruel and verbally abusive"	Lies to mother that she got pregnant after the wedding; birth of first child	Compliant, scared

Figure 11.6 Life Chart

Age				
28	Heaviest point: 265 pounds (lb.)	Bob occasionally shoves her	Birth of second child; "I channeled my energy into my daughters"	Hateful
32	"Eating a lot"	Husband hits her; she stands up to husband only once, to ask him to choose between her and alcohol	Does not tell anyone ("Nobody had a clue that we didn't have a wonderful marriage")	Scared
39		Bob no longer drinks but continues being verbally abusive Has sex with husband approximately 2 times a year	Continuing girl scout troop leader; very active in church Husband invests $80,000 of their joint money in real estate – all money lost; Debbie begins saving "every penny", sending $10,000 to her sister to open a savings account for Debbie; became a workaholic	Emotionally distant ("I made it happy for me") Fearful husband will hit her; obedient; proud at holding onto her feelings; derives esteem from keeping her trouble from her children and others
41	Eating as a way to "hold everything together"	Sexual relationship with Bob ends; Although she does not express anger, Bob yells at her, saying he can do whatever he wants with his money		
46	260 lbs., blood pressure increasing		Marital therapy with clergy for 3 months	
47	Loses 90 lbs. (170 lbs.); lowest adult weight	Debbie files for divorce		
50		Meets current boyfriend	Mother dies	Funeral is "a lot less stressful [than my grandfather's] because I knew it was ok to cry"
51		Moves in with current boyfriend		
52	Binge eating at night		Works 14+ hour days, not pausing to eat or rest during the day	
53	231 lbs., binges on objectively large amounts of food 3 times a week, binge eating its most frequent ever	Does not tell any family members she is seeking help		Feels satisfied with their relationship

Figure 11.6 (continued)

Next, the clinician explains the rationale of IPT, describing that therapy focuses on identifying and altering current dysfunctional interpersonal patterns related to eating disorder symptomatology.

Next, the clinician identifies a patient's specific problem area(s) by conducting an *interpersonal inventory*. The purpose of the interpersonal inventory is to make connections between life experiences and the development of eating disorder symptoms. Four separate histories are taken: a history of the eating problem and how it evolved; a history of the patient's interpersonal functioning prior to and since the development of BED; a history of significant life events; and a history of problems with self esteem and depression. At this point, the clinician also assesses the quality of the patient's current interpersonal functioning, and identifies precipitants of binge episodes. For each relationship, the clinician should assess the frequency of contact, activities shared, satisfactory and unsatisfactory aspects of the relationship, and ways in which the patient wishes to change the relationship. The information obtained from the interpersonal inventory can be put together into a life chart (see Figure 11.6). The life chart is an exploratory tool that is used to make connections between interpersonal events and the onset and maintenance of the eating disorder. It is a working document that provides important insights for both the clinician and the patient. Conducting a comprehensive interpersonal inventory is extremely important, as accurate identification of the patient's primary problem area(s) is crucial to successful treatment.

The clinician and patient will then develop a written *interpersonal formulation*, which includes the identification of the patient's primary problem area. Many patients may present with multiple problem areas, but since treatment is time-limited, the clinician should focus on the problem area that impacts the patient's interpersonal functioning most, and is most closely linked to the onset and maintenance of the eating disorder. The clinician and patient agree upon and can write up goals, which serve as a "treatment contract". Forming this contract can help the patient and clinician maintain focus on the connection between the eating disorder and interpersonal problem area, and guides the patient throughout the course of treatment (Wilfley *et al.* 2002).

During the initial phase of treatment, our case study Barb and her clinician noticed that Barb had a history of avoiding conflict, a fear of criticism, and a tendency to disregard her own needs. In this way, interpersonal deficits were identified as her primary problem area. This problem area applies to patients with a long-standing history of social isolation, low self-esteem, loneliness, and an inability to form or maintain intimate relationships. Barb, like many patients with eating disorders, reported having a large social network with many friends. However, Barb's relationships were chronically unsatisfying and lacked intimacy. She set the following goals: to become more aware of the feelings that preceded her binge eating; to share her feelings with others rather than avoiding conflict; and to find ways to nurture herself instead of expending all of her energy on others.

Intermediate phase

The intermediate phase of IPT is considered the "work" phase of treatment. The clinician's essential task in this phase is to assist the patient in understanding the connection between difficulties in interpersonal functioning and BED symptoms. The clinician uses the strategies specific to the patient's problem area to help the patient achieve his or her goals (see Table 11.3).

Once strategies for tackling the patient's specific problems are identified, the clinician facilitates the patient's work on these goals. Each week, the clinician maintains a focus on how the patient is working on his or her agreed-upon goals between sessions. Patients are encouraged to be responsible for their treatment, and to recognize that it requires attention and persistence. Clinicians can use phrases such as "moving forward on your goals" or "making important changes" in order to help the patient remain goal-oriented and focused. Midway through treatment, the patient is encouraged to complete a form that reflects on treatment to date and to plan for future gains (see Figure 11.7). The patient can fill out the reflection form between sessions 10 and 11 and bring it to session to discuss progress.

Table 11.3 IPT problem areas and corresponding goals

Problem area	Description	Strategies/Goals
Grief	Complicated bereavement following the death of a loved one	• Facilitate mourning • Help the patient to find new activities and relationships to substitute for the loss
Interpersonal role disputes	Disputes with significant other (e.g., partner, family member, coworker, friend) which emerge from differences in expectations about the relationship	• Identify the dispute • Weigh options to resolve the dispute • Modify expectations and faulty communication to bring about a satisfactory resolution
Role transitions	Difficulties resulting from a change in life status (e.g., divorce, retirement, moving, diagnosis of medical illness)	• Recognize positive and negative aspects of the new role • Mourn and accept loss of the old role • Restore self-esteem by developing a sense of mastery in the new role
Interpersonal deficits	A long-standing history of social isolation, low self-esteem, loneliness, and an inability to form or maintain intimate relationships	• Reduce the patient's social isolation by helping enhance the quality of existing relationships • Encourage the formation of new relationships

Area #1: Share your feelings with others rather than avoiding conflict. For example, you can practice confronting significant others in your life (e.g., boyfriend, sisters) when you are upset. You can also practice saying "No" to people, like your customers at the salon.

1 In what ways have you used treatment to work on this goal?	I've worked on sharing more with my boyfriend. Once, I confronted him when I thought he overreacted to something I said, and I could get through him being upset with me. I'm also talking more with my sisters. I even told my sister that she hurt my feelings.
2 How has work on this goal been connected to decreasing your problems with binge eating?	Instead of eating when I'm upset, I can sometimes talk to my boyfriend about my feelings.
3 In your social network, what changes have you noticed as a result of your work on this problem?	My relationships are going a little better with my sisters and my boyfriend.
4 In what ways have you been unable to work on this problem?	I still have a hard time not working a lot of hours and saying "No" to people.
5 What specific plan do you have for continuing to work on this problem over the next ten weeks?	I'll try to set some boundaries with my customers, and I want to share more with my daughters.

Figure 11.7 Mid-treatment Goal Reflection

The clinician continually encourages the patient to identify connections between eating disorder symptoms and interpersonal events during the week. As patients learn to make these connections, the clinician should guide them in developing strategies to alter the interpersonal context in which BED symptoms occur. For example, Barb realized that working 14-hour days to please her clients often resulted in feelings of resentment and frustration, which often led to bingeing. Throughout this phase, Barb was encouraged to set limits with her customers by refusing some of their requests.

Additionally, one of the clinician's most important jobs is to redirect discussions to highlight the connections between binge eating and interpersonal events. Patients may bring up distressing aspects of their BED symptoms and want to engage in extended discussion related to these symptoms. When this occurs, however, the clinician is to redirect the patient to link their symptoms to the interpersonal context, and to gently guide the patient toward discussion of treatment goals. Barb's clinician was often able to help Barb refocus and realize why she was bingeing:

Barb: So I got off work at 8 and since I hadn't eaten all day I picked up a pizza and ate that while I drove home. But then I got back and Denny had cooked dinner, so I ate with him again. So I had a whole pizza, then I ate the chicken that he made, and the macaroni, and we had a bunch of cookies for dessert … I was just so hungry …

Clinician: Sounds to me again like you overextended yourself and you allowed your customers to kind of box you in. You were probably really frustrated and really tired …

Barb: No, I am never frustrated with my clients. I like to help them …

Clinician: Yeah but then what happens is you exhaust yourself, because you're taking care of other people, not yourself. Look what happens, you're tired, you ate pizza and then you ate with Denny because you felt bad. You can see what happens when you have a hard time setting boundaries with other people.

Termination phase

The purpose of the termination phase is to consolidate gains made throughout treatment and to establish future goals for continued work. The clinician should begin to discuss termination early and clearly, and should address any anxiety or grief the patient may be experiencing related to the end of treatment. This is crucial because when feelings of sadness or loss are not acknowledged, they may lead to fears of relapse or an increase in symptoms.

In the four to five sessions of the termination phase, the patient is encouraged to reflect on the progress and changes he or she has made during treatment. It is especially important for the clinician to emphasize that the patient has begun to successfully manage relationships and emotions. It is not uncommon for a person with BED to attribute changes in treatment to the therapist rather than their own hard work, which may erode the patient's confidence in his or her ability for continued success and improvement after treatment.

Because there are always goals that are not accomplished within the time frame of IPT, termination should also include a discussion of strategies to prevent relapse and plans for continued work after treatment has ended. Patients should be realistic and predict that setbacks will occur, but that with continued effort, change and progress can be sustained. The clinician should guide the patient in a discussion of contingencies for handling future problems, as this will bolster feelings of competence. It is vital to assist patients in thinking about warning signs and symptoms that suggest a need for action on their part.

By the end of treatment, Barb had made many positive changes that led her to stop binge eating. She took better care of herself by decreasing her work hours, was able to tend to negative feelings without feeling overwhelmed, and recognized that making more time for herself allowed her to attend to these feelings and needs. She was encouraged to move work forward on her goals, and a year later Barb was still binge-free and had lost 70 pounds since the start of treatment.

Conclusion

In sum, the goals of CBT are to identify patterns of over-restriction and under-restriction, normalize eating patterns, teach cognitive skills to counter negative thoughts, and use cognitive restructuring to promote the acceptance of diverse body sizes. Conversely, IPT treats binge eating by intervening at the level of a patient's social network and emphasizing the link between interpersonal stressors and binge eating throughout treatment. CBT and IPT have the strongest empirical base of all studied psychological treatments for BED. Given the breadth and sustainability of treatment effects, both should be considered "first-line" treatments for patients with BED.

When determining what treatment to employ with a given patient, a number of factors should be considered. First, the clinician should examine his or her level of expertise with each modality. Both therapies are specialty treatments that should be delivered by trained professionals. However, it has been argued that experienced clinicians trained in other modalities tend to learn IPT quickly and are able to implement IPT with a high degree of integrity (Birchall 1999). Additionally, studies suggest that IPT may be more acceptable than CBT to African Americans (Chui et al. 2002; Wilson et al. 2010) and individuals with lower levels of education (Franko et al. 2012). Both CBT and IPT appear to be more effective than generalist (e.g., fluoxetine, behavioral weight loss) and non-specialist treatments (e.g., guided self-help) for individuals with more severe eating disorder presentations and general psychopathology (Grilo et al. 2012; Wilson et al. 2010). Ultimately, the choice of what modality to implement should be a collaborative decision determined by the clinician and patient based on the clinician's expertise, as well as the patient's presenting features, preferences, and skills.

Finally, there is a need to translate evidence-based treatments for BED into clinical settings in order to increase access to care. The use of specialist treatment for BED in clinical practice is relatively scarce (Kazdin 2008). Dissemination and implementation research will provide an avenue for translating evidence-based treatments into routine care so as to ensure treatment fidelity and sustainability of practice. One direction of this research has been examining the feasibility of training provider with differing levels of expertise. For example, community members with no mental health experience in Uganda and India have been successfully trained to competency in IPT (Bolton et al. 2003; Patel et al. 2011). Furthermore, new technologies may enable wider access to effective treatments. The potential for harnessing electronic-health (eHealth) and mobile-health (mHealth) technologies to enhance access to treatments for BED is a burgeoning area of research. Studies have demonstrated that therapies for BED and other psychological problems can be enhanced through the use of technology, including text messaging, Internet, and e-mail (Carrard et al. 2011; Ljotsson et al. 2007; Robinson and Serfaty 2008). Additionally, adaptations for these treatments for loss of control eating in child and adolescent populations should be explored, as early intervention to prevent development of binge eating disorder, weight gain, and associated psychopathology is a crucial direction for future research in the field.

Resources

In order to be competent in the delivery of CBT and IPT for BED, expertise with cognitive behavioral therapy and interpersonal psychotherapy protocols is needed. Clinicians should contact the authors for access to unpublished manuals for both treatments (Kenny 2011; Wilfley *et al.* 2010). Furthermore, the *Casebook of Interpersonal Psychotherapy* (Markowitz and Weissman 2012) includes more in-depth clinical guidelines for the use of IPT with patients with BED in both individual and group settings. The book *Interpersonal Psychotherapy for Group* (Wilfley 2000) is an excellent resource detailing the modification of IPT for group settings. Finally, the International Society for Interpersonal Psychotherapy (http://interpersonalpsychotherapy.org/) provides frequent opportunities around the world for certification in the delivery of IPT for a range of psychological problems.

Acknowledgments

We acknowledge Rick Stein and Robinson Welch for their invaluable clinical expertise, as well as the patients who have shared their stories with us. We also acknowledge the following grant funding: 5K24MH070446-09, 5T32HL007456-27, and the Washington University Chancellor's Graduate Fellowship Program.

References

Agras, W. S., Telch, C. F., Arnow, B., Eldredge, K., and Marnell, M. (1997) "One-year follow-up of cognitive-behavioral therapy for obese individuals with binge eating disorder", *Journal of Consulting and Clinical Psychology* 65: 343–7.

Agras, W. S., Telch, C. F., Arnow, B., Eldredge, K., Wilfley, D. E., Raeburn, S. D., *et al.* (1994) "Weight loss, cognitive-behavioral, and desipramine treatments in binge eating disorder: an additive design", *Behavior Therapy* 25: 225–38.

Arnow, B., Kenardy, J., and Agras, W. S. (1995) "The emotional eating scale: the development of a measure to assess coping with negative affect by eating", *International Journal of Eating Disorders* 18: 79–90.

Birchall, H. (1999) "Interpersonal psychotherapy in the treatment of eating disorders", *European Eating Disorders Review* 7: 315–20.

Blomquist, K. K., and Grilo, C. M. (2011) "Predictive significance of changes in dietary restraint in obese patients with binge eating disorder during treatment", *International Journal of Eating Disorders* 44: 515–23.

Bolton, P., Bass, J., Neugebauer, R., Verdeli, H., Clougherty, K. F., Wickramaratne, P., *et al.* (2003) "Group interpersonal psychotherapy for depression in rural Uganda:

a randomized controlled trial", *Journal of the American Medical Association* 289: 3117–24.

Carrard, I., Crépin, C., Rouget, P., Lam, T., Golay, A., and Van der Linden, M. (2011) "Randomised controlled trial of a guided self-help treatment on the internet for binge eating disorder", *Behaviour Research Therapy* 49: 482–91.

Chui, W., Safer, D. L., Bryson, S. W., Agras, W. S., and Wilson, G. T. (2007) "A comparison of ethnic groups in the treatment of bulimia nervosa", *Eating Behaviors* 8: 485–91.

Cooper, Z., and Fairburn, C. (1987) "The eating disorder examination: a semi-structured interview for the assessment of the specific psychopathology of eating disorders", *International Journal of Eating Disorders* 6: 1–8.

Devlin, M. J., Goldfein, J. A., Pekova, E., Jiang, H., Raiszman, P. S., Wolk, S., *et al.* (2005) "Cognitive behavioral therapy and fluoxetine as adjuncts to group behavioral therapy for binge eating disorder", *Obesity Research* 13: 1077–88.

Devlin, M. J., Goldfein, J. A., Petkova, E., Liu, L., and Walsh, B. T. (2007) "Cognitive behavioral therapy and fluoxetine for binge eating disorder: two-year follow-up", *Obesity (Silver Spring)* 15: 1702–9.

Dingemans, A. E., Spinhoven, P., and van Furth, E. F. (2007) "Predictors and mediators of treatment outcome in patients with binge eating disorder", *Behaviour Research and Therapy* 45: 2551–62.

Eldredge, K. L., and Agras, W. S. (1997) "The relationship between perceived evaluation of weight and treatment outcome among individuals with binge eating disorder", *International Journal of Eating Disorders* 22: 43–9.

Fairburn, C. G., Doll, H. A., Welch, S. L., Hay, P. J., Davies, B. A., and O'Connor, M. E. (1998) "Risk factors for binge eating disorder: a community-based, case-control study", *Archives of General Psychiatry* 55: 425–32.

Fairburn, C. G., Welch, S. L., Doll, H. A., and O'Connor, M. E. (1997) "Risk factors for bulimia nervosa: a community-based case-control study", *Archives of General Psychiatry* 54: 509–17.

Franko, D. L., Thompson-Brenner, H., Thompson, D. R., Boisseau, C. L., Davis, A., Forbush, K. T., *et al.* (2012) "Racial/ethnic differences in adults in randomized clinical trials of binge eating disorder", *Journal of Consulting and Clinical Psychology* 80: 186–95.

Gorin, A. A., Le Grange, D., and Stone, A. A. (2003) "Effectiveness of spouse involvement in cognitive behavioral therapy for binge eating disorder", *International Journal of Eating Disorders* 33: 421–33.

Grilo, C. M., and Masheb, R. M. (2005) "A randomized controlled comparison of guided self-help cognitive behavioral therapy and behavioral weight loss for binge eating disorder", *Behavior Research and Therapy* 43: 1509–25.

Grilo, C. M., Masheb, R. M., and Crosby, R. D. (2012) "Predictors and moderators of response to cognitive behavioral therapy and medication for the treatment of binge eating disorder", *Journal of Consulting and Clinical Psychology*: e-pub ahead of print.

Grilo, C. M., Masheb, R. M., Wilson, G. T., Gueorguieva, R., and White, M. A. (2011) "Cognitive–behavioral therapy, behavioral weight loss, and sequential treatment for obese patients with binge-eating disorder: a randomized controlled trial", *Journal of Consulting and Clinical Psychology* 79: 675–85.

Hilbert, A., Bishop, M. E., Stein, R. I., Tanofsky-Kraff, M., Swenson, A. K., Welch, R. R. *et al.* (2012) "Long-term efficacy of psychological treatments for binge eating disorder", *British Journal of Psychiatry* 200: 232–7.

Horowitz, L. M., Rosenberg, S. E., Baer, B. A., Ureno, G., and Villasenor, G. (1988) "Inventory of interpersonal problems: psychometric properties and clinical applications", *Journal of Consulting and Clinical Psychology* 56: 885–92.

Iacovino, J. M., Gredysa, D. M., Altman, M., and Wilfley, D. E. (in press) "Psychological treatments for binge eating disorder", *Current Psychiatry Reports*.

Kazdin, A. E. (2008) "Evidence-based treatment and practice: new opportunities to bridge clinical research and practice, enhance the knowledge base, and improve patient care", *American Psychologist* 63: 146–59.

Kenardy, J., Mensch, M., Bowen, K., and Walton, J. (2002) "Group therapy for binge eating in Type 2 diabetes: a randomized trial", *Diabetes Medicine* 19: 234–9.

Kenny, P. J. (2011) "Common cellular and molecular mechanisms in obesity and drug addiction", *Nature Reviews Neuroscience* 12: 638–51.

Ljotsson, B., Lundin, C., Mitsell, K., Carlbring, P., Ramklint, M., and Ghaderi, A. (2007) "Remote treatment of bulimia nervosa and binge eating disorder: a randomized trial of Internet-assisted cognitive behavioural therapy", *Behavior Research and Therapy* 45: 649–61.

Markowitz, J. C., and Weissman, M. M. (2012) *Casebook of Interpersonal Psychotherapy*, Oxford: Oxford University Press.

Munsch, S., Biedert, E., Meyer, A., Michael, T., Schlup, B., Tuch, A., and Margraf, J. (2007) "A randomized comparison of cognitive behavioral therapy and behavioral weight loss treatment for overweight individuals with binge eating disorder", *International Journal of Eating Disorders* 40: 102–13.

Patel, V., Chowdhary, M., Rahman, A., and Verdeli, H. (2011) "Improving access to psychological treatments: lessons from developing countries", *Behavior Research and Therapy* 49: 523–8.

Rieger, E., Van Buren, D. J., Bishop, M., Tanofsky-Kraff, M., Welch, R., and Wilfley, D. (2010) "An eating disorder-specific model of interpersonal psychotherapy (IPT-ED): causal pathways and treatment implications", *Clinical Psychology Review* 30: 400–10.

Rieger, E., Wilfley, D. E., Stein, R. I., Marino, V., and Crow, S. J. (2005) "A comparison of quality of life in obese individuals with and without binge eating disorder", *International Journal of Eating Disorders* 37: 234–40.

Robinson, P., and Serfaty, M. (2008) "Getting better byte by byte: a pilot randomised controlled trial of email therapy for bulimia nervosa and binge eating disorder", *European Eating Disorders Review* 16: 84–93.

Schlup, B., Munsch, S., Meyer, A. H., Margraf, J., Wilhelm, F. H. (2009) "The efficacy of a short version of a cognitive-behavioral treatment followed by booster sessions for binge eating disorder", *Behavior Research and Therapy* 47: 628–35.

Steiger, H., Gauvin, L., Jabalpurwala, J.R., Sequin, J. R., and Stotland, S. (1999) "Hypersensitivity to social interactions in bulimic syndromes: relationship to binge eating", *Journal of Consulting and Clinical Psychology* 67: 765–75.

Tanofsky-Kraff, M., Wilfley, D. E., and Spurrell, E. (2000) "Impact of interpersonal and ego-related stress on restrained eaters", *International Journal of Eating Disorders* 27: 411–18.

Tanofsky-Kraff, M., Wilfley, D. E., and Young, J. F., Mufson, L., Yanovski, S. Z., Glasofer, D. R., Salaita, C. G., and Schvey, N. A. (2009) "A pilot study of interpersonal psychotherapy for preventing excess weight gain in adolescent girls at-risk for obesity", *International Journal of Eating Disorders* (e-pub ahead of print).

Telch, C. F., Agras, W. S., Rossiter, E. M., Wilfley, D. E., and Kenardy, J. (1990) "Group cognitive-behavioral treatment for the nonpurging bulimic: an initial evaluation", *Journal of Consulting and Clinical Psychology* 58: 629–35.

Wilfley, D. E. (2000) *Interpersonal Psychotherapy for Group*, New York: Basic Books.

Wilfley, D. E. (2002) "Psychological treatment of binge eating disorder", in K. D. Brownell and C. G. Fairburn (eds) *Eating Disorders and Obesity* (pp. 350–53), New York: The Guilford Press.

Wilfley, D. E., Agras, W. S., Telch, C. F., Rossiter, E. M., Schneider, J. A., Cole, A. G., *et al.* (1993) "Group cognitive-behavioral therapy and group interpersonal psychotherapy for the nonpurging bulimic individual: a controlled comparison", *Journal of Consulting and Clinical Psychology* 61: 296–305.

Wilfley, D. E., Stein, R., and Welch, R. (2005) "Interpersonal psychotherapy", in J. Treasure, J., U. Schmidt, and E. van Furth (eds) *The Essential Handbook of Eating Disorders* (pp. 137–54), West Sussex, UK: John Wiley & Sons.

Wilfley, D. E., Van Buren, D. J., Theim, K. R., Stein, R. I., Saelens, B. E., Ezzet, F., *et al.* (2010) "The use of biosimulation in the design of a novel multilevel weight loss maintenance program for overweight children", *Obesity (Silver Spring)* 18 Suppl 1: S91–8.

Wilfley, D. E., Welch, R. R., Stein, R. I., Spurrell, E. B., Cohen, L. R., Saelens, B. E., *et al.* (2002) "A randomized comparison of group cognitive-behavioral therapy and group interpersonal psychotherapy for the treatment of overweight individuals with binge-eating disorder", *Archives of General Psychiatry* 59: 71321.

Wilson, G. T., and Shafran, R. (2005) "Eating disorders guidelines from NICE", *Lancet* 365: 79–81.

Wilson, G. T., Wilfley, D. E., Agras, W. S., and Bryson, S. W. (2010) "Psychological treatments of binge eating disorder", *Archives of General Psychiatry* 67: 94–101.

Chapter 12

Pharmacologic treatment of binge eating disorder

Scott Crow

Case study

I'm a 45-year-old woman who presented for treatment of BED at a multi-disciplinary eating disorder treatment program. I began engaging in episodes of binge eating in the seventh grade. About three times a week I eat a large amount of food with loss of control, usually in secret. I don't have a history of purging, except for brief experimentation when I started college. I have begun psychotherapy sessions and have been working with a dietician about two months prior to this latest medication evaluation. I feel my "relationship with food" has improved substantially, and the amount of time I spend thinking about eating, weight, and shape-related issues has diminished somewhat. The frequency of eating binges has gone from four or five times a week down to three a week, but I believe this has plateaued.

I have had "lifelong depression", which my therapist says sounds like recurring episodes of major depression, about nine bouts in total, each lasting six months to a year. I've no history of substance use disorder except for a drinking pattern suggestive of alcohol abuse in college. I've had occasional panic attacks and some diffuse anxiety, primarily focused on eating-related issues. My therapist says I've no OCD, no PTSD, and no social phobia.

I'm interested in considering medication to try to get my binge eating under better control, and I want to lose at least 50lbs (my current height is 5'5" and my current weight is 212lbs for a BMI of 35.3). My therapist and dietician are somewhat hesitant about desire for weight loss; the internist feels that I should consider trying to lose weight, but suggests a weight loss goal of between 15 and 20lbs.

Miss A

Introduction

Medications provide one potential treatment approach for BED. As with other eating disorders, medications play a less prominent role than psychotherapy and/

or changes in nutritional patterns. However, there are specific situations in which medications may be particularly useful. Certainly, the other approaches do not work optimally for every person with binge eating disorder (this may be particularly true when weight change is the desired outcome). Effective pharmacologic treatments are available essentially anywhere, in contrast to specialized psychotherapies. Also, medicines may be useful in treating comorbid conditions such as depression or anxiety disorders.

For all these reasons, medication treatment represents a viable approach to BED. This chapter reviews the rationale for and potential goals of medication treatment for BED. The existing literature regarding controlled trials of medications for BED will be discussed, and its strengths and limitations reviewed. Finally, summary recommendations will be made.

Rationale for and goals of medication treatment for BED

Several clinical situations may prompt consideration of medication treatment for BED. First, while response rates to psychotherapy and dietary interventions for binge eating reduction and abstinence are impressive, a significant number of patients do not improve fully in terms of binge eating when receiving those other treatments. This may prompt consideration of medication treatment to address binge eating symptoms, or perhaps associated eating disorder cognitions. In addition, psychotherapy for BED typically is associated with degrees of weight loss which fall far short of even minimally desired amounts of weight loss for individuals receiving treatment. As the following review will show, currently available medications that have been studied for BED vary widely in terms of their impact of weight, but some do appear to be associated with significant amounts of weight loss in short term treatment. Therefore, certain medication choices may be useful when weight loss is desired. Third, as discussed elsewhere in this volume, BED is strongly associated with forms of psychopathology; medications may be quite useful in treating these other forms of psychopathology. Often, it's possible to identify medication options which would have the potential to improve multiple types of psychopathology encountered in the same person. Last, while a number of effective psychotherapy approaches and nutritional approaches to binge eating disorder have been identified (as discussed elsewhere in this volume), they typically require significant amounts of training and experience to execute properly and, as such, these treatments are typically most readily found in specialized eating disorder centers. While many such centers now exist, it seems likely that most people in most countries do not have practical access to such treatments, simply for geographical reasons. The situation is potentially far better for medications. In other areas (bulimia nervosa, for example) there is evidence that pharmacologic treatments are not always used optimally (for example, see Crow *et al.* 1999). However, while they often may not be employed optimally, they are available to be used in an optimal fashion at essentially any pharmacy; therefore, pharmacologic treatments are much more widely available. Furthermore, it would likely be easier to train a non-specialist practitioner to provide adequate pharmacotherapy (for example, adequate doses of SSRI's) than it would be to train a non-specialist practitioner to effectively employ a manual-based psychotherapy.

There are several potential goals for medication treatment. A first goal, assessed in nearly all controlled trials conducted so far, is the cessation of binge eating. Much emphasis in this area has been placed on abstinence from binge eating (just as in bulimia nervosa) relating to a concern that persisting binge eating (even at low rates) at the end of treatment may be associated with a high rate of relapse. Most trials also report information on the percentage decrease in binge eating. Both are potentially useful pieces of information, as it is not formally known whether patients receiving treatment value full abstinence from binge eating substantially more highly than marked decreases in the rate of binge eating. A second potential goal of treatment is the reduction in eating disorder cognitions related to BED, though this overall has received less attention in pharmaco-therapy trials to date. Third, another critical potential outcome variable is change in weight. Given that weight loss might carry significant medical benefit for many obese individuals with binge eating disorder, most trials conducted in this area have reported data on weight loss. Clinically, this is a particularly salient outcome since it appears that many, perhaps most people seeking treatment for binge eating disorder, would categorize weight loss as being of equal or more impor-tance to them as cessation of binge eating. A final goal of medication treatment, as referenced above, could be the treatment of comorbid psychopathology (particu-larly mood and anxiety disorders).

Review of controlled treatment trials for binge eating disorder

Initial medication development in this area followed along the lines of that conducted in bulimia nervosa. As such, the work focused initially on antidepres-sants but in more recent years, medications with the potential to impact food intact directly have also been examined. These studies will be reviewed here in brief and are summarized in Table 12.1.

SSRI trials

Multiple SSRIs have been studied, and these represent the largest number of trials in BED at this point. Marcus and colleagues conducted the initial trial of fluoxetine (1990). Twenty-two people participated in this year-long trial, in which improvements in binge eating were seen, but abstinence rates were not reported. Weight loss was significantly greater in the active drug than the placebo-treated group. Three subsequent trials have also examined fluoxetine (Arnold *et al.* 2002; Devlin *et al.* 2004; Grilo, Masheb and Wilson 2005). The Arnold *et al.* study examined medication treatment alone in 60 participants over 6 weeks of treatment and both binge-eating abstinence and weight change favored the active drug. Both the Grilo and Devlin studies combined pharmacotherapy treatment with cognitive behavioral treatment and each lasted somewhat longer (16 and 20 weeks, respectively), but neither found significant benefit for fluoxetine.

A second SSRI receiving attention is fluvoxamine with a 9-week study in 85 subjects finding greater efficacy for active drug in binge abstinence and weight loss (Hudson *et al.* 1998) but a substantially smaller (20 subject) study finding no difference between active drug and placebo (Pearlstein *et al.* 2003). Smaller studies have been conducted using citalopram (McElroy *et al.* 2003) and escitalopram (Guerdjikova *et al.* 2008). In each of these trials, abstinence rates were substantially higher with active drug than placebo and weight loss results modestly favored active drug. Finally, one study has examined sertraline (McElroy *et al.* 2000); in this small study, binge eating outcomes favored active drug and weight loss was greater with active drug than placebo.

In summary, many of these trials have found some advantage for active drug over placebo in terms of cessation of binge eating, but weight loss results have been for the most part quite modest.

Other antidepressants

An early study of desipramine was conducted by Agras and colleagues (1994). The design was an additive one, wherein participants were randomized to receive or not receive desipramine; all received CBT. Notably, the treament was not placebo-controlled, but binge eating and weight loss outcomes were more favorable in those receiving desipramine.

Other agents

One study has examined atomoxetine for BED (McElroy, Guerdjikova *et al.* 2007). This 10-week study included 40 people and abstinence rates were substantially higher with active drug compared with placebo, with modest weight losses in the active drug group and no weight change with placebo.

Agents selected for weight loss properties

A number of studies have employed agents selected at least in part for their tendency to cause weight loss and/or diminish appetite. In this group, however, some of the studied agents also have other putative mechanisms including direct impact on binge eating (topiramate) or indirect impact to diminish binge eating by virtue of adverse consequences of binge eating while on the active agent (orlistat). Notably, two of the agents in this group have been withdrawn from the market for safety reasons (sibutramine and d-fentluramine). The currently available agents and withdrawn agents will be reviewed separately.

Agents currently available

One medication that has received substantial attention is the anticonvulsant topiramate, selected in large part for its tendency to diminish appetite and weight (first noted in studies of people with seizure disorders). A total of three studies have been conducted (Claudino *et al.* 2007; McElroy *et al.* 2003; McElroy, Hudson *et al.* 2007), and long-term outcome is available from one of these studies (McElroy *et al.* 2006). In each of these studies, substantially greater rates of abstinence from binge eating behavior were observed with active drug than placebo, and weight loss also favored active drug. Moreover, in the long-term extension and follow-up study reported by McElroy *et al.* (2006) it appeared that a substantial amount of the benefit was preserved and moreover that subjects who crossed over to placebo experienced some improvement.

Two studies have examined orlistat (Golay *et al.* 2005; Grilo, Masheb, and Salant 2005). In each of these studies greater weight loss and greater binge eating abstinence was seen with active drug.

Agents withdrawn from the market

Stunkard and colleagues (1996) described the results of a study of d-fenfluramine for the treatment of BED. Notably, although benefits were observed with regard to binge eating, no statistically or clinically significant difference in weight change was seen between active drug and placebo (albeit in a relatively brief, eight-week study). More recently, several studies examined sibutramine, a noradrenergic and serotonergic reuptake inhibitor subsequently withdrawn from the market because of concerns about impact on blood pressure. In these studies, higher rates of abstinence from binge eating were seen with active drug than placebo, and weight loss results also favored active drug (Appolinario *et al.* 2003; Milano *et al.* 2005; Wifley *et al.* 2008).

Limitations of the existing literature

As the above section details, there is ample knowledge about pharmacologic treatments for BED. However, the existing literature is marked by several very significant limitations. These limitations do not invalidate the existing literature but they do tend to limit somewhat how well it can inform current practice.

First, placebo rate response rates are high, perhaps higher than that seen in some other areas of psychopharmacology research. This sometimes has been used to argue for diminished importance for BED, yet examination of the outcome of placebo responders suggests that most people with BED who have placebo response revert to symptomatic status relatively promptly (Jacobs-Pilipski *et al.* 2007). Such a high placebo response rate might be better viewed not as an indictment of BED as a diagnostic construct but rather as a significant

Table 12.1 Controlled Pharmacotherapy Trials for BED

Author	Year	n	Drug	Duration (Weeks)	% Abstinent		Weight Change	
					Drug	Placebo	Drug	Placebo
Appolinario et al.	2003	60	Sibutramine	12	52	32	-7.4 kg	1.4 kg
Arnold et al.	2002	60	Fluoxetine	6	45	24	-3.3 kg	0.7 kg
Grilo, Masheb & Wilson	2005	108	Fluoxetine	16	29	30	-0.8 kg	0 kg
Guerdjikova et al.	2008	44	Escitalopram	12	50	26	-1.0 kg	0.6 kg
Hudson et al.	1998	85	Fluvoxamine	9	45	24	-2.7 kg	-0.3 kg
McElroy et al.	2000	34	Sertraline	6	NR	NR	+2.3[a] kg	-5.3 a kg
McElroy et al.	2003	38	Citalopram	6	47	21	-2.1 kg	0.2 kg
McElroy et al.	2003	61	Topiramate	14	64	30	-5.9 kg	-1.2 kg
McElroy, Hudson et al.	2007	394	Topiramate	16	58	29	-4.5 kg	0.2 kg
McElroy et al.	2006	60	Zonisamide	16	54	45	-4.8 kg	-1.0 kg
McElroy, Guerdjikova et al.	2007	40	Atomoxetine	10	70	32	-2.7 kg	-0.0 kg
Milano et al.	2005	20	Sibutramine	12	NR	NR	-4.5 kg	-0.6 kg
Pearlstein et al.	2003	25	Fluvoxamine	12	50	50	-.4 kg	+1.8 kg
Stunkard et al.	1996	28	d-fenfluramine	8	NR	NR	-0.02 kg	0.06
Wilfley et al.	2008	304	Sibutramine	24	59	43	-4.3 kg	-0.8 kg
Golay et al.	2005	89	Orlistat	24	NR	NR	-7.4%	-2.3%
Agras et al.	1994	108	Desipramine	36	41	37	-6.0 kg	-1.6 kg
Grilo, Masheb & Salant	2005	50	Orlistat	12	64	36	-3.5 kg	-1.6 kg
Claudino et al.	2007	73	Topiramate	21	84	61	6.8%	4.1%
Devlin et al.	2005	116	Fluoxetine	20	52	41	-4.1 kg	-1.9 kg
Marcus et al.	1990	45	Fluoxetine	52	NR	NR	-13.9 kg	0.6 kg

[a] estimated

NR = not reported

practical challenge to researchers attempting to identify potentially effective treatments for BED.

A second major limitation regards the duration of trials. As Table 12.1 shows, most studies have been relatively short, with the duration best measured in weeks. The optimal length of time for medication treatment aimed at binge eating symptoms has not been firmly established, yet it seems unlikely to be substantially shorter than the optimal length of time for the treatment of mood or anxiety disorders (and, one must recall that treatment of those disorders is often a secondary target of BED pharmacotherapy). Viewed from that perspective, almost none of the trials conducted so far would qualify as an "adequate" medication trial in terms of length. Considered from the standpoint of obesity pharmacotherapy, most thinking in the obesity pharmacotherapy field has tended to conceptualize of weight loss medications as similar to antihypertensives or anti-diabetic agents, in the sense that they must continually be taken in order to gain benefit. This perspective, too, would suggest that the existing trials are far too short.

As in bulimia nervosa (Mitchell *et al.* 1997) many trials have employed relatively restrictive inclusion and exclusion criteria which likely result in clinical trial samples bearing limited relationship to commonly encountered clinic samples (see Guerdjikova and McElroy 2009). Similarly, the existing trials have generally looked at one (binge eating) or two (binge eating and weight loss) outcomes. But in clinical practice, it is common to look at treatment of comorbid psychopathology and only very limited work in this area has been conducted to date (Guerdjikova *et al.* 2012). Further studies of this sort would be welcome. Additionally, such studies might well consider quality of life as an important outcome as this also has been examined only to a limited degree.

Conclusion

A growing literature generally supports the efficacy of SSRIs, topiramate, and orlistat as treatments for BED. Decreases in binge eating and modest weight loss have been observed, with weight loss more prominent generally in the topiramate and orlistat studies. The existing evidence is over short treatment duration, generally, but effective pharmacotherapy for BED likely requires at least months of treatment. In sum, medications represent a useful treatment option for BED.

References

Agras, W. S., Telch, C. F., Arnow, B., Eldredge, K., Wilfley, D. E., Raeburn, S. D., *et al.* (1994) "Weight loss, cognitive-behavioral, and desipramine treatments in binge eating disorder: an additive design", *Behavior Therapy* 25: 225–38.

Appolinario, J. C., Bacaltchuk, J., Sichieri, R., Claudino, A. M., Godoy-Matos, A., Morgan, C., *et al.* (2003) "A randomized, double-blind, placebo-controlled study of sibutramine in the treatment of binge-eating disorder", *Archives of General Psychiatry* 60(11): 1109–16.

Arnold, L. M., McElroy, S. L., Hudson, J. I., Welge, J. A., Bennett, A. J., and Keck, P. E. (2002) "'placebo-controlled, randomized trial of fluoxetine in the treatment of binge-eating disorder", *Journal of Clinical Psychiatry* 63(11): 1028–33.

Claudino, A. M., de Oliveira, I. R., Appolinario, J. C., Cordas, T. A., Duchesne, M., Sichieri, R., *et al.* (2007) "Double-blind, randomized, placebo-controlled trial of topiramate plus cognitive-behavior therapy in binge-eating disorder", *Journal of Clinical Psychiatry* 68(9): 1324–32.

Crow, S., Mussell, M. P., Peterson, C., Knopke, A., and Mitchell, J. (1999) "Prior treatment received by patients with bulimia nervosa", *International Journal of Eating Disorders* 25(1): 39–44.

Devlin, M. J., Goldfein, J. A., Petkova, E., Jiang, H., Raizman, P. S., Wolk, S., *et al.* (2005) "Cognitive behavioral therapy and fluoxetine as adjuncts to group behavioral therapy for binge eating disorder", *Obesity Research* 13(6): 1077–88.

Georgoulias, V., and Crown, J. P. (1999) "Increasing options in cancer therapy: current status and future prospects", *Anti-Cancer Drugs* 10 Suppl 1: S1–3.

Golay, A., Laurent-Jaccard, A., Habicht, F., Gachoud, J. P., Chabloz, M., Kammer, A., *et al.* (2005) "Effect of orlistat in obese patients with binge eating disorder", *Obesity Research* 13(10): 1701–8.

Grilo, C. M., Masheb, R. M., and Salant, S. L. (2005) "Cognitive behavioral therapy guided self-help and orlistat for the treatment of binge eating disorder: a randomized, double-blind, placebo-controlled trial", *Biological Psychiatry* 57(10): 1193–201.

Grilo, C. M., Masheb, R. M., and Wilson, G. T. (2005) "Efficacy of cognitive behavioral therapy and fluoxetine for the treatment of binge eating disorder: a randomized double-blind placebo-controlled comparison", *Biological Psychiatry* 57(3): 301–9.

Grilo, C. M., Masheb, R. M., and Wilson, G. T. (2006) "Rapid response to treatment for binge eating disorder", *Journal of Consulting and Clinincal Psychology* 74(3): 602–13.

Guerdjikova, A. I., and McElroy, S. L. (2009) "Binge eating disorder pharmacotherapy clinical trails – who is left out?", *European Eating Disorders Review* 17(2): 101–8.

Guerdjikova, A. I., McElroy, S. L., Kotwal, R., Welge, J. A., Nelson, E., Lake, K., *et al.* (2008) "High-dose escitalopram in the treatment of binge-eating disorder with obesity: a placebo-controlled monotherapy trial", *Human Psychopharmacology* 23(1): 1–11.

Guerdjikova, A. I., McElroy, S. L., Winstanley, E. L., Nelson, E. B., Mori, N., McCoy, J., *et al.* (2012) "Duloxetine in the treatment of binge eating disorder with depressive disorders: a placebo-controlled trial", *International Journal of Eating Disorders* 45(2): 281–9.

Hudson, J. I., McElroy, S. L., Raymond, N. C., Crow, S., Keck, P. E. Jnr, Carter, W. P., *et al.* (1998) "Fluvoxamine in the treatment of binge-eating disorder: a multicenter placebo-controlled, double-blind trial", *American Journal of Psychiatry* 155(12): 1756–62.

Jacobs-Pilipski, M. J., Wilfley, D. E., Crow, S. J., Walsh, B. T., Lilenfeld, L. R., West, D.S., *et al.* (2007) "Placebo response in binge eating disorder", *International Journal of Eating Disorders* 40(3): 204–11.

Marcus, M. D., Wing, R. R., Ewing, L., Kern, E., McDermott, M., and Gooding, W. (1990) "A double-blind, placebo-controlled trial of fluoxetine plus behavior modification in the treatment of obese binge-eaters and non-binge-eaters", *American Journal of Psychiatry* 147(7): 876–81.

McElroy, S. L., Casuto, L. S., Nelson, E. B., Lake, K. A., Soutullo, C. A., Keck, P. E. Jnr, *et al.* (2000) "Placebo-controlled trial of sertraline in the treatment of binge eating disorder", *American Journal of Psychiatry* 157(6): 1004–6.

McElroy, S. L., Guerdjikova, A., Kotwal, R., Welge, J. A., Nelson, E. B., Lake, K. A., *et al.* (2007) "Atomoxetine in the treatment of binge-eating disorder: a randomized placebo-controlled trial", *Journal of Clinical Psychiatry* 68(3): 390–98.

McElroy, S. L., Hudson, J. I., Capece, J. A., Beyers, K., Fisher, A. C., and Rosenthal, N. R. (2007) "Topiramate for the treatment of binge eating disorder associated with obesity: a placebo-controlled study", *Biological Psychiatry* 61(9): 1039–48.

McElroy, S. L., Hudson, J. I., Malhotra, S., Welge, J. A., Nelson, E. B., and Keck, P. E. Jnr (2003) "Citalopram in the treatment of binge-eating disorder: a placebo-controlled trial", *Journal of Clinical Psychiatry* 64(7): 807–13.

McElroy, S. L., Kotwal, R., Guerdjikova, A. I., Welge, J. A., Nelson, E. B., Lake, K. A., *et al.* (2006) "Zonisamide in the treatment of binge eating disorder with obesity: a randomized controlled trial", *Journal of Clinical Psychiatry* 67(12): 1897–906.

Milano, W., Petrella, C., Casella, A., Capasso, A., Carrino, S., and Milano, L. (2005) "Use of sibutramine, an inhibitor of the reuptake of serotonin and noradrenaline, in the treatment of binge eating disorder: a placebo-controlled study", *Advances in Therapy* 22(1): 25–31.

Mitchell, J. E., Maki, D. D., Adson, D. E., Ruskin, B. S., and Crow, S. (1997) "The selectivity of inclusion and exclusion criteria in bulimia nervosa treatment studies", *International Journal of Eating Disorders* 22(3): 243–52.

Pearlstein, T., Spurell, E., Hohlstein, L. A., Gurney, V., Read, J., Fuchs, C., *et al.* (2003) "A double-blind, placebo-controlled trial of fluvoxamine in binge eating disorder: a high placebo response", Archives of Women's Mental Health 6(2): 147–51.

Reas, D. L., and Grilo, C. M. (2008) "Review and meta-analysis of pharmacotherapy for binge-eating disorder", *Obesity (Silver Spring)* 16(9): 2024–38.

Ruof, J., Golay, A., Berne, C., Collin, C., Lentz, J., and Maetzel, A. (2005) "Orlistat in responding obese type 2 diabetic patients: meta-analysis findings and cost-effectiveness as rationales for reimbursement in Sweden and Switzerland", *International Journal of Obesity* 29(5): 517–23.

Stunkard, A., Berkowitz, R., Tanrikut, C., Reiss, E., and Young, L. (1996) "d-fenfluramine treatment of binge eating disorder", *American Journal of Psychiatry* 153(11): 1455–9.

Wilfley, D. E., Crow, S. J., Hudson, J. I., Mitchell, J. E., Berkowitz, R. I., Blakesley, V., *et al.* (2008) "Efficacy of sibutramine for the treatment of binge eating disorder: a randomized multicenter placebo-controlled double-blind study", *American Journal of Psychiatry* 165(1): 51–8.

Chapter 13

Loss of control and binge eating in children and adolescents

Children and adolescents: interventions

Robyn Osborn, Rachel Miller, Anna Vannucci,
Andrea B. Goldschmidt, Kerri Boutelle
(with Stephanie Knatz and Jennifer Madowitz) and
Marian Tanofsky-Kraff

Introduction

Full-syndrome binge eating disorder (BED) is rarely diagnosed among children and adolescents. Yet episodes of loss of control (LOC) eating are often reported by youth (Tanofsky-Kraff *et al.* 2004). As described more fully in the first part of this chapter, when children and adolescents report experiencing an inability to stop eating once started, the eating can be characterized as a LOC episode, which can occur irrespective of amount of food consumed. In other words, children experience LOC with or without consuming an unambiguously large amount of food, so including both large episodes of binge eating and not large episodes. Given the psychological (e.g. depressive symptoms), social (difficult relationships), and health (obesity) problems associated with LOC eating in youth (see the first part of this chapter), it is crucial for clinicians to assess for the presence of LOC eating and to implement interventions focused on reducing LOC eating and associated problems, such as excessive weight gain.

Youth reporting LOC eating are more likely to be overweight or obese compared to youth without this behavior and often participate in behavioral weight loss programs due to their weight status. However, some behavioral weight loss programs for children and adolescents have demonstrated limited impact on LOC eating and weight loss outcomes among youth with LOC eating (Epstein *et al.* 2001; Ranzenhofer *et al.* 2008; Wildes *et al.* 2010). These findings are comparable in obese adults with BED (Blaine and Rodman 2007; Gorin *et al.* 2008; White *et al.* 2010; Wilson *et al.* 2010). Therefore, interventions aimed primarily at modifying energy intake and physical activity in youth for weight management may be less effective than treatments that specifically target aberrant eating patterns such as LOC or binge eating.

This chapter reviews evidence-based intervention strategies for LOC eating in youth. Two primary types interventions are discussed: cognitive behavioral therapy (CBT) and interpersonal psychotherapy (IPT) for BED, both of which have been more extensively reviewed elsewhere (Tanofsky-Kraff, Wilfley *et al.* 2007; Wilfley *et al.* 2011). Intervention strategies for disinhibited eating behaviors that often overlap with loss of control eating are be reviewed.

Cognitive behavioral therapy

Like most cognitive behavioral therapy (CBT) treatment protocols, CBT for BED targets specific thoughts and behaviors that are directly associated with the disorder (Fairburn 2008). For example, many people who have BED report periods of overeating followed by periods of under-eating (restriction); these periods of under-eating and restriction can trigger a binge episode (Herman and Polivy 1980). A cycle of dietary restriction and binge eating is created that maintains bingeing behavior. One behavioral therapeutic focus for BED is to emphasize moderation of food intake (Wilfley *et al.* 2002). With regard to cognitions and emotions, binge eating episodes are frequently preceded by negative affect (for a review, see Wolfe *et al.* 2009). Negative cognitions and self-talk about body shape and weight, low self-esteem, and negative affect are targeted in CBT for BED to reduce dysfunctional thinking patterns that perpetuate the binge cycle (Stein *et al.* 2001; Wilfley *et al.* 2011). See Chapter 11 for a full description of CBT for adult BED.

Very few studies have examined CBT for children and adolescents with LOC eating behaviors. Jones *et al.* (2008) evaluated an Internet-facilitated weight management program aimed at reducing binge eating, overeating and weight gain among overweight high school students. Compared to waitlist controls, adolescents receiving CBT displayed significant reductions in BMI, binge eating, and shape and weight concerns. However, participants rarely logged on to the CBT online program, leaving the mechanism of change unclear. Nevertheless, additional data evaluating CBT modification programs among overweight adolescents have revealed similar findings. Moens and colleagues reported weight loss and/or maintenance over an eight-year follow up using a multidisciplinary outpatient CBT program for obese children (mean age 10 years). Inpatient CBT programs also have shown some long-term (14-month) weight-loss outcomes (Braet et al. 2004; Ceilo-Doyle et al. 2008; Moens et al. 2010). As more trials are conducted, CBT interventions will continue to be viable options for children and adolescents with eating and weight concerns.

Interpersonal psychotherapy

Interpersonal psychotherapy (IPT) was originally developed for the treatment of depression (Weissman *et al.* 2000), modified for patients with bulimia nervosa (Fairburn *et al.* 1991), and later adapted into a group format for people with BED (Wilfley 2000). IPT for the Prevention of Excessive Weight Gain (IPT-WG) (Tanofsky-Kraff, Wilfley *et al.* 2007) was developed for teens experiencing LOC eating. IPT-WG was adapted directly from IPT for Adolescent Skills Training for the prevention of depression (Young *et al.* 2006) and IPT for BED (Wilfley 2000) and is aimed at reducing inappropriate weight gain as well as reducing disordered eating and the development of full-syndrome BED (Tanofsky-Kraff, in press). A pilot study of IPT-WG was conducted among adolescent girls (12–17 years) at risk for obesity (75th–97th body mass index percentile) with and without LOC eating (Tanofsky-Kraff *et al.* 2010). Among girls reporting LOC, those in IPT-WG exhibited greater reductions in LOC episodes as compared to girls in the health education group. Regardless of LOC status, girls in IPT-WG were less likely to experience excessive weight gain as compared to girls in the health education group at one-year follow-up. A full-scale randomized controlled trial is underway.

IPT is a brief, time-limited therapy that focuses on improving interpersonal functioning by relating symptoms to interpersonal problem areas and targeting strategies to improve these problems (Freeman and Gil 2004; Klerman *et al.* 1984). According to interpersonal theory as it relates to LOC eating, difficult interpersonal interactions, feelings of loneliness, or other negative emotions (e.g., feeling angry, bored or sad) trigger episodes of LOC eating, as people use food to cope with negative affect. Therefore, IPT is designed to improve interpersonal functioning and self-esteem, reduce negative affect and, in turn, decrease eating disorder symptoms.

IPT targets negative affect by addressing social interactions that are related to mood rather than directly targeting eating behaviors. It is based on the assumption that binge eating occurs in response to poor social functioning, such as isolation and rejection, and consequent negative moods (Wilfley *et al.* 1997). Interpersonal relationships and social functioning are of vital impor-tance to adolescents (Mufson *et al.* 2004) and many adolescents use peer relationships as a measure of self-evaluation; therefore, they may be more motivated to engage in treatment and prevention programs focusing on social relationships.

Overweight youth often have negative feelings about their body shape and weight (Fallon *et al.* 2005; Schwimmer *et al.* 2003; Striegel-Moore *et al.* 1986), are frequently subjected to teasing, and may have low self-esteem and increased negative affect compared to healthy weight adolescents (Strauss and Pollack 2003). To cope with negative emotions, some teens may use food to self-soothe. IPT focuses on increasing interpersonal skills and improving relationships with the aim of reducing negative affect and LOC eating. Given the time-limited nature of IPT, clinicians must quickly identify patterns in interpersonal relationships and link these patterns to eating disordered symptoms.

IPT-WG is delivered in a group format and begins with an "interpersonal inventory" (Weissman *et al.* 2000) to identify connections between interpersonal functioning, self-esteem and mood, and eating patterns. Using the inventory, the therapists (typically, two) learn about the patient's relationships and the context in which LOC episodes manifest, and are able to set goals for treatment. During this pre-group meeting, a timeline is created to help link significant events (e.g., parent divorce) to eating and weight related problems. As with all forms of IPT (Weissman *et al.* 2000) the manifestation of the patient's symptoms is then conceptualized in one of four problem areas: a) interpersonal deficits; b) interpersonal role disputes; c) role transitions; and d) grief.

Interpersonal deficits describe people who are either socially isolated or who are involved in chronically unfulfilling relationships, often resulting from poor or very limited social skills. Interpersonal role disputes refer to conflicts with a significant other (e.g., a parent) that emerge from differences in expectations about the relationship. Role transitions occur with changes in life status (e.g., changes in schools, graduation, moving, parental divorce). The problem area of grief is identified when the onset of the patient's symptoms is associated with either the recent or past loss of a person or a relationship. Making use of this framework for defining one or more interpersonal problem areas, IPT focuses on identifying and changing the maladaptive interpersonal context in which the eating problem has developed and been maintained (Tanofsky-Kraff and Wilfley 2009).

The group context for IPT-WG is important because members, particularly those with interpersonal deficits, are encouraged to use the group as a social network where they can work on decreasing social isolation while forming new social relationships, which could model such behaviors outside of the therapeutic context (Wilfley *et al.* 1998). IPT-WG is time-limited and lasts 12 weeks over three months. As with all IPT adaptations, IPT-WG is delivered in three phases. The *initial phase* is dedicated to identifying the problem area(s) that will be the target for treatment. The *intermediate phase* is devoted to working on the target problem area(s). The *termination phase* is devoted to consolidating gains made during treatment, and preparing patients for future work on their own. Throughout all phases of the treatment, the clinician is active and advocates for the patient rather than remaining neutral (Tanofsky-Kraff and Wilfley 2009).

Case study

Twelve-year-old "Becky" (continued from Chapter 12) presented for IPT-WG with recurrent LOC eating, "emotional eating", and weight concerns. She began her IPT-WG program by completing an interpersonal inventory with her two group leaders:

> Becky lives at home with her nine-year-old brother and parents. She has very close relationships with her mother and her aunt, but a strained, yet emotionally important, relationship with her brother. This stress is largely due to being responsible for her brother's care each day after school while waiting for their parents to return from work. Becky says her brother has often used this time to tease her about her weight and she tearfully recalls

him calling her a "big, fat, and stupid animal". She begins to connect how her brother's actions became a trigger for feelings of sadness, shame, and LOC eating. She recalls consuming lots of snack foods during this time, feeling out of control with her eating, and trying to hide the "evidence" of her eating by throwing away the food wrappers in her bedroom rather than placing them in the kitchen trash can.

Therapists

In completing the timeline component of the pre-group interview, Becky revealed that her first LOC eating episode occurred at age 10, the same year that her brother began to tease her about her weight (he was seven years old at the time). It was also during this time that Becky's care-taking responsibilities for her brother increased because her mother's new job required different and longer hours. Becky reported that over time, her brother's behavior intensified, and, as he grew older, he became more and more defiant until he was diagnosed with ADHD. Her mother often blamed Becky for her brother's behavior and would get angry with her when he did not complete his chores.

Conceptualization

Becky and her mother had difficulty negotiating their relationship and Becky's role as a young adolescent trying, albeit unsuccessfully, to assert independence ("role dispute"). She and her mother clearly held non-reciprocal expectations about the roles that they should play in the relationship. Becky felt unable to handle all the responsibility of caring for her brother, but her mother felt she was capable to do so. They experienced frequent conflicts over this issue. To deal with her negative feelings, Becky would avoid communication and turn to food.

Goals

The therapists and Becky agreed on the following therapy goals. First, Becky would more directly express to her mother how stressed and overwhelmed she felt about her role as her brother's caretaker. Moreover, she would work on expressing these feelings more consistently and without fear that she would be blamed for his actions (or inaction). Second, she would work to begin sharing her feelings more in order to reduce her feelings of being overwhelmed and decrease her frustration from building up and turning to food. She would work on this goal by talking to her friends as well as her mother.

Treatment

During the initial phase of group, Becky was encouraged to share her feelings of frustration about her situation at home with the other group members and to get their feedback on her situation. Next, we moved toward in-group role-plays of discussions she would have with her mother, which directly related to her first goal of expressing her frustration and feelings of being overwhelmed.

During the middle/work phase of the group, Becky experienced ups and downs with regard to her ability to work towards meeting her goals. Her work-at-home assignment to talk to her mother during week three did not occur, so time was spent during the middle phase discussing her resistance to speaking with her mother. With group encouragement, guidance from the group leaders, and additional role-plays to plan out how her conversations would go, Becky began to engage in productive dialogues with her mother. She described feeling so anxious before one conversation that she thought she would "panic", but eventually she was able to tell her mom how overwhelmed she felt in caring for her brother. Her mother's caring response and their problem-solving approach helped them reach the agreement that Becky would still be "in charge" during the two hours after school, and that her mother would not take out her frustration on Becky but would instead directly punish or praise her brother for his behavior. Becky described a sense of relief after this discussion with her mom. She reported during week seven that she felt that she had "always bottled up" her feelings and that made her "want to eat to push them down". By the final group phase, Becky was experiencing a significant decline in number of LOC episodes. She felt less anxious after school and could focus on other things besides food during this time. The final phase emphasized Becky's improved communication skills and repeated practice of using the skills to talk with her mother and other close interpersonal relationships. At this point, Becky began to feel more comfortable talking to others about her feelings, and our approach shifted towards enlisting social support, such as her peers, for her to talk to when feeling stressed.

Targeted intervention strategies for disinhibited eating behaviors

Among children and adolescents who, like Becky, experience LOC eating, there is increasing recognition that interventions may need to be tailored to address distinct patterns of disinhibited eating that may serve to maintain or enhance LOC eating. Disinhibited eating refers to occasions when youth eat food for reasons not motivated by biological hunger. Such occasions are often marked by feelings of "letting go" or a lack of restraint (Shomaker et al. 2011). In comparison to LOC eating, eating in the absence of hunger and emotional eating are two somewhat less pathological disinhibited eating behaviors that overlap significantly with LOC in children and adolescents (Shomaker et al. 2011). The emergence of eating in the absence of hunger may predate the onset of LOC eating in children, as this behavior appears to begin in preschool-aged children (Birch et al. 2003). Therefore, targeting these behaviors may serve as beneficial LOC prevention strategies in addition to alleviating maintenance factors associated with LOC eating.

Interventions for eating in the absence of hunger

Eating in the absence of hunger refers to eating in response to the presence of palatable foods despite an absence of physiological hunger (Kral and Faith 2007; Shomaker et al. 2010). For example, children who eat in the absence of hunger will eat lunch until they say they are completely full, but then continue to eat snacks available to them soon afterwards. Based on the internality–externality theory (Schachter 1971), it is thought that youth who eat in the absence of hunger are more responsive to external cues for hunger and fullness, such as the presence of food, and are less sensitive to internal cues, such as feeling their stomach rumble, than those who do not eat in the absence of hunger. External food cues include characteristics of food such as the sight, smell, and taste as well as the environment and cognitive-affective states associated with food.

Johnson (2000) provided six weeks of training to help preschool-age children identify internal hunger and fullness cues. In the first week, children participated in a skit with themes of hunger and fullness and were taught the meanings of the terms "mouth" (where you chew food), "esophagus" (where food goes when you swallow), and "stomach" (where swallowed food goes). Week two involved watching *Winnie the Pooh and the Honey Jar* and discussing hunger, overeating, and the results of chronic overeating. During week three, doll play was used to teach children about internal cues of hunger and fullness, and each child was asked to compare each of the dolls' stomachs to their own before and after snack-time and at different times during the day. Results from this study demonstrated that children improved their ability to compensate the amount they ate at lunch following a preload energy-dense drink (Johnson 2000).

Another program focused on improving awareness of internal cues in youth is the Children's Appetite Awareness Training program, or CAAT (Craighead and Allen 1996). The program's objective is to help children and adolescents regulate their eating by improving ability to respond to hunger. Youth are taught to recognize internal, physiological signals that their bodies are hungry and are taught how to use these bodily signals when deciding what and how much to eat. Among overweight children the program demonstrated preliminary efficacy in weight loss after six sessions when compared to waiting list controls (Bloom et al. 2005).

The Regulation of Cues program (ROC), developed by Boutelle and colleagues (see Boutelle and Tanofsky-Kraff 2010 for a review), targets eating in the absence of hunger in overweight children and their parents. ROC is based on the both the internality–externality theory and learning theory, which suggests external food cues elicit physiological responses which can be experienced as craving. The ROC program is focused on teaching children and their parents to be more sensitive to internal hunger and fullness cues and to learn to resist eating in the absence of hunger when exposed to external food cues. This program was adapted directly from the two programs in the pilot study comparing CAAT and a cue-responsivity program (Boutelle et al. 2011).

ROC is a 12-session intervention in which information is covered in separate parent and child groups. The first five sessions parallel the CAAT program described above, while the last seven sessions provide psycho-education and skills-based learning about overeating, craving, and environmental food cues. Children and parents are taught methods to manage "tricky hungers" such as distraction, activity substitution, relaxation, mindful eating, media awareness, and cost benefit analyses. Behavioral parenting skills implemented in ROC include daily meetings to discuss the family's ROC progress, positive reinforcement, self-monitoring, behavior modeling, stimulus control to decrease external food cues in the home, and a family-based rewards system. Individual parent/child dyads then engage in guided experiential learning, focused on helping children and parents learn to monitor internal hunger and fullness and to reduce responsiveness to hedonic food cues.

Future directions for LOC eating treatment

The identification of evidence-based treatments for pediatric LOC eating is in its early stages. Promising prevention and treatments efforts for LOC eating and other aberrant eating behaviors during childhood and adolescence have the potential to prevent the development of BED as well as the host of medical and psychosocial problems associated with LOC and BED (see Chapters 12 and 13). Moving forward, it is critical to continue to conduct research on LOC eating treatments as well as to develop preventive strategies for youth at high risk for LOC onset.

The identification of early childhood risk factors for LOC eating will assist in the identification of targeted prevention efforts. For example, emotional eating – defined as eating in response to negative affect – may represent a promising intervention target for the prevention of LOC, as emotional eating been shown to overlap with loss of control eating among youth (Tanofsky-Kraff, Theim et al. 2007) and to predict the onset of binge eating in adolescents (Stice et al. 2002). Additionally, a greater focus on the inclusion of the family in LOC interventions is likely to be important for enhancing treatment outcomes, especially among those reporting LOC in early and middle childhood. Although children with LOC eating report greater familial problems than those without LOC eating (Field et al. 2008; Goossens et al. 2011; Haines et al. 2006), parental involvement (e.g., regular family dinners, parental monitoring of food intake) has been shown to be a protective factor for binge eating and eating in response to negative affective states in youth (Farrow 2012; Haines et al. 2010). Research is also needed on alternative treatment modalities for LOC eating. Developmentally tailored treatments that have shown promise in the treatment of BED in adults, such as CBT and dialectical behavior therapy, are likely good starting points for future treatment work. Finally, the formation of collaborative partnerships between university researchers and clinicians working in the community is crucial as new interventions are being developed and tested, to help inform future dissemination and implementation efforts.

Conclusion

Interventions targeting aberrant eating patterns, such as LOC eating and eating in the absence of hunger, among children and adolescents are a promising area of work. Such eating styles have links with psychological and physical health, and therefore early intervention and prevention are critical. The case example of Becky highlights how interventions that are not specifically aimed at eating behavior may still have impact on eating and weight related outcomes. Understanding the many triggers and maintaining factors associated with aberrant eating behaviors, such as social interactions or negative affect, may assist clinicians in providing effective evidence-based care.

References

Birch, L. L., Fisher, J. O., and Davison, K. K. (2003) "Learning to overeat: maternal use of restrictive feeding practices promotes girls' eating in the absence of hunger", *American Journal of Clinical Nutrition* 78(2): 215–20.

Blaine, B., and Rodman, J. (2007) "Responses to weight loss treatment among obese people with and without BED: a matched-study meta-analysis", *Eating and Weight Disorders* 12(2): 54–60.

Bloom, T., Sharpe, L., Heriot, S., Zucker, N., and Craighead, L. (2005) "Children's appetite-awareness training (CAAT): a cognitive-behavioural intervention in the treatment of childhood obesity", presented at the WHO Expert Meeting on Childhood Obesity, Kobe, Japan, June.

Boutelle, K. N., and Tanofsky-Kraff, M. (2011) "Treatments targeting aberrant eating patterns in overweight youth", in D. Le Grange and J. Lock (eds), *Eating Disorders in Children and Adolescents: A Clinical Handbook* (pp. 381–401), New York: The Guilford Press.

Boutelle, K. N., Zucker, N. L., Peterson, C. B., Rydell, S. A., Cafry, G., and Harnack, L. (2011) "Two novel treatments to reduce overeating in overweight children: a randomized controlled trial", *Journal of Consulting and Clinical Psychology* 79(6): 759–71.

Braet, C., Tanghe, A., Decaluwé, V., Moens, E., and Rosseel, Y. (2004) "Inpatient treatment for children with obesity: Weight loss, psychological well-being, and eating behaviour", *Journal of Pediatric Psychology* 29(7): 519–29.

Ceilo-Doyle, A., Goldschmidt, A. B., Huang, C., Winzelberg, A. J., Taylor, C. B., and Wilfley, D. E. (2008) "Reduction of overweight and eating disorder symptoms via the internet in adolescents: a randomized controlled trial", *Journal of Adolescent Health* 43: 172–9.

Craighead, L. W., and Allen, H. N. (1996) "Appetite awareness training: a cognitive behavioural intervention for binge eating", *Cogitive and Behavioral Practice* 2(2): 249–70.

Epstein, L. H., Paluch, R. A., Saelens, B. E., Ernst, M. M., and Wilfley, D. E. (2001) "Changes in eating disorder symptoms with pediatric obesity treatment", *Journal of Pediatrics* 139(1): 58–65.

Fairburn, C. G. (2008) *Cognitive behaviour therapy and eating disorders*, New York: The Guilford Press.

Fairburn, C. G., Jones, R., Peveler, R. C., Carr, S. J., Solomon, R. A., O'Connor, M. E., *et al.* (1991) "Three psychological treatments for bulimia nervosa. a comparative trial", *Archives of General Psychiatry* 48(5): 463–9.

Fallon, E. M., Tanofsky-Kraff, M., Norman, A. C., McDuffie, J. R., Taylor, E. D., Cohen, M. L., *et al.* (2005) "Health-related quality of life in overweight and nonoverweight black and white adolescents", *Journal of Pediatrics* 147(4): 443–50.

Farrow, C. V. (2012) "Do parental feeding practices moderate the relationships between impulsivity and eating in children?", *Eating Behaviors* 13: 150–53.

Field, A. E., Javaras, K. M., Aneja, P., Kitos, N., Camargo, C. A., Taylor, C. B., and Laird, N. M. (2008) "Family, peer, and media predictors of becoming eating disordered", *Archives of Pediatrics & Adolescent Medicine* 162(6): 574–9.

Freeman, L. M. Y., and Gil, K. M. (2004) 'Daily stress, coping, and dietary restraint in binge eating', *International Journal of Eating Disorders* 36(2): 204–12.

Goossens, L., Braet, C., Bosmans, G., and Decaluwé, V. (2011) "Loss of control over eating in pre-adolescent youth: the role of attachment and self-esteem", *Eating Behaviors* 12(4): 289–95.

Gorin, A. A., Niemeier, H. M., Hogan, P., Coday, M., Davis, C., DiLillo, V. G., *et al.* (2008) "Binge eating and weight loss outcomes in overweight and obese people with type 2 diabetes: results from the Look AHEAD trial", *Archives of General Psychiatry* 65(11): 1447–55.

Haines, J., Gillman, M. W., Rifas-Shiman, S., Field, A. E., and Austin, S. B. (2010) "Family dinner and disordered eating behaviours in a large cohort of adolescents", *Eating Disorders* 18(1): 10–24.

Haines, J., Neumark-Sztainer, D., Eisenberg, M. E., and Hannan, P. J. (2006) "Weight teasing and disordered eating behaviours in adolescents: longitudinal findings from Project EAT", *Pediatrics* 117(2): e209–15.

Herman, C. P., and Polivy, J. (1980) "Restrained eating", in A. J. Stunkard (ed.) *Obesity* (pp. 208–25), Philadelphia, PA: Saunders.

Johnson, S. L. (2000) "Improving preschoolers' self-regulation of energy intake", *Pediatrics* 106(6): 1429–35.

Jones, M., Luce, K. H., Osborne, M. I., Taylor, K., Cunning, D., Doyle, A. C., *et al.* (2008) "Randomized, controlled trial of an internet-facilitated intervention for reducing binge eating and overweight in adolescents", *Pediatrics* 121(3): 453–62.

Klerman, G., Weissman, M., Rounsaville, B., and Chevron, E. S. (1984) *Interpersonal Psychotherapy of Depression*, New York: Basic Books

Kral, T. V., and Faith, M. S. (2007) "Child eating patterns and weight regulation: a developmental behaviour genetics framework", *Acta Paediatrica* Suppl. 96(454): 29–34.

Moens, E., Braet, C., and Van Winckel, M. (2010) "An 8-year follow-up of treated obese children: children's, process and parental predictors of successful outcome", *Behavior Research and Therapy* 48(7): 626–33.

Mufson, L., Dorta, K. P., Moreau, D., and Weissman, M. M. (2004) *Interpersonal Psychotherapy for Depressed Adolescents* (2nd edn), New York: The Guilford Press.

Ranzenhofer, L. M., Tanofsky-Kraff, M., McDuffie, J. R., Checchi, J., Salaita, C., Yanoff, L. B., *et al.* (2008) "The impact of disordered eating pathology, depression, and anxiety on weight outcomes of overweight adolescents following weight loss treatment",presented at the Eating Disorders Research Society 14th Annual Meeting, Montreal, Canada, September.

Schachter, S. (1971) "Some extraordinary facts about obese humans and rats", *American Psychologist* 26(2): 129–44.

Schwimmer, J. B., Burwinkle, T. M., and Varni, J. W. (2003) "Health-related quality of life of severely obese children and adolescents", *Journal of the American Medical Association* 289(14): 1813–19.

Shomaker, L. B., Tanofsky-Kraff, M., and Yanovski, J. (2011) "Disinhibited eating and body weight in youth", in V. R. Preedy, R. R. Watson and C. R. Watson (eds) *International Handbook of Behaviour, Diet and Nutrition* (pp. 2183–200), New York: Springer Publishing Co.

Shomaker, L. B., Tanofsky-Kraff, M., Zocca, J. M., Courville, A., Kozlosky, M., Columbo, K. M., *et al.* (2010) "Eating in the absence of hunger in adolescents: intake after a large-array meal compared with that after a standardized meal", *American Journal of Clinical Nutrition* 92(4): 697–703.

Stein, R. I., Saelens, B. E., Dounchis, J. Z., Lewczyk, C. M., Swenson, A. K., and Wilfley, D. E. (2001) "'Treatment of eating disorders in women", *Counseling Psychology* 29(5): 695–732.

Stice, E., Presnell, K., and Spangler, D. (2002) "Risk factors for binge eating onset in adolescent girls: a 2-year prospective study", *Health Psychology* 21(2): 131–8.

Strauss, R. S., and Pollack, H. A. (2003) "Social marginalization of overweight children", *Archives of Pediatrics & Adolescent Medicine* 157(8): 746–52.

Striegel-Moore, R. H., Silberstein, L. R., and Rodin, J. (1986) "Toward an understanding of risk factors for bulimia", *American Psychologist* 41(3): 246–63.

Tanofsky-Kraff, M. (in press) "Psychosocial preventive interventions for obesity and eating disorders in youth", *International Review of Psychiatry*.

Tanofsky-Kraff, M., Theim, K. R., Yanovski, S. Z., Bassett, A. M., Burns, N. P., Ranzenhofer, L. M., *et al.* (2007) "Validation of the emotional eating scale adapted for use in children and adolescents (EES-C)", *International Journal of Eating Disorders* 40(3): 232–40.

Tanofsky-Kraff, M., and Wilfley, D. E. (2010) "Interpersonal psychotherapy for bulimia nervosa and binge-eating disorder", in C. M. Grilo and J. E. Mitchell (eds) *The Teatment of Eating Disorders: A Clinical Handbook* (pp.271–93), New York: The Guilford Press.

Tanofsky-Kraff, M., Wilfley, D. E., Young, J. F., Mufson, L., Yanovski, S. Z., Glasofer, D. R., and Salaita, C. G. (2007) "Preventing excessive weight gain in adolescents: Interpersonal psychotherapy for binge eating", *Obesity (Silver Spring)* 15(6): 1345–55.

Tanofsky-Kraff, M., Wilfley, D. E., Young, J. F., Mufson, L., Yanovski, S. Z., Glasofer, D. R., *et al.* (2010) "A pilot study of interpersonal psychotherapy for preventing excess weight gain in adolescent girls at-risk for obesity", *International Journal of Eating Disorders* 43(8): 701–8.

Tanofsky-Kraff, M., Yanovski, S. Z., Wilfley, D. E., Marmarosh, C., Morgan, C. M., and Yanovski, J. A. (2004) "Eating-disordered behaviours, body fat, and psychopathology in overweight and normal-weight children", *Journal of Consulting and Clinical Psychology* 72(1): 53–61.

Weissman, M. M., Markowitz, J. C., and Klerman, G. L. (2000) *Comprehensive Guide to Interpersonal Psychotherapy*, New York: Basic Books.

White, M. A., Kalarchian, M. A., Masheb, R. M., Marcus, M. D., and Grilo, C. M. (2010) "Loss of control over eating predicts outcomes in bariatric surgery patients: a prospective, 24-month follow-up study", *Journal of Clinical Psychiatry* 71(2): 175–84.

Wildes, J. E., Marcus, M. D., Kalarchian, M. A., Levine, M. D., Houck, P. R., and Cheng, Y. (2010) "Self-reported binge eating in severe pediatric obesity: impact on weight change in a randomized controlled trial of family-based treatment", *International Journal of Obesity* 34(7): 143–8.

Wilfley, D. E. (2000) *Interpersonal Psychotherapy for Group*, New York: Basic Books.

Wilfley, D. E., Frank, M., Welch, R., Spurrell, E., and Rounsaville, B. (1998) "Adapting interpersonal psychotherapy to a group format (IPT-G) for binge eating disorder: toward a model for adapting empirically supported treatments", *Psychotherapy Research* 8(4): 379–91.

Wilfley, D. E., Kolko, R. P., and Kass, A. E. (2011) "Cognitive-behavioural therapy for weight management and eating disorders in children and adolescents"', *Child and Adolescent Psychiatric Clinics of North America* 20(2): 271–85.

Wilfley, D. E., Pike, K. M., and Streigel-Moore, R. H. (1997) "Toward an integrated model of risk for binge eating disorder", *Journal of Gender, Culture and Health* 2: 1–3.

Wilfley, D. E., Welch, R. R., Stein, R. I., Spurrell, E. B., Cohen, L. R., Saelens, B. E., *et al.* (2002) "A randomized comparison of group cognitive-behavioural therapy and group interpersonal psychotherapy for the treatment of overweight people with binge-eating disorder", *Archives of General Psychiatry* 59(8): 713–21.

Wilson, G. T., Wilfley, D. E., Agras, W. S., and Bryson, S. W. (2010) "Psychological treatments of binge eating disorder", *Archives of General Psychiatry* 67(1): 94–101.

Wolfe, B. E., Baker, C. W., Smith, A. T., and Kelly-Weeder, S. (2009) "Validity and utility of the current definition of binge eating", *International Journal of Eating Disorders* 42(8): 674–86.

Young, J. F., Mufson, L., and Davies, M. (2006) "Efficacy of interpersonal psychotherapy-adolescent skills training: an indicated preventive intervention for depression"', *Journal of Child Psychology and Psychiatry* 47(12): 1254–62.

Chapter 14

Bariatric surgery

Scott Engel and James E. Mitchell

Case study

I have been quite overweight all of my life. I was teased about my weight in grade school and in high school. Besides eating too much most of the time I also went on eating binges several times a week, when I would consume very large amounts of food, such as one or two pizzas or a quart of ice cream. During these times I felt "driven", like I couldn't stop myself until the food was gone. I was very embarrassed by this and because of that I would isolate myself at home when no one else was around to do much of my eating. My parents worried about my weight and started encouraging me to diet during adolescence but nothing really seemed to work. I tried low-calorie diets, low-carbohydrate diets, low-fat diets, and just about everything else. I had a book shelf devoted just to self-help diet books. In my 20s my weight continued to increase and by the time I turned 30 I weighed about 300 pounds at 5'5" tall. My doctor was always telling me how I would develop health problems if I didn't lose weight and this eventually happened. That year I went in for a sinus infection and was told that I had high blood pressure and was started on medication. However, I continued to gain weight and a few years later when I turned 34 I was told that I had "early diabetes" and that I would have to follow a special diet and be on medication for that as well. My problems with binge eating continued and if anything seemed to get worse. I finally had had enough. I started reading about bariatric surgery for obesity on the web and eventually asked my physician for a referral to a surgeon who could do this procedure. After waiting for months, undergoing various steps in the evaluation and approval process, I underwent a Roux-en-Y gastric bypass procedure. Not only did I start to lose weight right away but also my blood sugars rapidly came under control without medication. Over the next six months I lost about 80 pounds and was able to go off my blood pressure medication. I felt great being thinner and in particular I felt wonderful being able to go out and socialize more and not be so embarrassed about my weight. I also found I wasn't hungry like before and didn't seem to crave the same foods. The weight loss continued, but during the second year after surgery I started having problems again with feeling "out of control" at times when I was eating and would eat more than I intended to. Because I had a stomach pouch I could no longer eat really huge amounts of food; however, I still ate more than I wanted to, and felt a desperate sense that I couldn't stop. I saw my bariatric surgeon and she said my problem was what she called "loss of control eating" that sometimes develops after bariatric surgery and suggested I see a counselor for the problem.

Dora, aged 42

Considerable empirical evidence suggests that severely obese patients seeking bariatric surgery commonly engage in problematic eating behaviors such as over-eating, binge eating, and eating with a sense of loss of control. Additionally, these patients are much more likely to meet criteria for binge eating disorder (BED) when compared to less severely obese individuals who are not candidates for bariatric surgery. Further, binge eating and BED diagnosis have been studied to determine the extent to which these behaviors predict outcome after bariatric surgery. Finally, while post-bariatric surgery patients may not be able to binge eat as they did before surgery because of the limited remaining gastric volume, some evidence suggests that they are at increased risk for other "addictive behaviors" after surgery. This chapter examines the empirical evidence related to the issues outlined, and discusses relevant conceptual issues to guide clinicians and researchers interested in this area.

Assessment issues

On first consideration the assessment of eating behavior may seem to be a relatively straightforward process which can be accomplished without much difficulty: simply determine what and how much food and drink a person has consumed during each meal and on any given day. Unfortunately, this is a misperception. The assessment of dietary intake is complex, and currently all typical methods of assessment have limitations. Much attention has been paid to these limitations, and many researchers have attempted to improve the assessment of dietary intake through the implementation of technological advances (Thompson et al. 2010). Binge eating, full syndromal BED, and loss of control are typically assessed with interviews or questionnaires. Importantly, both of these methods rely on self-report, and it has long been known that obese people (as well as most other groups of people) under-report their dietary intake (Buhl et al. 1995). There are many plausible reasons for obese people to under-report dietary intake, but some of the obvious ones are related to memory biases, simple forgetting, and "motivated forgetting" (i.e., intentionally not disclosing accurate information).

For an eating episode to be considered a binge eating episode it typically must meet two criteria. First, an objectively large amount of food must be consumed, and second, the person must experience a sense of loss of control during the eating episode (Fairburn and Cooper 1993). A key problem in the assessment of bariatric surgery patients is that many researchers have chosen, often by necessity, to employ different standards for what constitutes objectively large amount of food in the pre-surgery vs. the post-surgery condition. For example, some studies have considered binge eating episodes to have occurred after bariatric surgery when a patient has eaten a much smaller amount of food (compared to the amount he or she might have eaten in the pre-surgery condition), but has experienced a sense of loss of control while eating (e.g., Hsu, Betancourt and Sullivan 1996). Because of the changes to the digestive tract, post-bariatric surgery patients obviously are not able to consume the same amounts of food after surgery that they could before surgery. However, this is problematic in that it results in two different definitions of binge eating. This obfuscates both comparisons of binge eating frequencies before and after surgery as well as the diagnosis of BED in the pre- and post-surgery conditions.

Related to the difficulty of diagnosing BED, it is also unclear what constitutes eating disordered behavior after surgery. Further, since little is actually known about the details of eating behavior after surgery, it is difficult to identify atypical or abnormal eating behaviors. Clearly, specialized diets and medical complications after surgery may mimic symptoms of eating disorders. In fact, some relatively common problems after surgery, such as plugging, dumping, constipation, or dysphagia can result in patients engaging in compensatory behaviors and/or restrictive eating behaviors in an effort to deal with these symptoms. Finally, some patients receive suggestions from their surgery team to engage in behaviors that are usually considered inappropriate compensatory behaviors, for example that they "chew and spit out" food, and some have promoted the use of self-induced vomiting if feeling uncomfortable following a meal. While these behaviors have traditionally been considered pathological, to determine if they are problematic in nature in bariatric surgery patients one must better understand the motivation behind them. Are the behaviors driven by shape and body concerns, or are they simply a means of adjusting to the symptoms that can result from the digestive tract changes that occur during the surgery, and/or are suggested by members of the surgery team?

Binge eating, LOC eating, and BED

Pre-surgery

As already addressed, the "gold standard" definition of binge eating is an eating episode in which a person consumes an objectively large amount of food, in a discrete period of time, while experiencing a sense of loss of control over eating (Fairburn and Cooper 1993). BED is currently included in the *Diagnostic and Statistical Manual of Mental Disorders*, 4th edition, text revision (American Psychiatric Association 2000) and is listed as a disorder worthy of further study. BED, which is expected to be listed as an Axis I disorder in DSM-5, is characterized by episodes of binge eating that are not accompanied by compensatory behaviors such as those seen in patients with bulimia nervosa.

It is well known that binge eating behavior and BED are common among obese patients who seek bariatric surgery (de Zwaan 2005). We recently reviewed the relevant published data from 1995 to 2012 that examined binge eating frequency in pre-surgery bariatric surgery patients. Frequency of binge eating was estimated from as low as 6 per cent (Allison *et al.* 2006; Sansone *et al.* 2008) to as high as 69 per cent (Adami *et al.* 1995), with an average across all studies of about 36 per cent. The large range in the estimates of binge eating prevalence is likely attributable to a wide variety of definitions of binge eating as well as varied methods of assessing the behavior. Assessment methods have also varied when attempting to diagnose BED, and some studies have used different diagnostic criteria as well. In the studies that identified syndromal BED in those seeking bariatric surgery, prevalence estimates ranged from as low as 1 per cent (Herpertz and Saller 2001) to as high as 49 per cent (Mitchell *et al.* 2001). The average rate of BED in bariatric surgery patients across all relevant studies has been approximately 25 per cent. However, it is worth noting the considerable variability in the rates reported across the studies. This is not surprising given the considerable variability in the assessment instruments used.

For some time it was assumed that binge eating was a contraindication for bariatric surgery. In recent years a number of studies have addressed this issue, and the findings cast doubt on this assumption. Admittedly, the findings are not

Table 14.1 Binge Eating and surgical intervention – Predictability of Weight Outcome

Authors	Method	N	Follow-up Duration	Is BE(D) Predictive of Weight Outcome?
Wadden et al., 2011	Roux-en-Y + Banding	36	12 mos	No
de Zwaan et al., 2010	Roux-en-Y	59	2 yrs	No
White et al., 2009	Roux-en-Y	361	1 and 2 yrs	No
Kalarchian et al., 2008	Roux-en-Y	207	6 mos	No
Sallet et al., 2007	Roux-en-Y	216	2 yrs	Yes
Bocchieri-Ricciardi et al., 2006	Roux-en-Y	72	18 mos	No
Malone & Alger-Mayer, 2005	Roux-en-Y	109	12 mos	No
Busetto et al., 2005	Banding	379	5 yrs	No
Burgmer et al., 2005	Banding	118	> 12 mos	No
Green et al., 2004	Roux-en-Y	65	6 mos	Yes
Boan et al., 2004	Roux-en-Y	40	6 mos	No
Sabbioni et al., 2002	Gastroplasty	82	2 yrs	No
Busetto et al., 2002	Banding	260	3 yrs	No
Dymek et al., 2001	Roux-en-Y	32	6 mos	Yes
Powers et al., 1999	VBG	72	5.5 yrs	No
Hsu et al., 1997	Roux-en-Y	27	21 mo	Yes
Hsu et al., 1996	Gastroplasty	24	3.5 yrs	No

completely consistent, but they seem to suggest that there is either only a very weak relationship between pre-surgery binge eating and weight loss or weight regain, or no relationship at all (see Table 14.1). Most studies have found no relationship between pre-surgery binge eating and weight loss or weight regain (Busetto *et al.* 2005; Hsu, Betancourt, and Sullivan 1996; Powers *et al.* 1999; Busetto *et al.* 2002; Sabbioni *et al.* 2002; Boan *et al.* 2004; Burgmer *et al.* 2007; Wadden *et al.* 2011). Only four of the studies found that pre-surgery binge eating significantly predicted weight loss or regain (Hsu *et al.* 1997; Dymek *et al.* 2001; Green *et al.* 2004; Sallet *et al.* 2007). Of these studies, it is important to note that two included relatively small sample sizes: one had 27 research participants (Hsu *et al.* 1997) and the other had 32 (Dymek *et al.* 2001). Given the large number of studies that found no relationship, we conclude that the findings generally suggest no meaningful association between pre-surgery binge eating and weight loss or regain.

Post-surgery

As previously mentioned, assessing binge eating after bariatric surgery is a potential problem. While binge eating is often assessed, loss of control eating is also of particular relevance. Given that post-bariatric surgery patients are usually physically unable to consume a volume of food that is considered objectively large, some research has examined whether eating with a sense of loss of control predicts less weight loss or greater regain after surgery. In reviewing this topic, Marino and colleagues (in press) recently concluded that patients who experience a sense of loss of control while eating after surgery are more likely to experience less weight loss or greater weight regain. Table 14.2 reviews those published studies. Unlike pre-surgery, binge eating as defined by loss of control eating after surgery has consistently been shown to be a significant predictor of post-surgery weight outcome.

Table 14.2 Binge Eating and Loss of Control – Predictability of Weight Outcome.

Authors	Method	N	Follow-up Duration	Is BE(D)/LOC Predictive of Weight Outcome?
Kofman *et al.*, 2010	Roux-en-Y	100	3–10 yrs	Yes
de Zwaan *et al.*, 2010	Roux-en-Y	59	2 yrs	Yes
White *et al.*, 2009	Roux-en-Y	361	1 and 2 yrs	Yes
Larsen *et al.*, 2004, 2006	Banding	157	> 2 yrs	Yes
Guisado & Vaz, 2003	Gastroplasty	140	18 mos	Yes
Kalarchian *et al.*, 2002	Roux-en-Y	99	2–7 yrs	Yes
Mitchell *et al.*, 2001	Roux-en-Y	78	14 yrs	Yes
Hsu *et al.*, 1996	Gastroplasty	24	3.5 yrs	Yes
Pekkarinen *et al.*, 1994	Gastroplasty	27	5.4 yrs	Yes
Rowston *et al.*, 1992	BPD*	16	2 yrs	Yes

Other addictive behaviors and the Addiction Transfer Model

Bariatric surgery is quite effective for excess weight loss, and most patients not only lose a large percentage of excess weight but also experience the amelioration of a number of the health comorbidities associated with obesity (World Health Organization 2005). In spite of this, a number of concerning outcomes have been associated with bariatric surgery. For example, recent reports suggest that post-bariatric surgery patients may be at increased risk for suicide (e.g., Adams *et al.* 2007). Deitel (2002) found that eating disorder rates also increased after bariatric surgery. Perhaps most intriguing has been speculation, anecdotal evidence, and some empirical investigation that suggests that people who undergo bariatric surgery may experience a "transfer of addictions." As described below, a number of sources have recently suggested that, when faced with the inability to overeat and/or binge eat in the manner they could before surgery, some post-bariatric surgery patients seem to exchange these behaviors for other addictive behaviors, such as drug and/or alcohol abuse (Buffington 2007).

The popular media has devoted considerable attention to this topic. Although many other sources have mentioned this topic (e.g., Souter *et al.* 2007; Spencer 2006), perhaps Oprah Winfrey (*Oprah Winfrey Show* 2006) has been the best-known discussant. Oprah stated that 30 per cent of patients replace compulsive eating with compulsive drinking of alcohol after surgery. At that time there were virtually no data speaking to this issue, and to our knowledge there was no empirical evidence supporting her 30 per cent figure or even the basic idea that post-bariatric surgery patients may be at greater risk for alcoholism than a reasonable comparison group. However, these comments, and the attention paid to this topic by the popular press in general, was followed by preliminary research in the area.

A small number of studies have recently provided information about the frequency that post-bariatric surgery patients consume alcohol, and the changes that occur from pre- to post-surgery in the effects that alcohol has on these people. Buffington (2007) found that of the 318 patients who responded to a web-based questionnaire, 83 per cent said they "regularly" or "upon occasion" consumed alcohol. Of those patients who reported consuming at least one alcoholic drink per week, 84 per cent said that they were much more sensitive to the effects of alcohol compared to before surgery. Further, 45 per cent stated that they could "feel the effects of alcohol after only a few sips of alcohol".

Another study (Sogg 2007) found that 32 of 340 post-bariatric surgery patients reported consuming alcohol at a level defined as "problem drinking". Importantly, 19 of these 32 patients did not report pre-operative problem drinking. Using a different assessment than that was used in the Sogg article, Welch and colleagues (2011) found that only 1.3 per cent of post-bariatric surgery patients reported abusing alcohol. Also, in a relatively small study (n = 70) Ertelt and colleagues (2008) found that although seven post-bariatric surgery patients met criteria for alcohol abuse or dependence, approximately two-thirds of the sample (67.1 per cent) reported no significant change in their consumption of alcohol.

Three additional studies shed light on the topic. Suzuki, Haimovici, and Chang (2010) interviewed 51 post-bariatric surgery patients from a sample of 530. They found two key predictors of alcohol use disorder after surgery. First, patients who had a lifetime history of problems with alcohol were more likely to have an alcohol use disorder after surgery. Second, patients who underwent Roux-en-Y gastric bypass surgery were more likely to have an alcohol use disorder following surgery than those who underwent a laparoscopic adjustable gastric banding procedure.

Ostlund (2011) reported on 12,277 patients who underwent bariatric surgery. She found that those who underwent bariatric surgery were at a significantly greater risk for the inpatient treatment of alcoholism compared to a comparison group of 122,277 age and gender matched people from the general population. She also reported that patients who underwent gastric bypass were 2.3 times more likely to have significant problems with alcohol. Consistent with the findings reported above, patients who had Roux-en-Y gastric bypass surgery were 2.5 times more likely to be treated for substance abuse than those who underwent a laparoscopic adjustable banding procedure.

Finally, the Longitudinal Assessment of Bariatric Surgery Consortium recently presented data on sample of 1945 participants, finding 9.6 per cent of participants had alcohol problems two years after bariatric surgery (King *et al.* 2012). In patients who did not have a history of alcohol problems before surgery, pre-surgery predictors of alcohol problems after surgery included male sex (odds ratio = 2.2), younger age (odds ratio = 2.0), regular alcohol consumption (odds ratio = 8.6), recreational drug use (odds ratio = 2.5), lower interpersonal support (odds ratio = 1.1), and having had Roux-en-Y gastric bypass (odds ratio = 3.1; the reference group was laparoscopic adjustable gastric band).

Increased risk for alcohol problems after bariatric surgery: possible mechanisms for the Addiction Transfer Model

As suggested by the empirical evidence above, there appears to be support for a loose interpretation of the Addiction Transfer Model. The data suggest that patients who undergo bariatric surgery, in particular Roux-en-Y gastric bypass, are at an increased risk for developing significant problems with alcohol. However, data are extremely limited in several areas related to this, and the causal mechanisms for this phenomenon are largely unknown. The King *et al.* (2012) data suggests that in patients who do not have a history of alcohol problems, regular pre-surgery alcohol consumption is a strong predictor post-surgery alcohol problems.

Another body of research has shown that the pharmacokinetics of alcohol are changed in post-bariatric surgery patients. Both Roux-en-Y and gastric sleeve patients get intoxicated more quickly and reach higher blood/breath alcohol concentrations after consuming alcohol than before surgery or compared to weight-matched controls (Hagedorn *et al.* 2007; Klockhoff *et al.* 2002; Maluenda *et al.* 2010). Coupling the findings from these two areas of research leads one to speculate if patients who drink alcohol regularly before surgery, and experience the predicted pharmacokinetic changes after surgery but fail to down regulate their alcohol consumption appropriately, will be the ones who most frequently develop such problems. Another variable of interest that may play a role relates to the subjective experience associated with the pharmacokinetic changes that occur after surgery. Some patients likely experience the more rapid acceleration and greater peak blood alcohol concentrations as aversive, while others may respond more positively. We speculate that the interaction of the pharmacokinetic changes and the more positive subjective experiences that occurs in some people when consuming alcohol after bariatric surgery may put them at increased risk for an alcohol use disorder.

Numerous other important questions remain unanswered on the topic. For example, could poor social support play a role in the development of alcohol problems after surgery? Might the extent to which a person employs eating to cope with stress or negative effects before surgery predict their likelihood of developing problems with alcohol after surgery? Surely these people continue to experience stress and negative emotional states: how do they cope with these experiences given their lack of ability to use eating behaviors to cope? Unfortunately, little is known regarding the answer to these questions and much research is needed to explain the reasons for an increased risk in people after surgery.

Conclusion

Patients who are candidates for bariatric surgery commonly engage in binge eating behavior. However, pre-surgery binge eating and the pre-surgery diagnosis of BED do not appear to be particularly informative about weight outcomes after surgery. On the other hand, eating behavior after surgery is consistently predictive of post-surgery outcome. The interesting notion that binge eating before surgery morphs into different problematic behaviors, particularly problematic alcohol consumption, after surgery has been proposed and there appears to be some support for this hypothesis. Further study is needed on the topic.

References

Adami, G. F., Gandolfo, P., Bauer, B., and Scopinaro, N. (1995) "Binge eating in massively obese patients undergoing bariatric surgery", *International Journal of Eating Disorders* 17: 45–50.

Adams, T. D., Gress, R. E., Smith, S. C., Halverson, R. C., Simper, S. C., Rosamond, W. D., LaMonte, M. J., Stroup, A. M., and Hunt, S. C. (2007) "Long-term mortality after gastric bypass surgery", *New England Journal of Medicine* 357: 753–61.

Allison, K. C., Wadden, T. A., Sarwer, D. B., Fabricatore, A. N., Crerand, C. E., Gibbons, L. M., Stack, R. M., Stunkard, A. J., and Williams, N. N. (2006) "Night eating syndrome and binge eating disorder among persons seeking bariatric surgery: prevalence and related features", *Surgery for Obesity and Related Diseases* 2: 153–8.

American Psychiatric Association (2000) *DSM-IV-TR: Diagnostic and Statistical Manual of Mental Disorders*, 4th edn (Text Revision), Washington, DC: American Psychiatric Press.

Boan, H., Kolotkin, R. J., Westman, E. C., McMahon, R. I., and Grant, J. P. (2004) "Binge eating, quality of life and physical activity improve after Roux-en-Y gastric bypass for morbid obesity", *Obesity Surgery* 14: 975–85.

Buffington, C. K. (2007) "Alcohol use and health risks: survey results", *Bar Times* 4: 21–3.

Buhl, K. M., Gallagher, D., Hoy, K., Mathews, D. E., and Heymsfield, S. B. (1995) "Unexplained disturbance in body weight regulation: diagnostic outcome assessed by doubly labeled water and body composition analyses in obese patients reporting low energy intakes", *Journal of the Academy Nutrition and Dietetics* 12: 1393–400.

Burgmer, R., Petersen, I., Burgmer, M., de Zwaan, M., Wolf, A. M., and Herpertz, S. (2007) "Psychological outcome two years after restrictive bariatric surgery', *Obesity Surgery* 17: 785–91.

Busetto, L., Segato, G., De Luca, M., Marchi, F. D., Foletto, M., Vianello, M., Valeri, M., and Enzi, G. (2005) "Weight loss and postoperative complications in morbidly obese patients with binge eating disorder treated by laparoscopic adjustable gastric banding", *Obesity Surgery* 15: 195–201.

Busetto, L., Segato, G., De Marchi, F., Foletto, M., De Luca, M., Caniato, D., Favretti, F., Lise, M., and Enzi, G. (2002) "Outcome predictors in morbidly obese recipients of an adjustable gastric band", *Obesity Surgery* 12: 83–92.

de Zwaan, M. (2005) 'Weight and eating changes after bariatric surgery', in J. E. Mitchell, and M. de Zwaan (eds) *Bariatric Surgery: A guide for Mental Health Professionals* (pp. 77–100), New York: Hove Routledge.

Deitel, M. (2002) "Anorexia nervosa following bariatric surgery" (Editorial), *Obesity Surgery* 12: 729–30.

Dymek, M. P., Le Grange, D., Neven, K., and Alverdy, J. (2001) "Quality of life and psychosocial adjustment in patients after Roux-en-Y gastric bypass: a brief report", *Obesity Surgery* 11: 32–9.

Ertelt, T. W., Mitchell, J. E., Lancaster, K., *et al.* (2008) "Alcohol abuse and dependence before and after bariatric surgery: a review of the literature and report of a new data set"', *Surgery for Obesity and Related Diseases* 4: 647–50.

Fairburn, D., and Cooper, Z. (1993) "The eating disorder examination', in C. G. Fairburn and G. T. Wilson (eds) *Binge Eating: Nature, Assessment and Treatment* (pp. 317–60), New York: Guilford.

Green, A., Dymek-Valentine, M., Le Grange, D., Pyluk, S., and Alverdy, J. (2004) "Psychosocial outcome of gastric bypass surgery for patients with and without binge eating", *Obesity Surgery* 14: 975–86.

Hagedorn, J. C., Encarnacion, B., Brat, G. A., and Morton, J. M. (2007) "Does gastric bypass alter alcohol metabolism?", *Surgery for Obesity and Related Diseases* 3: 543–8.

Herpertz, S., and Saller, B. (2001) "Psychosomatic aspects of obesity", *Psychother Psychosom Med Psychol* 51: 336–49.

Hsu, L., Betancourt, S., and Sullivan, S. (1996) "Eating disturbances before and after vertical banded gastroplasty: a pilot study", *International Journal of Eating Disorders* 19: 23–34.

Hsu, L. K., Sullivan, S. P., and Benotti, P. N. (1997) "Eating disturbances and outcome of gastric bypass surgery: a pilot study", *International Journal of Eating Disorders* 21: 385–90.

King, W. C., Kalarchian, M. A., Chen, A. P., Courcoulas, A. P., Engel, S. G., Mitchell, J. E., Pories, W. J., Steffen, K., and Yanovski, S. (2012) "Alcohol problems before and in the first two years following bariatric surgery", presented at the American Society for Metabolic and Bariatric Surgery Annual Conference, San Diego, CA, June.

Klockhoff, H., Naslund, I., and Jones, A. (2002) "Faster absorption of ethanol and higher peak concentration in women after gastric bypass surgery", *British Journal of Clinical Pharmacology* 54: 587–91.

Maluenda, F., Csendes, A., De Aretxabala, X., Poniachik, J., Salvo, K., Delgado, I., and Rodriguez, P. (2010) "Alcohol absorption modification after a laparoscopic sleeve gastrectomy due to obesity", *Obesity Surgery* 20: 744–8.

Marino, J. M., Ertelt, T. W., Lancaster, K., Steffen, K., Peterson, L., de Zwaan, M., and Mitchell, J. E. (in press) "The emergence of eating pathology after bariatric surgery: a rare outcome with important clinical implications", *International Journal of Eating Disorders*.

Mitchell, J. E., Lancaster, K. L., Burgard, M. A., Howell, L. M., Krahn, D. D., Crosby, R. D., Wonderlich, S. A., and Gosnell, B. A. (2001) "Long-term follow-up of patients' status after gastric bypass", *Obesity Surgery* 11: 464–8.

Oprah Winfrey Show (2006) (television program), Oprah Winfrey Network, US, 24 October.

Ostlund, M. (2011) "Risk of alcohol problems after bariatric surgery", presented at Digestive Disease Week, Chicago, IL, May.

Powers, P. S., Perez, A., Boyd, F., and Rosemurgy, A. (1999) "Eating pathology before and after bariatric surgery: a prospective study", *International Journal of Eating Disorders* 25: 293–300.

Sabbioni, M. E. E., Dickson, M. H., Eychmuller, F. D., Goetz, S., Hurny, C., Naef, M., Balsiger, B., de Marco, D., Burgi, U., and Buchler, M. W. (2002) "Intermediate results of health related quality of life after vertical banded gastroplasty", *International Journal of Obesity* 26: 277–80.

Sallet, P. C., Sallet, J. A., Dixon, J. B., *et al.* (2007) "Eating behaviour as a prognostic factor for weight loss after gastric bypass", *Obesity Surgery* 17: 445–51.

Sansone, R. A., Schumacher, D., Wiederman, M. W., and Routson-Weichers, L. (2008) "The prevalence of binge eating disorder and borderline personality symptomatology among gastric surgery patients", *Eating Behaviors* 9: 197–202.

Sogg, S. (2007) "Alcohol misuse after bariatric surgery: epiphenomenon or 'Oprah' phenomenon?", *Surgery for Obesity and Related Diseases*, 3: 366–8.

Souter, E., Shapiro, E., Sheff-Cahan, V. (2007) "Trading one addiction for another", *People* 67: 60–65.

Spencer, J. (2006) "After weight-loss surgery, some find new addictions". Online. Available: http:// http://old.post-gazette.com/pg/06199/706662-114.stm (accessed 7 April 2012).

Suzuki, J., Haimovici, F., and Chang, G. (2010) "Alcohol use disorders after bariatric surgery", *Obesity Surgery* 22: 201–7.

Thompson, F. E., Subar, A. F., Loria, C. M., Reedy, J. L., and Baranowski, T. (2010) 'Need for technological innovation in dietary assessment', *Journal of the American Dietetic Association* 110: 48–51.

Wadden, T. A., Faulconbridge, L. F., Jones-Corneille, L. R., Sarwer, D. B., Fabricatore, A. N., Thomas, G. J., *et al.* (2011) "Binge eating disorder and the outcome of bariatric surgery at one year: a prospective, observational study", *Obesity* 19: 1220–28.

Welch, G., Wesolowski, C., Zagarins, S., Kuhn, J., Romanelli, J., Garb, J., and Allen, N. (2011) "Evaluation of clinical outcomes for gastric bypass surgery: results from a comprehensive follow-up study", *Obesity Surgery* 21: 18–28.

World Health Organization (2005) *World Health Report 2005.* Online. Available: http://www.who.int/whr/2005/en/index.html (accessed 3 June 2012).

Chapter 15

Behavioral weight loss

Erin C. Accurso and Lisa Sanchez-Johnsen

Case study

I am 25 years old and, since I was 13 or 14, all of my doctors have said that I need to lose weight. I come from a traditional Mexican family and many of my family members and relatives are overweight, so I thought that was normal. I tried many diets, starting in early adolescence, but I always ended up gaining the weight back. Initially, I think I gained weight as a way to protect myself. My life has not been easy. I was sexually abused as a child, and men would always make sexual comments about my body. Those comments seemed to stop as I gained weight. It is also hard for me to lose weight because I love the taste of food, especially sweet and salty snacks!

Over time, I learned that food could be comforting. When I had a stressful day or felt depressed, fantasizing about what I would eat after work was helpful. And then, when I ate the food, I felt even happier and did not have to think about my problems. Things eventually got to the point where my eating felt completely out of control, and I couldn't stop myself from eating my way through the entire pantry. When I was 17, Mom was cleaning my bedroom and found a food stash under my bed – a big box filled with bags of *chicharrón* (fried pork skin), candy bars, Mexican cookies, and all sorts of other junk food. It was obvious that some of the food had been eaten, because there was a whole pile of empty wrappers hidden under there too. When Mom asked me about this, I knew I could no longer hide my problem with overeating. I felt so ashamed and embarrassed. I still eat like that sometimes … mostly when I'm alone after I get home from work. Like last month, I was kind of nervous about my first appointment here, so I drove through McDonald's on my way home. I ordered my food and then parked in the empty corner of the parking lot so that no one could see me eating. I feel disgusted and ashamed of myself when I eat like this.

My parents were born and raised in Mexico, and are very traditional in their values. They also believe that problems should be discussed in the family, so I was surprised when Mom took me to see a psychologist. The doctor told me that I had this thing called Binge Eating Disorder. I didn't get treatment at the time because I was too embarrassed to talk about my eating, but this time I really needed to take action. I had been gaining more weight and it scared me that I could lose control over my eating so easily. Through therapy, I am beginning to understand my emotional eating better and the difference between bingeing and overeating. With practice, I am gaining better control of my emotions, my eating, and my weight. I feel really motivated to get this under control and improve my overall health, for myself and for my family.

Rosa

Introduction

Binge eating disorder (BED) is characterized by recurrent binge eating episodes in the absence of inappropriate compensatory weight control methods (American Psychiatric Association 2000). Binge eating episodes are defined as eating an unusually large amount of food, accompanied by a sense of lack of control and significant distress. While obesity is not a criterion for BED, it is prevalent among people with BED (Johnson et al. 2001). Indeed, the prevalence of BED appears to increase as the degree of obesity increases (Giusti et al. 2004; Hay 1998; Hay and Fairburn 1998; Telch et al. 1988). Among people seeking bariatric surgery, close to 30 per cent also meet criteria for BED, with prevalence rates of 4 to 8 per cent in community samples of people with obesity (Kalarchian et al. 2007; Marcus and Levine 2004). Despite differences in obese people with and without BED, it is believed that similar treatment approaches may be efficacious for both groups. The focus of this chapter is on empirically supported behavioral and cognitive interventions for weight loss among overweight and obese people with BED; it does not address people with BED who are normal weight or underweight. Future directions for weight loss interventions will also be discussed, with an emphasis on culturally-tailored interventions for overweight people with BED.

Differences in obese people with and without BED

BED is associated with greater psychiatric comorbidity than is present in obesity without BED, including greater psychological distress (Ramacciotti et al. 2008), greater psychosocial impairment (Hsu et al. 2002; Ramacciotti et al. 2008; Rieger et al. 2005; Riener et al. 2006), greater impairment at work (Rieger et al. 2005), greater self-evaluation based on weight and shape concerns (Ramacciotti et al. 2008), and poorer overall quality of life (Rieger et al. 2005). Additional factors that might impact the course of treatment in BED include poorer interoceptive awareness, greater perceived ineffectiveness, and tendency to use all-or-nothing thinking (Ramacciotti et al. 2008). In addition to psychological factors, research has shown that there are differences in obesity onset and weight trajectories among people with and without BED. People with BED may have an earlier onset of obesity than those without BED (Tseng *et al.* 2004; Wilfley *et al.* 2003), with the majority having gained a significant amount of weight in the year prior to seeking treatment (Barnes *et al.* 2011). Although adults tend to gradually gain weight over time (one to two pounds a year; Williamson *et al.* 1991), weight gain in those with BED is much greater. People with BED also consume significantly more calories at both regular meals and binge meals than weight-matched controls (Guss *et al.* 2002; Walsh and Boudreau 2003). Finally, binge eating is associated with significant weight cycling (Marchesini *et al.* 2004; Venditti *et al.* 1996).

Current treatments for BED

Understanding the range of differences between obese people with and without BED is essential to inform appropriate treatment approaches and treatment goals. While treatment of binge eating alone can help to prevent further weight gain (Yanovski 2003), it is not adequate in addressing obesity. Binge eating is the initial target of cognitive behavioral treatment (CBT) for BED, which is considered to be the gold standard of treatment for BED (NICE 2004; Wilson and Fairburn 2000). This treatment approach conveys a firm stance toward first eliminating binge eating and establishing healthier eating patterns *before* engaging in weight loss attempts. While CBT does provide psycho-education about nutrition and incorporates regular exercise, the target of the treatment is not to reduce weight but rather to improve control over binge eating and promote acceptance of larger than average body size (Fairburn *et al.* 1993). Other psychological treatments for BED with initial evidence include interpersonal psychotherapy (Wilfley *et al.* 2002) and dialectical behavior therapy (Telch *et al.* 2001). In addition, psychotropic medications have demonstrated some promise in reducing binge eating but only small or non-significant effects for weight loss (Arnold *et al.* 2002; McElroy *et al.* 2000; McElroy, Arnold *et al.* 2003; McElroy, Hudson *et al.* 2003; Pearlstein *et al.* 2003).

Due to the multiple problems associated with BED (i.e., binge eating, psychological distress, and obesity), it has been suggested that binge cessation be achieved through psychological treatment before attempting weight loss (Agras *et al.* 1994). Certainly, abstinence from binge eating is associated with greater weight loss (Grilo *et al.* 2005; Wilfley *et al.* 2002). While this sequence of treatments seems logical, research has found little additional benefit to this progression of treatment (de Zwaan *et al.* 2005; Grilo *et al.* 2011). Although there might be concern about weight loss programs exacerbating binge eating in those with BED, research has found that weight loss and caloric restriction are not associated with worsened binge eating in those with BED (de Zwaan *et al.* 2005; Raymond *et al.* 2002; Wadden *et al.* 2004). Indeed, CBT for binge eating and behavioral weight loss (BWL) interventions in isolation have both been shown to be efficacious in reducing binge eating and eating disorder psychopathology (Grilo *et al.* 2011; Marcus *et al.* 1995; Munsch *et al.* 2007). While CBT for binge eating is associated with greater reductions in binge eating (Devlin *et al.* 2005; Grilo *et al.* 2011; Munsch *et al.* 2007), BWL interventions are associated with greater weight loss at completion of treatment (Grilo *et al.* 2011; Marcus *et al.* 1995; Munsch *et al.* 2007). Therefore, BWL treatment may be appropriate for patients with obesity and BED because it specifically targets eating behavior to establish regular eating habits, thereby reducing disorganized eating and binge eating. Indeed, when administered as a first-line treatment, BWL also reduces binge eating frequency (Devlin *et al.* 2005; Grilo *et al.* 2011; Munsch *et al.* 2007; Nauta *et al.* 2001). Despite reductions in weight and binge eating for those with obesity and BED, it is important to note that BED moderates weight loss treatment effects – people with BED have poorer weight loss treatment response than those without (Blaine and Rodman 2007).

Description of behavioral weight loss

Patients with BED and obesity typically have weight loss as their primary goal (Fairburn *et al.* 1993). Although previous recommendations were that binge eating should be addressed first (Agras *et al.* 1994), studies have found that weight loss treatment can simultaneously improve binge eating and reduce weight. Behavioral and cognitive behavioral interventions are largely overlapping and have shown success with overweight or obese patients with BED before or after psychological treatment of binge eating. BWL treatments aim to modify both eating and exercise habits to produce a negative energy balance through reduced caloric intake and increased energy expenditure through physical activity (Brownell 2000).

However, people with BED and obesity typically have weight loss expectations that "far exceed expert and governmental guidelines" (Masheb and Grilo 2002), which may result in disappointment and decreased motivation for weight loss. Therefore, CBT for obesity focuses on encouraging greater self-acceptance and modifying unrealistic weight loss expectations, which may be particularly salient for those with obesity and BED. BWL treatments also focus on modifying cognitions but to a lesser extent. While CBT for obesity may be an appropriate treatment for BED (Cooper *et al.* 2003), there is relatively less research on CBT than BWL treatment in those with BED and obesity. Therefore, this section will focus on BWL treatment, in particular Brownell's (2000) LEARN program, which is considered the "gold standard" of CBTs for weight loss. The LEARN program has been adapted for use in both research and clinical settings.

BWL programs are typically delivered in a group format and range from four to six months of weekly sessions. Setting specific, concrete, and achievable goals is an important first step in BWL treatment. For example, Rosa might initially formulate a goal of wanting to feel more in control of her life. In determining factors that may increase her sense of control, she may incorporate an exercise goal into her routine (e.g., "I will walk for at least 15 minutes four days per week"). A key component of BWL is daily self-monitoring of food intake and physical activity. Self-monitoring is an important part of assessment, which can guide the use of behavioral interventions and is an important part of the behavior change process. It provides information on progress towards goals (e.g., the number of days for which Rosa able to achieve her walking goal). In reviewing food and activity logs, factors associated with success can be reinforced and barriers to success can be identified. Once barriers are identified, problem-solving skills are taught to increase behavioral adherence to the program. If Rosa is having difficulty with motivating herself to walk after returning home from work, she might consider rescheduling her walk for another time of the day. If bad weather is interfering with walking, treatment may help Rosa to consider other types of activities that she can do indoors.

While the program is largely behavioral in focus, cognitive restructuring is also incorporated to identify and modify dysfunctional thoughts about weight regulation and other weight-related goals. Treatment focuses on modifying unrealistic goals (e.g., "I'll never eat cake again" or "I will always be able to control my mood to avoid eating in the absence of hunger") and shaping them towards realistic ones (e.g., "I will eat only a sliver of cake at my son's birthday party"). In addition, BWL treatment encourages positive self-talk related to progress towards realistic goals. Body image and self-esteem are also addressed. For example, BWL treatment would help Rosa to focus on how her body is a gift, rather than on how it has attracted unwanted attention, and address faulty beliefs about being able to control her social life through controlling her appearance. Interpersonal relationships are also discussed to aid coping with interpersonal triggers for overeating and increase social support for weight control. Additional BWL techniques include self-regulatory strategies such as stimulus control (i.e., limiting exposure to unhealthy foods) to reduce overeating. Brownell's (2000) BWL program also helps participants to distinguish between food cravings and physical hunger, then teaches how to target cravings through distraction (e.g., thinking about an upcoming pleasant social event) or confrontation (e.g., "You [craving] are trying to trick me into eating ice cream, but I'm not hungry so I won't be fooled!"), as well as learning new strategies to coping with stress (e.g., engaging in a relaxing activity other than eating).

BWL programs such as LEARN (Brownell 2000) emphasize moderate caloric restriction and increased activity level. Although BWL has also been combined with very low-calorie diets, it traditionally endorses balanced and flexible food choices rather than rigid dieting. Homework, such as self-monitoring, is a critical component of BWL treatment to change eating, activity, and thinking habits. Weekly visits allow for frequent review of goals and homework assignments (e.g., self-monitoring). Weekly visits also allow for consistent use of reinforcement contingencies for homework completion. In addition, weekly assessment of a patient's weight provides a concrete measure of adherence to the program and helps to increase patient motivation to follow behavioral prescriptions. While the treatment itself is time-limited, BWL treatments emphasize long-term modification of eating and exercise patterns as a lifestyle for sustained weight loss and/or maintenance. Therefore, the last phase of treatment underscores relapse prevention strategies to promote weight loss maintenance.

When BWL is delivered individually, sessions cover the same psycho-educational material but are typically shorter in duration than when delivered in groups (e.g., 45 minutes versus 90 minutes) and include more individualized review of homework. Individual therapy allows for greater flexibility and treatment individualization in addressing personal issues related to weight or weight loss efforts. When delivered in a group format, group cohesion and support are developed and fostered throughout treatment. Closed groups are typically preferable in order to promote group cohesion and present material in a sequence of stages that builds upon previously presented material. Furthermore, groups allow for members to learn and benefit from others' experiences. While BWL treatment can be delivered individually, research has found that group treatment for BED results in greater weight loss than individual treatment, regardless of patient preference for individual or group treatment (Renjilian *et al.* 2001). In addition, group treatment is more cost-effective than individual treatment.

One of the potential advantages to BWL over more specialized treatments (e.g., CBTs for binge eating or weight loss) is that it can be more readily disseminated in community settings. The treatment can be delivered by a broader group of health professionals because it does not require the same level of clinical expertise. In addition, it is easily delivered in a group format and less expensive to implement than psychological treatments. Furthermore, weight loss achieved at the end of BWL treatments is greater than that found in other psychological interventions (Grilo *et al.* 2011; Marcus *et al.* 1995; Munsch *et al.* 2007). Certainly, clinical judgment should be used to determine whether weight loss should be attempted prior to targeted treatment of binge eating, or whether a patient would benefit from additional treatment targeted at binge eating should these symptoms remain problematic during the course of, or following, BWL treatment. Clinical judgment is also necessary to culturally tailor interventions as appropriate. For example, the clinician treating Rosa may offer family therapy as an option given the high value placed on interdependence and family in Latinos (Sanchez-Johnsen 2011). Other cultural considerations include conducting bilingual therapy and integrating other cultural values into treatment, with attention to how these factors may influence thoughts about diet, eating patterns, and physical activity.

Short-term and long-term outcomes

Short-term weight loss is greater for people with obesity and BED in BWL treatments compared to CBT for binge eating (Grilo *et al.* 2011; Munsch *et al.* 2007). This is also true for behavioral treatment versus purely cognitive treatment (Nauta *et al.* 2000). However, differences become non-significant within six months to one year (Grilo *et al.* 2011; Munsch *et al.* 2007), partially due to some weight regain in the behavioral treatment group (Marcus *et al.* 1995; Munsch *et al.* 2007; Nauta *et al.* 2000). While both CBT for binge eating (Adriaens *et al.* 2008; Grilo *et al.* 2005; Marchesini *et al.* 2002) and BWL treatments (Blaine and Rodman 2007; Devlin *et al.* 2005; Grilo *et al.* 2011; Munsch *et al.* 2007; Nauta *et al.* 2001) result in weight loss for those with obesity and BED, the weight loss is generally minimal to modest. A large meta-analysis confirmed this trend, finding that weight loss treatment resulted in negligible weight loss for individuals with obesity and BED, despite good weight loss outcomes for individuals without BED (Blaine and Rodman 2007). Nevertheless, BWL appears to be the most promising short-term intervention for weight loss in BED. Indeed, a recent meta-analysis of 38 studies found that no current psychological or pharmacological interventions other than BWL treatments (with or without a prescribed diet) resulted in considerable weight loss for overweight patients with BED (Vocks *et al.* 2010).

The long-term effects of BWL treatment on binge eating have not been well investigated. However, long-term weight loss among obese people with and without BED is generally poor. In one randomized controlled trial, remission rates of binge eating were similar across psychological treatments and BWL at post-treatment and one-year follow-up (Wilson *et al.* 2010). However, BWL resulted in significantly better weight loss, with more than twice as many patients achieving at least a five-per cent weight loss in the BWL condition when compared to psychological treatments (e.g., CBT for binge eating; Wilson *et al.* 2010). Weight loss differences were no longer significant at two-year follow-up, while those in psychological treatment conditions had better binge eating outcomes. Unfortunately, no psychological or behavioral treatment to date has resulted in significant long-term weight loss or maintenance in people with obesity, with or without binge eating. Furthermore, binge eating is uniquely associated with poorer long-term weight loss outcomes (Sherwood *et al.* 1999) and higher treatment dropout (Melchionda *et al.* 2003). Even obese people without BED participating in behavioral treatments (spanning 14 to 32 sessions) maintained an average weight loss of less than four pounds approximately four years post-treatment (see Perri and Corsica 2002 for a review). There appears to be improved maintenance of weight loss when traditional behavioral treatment is augmented with problem-solving therapy (Perri *et al.* 2001), particularly for those with better problem-solving skills (Murawski *et al.* 2009). Additional research is needed to examine how long-term maintenance of weight loss can be improved for people with BED.

Future directions

Most patients with BED are not currently receiving evidence-based treatment. The gap between research and clinical practice remains a serious problem, with most research examining interventions in the context of clinical trials rather than "real-world" community settings (Wilson *et al.* 2007). Therefore, future research should investigate treatments for BED in community-based settings. In addition, guided self-help interventions have potential to help bridge the research–practice gap in that they are more cost-effective and have improved feasibility. Guided self-help BWL has not proved as efficacious as guided self-help CBT in reducing binge eating, but it is equally efficacious with respect to weight loss (Grilo and Masheb 2005). Although BED treatments are typically assessed with binge eating and weight as outcomes, more attention should be paid to a greater range of outcomes, including psychological and emotional health, as well as indicators of physical health other than weight. Finally, the role of culture in treatment should be investigated. Since culture is a complex and multidimensional concept, interventions should focus on the internal representations of culture, such cultural values, beliefs, and attitudes. To date, the majority of BWL treatments for obesity with or without BED have not considered the influence of culture or cultural values. Certain ethnic minority groups such as Latinos, African Americans, Native Americans, and Native Hawaiian/Pacific Islanders have disproportionate rates of overweight and obesity compared to non-Hispanic Whites (Wang and Beydoun 2007). As such, culturally competent weight loss interventions that systematically consider the role of culture, cultural values, and acculturation need to be developed for people with BED.

References

Adriaens, A., Pieters, G., Vancampfort, D., Probst, M., and Vanderlinden, J. (2008) "A cognitive-behavioural program (once a week) for patients with obesity and binge eating disorder: short-term follow-up data", *Psychol Top* 17: 361–71.

Agras, W. S., Telch, C. F., Arnow, B., Eldredge, K., and Wilfley, D. E. (1994) "Weight loss, cognitive-behavioral, and desipramine treatments in binge eating disorder: an additive design", *Behavior Therapy* 25: 225–38.

American Psychiatric Association (2000) *Diagnostic and Statistical Manual of Mental Disorders (DSM-IV-TR)* (4th edn, text revision), Washington, DC: American Psychiatric Association.

Arnold, L. M., McElroy, S. L., Hudson, J. I., Welge, J. A., Bennett, A. J., and Keck, P. E. (2002) "A placebo-controlled, randomized trial of fluoxetine in the treatment of binge-eating disorder", *Journal of Clinical Psychiatry* 63: 1028–33.

Barnes, R. D., Blomquist, K. K., and Grilo, C. M. (2011) "Exploring pretreatment weight trajectories in obese patients with binge eating disorder", *Comprehensive Psychiatry* 52: 312–18.

Blaine, B., and Rodman, J. (2007) "Responses to weight loss treatment among obese individuals with and without BED: a matched-study meta-analysis", *Eating and Weight Disorders* 12: 54–60.

Brownell, K. D. (2000) *The LEARN Program for Weight Management*, Dallas, TX: American Health Publishing Company.

Cooper, S., Fairburn, C. G., and Hawker, D. M. (2003) *Cognitive-behavioral treatment of obesity*, New York: The Guilford Press.

Devlin, M. J., Goldfein, J. A., Petkova, E., Jiang, H., Raizman, Wolk, S., *et al.* (2005) "Cognitive behavioral therapy and fluoxetine as adjuncts to group behavioral therapy for binge eating disorder", *Obesity Research* 13: 1077–88.

de Zwaan, M., Mitchell, J. E., Crosby, R. D., Mussell, M. P., Raymond, N. C., Specker, S. M., *et al.* (2005) "Short-term cognitive behavioral treatment does not improve outcome on a comprehensive very-low-calorie diet program in obese women with binge eating disorder", *Behavior Therapy* 36: 89–99.

Fairburn, C. G., Marcus, M. D., and Wilson, G. T. (1993) "Cognitive-behavioral therapy for binge eating and bulimia nervosa: a comprehensive treatment manual", in C. G. Fairburn and G. T. Wilson (eds) *Binge Eating: Nature, Assessment, and Treatment* (pp. 361–404), New York: The Guilford Press.

Giusti, V., Héraïef, E., Gaillard, R. C., and Burckhardt, P. (2004) "Predictive factors of binge eating disorder in women searching to lose weight", *Eating and Weight Disorders* 9: 44–9.

Grilo, C. M., and Masheb, R. M. (2005) "A randomized controlled comparison of guided self-help cognitive behavioral therapy and behavioral weight loss for binge eating disorder", *Behavior Research and Therapy* 43: 1509–25.

Grilo, C. M., Masheb, R. M., and Wilson, G. T. (2005) "Efficacy of cognitive behavioral therapy and fluoxetine for the treatment of binge eating disorder", *Biological Psychiatry* 57: 301–9.

Grilo, C. M., Masheb, R. M., Wilson, G. T., Gueorguieva, R., and White, M. A. (2011) "Cognitive-behavioral therapy, behavioral weight loss, and sequential treatment for obese patients with binge-eating disorder", *Journal of Consulting and Clinical Psychology* 79: 675–85.

Guss, J. L., Kissileff, H. R., Devlin, M. J., Zimmerli, E., and Walsh, B. T. (2002) "Binge size increases with body mass index in women with binge-eating disorder", *Obesity Research* 10: 1021–9.

Hay, P. (1998) "The epidemiology of eating disorder behaviors: an Australian community-based survey", *International Journal of Eat Disorders* 23: 371–82.

Hay, P., and Fairburn, C. (1998) "The validity of the DSM-IV scheme for classifying bulimic eating disorders", *International Journal of Eating Disorders* 23: 7–15.

Hsu, L. K., Mulliken, B., McDonagh, B., Krupa Das, S., Rand, W., Fairburn, C. G., *et al.* (2002) "Binge eating disorder in extreme obesity", *International Journal of Obesity Related Metabolic Disorders* 26: 1398–403.

Johnson, J. G., Spitzer, R. L., and Williams, J. B. (2001) "Health problems, impairment and illness associated with bulimia nervosa and binge eating disorder among primary care and obstetric gynaecology patients", *Psychological Medicine* 31: 1455–66.

Kalarchian, M. A., Marcus, M. D., Levine, M. D., Courcoulas, A. P., Pilkonis, P. A., Ringham, R. M., *et al.* (2007) "Psychiatric disorders among bariatric surgery candidates: relationship to obesity and functional health status", *American Journal of Psychiatry* 164: 328–34.

Marchesini, G., Cuzzolaro, M., Mannucci, E., Dalle Grave, R., Gennaro, Tomasi, F., *et al.* (2004) "Weight cycling in treatment-seeking obese persons: data from the QUOVADIS study", *International Journal of Obesity* 28: 1456–62.

Marchesini, G., Natale, S., Chierici, S., Manini, R., Besteghi, L., Di Domizio, S., *et al.* (2002) "Effects of cognitive-behavioural therapy on health related quality of life in obese subjects with and without binge eating disorder", *International Journal of Obesity* 26: 1261–7.

Marcus, M. D., and Levine, M. (2004) "Obese patients with binge-eating disorder", in D. J. Goldstein (ed.) *The Management of Eating Disorders and Obesity* (2nd edn) (pp. 143–60), Totowa, NJ: Humana Press.

Marcus, M. D., Wing, R. R., and Fairburn, C. G. (1995) "Cognitive treatment of binge-eating v. behavioral weight control in the treatment of binge eating disorder", *Annals of Behavioral Medicine* 17: S090.

Masheb, R. M., and Grilo, C. M. (2002) "Weight loss expectations in patients with binge-eating disorder", *Obesity Research* 10: 309–14.

McElroy, S. L., Arnold, L. M., Shapira, N. A., Keck, P. E., Rosenthal, N. R., Karim, M. R., et al. (2003) "Topiramate in the treatment of binge eating disorder associated with obesity", *American Journal of Psychiatry* 160: 255–61.

McElroy, S. L., Casuto, L. S., Nelson, E. B., Lake, K. A., Soutullo, C. A., and Keck, P. E. Jnr (2000) "Placebo-controlled trial of sertraline in the treatment of binge eating disorder", *American Journal of Psychiatry* 157: 1004–6.

McElroy, S. L., Hudson, J. I., Malhotra, S., Welge, J. A., Nelson, E. B., and Keck, P. E. Jnr (2003) "Citalopram in the treatment of binge-eating disorder", *Journal of Clinical Psychiatry* 64: 807–13.

Melchionda, N., Besteghi, L., Di Domizio, S., Pasqui, F., Nuccitelli, C., Migliorini, S., et al. (2003) "Cognitive behavioural therapy for obesity: one-year follow-up in a clinical setting", *Eating and Weight Disorders* 8: 188–93.

Munsch, S., Biedert, E., Meyer, A., Michael, T., Schlup, B., Tuch, A., et al. (2007) "A randomized comparison of cognitive behavioral therapy and behavioral weight loss treatment for overweight individuals with binge eating disorder", *International Journal of Eating Disorders* 40: 102–13.

Murawski, M. E., Milsom, V. A., Ross, K. M., Rickel, K. A., DeBraganza, N., Gibbons, L. M., et al. (2009) "Problem solving, treatment adherence, and weight-loss outcome among women participating in lifestyle treatment for obesity", *Eating Behaviors* 10: 146–51.

National Institute for Clinical Excellence (NICE) (2004) *Eating Disorders: Core Interventions in the Treatment and Management of Anorexia Nervosa, Bulimia Nervosa and Related Eating Disorders: Clinical Guideline No. 9*, London: NICE. Online. Available: http://publications.nice.org.uk/eating-disorders-cg9 (accessed 15 January 2012).

Nauta, H., Hospers, H., and Jansen, A. (2001) "One-year follow-up effects of two obesity treatments on psychological well-being and weight", *British Journal of Health Psychology* 6: 271–84.

Nauta, H., Hospers, H., Kok, G., and Jansen, A. (2000) "A comparison between a cognitive and a behavioral treatment for obese binge eaters and obese non-binge eaters", *Behavior Therapy* 31: 441–61.

Pearlstein, T., Spurrell, E., Hohlstein, L. A., Gurney, V., Read, J., Fuchs, C., et al. (2003) "A double-blind, placebo-controlled trial of fluvoxamine in binge eating disorder", *Archives of Women's Mental Health*, 6: 147–51.

Perri, M. G., and Corsica, J. A. (2002) "Improving the maintenance of weight lost in behavioral treatment of obesity", in T. A. Wadden and A. J. Stunkard (eds) *Handbook of Obesity Treatment* (pp. 357–79), New York: The Guilford Press.

Perri, M. G., Nezu, A. M., McKelvey, W. F., Shermer, R. L., Renjilian, D. A., and Viegener, B. J. (2001) "Relapse prevention training and problem-solving therapy in the long-term management of obesity", *Journal of Consulting and Clinical Psychology* 69: 722–6.

Ramacciotti, C. E., Coli, E., Bondi, E., Burgalassi, A., Massimetti, G., Dell'osso, L., *et al.* (2008) "Shared psychopathology in obese subjects with and without binge-eating disorder", *International Journal of Eating Disorders* 41: 643–9.

Raymond, N. C., de Zwaan, M., Mitchell, J. E., Ackard, D., and Thuras. P. (2002) "Effect of a very low calorie diet on the diagnostic category of individuals with binge eating disorder", *International Journal of Eating Disorders* 31: 49–56.

Rieger, E., Wilfley, D. E., Stein, R. I., Marino, V., and Crow, S. J. (2005) "A comparison of quality of life in obese individuals with and without binge eating disorder", *International Journal of Eating Disorders* 37: 234–40.

Riener, R., Schindler, K., Ludvik, B. (2006) "Psychosocial variables, eating behavior, depression and binge eating in morbidly obese subjects", *Eating Behaviors* 7: 309–14.

Renjilian, D. A., Perri, M. G., Nezu, A. M., McKelvey, W. F., Shermer, R. L., and Anton, S. D. (2001) "Individual versus group therapy for obesity: effects of matching participants to their treatment preferences", *Journal of Consulting and Clinical Psychology* 69: 717–21.

Sanchez-Johnsen, L. (2011) "The Hispanics", in J. F. McDermott and N. N. Andrade (eds) *People and Cultures of Hawai'i: The Evolution of Culture and Ethnicity* (pp. 152–75), Honolulu: University of Hawai'i Press.

Sherwood, N. E., Jeffery, R. W., and Wing, R. R. (1999) "Binge status as a predictor of weight loss treatment", *International Journal of Obesity* 23: 485–93.

Telch, C. F., Agras, W. S., and Linehan, M. M. (2001) "Dialectical behavior therapy for binge eating disorder", *Journal of Consulting and Clinical Psychology* 69: 1061–5.

Telch, C. F., Agras, W. S., and Rossiter, E. M. (1988) "Binge eating increases with increasing adiposity", *International Journal of Eating Disorders* 7: 115–19.

Tseng, M., Lee, M., Chen, S., Lee, Y., Lin, K., Chen, P., *et al.* (2004) "Response of Taiwanese obese binge eaters to a hospital-based weight reduction program", *Journal of Psychosomatic Research* 57: 279–85.

Venditti, E. M., Wing, R. R., Jakicic, J. M., Butler, B. A., and Marcus, M. D. (1996) "Weight cycling, psychological health, and binge eating in obese women", *Journal of Consulting and Clinical Psychology* 64: 400–405.

Vocks, S., Tuschen-Caffier, B., Pietrowsky, R., Rustenbach, S. J., Kersting, A., and Herpertz, S. (2010) "Meta-analysis of the effectiveness of psychological and pharmacological treatments for binge eating disorder", *International Journal of Eating Disorders* 43: 205–17.

Wadden, T. A., Foster, G. D., Sarwer, D. B., Anderson, D. A., Gladis, M., Sanderson, R. S., *et al.* (2004) "Dieting and the development of eating disorders in obese women: results of a randomized controlled trial", *American Journal of Clinical Nutrition* 80: 560–68.

Walsh, B. T., and Boudreau, G. (2003) "Laboratory studies of binge eating disorder", *International Journal of Eating Disorders 34:* S30–38.

Wang, Y., and Beydoun, M.A. (2007) "The obesity epidemic in the United States – gender, age, socioeconomic, racial/ethnic, and geographic characteristics: a systematic review and meta-regression analysis", *Epidemiology Review* 29: 6–28.

Wilfley, D. E., Welch, R. R., Stein, R. I., Spurrell, E. B., Cohen, L. R., Saelens, B. E., *et al.* (2002) "A randomized comparison of group cognitive-behavioral therapy for obese individuals with binge eating disorder", *Archives of General Psychiatry* 59: 713–21.

Wilfley, D. E., Wilson, G. T., and Agras, W. S. (2003) "The clinical significance of binge eating disorder", *International Journal of Eating Disorders* 34: S96–106.

Williamson, D. F., Kahn, H. S., and Byers, T. (1991) "The 10-year incidence of obesity and major weight gain in black and white US women aged 30–55 years", *American Journal of Clinical Nutrition* 53 (Suppl. 6): 1515–18.

Wilson, G. T., and Fairburn, C. G. (2000) "The treatment of binge eating disorder", *European Eating Disorders Review* 8: 351–4.

Wilson, G. T., Grilo, C. M., and Vitousek, K. M. (2007) "Psychological treatment of eating disorders", *American Psychologist* 62: 199–216.

Wilson, G. T., Wilfley, D. E., Agras, W. S., and Bryson, S. W. (2010) "Psychological treatments of binge eating disorder", *Archives of General Psychiatry* 67: 94–101.

Yanovski, S. Z. (2003) "Binge eating disorder and obesity in 2003: could treating an eating disorder have a positive effect on the obesity epidemic?", *International Journal of Eating Disorders* 34: S117–20.

Chapter 16

Intuitive eating and movement in the therapeutic milieu

A synergistic paradigm for healing in the treatment of binge eating disorder

Amy Pershing

Case study

> This feels so weird to tell someone this stuff. I don't even tell myself this stuff. I don't know me, and I don't know you, but here goes: I hate my bingeing, but I have no idea how to stay on a diet. Every time I try, I binge worse than ever. It's like part of me says: "No way. This is mine. Nobody's taking this away." But my body is tired and too heavy. I just don't know any other way.
>
> Anna

Introduction

Binge Eating Disorder (BED) has myriad causal factors. Biology, genetics, weight stigma and weight-related bullying, cultural pressures to be thin, a history of trauma, and family dynamics may all play a part. We know, too, that the specific combination of these factors varies a lot from person to person. Clinically we see some specific psychological factors that present with particular frequency in the adult population of patients with BED. Problematic attachment styles and an inability to set and maintain appropriate relational boundaries are often of particular concern. Somatic disconnection and dissociative behavior is also common; especially for survivors of abuse, powerful feelings of shame may elicit use of food to disconnect. In these cases, BED is often a power-fully *protective* mechanism, and one that patients quite wisely do not give up easily.

In the therapy office, BED patients often present with exceptional affective attunement to "other". Where some eating disorders can be more clinically narcissistic in presentation, patients with BED are often "caretakers", the child whose role was often that of "oldest", regardless of birth order. These children can sometimes be described as "15 going on 40". They are typically exceptionally responsible adults, rarely asking for needs to be met in interpersonal relation-ships, and have a great deal of difficulty either knowing or tolerating their own internal needful "child" part. They also often present as profoundly somatically disconnected, particularly unaware of hunger and fullness cues, as well as other physical, and emotional, needs and preferences.

This inability to connect to affective and somatic cues is often at the heart of BED. With minimal conscious access to internal needs, desires, fears and hopes, little protective guidance is available from the Self. For this chapter, Self refers to Jung's concept of the regulating center of the psyche and facilitator of individuation. It represents all that is unique within a human being, and its discovery and valuation is central to any therapeutic process. Although, according to Jung, a person is a collection of all the archetypes and what they learn from the collective unconscious, the Self is what makes that person an "I" (Jung 1983). For recovery to take place, treatment must have as a primary goal the repair of the patient's ability to compassionately connect to and trust this Self at all levels, including cognitive, affective, and somatic. Interventions of any kind do best when they help a patient move toward this goal. A variety of therapeutic schools of thought (psychodynamic, Jungian, IFS, Self Psychology) help patients move toward the goal of connection with Self on the psychological front, but only one orientation on the symptom front enables taking this wisdom into account. Research is bearing out the clinical wisdom for this orientation, called Intuitive Eating and Movement (IEM).

Intuitive Eating began as a response to the long-term inefficacy of low- and moderate-calorie diets and other restrictive measures in the non-eating disorder population. Many studies have shown extremely high rates of weight regain following restrictive programs in the general population (Tomiyama and Mann 2008), and this is certainly the case in people with BED as well. Diet regimens are predicated on adherence to an external set of rules and protocols. They do not provide for individual variance of food desires, nutrition, or caloric needs. The foods and amounts that a person finds satisfying (a key concept in lessening the likelihood of a binge) may change from day to day, season to season. Diets cannot adjust to this idiosyncratic reality. In addition, for those with BED, dieting further reinforces the shame cycle. The black and white nature of success and failure, and the implication that the body must be *changed* instead of *heard*, is often a powerful reinforcement of the very messages that are at the heart of BED. Dieting itself becomes another reinforcement for eating disorder psychology. It is important to note as well that dieting is considered a "gateway" to both anorexia and bulimia (Utter *et al.* 2003), and is seen as symptomatic of the presence of eating disorder pathology. It makes little sense therefore that we prescribe to those with BED what we otherwise recognize as fundamentally symptomatic of pathology.

Intuitive Eating, originally proposed by Evelyn Tribole and Elyse Resch (2003) to address the extremely low rates of long-term "success" of dieting, provides a system in excellent alignment with the underlying psychological work of recovery from BED. Basically stated, Intuitive Eating is a nutrition philosophy based on the premise that becoming attuned to the body's needs allows for maintenance of a healthy weight (*as defined by the body*), a decrease in food and weight obsession, a decrease in overeating/binge eating, and a more peaceful relationship with food and one's physical body. To date, there are more than 25 studies on Intuitive Eating (covered by many of the references listed at the end of this chapter, e.g. Bacon 2005; Ciampolini*et al.* 2010; Cole and Horacek 2010) which, combined, show that intuitive eaters have lower body mass index levels (without internalizing the thin ideal), lower rates of disordered eating and eating disorders, eat a variety of foods, enjoy the experience of eating, and show a higher psychological hardiness which includes well-being and resilience (Tribole and Resch 2003). The author of this chapter has added a movement component to the original concept of "intuitive eating", referring instead to Intuitive Eating and Movement (IEM). This model, modified for use with BED, has several discreet tenets. These tenets, and the psychotherapeutic implications of each, will be discussed. The tenets may be only marginally linear. Patients do them in their own way, in their own order, typically revisiting each many times along the journey of recovery. In fact, it can prove clinically informative to notice the steps to which a patient may first be drawn, and those they may save until a later time.

It is important to consider that IEM is often profoundly unnerving to patients with BED. Typically with long histories of weight cycling, most patients with BED believe if they are not dieting, they will *necessarily* gain weight. This has often seemingly proved true; for both biological and psychological reasons, dieting is followed by overeating and weight gain. Typically, however, patients with BED are convinced – by their culture, the medical community and the common mythology of the diet industry – that any weight gain is about a lack of willpower. Therefore, they believe that if eating is left under their body's jurisdiction, disaster will result. This corresponds with the common belief for patients that listening to the Self in any way will result in significant danger to their overall safety in the world.

Those not fully familiar with the IEM model sometimes suggest that it is nutritionally irresponsible, and that patients cannot trust their bodies to make good decisions. With the engineering of many foods to be so highly palatable, they ask is it even possible to eat intuitively? Won't patients simply be unable to stop eating the foods that should be "limited" for good health? This is not the clinical experience of this author, nor is the research bearing out such a conclusion. In fact, patients are astounded to discover how little of the foods they have forbidden they actually wish to eat. When patients learn to eat mindfully, to allow themselves to listen to their entire body when eating various foods, they eat very well. If patients consider the response of their palate, their stomach and their energy level as they eat, they learn how they want to feel, and what will create that feeling.

Clinicians may have similar concerns about patients who struggle with conditions such as Celiac disease, diabetes, or other food allergies or intolerances. IEM elegantly addresses these issues by using the body's natural systems of alert and warning. In the author's 20 years of clinical experience, people with diabetes or

Celiac disease, for example, often come to be very aware of their body's response to sugar or gluten. They have typically known it all along. When we "forbid" a food, we want it all the more. This becomes the "evidence" that the body cannot be trusted. In fact, when patients finally tune in, they find their body has not wanted toxins all along. Forbidding is anathema to recovery.

IEM is sometimes misunderstood to mean that immediate body cues are the *only* source of information to be used in determining food intake. In fact, patients develop an overall body wisdom that they regularly use to make informed decisions. This wisdom is based on experience of their body's reactions over time, and knowledge of their basic nutritional needs. From this, as well as recognition of immediate body desires for food type and amount, decisions can be made that most allow for overall health and satiety.

In clinical practice, several underlying fears may be triggered with the introduction of IEM. Clinicians must keep in mind the psychological material that may correspond to any proposed aspect of IEM, and process this directly with patients. The most common fears of IEM, followed by corresponding (often preconscious) fears from the deeper work of recovery, are listed here:

- Continuous, uncontrollable weight gain (*my feelings will overwhelm me!*).
- What else is there if I don't diet (*is a Self even there?*)?
- Giving up on weight change as the solution to problems (*grief*).
- Loss of the dream of the "ideal" (*letting go of pointless hope*).
- Lack of support for not dieting (*will I still be loveable if I'm just "me"?*).

The tenets of IEM and clinical implications

For most patients with BED, IEM is revolutionary, and takes place over a significant period of time. The internal diet voice is unlikely to entirely disappear for some time, if ever; as with any change of long-held belief, the challenge is to know how to address the voice when it inevitably arises.

We can consider the "diet paradigm", adapted from Nancy King's excellent description (Kratina *et al.* 2003), as follows:

- Achieving an "ideal" weight (as determined by external factors of varying kinds) is the essential measure of success.
- Hunger is suppressed or ignored. "Transgressions" are associated with lack of willpower or "giving in". Physical and emotional hunger are confused.
- Fullness/satiety are irrelevant to food choices.
- Reaching and maintaining goal weight is typically dependent on exercise, which is often dropped when a patient falls off the diet. It is seen as a "have to" or "should".
- Food is moralized as good/bad, illegal/legal, should/shouldn't, on/off diet. Variety, quantity, calories, fat grams, and so on are determined by an external source.

- The patient may gain a brief, false sense of power and control with weight loss, adherence to diet, and exercise plan. Self-esteem and body acceptance do not improve.
- The patient comes to distrust body and sense of judgment, especially with history of failure. Trust typically is placed in the diet or other outside source.

In contrast, the IEM paradigm invites the patient to become the expert on his or her body. A general description follows:

- The body naturally seeks a weight that is appropriate and healthful as food is eaten mostly in response to hunger and fullness cues and knowledge of body needs.
- The relationship to food and movement, however that goal may manifest, is overall health and wellbeing.
- Physical activities, listening to the body, seeking play, and natural movement are all explored. Movement is connected to health, strength and joy (instead of weight loss or body shame).
- ALL food is acceptable. Quantity, quality, and frequency are determined by the patient exploring and responding to physical cues, sense of well-being, taste, overall physiological response to specific foods, and blood glucose levels. Food intake is self-regulated, internally cued, and non-restrained. Body wisdom, unique to each person (e.g., discovering the importance of protein for breakfast, working out to relieve symptoms of anxiety), is incorporated into decision-making over time.
- A consistent challenging of concepts of willpower and obedience ("good day" vs. "bad day"), judgment, or shame in relation to food and movement choices is critical to long-term change.

The parallel clinical material relevant to this paradigm change is profound. Change to an IEM paradigm invites patients to listen to inner experience while placing judgments aside, to value that inner experience as wise, and, over the course of treatment, to come to believe in their ability to protect that inner experience from corruption by the needs of others. These are also the essential tenets of the reclaiming of the Self.

Tenet One: relearning hunger

Case Study

Hunger? Hunger is what you feel when your diet is working. It means you're doing something right. I don't know what to do with it except try and keep it going.

Sarah

For most patients with BED, as with other physical and emotional needs, hunger may be elusive or may be misunderstood as "success." As with other intense feelings the patient may be avoiding, such as grief, terror, rage or shame, hunger may be frightening. For some patients, acknowledgement of the presence of a desire may connect them with unmet needs of other kinds, and leave them feeling vulnerable and out of control. Working with hunger recognition corresponds beautifully with learning to allow needs and desires of all kinds. It also provides opportunities to recognize true present-moment needs (i.e. physical hunger) from emotional needs that may feel somewhat similar. In the therapeutic milieu, drawing these parallels helps patients further understand the need for the eating disorder, and an intuitive path toward change, creating hope and lessening shame. The tasks and tools of this step may include:

- Education regarding the importance of keeping the body nourished and sated.
- Identification of somatic hunger cues and patterns (Where does their hunger manifest in their body? What does a little hungry vs. very hungry feel like? When is food most satisfying?).
- Hunger scale (1–10) or log.
- Learning to differentiate hunger from other needs.
- Planning for hunger needs.
- Learning to see hunger (and feelings) as temporary and safe to experience.

The goals of step one, then, both on somatic and psychological fronts, are an increased awareness of inner experience, a growing acceptance of feelings and desires, and slowly allowing one's inner world to impact outer behavior.

Tenet Two: making peace with food and challenging the "food police"

Case study

> This was the hardest thing for me. I still have to remember it's ok to eat a cookie sometimes. But I know as soon as it's NOT ok to eat that cookie, something changes. I want ten!
>
> Rhonda

This step, as the first, is often met with trepidation. Patients need to be reminded that this can be a gradual process, and is really a period of discovery, of listening to the body's cues and reactions to all foods, and learning its likes and dislikes which have typically been unheard, or decided based on being in either "diet" or "binge" modes. This step requires, first and foremost, allowing all foods without judgment, *but with attention*. Foods that have been forbidden typically are eaten only during a binge, and "acceptable" foods eaten only during times of dieting or restriction. It is imperative to allow unconditional permission to eat without "penance" or some form of compensation.

Patients must also give themselves permission to explore the physical experience of different foods. How do salads make me feel? How does a brownie make me feel? How does the body react to each? What tastes good? What does not? When? Patients may be surprised at this information, their expectations differing greatly from their actual somatic reactions to various foods. The discovery that the body does not actually want to eat only binge foods allows for body trust to begin building. Also during this stage, diet rules need to be identified and challenged. Some of them may be in integrity with the body; many will not. Patients may wish to list these "rules" as they are discovered. A recovery group facilitated by the author created this list:

- "White food is bad!"
- "Bread (beans, chips, cake, etc) is fattening."
- "It's too late to eat."
- "I must have 10 servings of vegetables and 8 glasses of water every day!"
- "No salt!"
- "I only walked 20 minutes, so no dessert." (The karma rule.)
- "No snacking."
- "Exactly three snacks."

It is imperative that patients not make IEM another set of rules, but allow for a process of learning and listening.

The psychological parallels to this tenet are significant. This work involves the patient hearing his or her *own* story, own true needs, and ideas. It is also about the recognition of the body as a source of wisdom and protection, especially relevant for survivors of physical and sexual trauma. The development of curiosity (as opposed to judgment) about internal experience is developed, together with recognition of the reinforcement of internal judgment and shame by the dieter voice.

Tenet Three: satiety and satisfaction

Case study

> The big moment for me was eating chocolate in your office. I really tasted it, I think for the first time. I realized what kind I like best, and actually felt myself lose interest after several bites. The taste of it really changed. It became kind of too sweet. I'd never noticed that before. I was actually done.
>
> Monica

Satiety and satisfaction are critical elements to the prevention of binge eating in and of themselves. For many people with BED, the notion of what they might really *want* to eat is foreign. The sensual quality of foods matters; what temperature, texture, seasoning, and combination of flavors is desired is very important. Being able to determine fullness effectively is not only about amount, but also about the more elusive sense of being "satisfied". It is helpful if a patient can meet their satiety needs as often as possible at this stage of learning. Over time, as the patient comes to trust their ability and desire to meet their needs, postponing a desire is not a triggering event.

Mindfulness strategies can be learning tools in this step. Suggestions that patients find helpful include:

- Sight – look at food's color and shape with full concentration.
- Smell – a food's aroma, both cooked and uncooked. Can you tell when something is fresh or spoiled?
- Taste – let food linger in your mouth for a long time, chewing it and extracting all the flavor it has to give you. Do you like (or dislike) it?
- Experience – note a food's texture and sound as you chew.
- Hear – the sounds of food as you pop it in your mouth and crunch and munch.
- Keep checking in for taste. Ask: "Am I finished? Do I need more? Do I want more?"

Being mindful and aware of satiety and satisfaction can be revolutionary for patients. The connection to internal desires, the meeting of needs, and the experience of joy are powerful concepts in the therapeutic milieu. They can allow patients to hope, find courage to pass through pain, and realize they can move beyond loss and grief. Topics worthy of exploration in the creation of satiety in a variety of areas include:

- Where does/did the patient experience joy? Passion?
- Positive experiences of physical pleasure?
- Where does/did the patient experience peace?
- Does the patient create (art, craft, writing, movement, music)?
- Experiences of true love (including friends, partners and spouses, family members/caretakers, animals)?
- Transformative successes (i.e. finishing a project, graduating from school)?

Tenet Four: learning and respecting fullness

Case study

> I never thought I'd understand "full". I only knew what it was like to feel stuffed after a binge, or to want more of something that I wasn't supposed to eat.
>
> Sarah

Familiarity with hunger is often useful for patients before this tenet, because eating when hungry allows for cues of fullness to be most clear. Patients need to recognize that, like hunger, fullness is not a point but a range. Patients may wish to ask before eating: "How do I want to feel when I'm done with this meal? What level of fullness does my body seem to desire right now?" If they eat beyond where their body feels best, they will simply get hungry at a later time. There is no "making a mistake" in this process, only education. Patients will learn their body's fullness cues along the way, and so be better equipped to make these decisions. Again, always invite awareness and curiosity about their body's response. It helps to challenge the diet rules that hinder progress, such as "the clean plate club" or eating more than one wants "in order to be polite". Sometimes, scarcity eating ("I won't let myself have this again, so I better eat it now") factors in.

This stage is fundamentally about boundary setting. Honoring the ability to say "enough" both to self and others is a profoundly powerful important step in recovery. Patients come to trust themselves to a far greater degree, knowing they possess the ability to compassionately say "no" to both intrusion by others, as well as by the eating disorder itself.

Tenet Five: respect your body's true shape and size

Case study

> I don't even know what my own body looks like anymore. It has changed so many times.
>
> Jonna

Step five happens during therapy and long after, as patients will be confronted with cultural messages well into the foreseeable future. Challenging the status quo of beauty, and defining beauty for oneself, is central to finding a healthier body image and is a long-term journey for most people. In addition, a healthy body image greatly enhances the both the efficacy and endurableness of recovery (National Eating Disorders Association 2009).

Patients with BED have often been the victims of weight stigma, especially as children (Puhl and Heuer 2009). One study suggests 65 per cent of people with eating disorders have experienced weight-related bullying as children (Puhl and Heuer 2009). We must be mindful that weight stigma affects patients of all sizes; they may be in constant fear of either becoming "fat", or indeed already be deemed so. Either way, there is impact. These experiences are often traumatic in the clinical sense, and require exploration and processing in therapy. It is valuable to ask about weight-related bullying and stigma as a regular part of a BED intake interview. Besides providing important information, the questioning allows the patient to feel they are with someone who understands and has compassion for the experience of living in a larger body in this culture. Weight stigma also features highly in experiences of adults with BED who may be large: airplane seats, restaurant booths, and shopping for clothing can be shaming experiences, and can lead to a considerably restricted social life to avoid that pain. To move from pain to compassion, and ultimately challenger of the system, is the work of this step.

Ideas that patients might explore include:

- Look for expressions of beauty in everyone you meet. All ages, all races and colors, both genders. See what creates beauty for you.
- Wear clothing that fits, and is comfortable, in colors you love.
- If size tags are distressing, cut the labels out of your clothing.
- Stay away from fashion magazines, or any media source that narrows your ideas of beauty.
- If the scale will impact *anything* about how you feel, stay off.
- Think about your body as your home, not an object. Note changes in attitude to, and treatment of, Self.
- Become a critical consumer of cultural messages. Ask: Why is this source telling me this message about beauty? Who will benefit?

The IEM paradigm again powerfully reinforces the deeper work of recovery. This tenet is a metaphor for valuing the Self as a whole, not something in need of "fixing", but instead something to discover, honor and protect. This orientation is healing of self-esteem and self-efficacy. It challenges perfectionism and black and white thinking by finding value beyond that which is acceptable by the dominant paradigm. This is an important experience, especially for patients who need to challenge their roles in relationships, both past and present.

Tenet Six: reclaiming movement

Case study

> I always wanted to dance Flamenco. But in this body? No way! So I started with an instructional video in my basement, and no mirrors anywhere. I just did the dance. It felt so amazing! My body was meant to Flamenco!
>
> Lori

Patients with BED, especially those in culturally unacceptable bodies, may have experienced exercise as a "have to", something perhaps pursued for weight loss, but rarely for pleasure. Movement is rarely about enjoyment or play, or even the fun elements of competition. Choices are often repetitive and dull, serving to "burn" calories or define muscles. Sometimes, too, patients feel the venues (gyms and workout clubs) are unwelcoming.

This step is important to encourage patients to develop a greater appreciation of the value of "movement" in their lives. "Exercise" may be described as "to use repeatedly" in order to strengthen or develop. "Movement", on the other hand, can be described as merely "the act or process of moving" (*Merriam-Webster Online* 2012). It necessarily includes any and all forms of motion, without care for interval, intensity, or specific outcome. It can be useful to help patients at the beginning of this tenet to likewise to allow themselves as many movement forms as they like when considering how to best care for their body. Gardening, mountain climbing, NIA, yoga, walking, dancing, lifting weights, and even cooking and shopping can all be forms of movement. Again, ask patients to allow their bodies to define the length of time and frequency of movement as much as possible. "Play" is another good word to use with patients. What types of play do they remember enjoying from childhood? Do they remember days when movement was about exploration and joy? Over time, patients will learn the amount of movement that makes them feel best, and how to incorporate that knowledge into their lives.

The therapeutic parallels with this step typically grow throughout treatment and beyond. Movement can be a powerful gateway for a variety of desires, including sexuality and sexual expression. Patients with abuse histories need to proceed slowly with this step, but it is often a profound reminder that they control their own body now. An internal sense of power and efficacy is often reinforced as people step into a stronger, more capable body. Discipline and setting of goals in other areas of life can be reinforced too.

Conclusion

As this overview suggests, IEM offers a powerful paradigm for working with "symptom as metaphor" in the treatment of BED. As noted, research is bearing out that which we have seen in the therapy office for some time. It must be noted that IEM works best when practiced by clinicians using the model in their own lives. To experience changing from a weight loss focus to a body wisdom focus allows for invaluable credibility. A therapist who is comfortable in her or his body brings a very different energy to the therapeutic milieu; empathy for the process of change born of experience is, as is typically the case, of profound significance. Clinically informed self-disclosure provides a needed role model when a patient has very few mirrors as yet for doing this work. Acceptance of IEM, culturally and clinically, is growing rapidly.

Recovery from BED is fundamentally about hearing the Self and all our internal "parts" (to borrow an IFS term) with curious, compassionate ears. It is about hearing and honoring somatic cues *most* of the time, slowly taking judgment and obsession out of eating and movement. Recovery is learning to challenge cultural ideals of beauty, recognize the damage of weight stigma on body image, and heal from the experiences. Recovery is not about eating "perfectly" intuitively, nor is its *purpose* weight loss (although it may occur). Instead, IEM, interwoven with the work of insight-focused psychotherapy, elegantly brings patients faith that their needs and desires will lead them not to danger, but to a more compassionate relationship with body, heart and mind.

References

Augustus-Horvath, C. L., and Tylka, T. (2011) "The acceptance model of intuitive eating: a comparison of women in emerging adulthood, early adulthood, and middle adulthood", *Journal of Counseling Psychology* 58(1): 110–25.

Avalos, L. C., and Tylka, T. (2006) "Exploring an acceptance model of intuitive eating with college women", *Journal of Counseling Psychology* 53(4): 486–97.

Bacon, L. (2005) "Size acceptance and intuitive eating improve health in obese female chronic dieters", *Journal of the American Dietetic Association* 105: 929–36.

Bacon, L., and Aphramor, L. (2011) "Weight science: evaluating the evidence for a paradigm shift", *Nutrition Journal* 10: 9.

Ciampolini, M., and Bianchi, R. (2006) "Training to estimate blood glucose and to form associations with initial hunger", *Nutrition & Metabolism* 3: 42.

Ciampolini, M., Lovell-Smith, D., Bianchi, R. *et al.* (2010) "Sustained self-regulation of energy intake: initial hunger improves insulin sensitivity", *Journal of Nutrition and Metabolism* Article ID 286952.

Ciampolini, M., Lovell-Smith, D., and Sifone, M. (2010) "Sustained self-regulation of energy intake. Loss of weight in overweight subjects. Maintenance of weight in normal-weight subjects", *Nutrition & Metabolism* 7: 4.

Cole, R., and Horacek, T. (2009) "Applying PRECEDE-PROCEED to develop an intuitive eating nondieting approach to weight management pilot program", *Journal of Nutrition Education and Behavior* 41(2): 120–26.

Cole, R., and Horacek, T. (2007) "Effectiveness of the 'My body knows when' intuitive eating non-dieting weight management pilot program", *Journal of the American Dietetic Association* 107(August Suppl): A90.

Cole, R. E., and Horacek, T. "Effectiveness of the 'My body knows when' intuitive-eating pilot program", *American Journal of Health Behavior* 34(3): 286–97.

Cusumano D., and Thompson J. (1997) "Body image and body shape ideal in magazines: exposure, awareness, and internalization", *Sex Roles* 37: 701–21.

Hawks, S., Madanat, H., Hawks, J., and Harris, A. (2005) "The relationship between intuitive eating and health indicators among college women", *American Journal of Health Education* 36: 331–6.

Hawks, S. R. (2004) "Intuitive eating and the nutrition transition in Asia", *Asia Pacific Journal of Clinical Nutrition* 13(2): 194-203.

Hawks, S. R. (2004) "The intuitive eating validation scale: preliminary validation", *American Journal of Health Education* 35: 26–35.

Jung, C. G. (1983) *Alchemical studies* (R. F. C. Hull, trans.), Princeton NJ: Princeton University Press.

Kratina, K., King, N., and Hayes, D. (2003) *Moving Away from Diets* (2nd edn), Lake Dallas TX: Helm Seminars.

MacDougall, E.C. (2010) *An Examination of a Culturally Relevant Model of Intuitive Eating with African American College Women*, Akron OH: University of Akron.

Mathieu, J. (2009) 'What should you know about mindful and intuitive eating?', *Journal of the American Dietetic Association* 109(12): 1982–7.

Mensinger, J. L. (2009) "Intuitive eating: a novel health promotion strategy for obese women", presented at the American Public Health Association Conference, Philadelphia, November.

Merriam-Webster Online Online. Available: http://www.merriam-webster.com (accessed 30 March 2012).

National Eating Disorders Association (NEDA) (2009) *The Impact of Media Images on Body Image and Behaviors: A Summary of the Scientific Evidence, Committee Review*, New York: National Eating Disorders Association.

Puhl, Rebecca M., and Heuer, C. A. (2009) "The stigma of obesity: a review and update", *Obesity* 17(5): 941–64.

Smith, T., and Hawks, S. R. (2006) "Intuitive eating, diet composition, and the meaning of food in healthy weight promotion", *American Journal of Health Education* 37(3):130–36.

Smitham, L. A. (2008) *Evaluating an Intuitive Eating Program for Binge Eating Disorder: A Benchmarking Study*, South Bend IN: University of Notre Dame.

Stice, E., Rohde, P., Gau, J., and Shaw, H. (2009) "An effectiveness trial of a dissonance-based eating disorder prevention program for high-risk adolescent girls", *Journal of Consulting and Clinical Psychology* 77(5): 825–34.

Tomiyama, A. J., and Mann, T. (2008) "Focusing on weight is not the answer to America's obesity epidemic", *American Psychology*, 63: 203–4.

Tribole, E., and Resch, E. (2003) *Intuitive Eating: A Revolutionary Program that Works* (2nd edn), New York: St Martin's Griffin.

Tylka, T. L. (2006) "Development and psychometric evaluation of a measure of intuitive eating", *Journal of Counseling Psychology* 53(2): 226–40.

Tylka, T. L., and Wilcox, J. A. (2006) "Are intuitive eating and eating disorder symptomatology opposite poles of the same construct?", *Journal of Counseling Psychology* 53: 474–85.

Utter, J., Neumark-Sztainer, D., Wall, M., and Story, M. (2003) "Reading magazine articles about dieting and associated weight control behaviors among adolescents", *Journal of Adolescent Health* 32: 78–82.

Vanderlyden, J., and Vanderreycken, W. (1997) *Trauma, Dissociation, and Impulse Dyscontrol in Eating Disorders: New Visions in Theory, Practice, and Reality*, New York: Brunner/Mazel.

Weigenberg, M. J. "Intuitive eating is associated with decreased diposity" (Abstract) (2009) Online. Available: http://professional.diabetes.org/Abstracts_Display. aspx?TYP=1&CID=72812 (accessed 29 March 2012).

Young, S. (2011) "Promoting Healthy Eating Among College Women: Effectiveness of an Intuitive Eating Intervention" (dissertation), Iowa State University, AAT 3418683.

Chapter 17

Prevention

Alison E. Field and Kendrin R. Sonneville

Case study

> I have hated my body for as long as I can remember. I was heavier than most of the other girls in my class and I was teased constantly. I think my parents felt sorry for me and they let me try all sorts of crazy diets. I have dieted so much that I don't think I can eat normally anymore or if I can even tell when I am hungry or full. Most of the time, I can avoid sweets, but when I do eat them, I totally lose control. Once I take one bite, I just keep eating and eating and can't stop myself until I've eaten everything. I am mad at myself for letting things get so out of control. I wonder if it would be this bad if I had never been teased or if my parents stopped me from dieting. I wish I had never hated my body in the first place.
>
> Brianna, 19 years old

Binge eating disorder (BED) is more common than bulimia nervosa (BN) and anorexia nervosa (AN). Although the prevalence of BED is higher in women than men, the gender difference in prevalence is smaller than that for BN and AN (Hudson *et al.* 2007; Swanson *et al.* 2011). Despite the higher incidence of BED, public health efforts and targeted prevention programs focused on preventing the onset of binge eating are lacking. As such, greater attention to eating disorder prevention is warranted.

BED risk factors

Relatively little is known about the risk factors for binge eating disorder. Most studies have been cross sectional, had treatment-seeking samples, or used a broader outcome definition (i.e., binge eating, disordered eating, etc.). Nevertheless, a handful of risk factors have been identified. In treatment seeking samples the binge eating onset, as well as the risk factors, must be recalled, and so this type of research is highly susceptible to recall bias. Moreover, since only the minority of people with binge eating disorder seeks treatment (Hudson *et al.* 2007; Swanson *et al.* 2011), it is unclear whether the results from treatment seeking cases are generalizable to all cases. Therefore, community- and population-based samples should be used to identify non-genetic determinants of binge eating disorder. Other than for factors that do not change over time, such as gender, race, and genes, cross-sectional studies are not appropriate for identifying risk factors because it is unclear whether binge eating started before or after the "risk factor". By risk factor we mean a variable that even, after accounting for differences between people with and without the factor, predicts starting to binge eat. Therefore we have limited the literature reviewed to prospective studies of possible risk factors that can change over time, such as dieting, and cross-sectional and prospective studies of possible risk factors that do not change over time, such as race/ethnicity. Prospective studies have identified several modifiable risk factors for binge eating disorder which are promising prevention targets.

Sex

Findings from a cross-sectional analysis of a large, representative sample of US adolescents indicate that full-syndrome binge eating disorder is more prevalent in girls (2.3 per cent) than boys (0.8 per cent), but that there are no sex differences in the prevalence of subthreshold binge eating disorder (2.6 per cent versus 2.3 per cent) (Swanson et al. 2011). Similar results were observed in a large nationally representative sample of adults. Hudson et al. (2007) found that BED was more common among women (3.5 per cent) than men (2.0 per cent); however, the prevalence of subthreshold BED was higher in males (1.9 per cent vs. 0.6 per cent), so the prevalence of meeting full or subthreshold criteria was approximately equal among women and men.

Race/ethnicity

Although some studies of adults have found no racial/ethnic differences in the prevalence of recurrent binge eating (Reagan and Hersch 2005; Striegel-Moore et al. 2005), a nationally representative study of adolescents in the US found that BED was more common among Hispanics (2.4 per cent) than whites (1.4 per cent) or blacks (1.5 per cent), whereas subthreshold BED was slightly more common among blacks (3.5 per cent) than Hispanics (3.5 per cent) or whites (2.0 per cent) (Ricciardelli et al. 2007). Results from smaller or less-representative samples also have found race/ethnic differences in prevalence (Croll et al. 2002; French et al. 1997; Neumark-Sztainer, Croll et al. 2002; Story et al. 1995). Features of BED, such as including binge frequency, treatment-seeking behavior, and concerns with eating, weight, and shape, may differ by race/ethnicity (Pike et al. 2001)

In order to prevent BED and its consequences it is essential to identify modifiable risk factors on which to intervene. Since binge eating frequently begins in adolescence or early adulthood, prospective studies of youth and young adults are needed to identify modifiable risk factors for BED. To date there have been relatively few such studies, and few risk factors have been identified and confirmed by other studies. Next we review the evidence for the established and possible risk factors.

Dieting

Dieting has been postulated to promote binge eating because it required a shift from a reliance on physiological cues to cognitive control over eating behaviors, which leaves the individual vulnerable to loss of control eating when these cognitive processes are disrupted (Stice *et al.* 2002). Several studies have found that dieting predicts the onset of binge eating in adolescent girls (Field *et al.* 2008; Neumark-Sztainer *et al.* 1995a; Neumark-Sztainer, Wall, Haines, Story and Eisenberg 2007; Stice *et al.* 1998; Stice *et al.* 2002) and boys (Field *et al.* 2008; Neumark-Sztainer, Wall, Haines, Story and Eisenberg 2007).

Obesity

Numerous studies have found high rates of BED among men and women seeking weight-loss treatment (Vamado *et al.* 1997). In addition, many cross-sectional studies of adults have reported that BED is more common among people who are overweight (Hudson *et al.* 2007). FTO and MC4R are genes, which are strongly related to obesity (Loos *et al.* 2008; Saunders *et al.* 2007), have been found to be associated with binge eating (Branson *et al.* 2003; Tanofsky-Kraff, Han *et al.* 2009) in some, but not all, studies (Lubrano-Berthelier *et al.* 2006). However, genes do not entirely explain the association.

In samples of US adolescents, overweight youth were more likely to binge than their normal-weight peers (Field *et al.* 1999; Field *et al.* 2003; Neumark-Sztainer and Hannan 2000; Neumark-Sztainer, Story *et al.* 2002). However, in cross-sectional studies it is impossible to know whether the binge eating preceded the overweight or caused it. So, longitudinal studies are needed to draw inference on risk factors. There are relatively few prospective studies on the onset of binge eating.

Several studies of children and adolescents have found that binge eating predicts greater weight gain (Field *et al.* 2003; Haines *et al.* 2007; Neumark-Sztainer, Wall, Haines, Story and Eisenberg 2007; Tanofsky-Kraff, Yanovski *et al.* 2009); however, prospective studies of adolescents have shown that after controlling for dieting there is no association between overweight and starting to binge eat weekly (Field *et al.* 2008) or develop an eating disorder of at least subthreshold severity (Patton *et al.* 1999). Although dietary restraint and dieting increases risk for the onset of binge eating symptoms (Haines *et al.* 2010; Neumark-Sztainer, Wall *et al.* 2006; Neumark-Sztainer, Wall, Haines, Story, Sherwood *et al.* 2007; Stice *et al.* 1998), in randomized trials women randomized to a weight loss diet are likely to decrease their binge eating. This has been observed among overweight women (Goodrick *et al.* 1998; Klem *et al.* 1997) and healthy young women (Groesz and Stice 2007). A likely explanation is that self-selected diets tend to be of shorter duration and potentially involve more modest calorie reductions that those used in clinical trials. If women lose weight they may become less weight concerned and therefore less likely to diet and thereby reduce their risk of binge eating.

Weight concerns and body dissatisfaction

Weight concerns are inversely related to BMI, so it is not surprising that greater body dissatisfaction is seen in women with binge eating disorder than in overweight and obese women who do not binge (Lloyd-Richardson *et al.* 2000; Striegel-Moore *et al.* 1998; Wardle *et al.* 2001). Among 6185 females and 4902 males in the Growing Up Today Study (GUTS), those with high weight concerns were about three times more likely than their peers to start binge eating at least weekly (Field *et al.* 2008). Moreover, among overweight and obese adolescents in GUTS followed for 11 years, body satisfaction was protective against the onset of frequent binge eating (Sonneville *et al.* 2012). Further support for this association comes from a five-year longitudinal study of more than 2000 adolescents enrolled in the Project EAT cohort. That study reported lower body satisfaction predicted higher levels of binge eating among females, although the findings did not hold after adjusting for BMI (Neumark-Sztainer, Paxton *et al.* 2006). In males, lower body satisfaction predicted higher levels of binge eating after controlling for BMI (Neumark-Sztainer, Paxton *et al.* 2006).

Pressure to be thin

Stice and colleagues (2011) have shown that adolescent females reporting social pressure to be thin have a higher risk for onset of threshold or subthreshold binge eating disorder. Social pressures can include the influence of peers, parents, media, and the environment. Each domain has been investigated, but few studies have investigated multiple domains simultaneously. Future research should investigate the relative importance of each domain. In the Growing Up Today Study, media influences were a stronger predictor than perceived importance of weight to parents or peers of onset of frequent binge eating among adolescent and young adult women. None of these factors were related to risk among the males (Field *et al.* 2008).

Weight-related teasing

Weight-related teasing, which is most common for overweight and underweight youth (Neumark-Sztainer, Falkner *et al.* 2002), is associated with binge eating among overweight and non-overweight girls and boys (Neumark-Sztainer,

Falkner *et al.* 2002). The impact of weight-related teasing and other negative comments about weight can vary by whether the comments are made by peers, parents, or teachers. Little is known about the impact of negative comments by teachers, but weight teasing by parents is a risk factor for binge eating in girls and boys (Haines *et al.* 2010). In addition, among males, negative comments about weight by fathers is predictive of starting to binge at least weekly (Field *et al.* 2008). In a community-based case control study, subjects with binge eating disorder reported greater exposure than controls to critical comments by family about shape, weight, or eating and teasing about shape, weight, eating, or appearance (Fairburn *et al.* 1998).

Stress and negative affect

Few studies have studied the association between stress and the development of binge eating. In a cross sectional study of African American and Caucasian young adult women, recalled trauma and stress were significantly related to binge eating (Harrington *et al.* 2006). In addition, among 5692 adults in the National Comorbidity Survey-Replication Study, 3.5 per cent of the women and 2.0 per cent of the men reported a lifetime history of BED. Approximately 90 per cent of women and 98 per cent of men with a lifetime history of BED reported past trauma and 26 per cent of the women and 24 per cent of the men reported a lifetime history of PTSD (Mitchell *et al.* 2012). However, due to the study design the temporal relationship between stress and binge eating is not entirely clear.

Depressive symptoms and other measures of negative affect have been investigated in many studies as a possible risk factor for an eating disorder. In a prospective study of adolescent girls, elevated depressive symptoms and low self-esteem, but not anxiety and anger, predicted binge eating onset (Stice *et al.* 2002). Consistent with those results, a prospective study of adolescents observed that those with high depressive symptoms were three times more likely than their peers to start binge eating; however, they also found that girls who engaged in binge eating were likely to develop high depressive symptoms.

Prevention programs

Eating disorder researchers have developed several prevention programs which have demonstrated a reduction in eating disordered behavior and eating disorder risk factors (Shaw *et al.* 2009). Intervention that decreased attitudinal risk factors and promoted healthy weight control appear to be particularly effective (Shaw *et al.* 2009). While most studies of eating disorder prevention program do not specifically focus on the prevention of binge eating disorder, several do show a reduction in binge eating disorder risk factors (Shaw *et al.* 2009) and there are a few examples of evidenced-based eating disorder prevention programs that have demonstrated a reduction in the risk for binge eating.

The Body Project

The Body Project is an interactive and brief (three or four sessions) intervention based on the social psychological principle of cognitive dissonance. It is designed for high school and college students and encourages them to explore the costs of pursuing the thin ideal. Among 481 adolescent girls with body dissatisfaction, this intervention significantly reduced the risk for onset of binge eating at six months and the development of obesity at one-year follow-up (Stice *et al.* 2006). Moreover, at the two- to three-year follow-up, adolescent girls who received the intervention had significantly lower thin-ideal internalization, body dissatisfaction, negative affect, bulimic symptoms, and psychosocial impairment relative to assessment-only controls (Stice *et al.* 2008). The intervention reduced the risk for onset of threshold and subthreshold eating disorders (including binge eating disorder) through a three-year follow-up compared with assessment-only controls (6 per cent versus 15 per cent), which represents a 60 per cent reduction in the number of expected cases (Stice *et al.* 2008).

Healthy weight intervention

The healthy weight intervention was originally included as a control group in a study testing The Body Project. The brief, four-session intervention aims to teach participants how to achieve and maintain a healthy weight through making small, gradual changes in diet and exercise. The intervention also incorporates social psychological principles, such as motivational interviewing and public commitments to change. Among the 481 adolescent girls with body dissatisfaction in the Body Project trial, the healthy weight intervention arm was found to reduce the future onset of both binge eating and obesity at one-year follow-up (Stice *et al.* 2006). At three-year follow-up, the healthy weight intervention was more effective in reducing risk for onset of binge eating, compensatory behaviors, and obesity than the Body Project.

Weigh to Eat

Weight to Eat is a school-based program aimed at the primary prevention of eating disturbances by targeting unhealthy dieting and binge-eating (Neumark-Sztainer *et al.* 1995b). The program consists of 10 weekly hour-long sessions implemented by a nutritionist/health educator and conducted within classes during the school day (Neumark-Sztainer *et al.* 1995b). The program is based on social-cognitive principles for behavioral change, and the goals are to change knowledge, attitudes, and behaviors related to nutrition and weight control; improve body and self-image; and promote greater self-efficacy in dealing with social pressures regarding excessive eating and dieting (Neumark-Sztainer *et al.* 1995b). An effectiveness trial held among 341 girls in 10th-grade, from 16 classes at three Jerusalem high schools, produced marked improvements in knowledge, healthy weight control behaviors, dieting, and binge eating at six-month follow-up, although only the effects for binge eating remained significant at the two-year follow-up (Neumark-Sztainer *et al.* 1995b).

Integrated prevention of BED and obesity

Greater than one-third of adolescents and young adults in the United States are overweight or obese (Flegal *et al.* 2012; Ogden *et al.* 2012), making obesity a major public health problem. The lifetime prevalence rate of binge eating disorder and sub threshold binge eating disorder during adolescence are 1.6 per cent and 2.5 per cent (Swanson *et al.* 2011). Among adults the rates are higher, with a lifetime prevalence of BED is 3.5 per cent among women and 2.0 per cent among men (Hudson *et al.* 2007). Since binge eating is most common among overweight and obese individuals (Neumark-Sztainer, Wall, Haines, Story, Sherwood *et al.* 2007) binge eating predicts excess weight gain (Tanofsky-Kraff *et al.* 2006), and the fact that obesity and binge eating share common risk factors, such as dieting (Field *et al.* 2003; Haines *et al.* 2010; Neumark-Sztainer, Wall, Haines, Story, Sherwood *et al.* 2007; Stice *et al.* 1999; Tanofsky-Kraff *et al.* 2006), weight concern (Neumark-Sztainer, Wall, Haines, Story, Sherwood *et al.* 2007), and weight-related teasing (Field *et al.* 2008), it would be prudent to have integrated approaches to the prevention of obesity and binge eating disorder. Further rationale includes that both obesity and eating disorders prevention share the core recommendations of promoting and sustaining healthful and balanced nutritional and physical-activity behaviors (Austin 2011; Schwartz and Henderson 2009). Therefore, future research trials should aim to design and test interventions aimed at preventing both obesity and binge eating disorder. If successful, these integrated interventions have a substantial public health impact (Stice *et al.* 2008).

Conclusion

Binge eating disorder is a relatively new diagnosis, so there is a limited amount of data on the prevention of the disorder. What is known suggests that prevention efforts should target children and adolescents and that both male and female participants should be included in prevention efforts. Most of the information on risk factors comes from observational studies and have not been investigated in clinical trials. More interventions, particularly those which target the prevention of both obesity and binge eating disorder, are needed.

References

Austin, S. B. (2011) "The blind spot in the drive for childhood obesity prevention: Bringing eating disorders prevention into focus as a public health priority", *American Journal of Public Health* 101: e1–4.

Branson, R., Potoczna, N., Kral, J. G., Lentes, K. U., Hoehe, M. R., and Horber, F. F. (2003) "Binge eating as a major phenotype of melanocortin 4 receptor gene mutations", *New England Journal of Medicine* 348: 1096–103.

Croll, J., Neumark-Sztainer, D., Story, M., and Ireland, M. (2002) "Prevalence and risk and protective factors related to disordered eating behaviours among adolescents: relationship to gender and ethnicity", *Journal of Adolescent Health* 31: 166–75.

Fairburn, C. G., Doll, H. A., Welch, S. L., Hay, P. J., Davies, B. A., and O'Connor, M. E. (1998) "Risk factors for binge eating disorder: a community-based, case-control study", *Archives of Gen Psychiatry* 55: 425–32.

Field, A. E., Austin, S. B., Taylor, C. B., Malspeis, S., Rosner, B., Rockett, H. R., Gillman, M. W., and Colditz, G. A. (2003) "Relation between dieting and weight change among preadolescents and adolescents", *Pediatrics* 112: 900–906.

Field, A. E., Camargo, C. A. Jnr, Taylor, C. B., Berkey, C. S., Frazier, A. L., Gillman, M. W., and Colditz, G. A. (1999) "Overweight, weight concerns, and bulimic behaviours among girls and boys", *Journal of the American Academy of Child and Adolescent Psychiatry* 38: 754–60.

Field, A. E., Javaras, K. M., Aneja, P., Kitos, N., Camargo, C. A. Jnr, Taylor, C. B., and Laird, N. M. (2008) "Family, peer, and media predictors of becoming eating disordered", *Archives of Pediatric and Adolescent Medicine* 162: 574–9.

Flegal, K. M., Carroll, M. D., Kit, B. K., and Ogden, C. L. (2012) "Prevalence of obesity and trends in the distribution of body mass index among US adults, 1999–2010", *Journal of the American Medical Association* 307: 491–7.

French, S. A., Story, M., Neumark-Sztainer, D., Downes, B., Resnick, M., and Blum, R. (1997) "Ethnic differences in psychosocial and health behaviour correlates of dieting, purging, and binge eating in a population-based sample of adolescent females", *International Journal of Eating Disorders* 22: 315–22.

Goodrick, G. K., Poston, W. S. C. II, Kimball, K. T., Reeves, R. S., and Foreyt, J. P. (1998) "Nondieting versus dieting treatment for overweight binge-eating women", *Journal of Consulting and Clinical Psychology* 66: 363–8.

Groesz, L. M., and Stice, E. (2007) "An experimental test of the effects of dieting on bulimic symptoms: the impact of eating episode frequency", *Behavior Research and Therapy* 45: 49–62.

Haines, J., Kleinman, K. P., Rifas-Shiman, S. L., Field, A. E., and Austin, S. B. (2010) "Examination of shared risk and protective factors for overweight and disordered eating among adolescents", *Archives of Pediatric and Adolescent Medicine* 164: 336–43.

Haines, J., Neumark-Sztainer, D., Wall, M., and Story, M. (2007) "Personal, behavioural, and environmental risk and protective factors for adolescent overweight", *Obesity* 15: 2748–60.

Harrington, E. F., Crowther, J. H., Payne Henrickson, H. C., and Mickelson, K. D. (2006) "The relationships among trauma, stress, ethnicity, and binge eating", *Cultural Diversity and Ethnic Minority Psychology* 12: 212–29.

Hudson, J. I., Hiripi, E., Pope, H. G. Jnr, and Kessler, R. C. (2007) "The prevalence and correlates of eating disorders in the national comorbidity survey replication", *Biological Psychiatry* 61: 348–58.

Klem, M. L., Wing, R. R., Simkin-Silverman, L., and Kuller, L. H. (1997) "The psychological consequences of weight gain prevention in healthy, premenopausal women", *International Journal of Eating Disorders* 21: 167–74.

Lloyd-Richardson, E. E., King, T. K., Forsyth, L. H., and Clark, M. M. (2000) "Body image evaluations in obese females with binge eating disorder", *Eating Behaviors* 1: 161–71.

Loos, R. J., Lindgren, C. M., Li, S., Wheeler, E., Zhao, J. H., Prokopenko, I., *et al.* (2008) "Common variants near MC4R are associated with fat mass, weight and risk of obesity", *Nature Genetics* 40: 768–75.

Lubrano-Berthelier, C., Dubern, B., Lacorte, J. M., Picard, F., Shapiro, A., Zhang, S., Bertrais, S., Hercberg, S., Basdevant, A., Clement, K., and Vaisse, C. (2006) "Melanocortin 4 receptor mutations in a large cohort of severely obese adults: prevalence, functional classification, genotype-phenotype relationship, and lack of association with binge eating", *Journal of Clinical Endocrinology and Metabolism* 91: 1811–18.

Mitchell, K. S., Mazzeo, S. E., Schlesinger, M. R., Brewerton, T. D., and Smith, B. N. (2012) "Comorbidity of partial and subthreshold ptsd among men and women with eating disorders in the national comorbidity survey-replication study", *International Journal of Eating Disorders* 45: 307–15.

Neumark-Sztainer, D., Butler, R., and Palti, H. (1995a) "Dieting and binge eating: which dieters are at risk?", *Journal of the American Dietetic Association* 95: 586–9.

Neumark-Sztainer, D., Butler, R., and Palti, H. (1995b) "Eating disturbances among adolescent girls: evaluation of a school-based primary prevention program", *Journal of Nutrition Education* 27: 24–31.

Neumark-Sztainer, D., Croll, J., Story, M., Hannan, P. J., French, S. A., and Perry, C. (2002) "Ethnic/racial differences in weight-related concerns and behaviours among adolescent girls and boys: findings from Project EAT", *Journal of Psychosomatic Research* 53: 963–74.

Neumark-Sztainer, D., Falkner, N., Story, M., Perry, C., and Hannan, P. J. (2002) "Weight-teasing among adolescents: correlations with weight status and disordered eating behaviours", *International Journal of Obesity and Related Metabolic Disorders* 26: 123.

Neumark-Sztainer, D., and Hannan, P. J. (2000) "Weight-related behaviours among adolescent girls and boys: results from a national survey", *Archives of Pediatric and Adolescent Medicine* 154: 569–77.

Neumark-Sztainer, D., Paxton, S. J., Hannan, P. J., Haines, J., and Story, M. (2006) "Does body satisfaction matter? Five-year longitudinal associations between body satisfaction and health behaviours in adolescent females and males", *Journal of Adolescent Health* 39: 244–51.

Neumark-Sztainer, D., Story, M., Hannan, P. J., Perry, C. L., and Irving, L. M. (2002) "Weight-related concerns and behaviours among overweight and nonoverweight adolescents: Implications for preventing weight-related disorders", *Archives of Pediatric and Adolescent Medicine* 156: 171–8.

Neumark-Sztainer, D., Wall, M., Guo, J., Story, M., Haines, J., and Eisenberg, M. (2006) "Obesity, disordered eating, and eating disorders in a longitudinal study of adolescents: how do dieters fare 5 years later?", *Journal of the American Dietetic Association* 106: 559–68.

Neumark-Sztainer, D., Wall, M., Haines, J., Story, M., and Eisenberg, M. E. (2007) "Why does dieting predict weight gain in adolescents? Findings from Project EAT-II: a 5-year longitudinal study", *Journal of the American Dietetic Association* 107: 448–55.

Neumark-Sztainer, D. R., Wall, M. M., Haines, J. I., Story, M. T., Sherwood, N. E., and van den Berg, P. A. (2007) "Shared risk and protective factors for overweight and disordered eating in adolescents", *American Journal of Preventive Medicine* 33(5): 359–69.

Ogden, C. L., Carroll, M. D., Kit, B. K., and Flegal, K. M. (2012) "Prevalence of obesity and trends in body mass index among US children and adolescents, 1999–2010", *JAMA* 307: 483–90.

Patton, G. C., Selzer, R., Coffey, C., Carlin, J. B., and Wolfe, R. (1999) "Onset of adolescent eating disorders: population based cohort study over 3 years", *British Medical Journal* 318: 765–8.

Pike, K. M., Dohm, F. A., Striegel-Moore, R., Wilfley, D. E., and Fairburn, C. G. (2001) "A comparison of black and white women with binge eating disorder", *American Journal of Psychiatry* 158: 1455–60.

Reagan, P., and Hersch, J. (2005) "Influence of race, gender, and socioeconomic status on binge eating frequency in a population-based sample", *International Journal of Eating Disorders* 38: 252–6.

Ricciardelli, L. A., Mccabe, M. P., Williams, R. J., and Thompson, J. K. (2007) "The role of ethnicity and culture in body image and disordered eating among males", *Clinical Psychology Review* 27: 582–606.

Saunders, C. L., Chiodini, B. D., Sham, P., Lewis, C. M., Abkevich, V., Adeyemo, A. A., *et al.* (2007) "Meta-analysis of genome-wide linkage studies in BMI and obesity", *Obesity* 15: 2263–75.

Schwartz, M. B., and Henderson, K. E. (2009) "Does obesity prevention cause eating disorders?" *Journal of the American Academy of Child and Adolescent Psychiatry* 48: 784–6.

Shaw, H., Stice, E., and Becker, C. B. (2009) "Preventing eating disorders", *Child and Adolescent Psychiatric Clinics of North America* 18: 199–207.

Sonneville, K. R., Calzo, J. P., Horton, N. J., Haines, J., Austin, S. B., and Field, A. E. (2012) "Body satisfaction, weight gain, and binge eating among overweight adolescent girls", *International Journal of Obesity* doi: 10.1038/ijo.2012.68 (e-pub ahead of print).

Stice, E., Cameron, R. P., Killen, J. D., Hayward, C., and Taylor, C. B. (1999) "Naturalistic weight-reduction efforts prospectively predict growth in relative weight and onset of obesity among female adolescents", *Journal of Consulting and Clinical Psychology* 67: 967–74.

Stice, E., Killen, J. D., Hayward, C., and Taylor, C. B. (1998) "Age of onset for binge eating and purging during late adolescence: a 4-year survival analysis", *Journal of Abnormal Psychology* 107: 671–5.

Stice, E., Marti, C. N., and Durant, S. (2011) "Risk factors for onset of eating disorders: evidence of multiple risk pathways from an 8-year prospective study", *Behavior Research and Therapy* 49: 622–7.

Stice, E., Marti, C. N., Spoor, S., Presnell, K., and Shaw, H. (2008) "Dissonance and healthy weight eating disorder prevention programs: long-term effects from a randomized efficacy trial", *Journal of Consulting and Clinical Psychology* 76: 329–40.

Stice, E., Presnell, K., and Spangler, D. (2002) "Risk factors for binge eating onset in adolescent girls: a 2-year prospective investigation", *Health Psychology* 21: 131–8.

Stice, E., Shaw, H., Burton, E., and Wade, E. (2006) "Dissonance and healthy weight eating disorder prevention programs: a randomized efficacy trial", *Journal of Consulting and Clinical Psychology* 74: 263–75.

Story, M., French, S. A., Resnick, M. D., and Blum, R. W. (1995) "Ethnic/racial and socio-economic differences in dieting behaviours and body image perceptions in adolescents", *International Journal of Eating Disorders* 18: 173–9.

Striegel-Moore, R., Fairburn, C. G., Wilfley, D. E., Pike, K. M., Dohm, F. A., and Kraemer, H. (2005) "Toward an understanding of risk factors for binge-eating disorder in black and white women: a community-based case-control study", *Psychological Medicine* 35: 907–17.

Striegel-Moore, R. H., Wilson, G. T., Wilfley, D. E., Elder, K. A., and Brownell, K. D. (1998) "Binge eating in an obese community sample", *International Journal of Eating Disorders* 23: 27–37.

Swanson, S. A., Crow, S. J., Le Grange, D., Swendsen, J., and Merikangas, K. R. (2011) "Prevalence and correlates of eating disorders in adolescents: results from the National Comorbidity Survey Replication Adolescent Supplement", *Archives of General Psychiatry* 68: 714–23.

Tanofsky-Kraff, M., Cohen, M. L., Yanovski, S. Z., Cox, C., Theim, K. R., Keil, M., Reynolds, J. C., and Yanovski, J. A. (2006) "A prospective study of psychological predictors of body fat gain among children at high risk for adult obesity", *Pediatrics* 117: 1203–9.

Tanofsky-Kraff, M., Han, J. C., Anandalingam, K., Shomaker, L. B., Columbo, K. M., Wolkoff, L. E., Kozlosky, M., Elliott, C., Ranzenhofer, L. M., Roza, C. A., Yanovski, S. Z., and Yanovski, J. A. (2009) "The FTO gene rs9939609 obesity-risk allele and loss of control over eating", *American Journal of Clinical Nutrition* 90: 1483–8.

Tanofsky-Kraff, M., Yanovski, S. Z., Schvey, N. A., Olsen, C. H., Gustafson, J., and Yanovski, J. A. (2009) "A prospective study of loss of control eating for body weight gain in children at high risk for adult obesity", *International Journal of Eating Disorders* 42: 26–30.

Vamado, P. J., Williamson, D. A., Bentz, B. G., Ryan, D. H., Rhodes, S. K., O›Neil, P. M., Sebastian, S. B., and Barker, S. E. (1997) "Prevalence of binge eating disorder in obese adults seeking weight loss treatment", *Eating and Weight Disorders* 2: 117–24.

Wardle, J., Waller, J., and Rapoport, L. (2001) "Body dissatisfaction and binge eating in obese women: the role of restraint and depression", *Obesity* 9: 778–87.

Chapter 18

Complexities in binge eating disorder advocacy

Chevese Turner

A radio interviewer asked me if it is true that a majority of Americans have binge eating disorder. "Surely", the interviewer speculated, "if we have an obesity epidemic in our country and around the world, then binge eating disorder must be rampant."

Another common conversation takes place during Binge Eating Disorder Association (BEDA) outreach and educational work. People usually say something like this: "I definitely have an eating disorder. I eat too much and love food. I am an emotional eater and I need to stop." They usually goes on to inquire how BEDA can help them stop overeating and usually there is a request to suggest a diet and exercise regime that will result in permanent weight loss.

Clearly there are multiple layers of misunderstanding and complexity around this particular eating disorder that must be addressed. Emotional and overeating are not BED. The general public is uneducated about eating disorders in general and even further behind the curve when it comes to what qualifies as BED. This ignorance implies two areas of concern: 1) there is not the understanding of the severity of eating disorders; and 2) the casual use of the term undermines the ability of people to identify and understand that BED is a mental health issue that trained professionals must address.

From the perspective of an advocacy organization, it is imperative that we understand first and foremost what the BED community, made up of people with the disorder and their families, need and want. We also must understand the interface of this community with clinicians, researchers, advocates, and educators. The stakeholders bring complex perspectives about prevention, treatment, and public policy that keep an advocacy and educational organization like BEDA busy in its efforts to provide information about the need for increased research, treatment resources, and a message of hope.

It's an eating disorder, stupid

Borrowing from former US President Bill Clinton's 1992 campaign slogan, "It's the Economy, Stupid", the title of this section is meant to bring attention to the fact that far too often we hear and read information about binge eating disorder that is conflated with obesity. Binge eating disorder is relatively rare, despite being the most prevalent eating disorder. This said, it is often discussed within the context of obesity lending to confusion among healthcare providers and the general public. This alone may be preventing people with BED from getting access to care and/or appropriate treatment. The "voice" of obesity concerns are much louder, well funded, and represent a larger number of people. We must clarify and define the issue so that progress can be made in both prevention and treatment.

It is important to note that not all people with BED are obese and not everyone who is obese has BED (Hudson *et al.* 2007). Despite this knowledge, BED is underrepresented at major eating disorder and mental health conferences while obesity is often a headlining topic. I note that obesity, at this time, is not considered a mental health or eating disorder. Clearly, mental health issues such as depression plague those living in larger bodies, but as of this writing there is not enough evidence to classify it as such. This lack of clear communication about clinical presentation, treatment modalities, and recovery tools leaves clinicians without the understanding of the nuances of BED that are critical knowledge for effective care. They are left uneducated and unskilled about how to help those with the most prevalent eating disorder.

Funding for eating disorders research as a whole is dismal, so funding for large, multi-center trials on BED is unlikely to take place anytime soon. It only makes sense, therefore, that researchers and institutions would look to large obesity trials as a way to carve out information that can lend to some understanding and prevention of BED. The concern with this approach is the lack of information from inclusion of people with the disorder who are not obese. It is a dilemma that will limit or fractionate our knowledge to some extent.

Recognition that overeating is a part of normal eating is important, since most people overeat from time to time. Binge eating to cope with unpleasant feelings or situations is abnormal and falls in line within its designation as a mental health issue rather than an issue of weight. Bingeing for someone with an eating disorder provides temporary relief from stress around difficult emotions and feelings. The resulting distress around the behavior affects the person's self and body esteem to the extent that is mentally crippling.

Like any mental health disorder or physical disease, one treatment will not be appropriate for every patient, just as the experience of the disorder is not uniform. As with all eating disorders, there is much to learn about both BED's biological and environmental underpinnings.

Those of us in the advocacy field know that any issue requires education of the public to address misconceptions and realities through evidence-based research, clinical wisdom, and stories from those who have lived the issue at hand. BED is no different and the work has only just begun.

Advocacy for the most prevalent eating disorder is in its infancy compared with that of anorexia and bulimia. There are vast misconceptions in the general public and among healthcare providers about everything from BED's status as a true eating disorder, pathology, and treatment methods, to expected outcomes of treatment.

We must, on behalf of those struggling, communicate that BED is a serious mental health disorder that does not discriminate according to shape or size. While obesity may be a part of the patient's concern for his or her wellbeing, it is not the only factor with regard to identification, treatment, and recovery.

So, why is there misunderstanding and no clear communication around what BED is and is not? Simply put, it is a combination of the disorder only recently being recommended as its own distinct diagnosis in the Fifth Edition of the *Diagnostic and Statistical Manual of Mental Illnesses* (DSM-5), a lack of research and clinical expertise, and a public conversation around obesity that increasingly overshadows concern for eating disorders. Hallmarks of eating disorders are evident in those with BED, but it will take a considerable amount of time to educate those on the front lines, like primary care physicians, to look beyond weight and ask the questions that are critical to identifying an eating disorder.

There is one more critical issue standing in the way of full recognition of BED and the ability to bring it from the shadows of shame and isolation. This issue is weight stigma which, by its definition, places blame on the person with the illness and diminishes his or her social identity, and adds fuel to the fire.

Weight stigma by any other name is weight stigma

Canadian-born sociologist and writer Erving Goffman described stigma as "the process by which the reactions of others spoil normal identity" (Goffman 1963). BEDA and others recognize that the designation of BED as a mental health disorder alone provides an immediate level of stigma for those suffering. What is not always understood, even among some eating disorders clinicians and researchers, is the additional layer of stigma placed on the person with BED who is living in a larger body and what this means to the possibility of recovery. This external manifestation of size often results in multiple insults to a person's sense of self and mental/physical health status on a daily basis.

When BEDA first decided to address the issue of weight stigma, based on the mounting evidence it contributes to the expression and entrenchment of BED, and announced its first annual Weight Stigma Awareness Week in September of 2011, we were asked on several occasions why we would address an issue that clearly belonged in the field of obesity. The question was appropriate as BEDA clearly wants BED to be recognized as a mental health disorder so that effective treatments can be administered. Are we talking out of both sides of our mouths?

Weight stigma is not an issue that is exclusive to those who are obese. It is impossible to talk about body image or esteem issues and not talk about weight stigma. People all along the spectrum of eating disorders are fearful of living in a larger body. A percentage of those with BED are not only afraid, but actually realize the severe disapproval of others based on the characteristic of size. A plethora of research and emerging evidence confirms that this is an important issue for the BED community and, BEDA would argue, the eating disorders community as a whole.

A study published in the 2012 April *International Journal of Eating Disorders* found that Internalized Weight Bias (IWB) in Obese Patients with BED "was positively associated with eating disorder psychopathology, fat phobia, and depression, and negatively associated with self-esteem. IWB made significant independent contributions to the variance in eating disorder psychopathology even after accounting for fat phobia, depression, and self-esteem" (Durso *et al.* 2012).

Our society promotes and encourages weight stigma. The external becomes an internal expression of low self-esteem and increased anxiety that can only be addressed through mechanisms to decrease stress and disassociate from the pain that is a result of stigma and bias (Puhl and Brownell 2006).

Maladaptive eating behaviors become the primary coping mechanism for people who experience and internalize weight stigma (Haines *et al.* 2006; Neumark-Sztainer *et al.* 2002; Puhl and Brownell 2006). People who live in larger bodies can attest to the fact that on a daily basis they are bullied, harassed, or discriminated against either directly or indirectly through the media, television shows, advertising, movies, jokes, family members, friends, and healthcare providers.

BEDA challenges you to take a day and count how many times you hear a fat joke, fat talk, a discussion about someone's will-power, motivation, or abilities based on their size. Notice how many commercials for diet and fitness programs you see in a day's time, and take some special time to watch a larger person and the care he or she takes to not move in to another person's space. Most likely you will notice he or she is on high alert and monitoring the reactions of others to the space they take in the world. Food allows a temporary retreat from this heightened state.

Think about the moments you have experienced depression, anxiety, or sadness and how incapacitated you felt. Did someone react to you in a negative way as you were feeling your emotions? Did he or she make fun of you and tell you that you are unmotivated and call you names? Did you see constant ads about how you should feel and how little money it would cost you to use a program to solve how you are feeling? Was the implication made in these ads, news stories, or television programs that you feel the way you do because you are irresponsible, deviant, and lazy?

This is what people who are living in larger bodies experience on a daily basis. They are discriminated against in the workplace, given lower-quality healthcare, and experience disapproval, criticism, and bullying from family members, friends, and others. For the person struggling with an eating disorder this daily insult can be unbearable and further entrench a person's use of food as a coping mechanism, which leads to increased distress.

To diet or not to diet

Advocates, clinicians, and researchers are often asked if someone with BED who is also obese should diet. Whether binge eating is really an addiction or not is the next most common question. As with most other aspects of this disorder, there are no definitive answers in the research.

This said, there is no shortage of opinions. Most researchers in both eating disorders and obesity fields will acknowledge that whether you have an eating disorder or not, it is very unlikely that if you are overweight or obese that you will be able to maintain a weight loss for more than five years. It's a prime example of the biological instrument of species protection at play. Humans, over time, adapted to survive times of limited access to food. In an environment of plenty our bodies do not know to turn off the mechanisms that allowed us to store fuel for centuries. Our bodies are genetically wired to save fuel, some better than others.

At the same time, dopamine, a brain chemical that sends signals between nerve cells, is shown to increase in the brain when pleasurable foods are eaten. Dopamine plays a major role in the brain system that is responsible for reward driven learning. Therefore it would seem that foods can be addictive.

Both the difficulty in maintaining weight loss and the release of dopamine are traps for people who find themselves in the right environment for an eating disorder. They are motivated to eat highly palatable foods as a way to relieve anxiety and disassociate from difficult emotions.

For those who gain weight, the distress of their body size and shape fuels their determination to diet and maintain a body size that fits ideals about what is acceptable and a "healthy weight". Unfortunately, for someone with BED, this is often a set-up for increased eating disorder thoughts and behavior. For every person with BED, bingeing causes great distress, and often triggers a cycle of binge–diet–binge. Dieting or restriction is seen as a way to stop the behaviors, but ultimately the person returns to bingeing as a coping mechanism. It seems there is no clear path with regard to how to "treat" obesity, much less how to treat an eating disorder that sometimes involves obesity.

Treatment is in the eye of the beholder

The World Health Organization (WHO) defines health as being a state of complete physical, mental and social wellbeing, and not merely the absence of disease or infirmity. If this is the case, it is in the best interest of the treatment provider to offer a compassionate approach to any physical or mental health problem, including eating disorders.

Unfortunately, as we know, there are many ways in which economic interests direct healthcare, and for this reason it is imperative that the advocacy community continue to question the evidence around treatments being offered. Treatment protocols will benefit from increased communication around what BED is and is not.

The US government and third-party payers are poised to spend a great deal of money on obesity treatments and programs that have little or no evidence that they reduce weight permanently. Despite this knowledge, commercial interests continue to claim efficacy only to contribute to the cycle of gain–diet–gain, or yo-yo dieting. This is of particular concern to the eating disorders community for obvious reasons. Are we going to allow people with an eating disorder to engage in treatments that serve to change body size, but ultimately result in regain and a continuation of the binge cycle? How do BED patients who have participated in weight management programs fare two, five 10 years out? Is the goal of physical, mental, and emotional health achieved? There are many questions and concern that some treatment modalities ultimately may be a continuation of the problem. It would seem that stabilization would be a first-tier goal along with resolution of the eating disorder until there is evidence that an approach that includes weight loss has lasting effects and does not set a person up for relapse.

BEDA offers support to those seeking help and is involved with various eating disorders scientific and clinically oriented organizations that help guide our own understanding of the current knowledge and expert thought around treatment. We encourage people to do their homework utilizing resources provided by BEDA and others, and to educate themselves about the disorder, the evidence-based and clinically accepted treatment recommendations, and the risks and benefits of any given modality.

The cornerstone of treatment for any eating disorder is talk therapy. A multidisciplinary team approach is utilized by many out-patient, residential, and in-patient centers so that nutrition, medication, and co-morbid conditions can be assessed, monitored, and treated. This said, because BED often goes untreated for years, people often seek one or more of the following before realizing that another approach is necessary for overarching health: commercial diets, bariatric surgery, major dietetic changes like vegetarianism, veganism, no sugar or white flour, or low-fat and low-carbohydrate diets.

The goals we hear from those struggling is to stop bingeing, feel less anxious, have more time to do the things they want to do with their lives, and to feel comfortable with their bodies. This, unfortunately, is often a losing battle as the approaches mentioned previously provide no evidence to show resolution of the eating disorder nor do they address the purpose the binges serve. This failure solidifies the feelings of hopelessness and shame.

As advocates, we have grave concerns regarding the diet industry's level of voice and prominence and the lack of education around eating disorders in the healthcare community. A culture of "thin is beautiful and healthy" permeates our culture to the disadvantage of many. Across the spectrum of size, people feel and act on the desperation to be thin, often to the detriment of good health. A focus on one's wellbeing is paramount to health whereas size and body shape are not. We cannot determine a person's health status merely by looking at him or her. We can guess, but unless we examine the person, take his or her vitals, read his or her health history, and view his or her blood values, it is unlikely we know whether he or she is healthy or not.

While it is not appropriate for BEDA to determine what treatment model is appropriate for any person, it is essential that we advocate for treatments that do not cause harm, but rather improves the person's wellbeing. Treatment is an important decision that is made between the person and their family or loved ones. We support ongoing research and encourage people to consult with experts and look to those who have found recovery for ongoing support.

Show me the money ... or at a minimum, the costs

We hear an awful lot about the financial, personal, and societal costs of public health concerns like obesity, cancer, or diabetes. The cost to both the patient and society elevates as time passes and these conditions are left untreated. BED and other mental health conditions are no different.

A person with BED is likely to experience misdiagnosis and several rounds of dieting before they realize or are told that professional treatment is needed. This contributes to a sense of being different and alone. Stories of missed life opportunities like higher education and jobs are common among people who share their stories. Life goes on hold as the eating disorder takes up more and more of each passing moment.

It is important to evaluate the costs of this and other eating disorders within the context of the individual experience and societal responsibility. This estimate of the financial, emotional, mental, and physical toll can build a case to further explore effective prevention and treatment in an attempt to realize health.

Personal costs of the eating disorder may include all or some of the following:

- Increased psychological distress and co-morbid conditions
- Higher healthcare costs
- Inability to develop or maintain interpersonal relationships
- Family discord
- Isolation and shame
- Failure to thrive (school, career, social)
- Increased disability over time resulting in a decrease in resources and access to care
- Societal costs may include all or some of the following:
- Social functioning and ability to hold a job (lost wages)
- Disability funding by state and federal government for healthcare and living costs
- Decreased productivity by those who work
- Economic reality of length of treatment necessary for recovery
- Culture of stigma and blame on the individual

We are only just beginning to understand the costs of BED as people emerge from dark shame to the light of hope. Their stories are heart-felt and moving. Their pain is palatable. Their spirits are begging to heal.

So, where do we go from here?

Future directions for prevention, treatment and recovery

First and foremost, we must lift the shroud of secrecy around BED. We must normalize it to the extent that people are not inhibited to ask for help or information, and are willing to talk about their journey. BEDA has made every effort to create a culture of openness. We encourage open communication and community. We provide the tools which are essential to taking the first steps and encourage an environment that is not stigmatizing where every beautiful shape, size, color, and gender can gain self-acceptance: an important step toward change and recovery.

The following are some general steps that the BED advocacy is taking to create its community of support and knowledge:

- **Raise awareness in general public to include**
  Who is at risk
  Biological and environmental risk factors
  Diversity of individuals with BED
  Early signs and symptoms
  Treatment options and levels of care
  Differentiation between "normal" overeating and BED
  BED is not a "choice"
  Role of weight stigma

- **Raise awareness among mental health and allied health professionals, educators, payers and policy-makers**
  Who is at risk
  Cost to individual and society
  Need for increased research
  Treatment/Early interventions
  Referral and education sources
  BED with/out obesity
  Role of weight stigma

- **Increase advocacy, education and outreach to**
  National, regional, and local eating disorder organizations
  Mental health advocates
  Educational institutions
  Healthcare organizations
  Provider organizations

Athletic groups and clubs
Families

- **Provide health-focused prevention solutions that are integrated in to existing and future general and obesity-focused initiatives**

- **Confront, address and educate on the negative effects of weight stigma**

- **Continue to build BED community as a source of support for those struggling and their families**

As we realize DSM-5 recognition of BED, there is a sense of validation among those who are struggling or have struggled with this disorder. No longer is BED the "red-headed step child" of the eating disorders community. With validation, hope, and community it is possible to identify, prevent and treat BED with the ultimate goal of full recovery and a life of purpose and many gratifying moments.

So, how can advocacy help those with BED? How do we give them hope for a quality of life that includes the joy of good health and body movement? How do we encourage recovery and freedom for the cyclical pain of bingeing and dieting? How do we shield them from the effects of the stigma they will either encounter and/or fear?

BEDA aims to encourage people who are struggling with binge eating disorder to emerge from the shadows and become part of the BED community. We must provide resources and information so that people can have easy access and find help in their communities or via the internet. Educating the public is critical so that identification of the disorder comes earlier when intervention can have a long-term impact in a short amount of time. A community of people empowered to rebuke shame and build body and self-esteem are more resilient to the stigmas of body size and mental health. To realize one is not alone and that there are millions of others who are struggling is empowering. Stories are shared, tears are shed, and shame is discarded. This is the power of advocacy.

References

Durso, L. E., Latner, J. D., White, M. A., Masheb, R. M., Blomquist, K. K., Morgan, P. T., *et al.* (2012) "Internalized weight bias in obese patients with binge eating disorder: associations with eating disturbances and psychological functioning", *International Journal of Eating Disorders* 45(3): 423–7.

Goffman, I. (1963) *Stigma: Notes on the Management of Spoiled Identity*, Englewood Cliffs, NJ: Prentice-Hall.

Haines J., Neumark-Sztainer D., Eisenberg M. E., and Hannan P. J. (2006) "Weight teasing and disordered eating behaviours in adolescents: longitudinal findings from Project EAT (Eating Among Teens)", *Pediatrics* 117(2): e209–15.

Hudson, J. I., Hiripi, E., Pope, H. G., and Kessler, R. C. (2007) "The prevalence and correlates of eating disorders in the National Comorbidity Survey Replication", *Biological Psychiatry* 61(3): 348–58.

Neumark-Sztainer, D., Falkner N., Story M., Perry C., Hannan P. J., and Mulert S. (2002) "Weight-teasing among adolescents: correlations with weight status and disordered eating behaviours", *International Journal of Obesity* 26(1):123–31.

Puhl, R., and Brownell, K. (2006) "Confronting and coping with weight stigma: an investigation of overweight and obese adults", *Obesity* 14(10): 1802–15.

Chapter 19

Where to from here for binge eating disorder

Lynn Grefe

Sarah Palin, the unsuccessful nominee for Vice President in the United States in 2008 was asked: "How can you tell a 'hockey mom' from a pit bull?"

"Lipstick", she answered.

This whimsical, cutesy punch line was calculated to draw great applause at the Republican National Presidential Convention. The implication was clear: a hockey mom is every bit as tough as a pit bull, and therefore the same, except for a gloss of lipstick.

With the addition of Binge Eating Disorder (BED) to the *Fifth Edition of the Diagnostic and Statistical Manual of Mental Illnesses* (DSM-5) (American Psychiatric Association 2012), I am cautiously reminded of that kind of misinformed thinking which dangerously conflates two very different issues. We as a field face the challenge of showing the distinction between a serious mental disorder diagnosis of BED, and the much-debated weighty problems of an "obesity epidemic" (our society's words, not mine). The distinction is a whole lot more than lipstick, with many people already confusing a mental health problem with a weight status.

In 2012, I attended the conference of the International Association of Eating Disorders Professionals (iaedp) in Charleston, South Carolina. Hundreds of clinicians specializing in eating disorder treatment were there to receive information and updated training, inspiration and, of course, the support and hope we all share for better outcomes among those affected. Between sessions, I visited the Citadel, the military university. There, carved into one of the many walls of this pristine place, I came across some haunting words that pulled the whole trip together for me – "hope is not a course of action". I dwelled on those words for days, pondering their relevance to our field. The National Eating Disorders Association (NEDA) prides itself on providing hope, information, and support to people with eating disorders and their families. But, as we bring BED to the forefront, that phrase was a timely reminder that a plan of action is imperative in everything we do. We cannot just *hope* people get better. Rather, it is our responsibility to put into action programs that support, educate, and direct those affected to appropriate treatment, paving the way for them to get better.

The eating disorders field, as diverse and complicated as it is at times, is filled with dedicated and committed people. Yet, this newly declared diagnosis of BED is already creating misunderstandings and confusion within the field and certainly, one must think, to the general public. The confusion in many discussions stems from the lack of understanding of BED as a mental disorder versus the "obesity problem" – the latter continually reinforced in our mainstream media. Recent evidence has shown that weight-based discrimination is now on par with race- or gender-based discrimination (Puhl *et al.* 2008). So, being overweight brings enough problems of discrimination of its own and entering the possibility of a mental disorder, BED, adds to the confusion. There are questions as to whether there really can be health at any size, if diets are ever appropriate and for whom, whether health risks are visible based on appearance of a person's shape and size, and where and when interventions by physicians, family or friends should occur. Unfortunately, many people do not know that BED should not be treated with weight loss strategies, and much of the "obesity prevention" interventions and messages can inadvertently encourage weight cycling and dangerous eating disordered behaviors (Bacon and Aphramor 2011).

I remind people that we – NEDA – are not in charge of "National Eating", but rather represent an organization dedicating itself to serving those with eating disorders and their families. Therefore, as society tackles this so-called "obesity epidemic", our role is to protect those affected by BED and not allow them to get lost in the fray of inappropriate attention and treatment. This is no easy task, and it is often confusing in a weight-biased culture where the diet industry continues to be the only winner. Those in the eating disorder field know that 95 per cent of dieters regain their weight within five years (Grodstein *et al.* 1996; Neumark-Sztainer *et al.* 2007), and with shows like ABC TV's *The Biggest Loser* selling the myth that dramatic weight loss equals health and happiness, more and more people are likely to get caught in the "body mass confusion".

I am not here to resolve disagreements within the eating disorders field about weight versus health or the use of BMI but, overall, I believe our caring professionals have watched and experienced for too long, the indignities of a culture that demands we all strive to be a size zero and the stereotypes of a weight-obsessed culture. Further, clinicians know better than most how ravaged and pained their patients become as a result of those weight obsessions, and some patients sadly die. While some overweight people may or may not have the mental disorder of BED or another, those people who are perceived to be overweight (however that is defined) feel the stigmatization of our culture's impossible standards. History reminds us that generous weight was once a sign of success. Men had girth. Women were bosomy and round. A tour of art through the centuries exemplifies the beauty of the body, a body that in today's world would be demeaned as belonging to someone with no self-control.

Moving forward

So, what are we left with in moving forward? In the United States at least, we are subjected to far-reaching, misguided anti-obesity campaigns, which are targeted to *shame* children and their parents into losing weight; obesity prevention efforts that often do more harm than good; millions of children and adults with low self-esteem and negative body image; and nationally reported cost projections that state if nothing is done about the prevalence of obesity-related health problems one third of our population will suffer from diabetes by the year 2050. Meanwhile millions of people who suffer from a bona fide mental illness, such as BED or another eating disorder, some of whom may or may not be obese, or struggle with weight challenges, are lumped in with non-BED people who are obese.

Our goal, in the eating disorders field, must be to wade through the muck of ignorance and to pull our patients out of despair and into treatment – not weight loss treatment, but treatment of a mental disorder that affects the person's well-being and health, regardless of his or her size. Strikingly, weight is not necessarily an indicator of any eating disorder; rather, many other symptoms more accurately tell the story. As with other eating disorders, BED has more to do with how people think and feel about themselves, and use food to compensate for difficult emotions, than anything else. There is increasing evidence that biological forces are at play and that those who suffer from an eating disorders do not just lack the will to cope differently (for example, Mathes *et al.* 2009).

Another goal must be to steer all people with anorexia, bulimia, BED or eating disorder not otherwise specified (EDNOS) toward resources and support. We need to educate their families, friends, and professionals to ensure a support system with a nonjudgmental approach. But therein lies the first problem – our perception of an eating disorder sufferer (what he or she looks like) dramatically affects the intervention strategies that we consider acceptable among families and friends.

Two scenarios

Scenario one

Your roommate, who would be considered a thin person, experiences dizziness, fainting, mood swings, and often appears pale. You frequently witness this person avoiding the food on his or her plate or abstaining from meals all together. Worried that he or she might have an eating disorder, you approach your friend to set up a time to talk, you describe the behaviors you are worried about, and recommend that he or she make an appointment to see a professional opinion or get a physical exam.

Scenario two

Your roommate, who would be considered a larger person, often seems withdrawn and depressed. They frequently complain of stomach problems and you have noticed large quantities of food disappearing from your cabinets. You are worried about your friend's health, and suspect they might have an eating disorder, but you don't say anything because you fear they will think you are focusing on weight rather than being concerned about a serious mental disorder.

In the first scenario, you take every step that experts suggest taking when worried about a friend or loved one. In the second scenario, the friend is also displaying a number of possible eating disorders symptoms. However, your response changes. Why is this so?

As a starting point, the friend's larger size and our learned attitudes about people of size have influenced how we might go about helping them. We have come a long way in understanding that anorexia is a mental illness, but the false belief that people who suffer from this disorder have an "enviable willpower" remains prevalent among the general public. Because of the weight bias that exists in our society, the opposite is true with BED sufferers and to a lesser extend, bulimia sufferers. People who have eating disorders characterized by bingeing behavior are viewed as being "out of control" or "lacking self-discipline", as opposed to being people suffering from a mental disorder. This attitude is not confined to the public – studies have shown that physicians also demonstrate weight bias (Schwartz et al. 2003; Teachman and Brownell 2001). Something is very wrong with this picture, and it suggests a need for a new starting point in our approach to supporting people affected by BED.

Reflections

Ten years ago, when I entered this field, I had no knowledge that eating disorders had a stigma, were considered shameful or anything to hide. Why would I? My own child has suffered a serious eating disorder and I never once cringed or apologized. I saw that she was sick and needed help. But I learned quickly that I must have been blatantly naïve for I found many others around me were embarrassed and ashamed to ask for help. Parents cried for absolution that eating disorders were not their fault. It never occurred to me that I had caused my daughter's eating disorder because, gratefully, I knew eating disorders came from a complex interplay of factors.

From that time forward, I saw that the most important thing we as a community could do to help people recover was to de-stigmatize the issue, and secede from the union of ignorance and stereotypes. Invoking the "stigma card" is a crutch, meaning an excuse to not seek treatment, an excuse not to tell families, an excuse not to feel good about ourselves, because shame is a dark cloud, a place where we sit waiting for it to rain. It has been going on with anorexia, bulimia, and EDNOS for many years. But the good news is that, based on our surveys and focus groups, we have significantly improved public perceptions for anorexia and bulimia.

In 2003, we learned from focus groups that most people would never tell anyone that they or someone in their families had an eating disorder such as anorexia or bulimia – and that shame was a significant barrier to getting help. In a professionally conducted national survey seven years later, in 2010, most respondents indicated that they saw no reason to be embarrassed and would tell a friend to seek help if concerned they had anorexia or bulimia. We will hold the field and the diagnosis of BED back if we do not learn from these lessons and work to quickly remove stigma about this illness as well.

A culture that is strongly focused on obesity prevention and perpetuates the widespread and inaccurate message that thinness automatically equates to health, has made weight stigma a real problem. We must be proactive to prevent this same mistake permeating the general population perception of BED. Weight stigma and discrimination of any kind is appalling and has significant impacts. It has been found – like race or gender bias – to impact employment practices, access to education and many other facets of life. A health organization in Texas required a specific BMI for employment (until NEDA and others vehemently protested); a college in Pennsylvania requires a "passing" BMI to graduate; Whole Foods gives bonus point discounts to employees who reduce their BMI, with no dangerously low limit identified. The list goes on.

Hopefully we have progressed to the point where most people can acknowledge that parents are not directly at fault for their child's illness. That said, I am certain more than once my daughter in her youth heard me ask: "Do I look fat in this?" Would I ask that today? Of course not. Should I be burned at the stake? I hope not. My point is that we have to accept that we make mistakes at times as parents, professionals, and clinicians. We must learn from them and avoid reinforcing shame and embarrassment about weight and eating disorders. We have the choice to fuel the myths, or progressively shut down negative messaging, gossip about others' bodies, generalizations about people based on their size and shape, and involving our patients in the harmful messaging surrounding us about weight loss. Our patients with BED need treatment: no blame, no shame – simply, they need help.

A focus on weight loss is a strong precursor to dangerous dieting behaviors, weight cycling, and ultimately any one of the various eating disorders. People affected by BED now have a diagnosis, whether they know it yet or not, and, like other eating disordered patients, they are not easily identified by appearance. As with other eating disordered patients, stereotypes need to be diffused. It was often assumed that anorexia only affected young, rich, white girls. We now know that BED affects a disproportionate number of men in relation to other eating disorders and that EDNOS, hardly a household diagnosis, represents more than 50 per cent of all eating disorder cases (Wade *et al.* 2011). Thanks to emerging research, we also know that eating disorders affect people of all ethnicities and identity groups. We cannot automatically identify someone who has anorexia, bulimia, or EDNOS, and similarly, we cannot identify someone with BED, by appearance. It doesn't help that we have doctors and TV "gurus" advising us to "just get over it" and lose some weight. Add to this the many uninformed physicians who tell parents: "All the kids are on a diet, don't worry about it, your child looks great."

Hope into action

To increase understanding for BED we must expand our public education efforts to the same levels as offered for other eating disorders. NEDA has created a Binge Eating Disorder Task Force to include top clinicians and experts, and also families and sufferers. The goals of this task force are to identify how NEDA can develop the best possible resource base and deliver the information in the most effective way. While we included BED information in the past, this did not extend to a diagnosis for mental health insurance coverage; now that it is a diagnosis, we must feature it more prominently in all that we do. At NEDA, a spotlight is being placed on BED in all of our programs to ensure the public is aware of this serious illness and of the resources we offer for those affected. As the number of people affected by BED is much higher than other eating disorders, we are saying: "It's about time!" We also are incorporating a BED component into our National NEDA Navigator Program, which involves "trained friends" providing support to others. It is essential that our Navigators understand, as they support and guide those affected with BED and their families, that there are different aspects to BED. For example, BED patients may be of average weight, have no "physical symptoms" unless they are purging, or losing or gaining weight. In addition, if people with BED are overweight, at some point they may sadly have been subject to discrimination or bullying of some kind. Consequently, we need to recognize these possible differences, needs and concerns within this population.

Once again, the ultimate goal is to steer people toward appropriate treatment to achieve ultimately a long happy, healthy life. To be clear, this is health defined as overall physical and mental wellbeing, not size.

Early intervention

Another approach we must pursue is a genuine course of action for early intervention. If a child goes to school with bruises and cuts, we know that the school personnel would contact the authorities for child protective services. Yet, our population is restricting, purging, over-exercising, or bingeing with nobody raising concern. Not only are these dangerous behaviors overlooked, but new policies being put into place – like putting a student's "failing" BMI on his or her report card or publicly taking a student's weight – can exacerbate the problem.

Advocacy at all levels is required to overcome the ignorance in public understanding and improve access to treatment. For instance, NEDA is introducing legislation in states that requires eating disorder screenings in schools. If successful, we will need to provide easily implemented screening tools for eating disorders, including BED. Further, the education of all physicians must include these early diagnostic tools. We need them to recognize the signs and symptoms of BED as readily as one would recognize those of chicken pox. Interestingly, the concern and impediment, in some cases, is the fear that once we identify the students at risk, we won't have enough trained therapists to handle the cases. In addition, for the schools that are severely underfunded, there is a fear that this is one more thing on their "to do" list that they cannot handle. Our argument, of course, is twofold: currently BMI report cards are required in many schools, so this requirement is the antidote, so to speak. Eating disorders are potentially life threatening. Need we say more? To avoid diagnosing an illness because the current state of treatment is inadequate is no solution. Somehow, whether through legislation or mandated policy, we must intervene earlier to identify students at risk of all eating disorders before they become chronically ill.

In 2012, we successfully lobbied the American Medical Association (AMA) to launch an online course for the early recognition, diagnosis, and referral for eating disorders. We enlisted some of our NEDA professional members, who are also members of the Academy for Eating Disorders (AED), to work with the AMA to create this program. The AMA assured us that they would promote this widely, to inform physicians. Again, education is vital in every direction so that our patients have doors opened to them that never existed before, and so that physicians can become enlightened to the eating disorder diagnoses.

Finally, as we throw the lifeline to the BED population, our public education programs are likely to focus first among people who may be affected. You can be sure that many people who have BED do not even know that it has a name yet, or that their behaviors are recognized as any type of diagnosable illness or disorder. So, we will be negligent if we don't incorporate basic education about BED into all that we do. The self-revelation for the many people who have suffered secretly will be a new, wonderful day because they may now be able to access treatment.

That BED has become part of the DSM-5 is a significant step. However, until we *mainstream* the illness, and bring it into public understanding as we have with anorexia and bulimia, many people will remain untreated. There is much work to be done for all eating disorders, and BED is as serious and threatening as the others. For those of us who have suffered or have patients, friends, or loved ones who are suffering, the misinformation and social stigma that surround eating disorders can be frustrating and downright angering. However, let's channel that energy and passion into standing up for this significant population of people with BED who have been under-represented, misunderstood, and underserved for many years. I am confident that with the dedication, passion, and expertise in this field, we can succeed.

The next time we are asked the difference between obesity and BED, we can point to a true psychiatric diagnosis in the DSM-5.

References

American Psychiatric Association (2012) DSM-5 Proposed Diagnostic Criteria for Binge Eating Disorder. Online. Available: http://www.dsm5.org/ProposedRevisions/Pages/proposedrevision.aspx?rid=372# (accessed 18 May 2012).

Bacon, L., and Aphramor, L. (2011) "Weight science: evaluating the evidence for a paradigm shift", *Nutrition Journal* 10: 9.

Grodstein, F., Levine, R., Troy, L., Spencer, T., Colditz, G. A., and Stampfer, M. J. (1996) "Three-year follow-up of participants in a commercial weight loss program: can you keep it off?", *Archives of International Medicine* 156(12): 1302–6.

Mathes, W. F., Brownley, K. A., Mo, X., Bulik C. M. (2009) "The biology of binge eating", *Appetite* 52(3): 545–53.

Neumark-Sztainer, D., Wall, M., Haines, J., Story, M., and Eisenberg, M. E. (2007) "Why does dieting predict weight gain in adolescents? Findings from project EAT-II: a 5-year longitudinal study", *Journal of the American Dietetic Association* 107(3): 448–55.

Puhl, R. M., Andreyeva, T., and Brownell, K. D. (2008) "Perceptions of weight discrimination: prevalence and comparison to race and gender discrimination in America", *International Journal of Obesity* 32: 992–1000.

Schwartz, M. B., O'Neal, H., Brownell, K. D., Blair, S., and Billington, C. (2003) "Weight bias among health professionals specializing in obesity", *Obesity Research* 11: 1033–9.

Teachman, B. A., and Brownell, K. D. (2001) "Implicit anti-fat bias among health professionals: is anyone immune?", *International Journal of Obesity Related Metabolic Disorders* 25(10): 1525–31.

Wade, T. D., Keski-Rahkonen A., and Hudson J. (2011) "Epidemiology of eating disorders", in M. Tsuang and M. Tohen (eds) *Textbook in Psychiatric Epidemiology* (3rd edn) (pp. 343–60), New York: Wiley.

Afterword

Michael J. Devlin, Stephen A. Wonderlich,
B. Timothy Walsh and James E. Mitchell

The following dialogue takes place in an eating disorders clinic at an academic medical center, in the present time. The telephone rings.

Research
Assistant: Hello, Eating Disorders Treatment Research Program, RA speaking.

Caller: Hello, this is C. I've been struggling for more than 20 years with a terrible binge eating problem. You may remember me – I called your clinic back in 1990, and you had nothing to offer me. I'm still having exactly the same problems that I was having back then. Has anything gotten better in the meantime?

RA: I'm glad you called back, C, and I'm sorry you've been suffering for so long. I'm happy to say that the situation has indeed improved. For starters, we now have a name for what you have. It's called binge eating disorder, or BED, and we've developed a number of different treatment approaches, including different forms of psychotherapy, medication, and even self-help approaches. We'll need to meet with you to find out exactly what your goals are and what type of approach would be most helpful.

C: I'm glad I'm not the only person who has this problem.

RA: Far from it. Many people have had and continue to have similar problems. It's taken us a long time for us to realize what many of our colleagues in clinical practice have known for decades: that BED is a distinct problem and individuals with BED deserve help that is tailored to their particular struggles.

C: I wish I could say that I'd been able to figure out a way to get myself better in all this time, but I haven't. Why has this been such a difficult problem for me?

RA: Well, there are a lot of elements that can contribute in any given person – genetic risk factors, your individual experience, and the world we live in all play a role. The one thing I want to emphasize is that it's not due to a lack of will power.

C: That's a relief. I feel like I have a lot of will power in general, but

RA: this is something I just haven't been able to beat. So there are really other people out there with these kinds of problems?

RA: You bet, and there are organizations that bring together researchers who are interested in BED with people who have suffered or are currently suffering with the problem, family members, clinicians, and anyone who wants to make the make the world a place where we can all lead healthier lives and feel better about ourselves and each other.

C: That's great, because I'm not just interested in getting help. I'm interested in helping. I want to get better and I also want to make sure that others don't have to go through this. When can I come in? Thanks to this conversation I feel like, at last, I'm ready to start.

Like the dialogue that opened the book, this is not taken verbatim from an actual conversation, but is representative of the sorts of conversations that, given the past two decades of research, growing clinical experience, and advocacy, we are now able to have. In addition, it is intended to convey the generosity of spirit of many of the patients with whom we've worked who truly are interested not only in obtaining relief from their own suffering, but in helping one another and in bringing about lasting change in the community so that those who come after us can lead lives that are healthy, productive, and free from the suffering associated with BED.

The chapters in this volume have ably reviewed the many developments in our field that have taken place over the past two decades. In closing, we will share some thoughts regarding what lies ahead in four areas: (1) psychopathology and diagnosis; (2) pathophysiologic mechanisms, particularly the question of addiction (3) treatment, and (4) advocacy and community-level change.

Psychopathology and diagnosis of BED

Studies of the psychopathology characterizing BED have significantly clarified the nature of this relatively new eating disorder. We have acquired a clearer understanding of the nature of binge eating, the importance of loss of control of eating, and the distress surrounding binge eating episodes in individuals suffering from BED. We believe that several psychopathological concepts will continue to generate significant empirical research in the near future: 1) loss of control over eating; 2) overvaluation of shape and weight; 3) heterogeneity within the BED diagnosis and the possibility of subtypes; and 4) bio-behavioral dimensions or traits associated with BED.

As the chapters in this book have highlighted, loss of control (LOC) eating is an important aspect of the BED diagnosis which is associated with levels of current distress, comorbid psychopathology, and also appears predictive of negative medical and psychiatric outcomes in several populations. However, there remain significant issues regarding LOC eating which are not well understood. Is

LOC eating simply a loss of control over eating or is this phenomenon part of a larger construct of loss of control over various other behaviors? For example, is LOC related to loss of control over spending, substance use, gambling, or other behaviors reflecting general disinhibition? What is the relationship of LOC eating to various personality traits (e.g., impulsivity, affect regulation)? What profiles of psychiatric symptoms display the strongest association to LOC eating? All of these issues raise questions about the inherent nature of LOC eating, particularly discriminant validity. Clarifying whether LOC eating represents a construct that is specific to eating versus other behaviors will help clarify our understanding of this aspect of BED and inform future studies of eating behavior in BED.

Another feature of BED psychopathology that has recently emerged in the scientific literature is overvaluation of shape and weight. The absence of this cognitive feature in the diagnostic criteria set for DSM-IV and DSM-5 differentiates BED from the other eating disorders. Evidence for the clinical utility of overvaluation of shape and weight also continues to accumulate as this trait seems tied to clinical severity of BED and also predicts response to common treatments for BED. Although overvaluation of shape and weight has been considered as a diagnostic criterion for BED, this would potentially prohibit individuals with significant binge eating problems who lack such overvaluation from being diagnosed and receiving treatment. Consequently, researchers have alternatively suggested that overvaluation of shape and weight be considered as a specifier for the BED diagnosis, which would allow useful clinical information associated with this aspect of psychopathology to inform diagnostic and clinical decision making. As the relationship of BED and overvaluation of shape and weight is more fully understood across the eating disorder research community, this cognitive feature may ultimately enhance the diagnostic framework of BED, which could further hone targets for clinical interventions.

Additionally, within-diagnosis heterogeneity in psychopathology is likely to characterize BED in the same manner that it has bulimia nervosa (BN) and anorexia nervosa (AN). An accumulating number of empirical studies document several (often three) subtypes within the diagnoses of AN and BN. Furthermore, these subtypes differ in terms of clinical features, response to treatment, and longitudinal course. The diagnosis of BED has already been characterized as having clinically useful heterogeneity related to dietary restraint and mood disturbance. Such a model suggests that one type is characterized by high levels of dietary restraint and mood disturbance while another type is characterized by high levels of dietary restraint without mood disturbance. As noted previously, considerable variability is also associated with overvaluation of shape and weight within the BED construct and future studies may effectively identify other subtypes within BED, perhaps based on personality or cognitive traits. Clarifying such heterogeneity may enhance clinical interventions by targeting subtype specific psychopathology among people with BED.

Finally, such heterogeneity within the BED diagnosis raises the issues of variability along key underlying behavioral traits or dimensions associated with BED.

Dimensional approaches to understanding AN and BN have been considered for decades. Dimensional thinking has also been seen in the growing interest in endophenotypic traits associated with the eating disorders such as cognitive set shifting, central coherence, and impulsive disinhibition. Recently the role of traits and dimensions in all areas of psychopathology has been stimulated by the Research Domain Criteria (RDoC) initiative at the National Institute of Mental Health (NIMH) in the United States. The RDoC project was initiated to implement the NIMH strategic goal to develop, for research purposes, new ways of classifying mental disorders based on behavioral and neurobiological dimensions. RDoC is a dimensional classification system which does not rely on typical diagnostic categories and attempts to measure dimensions in terms of behavioral, genetic, brain circuitry, physiologic, and self-report assessment strategies. By studying behavioral dimensions associated with BED (e.g., negative emotionality or cognitive control), which not only characterize BED, but also are linked to other forms of psychopathology, we may learn how BED, and other eating disorders are situated in the broader range of psychopathology. Also, RDoC may ultimately help to identify dimensions of behavior which are specific to the eating disorders, and perhaps even specific to BED. Clearly, although RDoC is currently designed for research purposes, it does introduce a new way of thinking about psychopathology which differs from the category based system associated with the DSM and could ultimately inform clinical perspectives.

Mechanisms underlying BED: the question of addiction

There has been significant progress in identifying factors that contribute to the development and persistence of BED. As reviewed in Chapter 3, we now know that BED tends to run in families in patterns that suggest there is a genetic component, although no specific gene has been clearly identified and replicated. The occurrence of BED is clearly associated with that of obesity, but the nature of the association – what is cart and what is horse – has not yet been elucidated. There appears to be an increased frequency of substance use disorders among those with BED, and, as referenced in the Foreword, there have been reports that more than half of individuals with BED meet criteria for "food addiction". Indeed, there are striking parallels between the symptoms of people with BED and of those who abuse substances, including excessive consumption of, and craving for, food or the abused drug, respectively. It is very likely that this overlap of symptoms reflects the involvement of some of the same neural pathways in BED and in substance use disorders. Specifically, for example, dopamine is released in the ventral striatum (nucleus accumbens) in response to the intake of palatable food and in response to the administration of drugs of abuse. The activation of these and other reward centers is positively reinforcing and leads to increased and eventually repeated attempts to acquire palatable foods and drugs of abuse. The fact that both palatable foods and substances that are abused activate similar areas of the brain is virtually certain to account for the parallels in the clinical presentations and some of the difficulties faced by individuals with BED and those who abuse drugs.

Yet, it is critical to emphasize major differences. Drugs that are abused are substances that are not required to sustain life; people can abstain from cocaine, nicotine and alcohol with no adverse consequences, and, often, with an improvement in their general state of well-being. Needless to say, the consumption of food is required to sustain life. It has been argued that people with BED are "addicted" only to certain foods, such as highly palatable sweet foods. However, objective data from meals observed in a laboratory setting indicate that the foods preferred by people with BED are not significantly different from those preferred by comparable people without BED, and, while people with BED do, indeed, consume greater amounts of food, the pattern of food consumption does not appear disturbed. That is, there does not appear to be compelling evidence that a particular food or food component constitutes for people with BED the single substance that is abused – a significant difference from people who abuse substances.

Finally, successful treatment does not require that people with BED cease consuming foods that they prefer. Rather, a number of interventions documented to be successful encourage them to consume non-binge amounts of foods that were previously problematic. This approach is distinctly different from the typical approach recommended for people with substance abuse.

For these reasons, while it is critical to understand underlying disturbances in neural circuits that are likely to be similar in BED and in substance use disorders, it is important not to over-emphasize the parallels between these disorders. Viewing individuals with BED simply as being "addicted" is likely to do more harm than good.

Treatment of BED

As reviewed in this volume, there has been considerable progress in developing effective treatment approaches for patients with BED. These include pharmacological strategies, psychotherapeutic strategies, and combinations of these approaches. With an eye toward the future, we ask: Where are we heading with regard to psychotherapy and pharmacotherapy for BED? What are the next important questions to ask regarding treatment for BED, and how should we go about asking these questions? The comments that follow, while focused on BED, reflect the broader challenges of overall effectiveness, treatment matching, and availability in the community that exist across eating disorders and psychiatric disorders in general.

What lies ahead for psychotherapy?

As detailed above, a number of treatment approaches have been devised and studied which clearly impact on the course of BED. The literature has grown dramatically since the late 1990s. Cognitive behavioral therapy (CBT) remains the best established therapy. There is also strong evidence supporting the utility of interpersonal therapy (IPT) and there are suggestions that other sorts of therapy may be effective as well, including dialectic behavior therapy (DBT), therapies targeting eating awareness and mindfulness, and some recent modifications to CBT, including enhanced cognitive behavior therapy (CBT-E) and integrative cognitive affective therapy (ICAT). So, the field is making progress. However, a number of problems remain that we hope will be addressed soon:

1   We still have not developed effective ways to match patients to the optimal specific treatments. Unfortunately, so far in most of the psychotherapy literature, the obvious matching choices have not always turned out to be best. Part of this reflects the questions that have been asked, but much of the problem reflects the fact that most of the sample sizes in the available trials have made it impossible to parse the variables necessary to adequately examine this.

2   We still have very little knowledge about predictors of response to specific therapies or parts of therapies, or how therapies actually work. Prediction, mediation and moderation must be meaningfully examined to understand mechanisms. These are difficult issues to address because of sample size, cost, and the statistical methodologies involved, in that the process of studying such variables is still evolving. Therefore it is difficult to move forward with therapeutic techniques, except on a theoretical basis. This will continue until we actually know what changes mediate and moderate the effects of therapy and what variables predict response.

3   As has been widely recognized in recent years, clinical trials have demonstrated the efficacy of therapies for a variety of disorders including BED, yet these are not routinely employed in clinical practice. While some practitioners espouse a particular therapeutic orientation, many use amalgams of techniques acquired through professional training, continuing education workshops, and reading, and very rarely use manual-based therapies in the form in which they were studied. There are a number of reasons for this. First is the tension between tailoring treatment to the individual patient using familiar practices vs. employing a manual-based treatment in the form in which its efficacy has been demonstrated. Second, training is expensive and time consuming, and many existing psychotherapy training programs across disciplines do not yet include these approaches. The barriers to collaboration between clinical research and general practice communities must be understood and overcome. Fortunately, as detailed in the Introduction to Section 2, such efforts are underway.

4   Another major problem is the limited number of therapists, even in areas where the therapy network is well developed and practitioners are available. In many parts of the world, therapy is not available even to those with insurance or ability to pay out of pocket. There is a growing gulf between

what we know to work and what is actually available to patients. This cannot be addressed simply by training in available therapies but must additionally entail the implementation of methods of delivery of therapy that are far more cost effective and less dependent on the availability of individual practitioners. Such methods may include everything from telemedicine-based approaches, where therapy needs to be delivered to a distal area, to an increased utilization of group approaches, to manual- or computer-based self-help. The literature suggests that this is a growing yet largely untapped area where our expertise and our research have not caught up with the demand. To be able to meet the needs of our patients, not just now but in the future, we increasingly need to think about not only what we deliver but also how we can deliver therapy more widely and cost effectively.

What lies ahead for pharmacotherapy?

Although we posit specific linkages between given drugs and given illnesses, most of the psychopharmacological agents that we have currently are nonspecific in their effects, and not uncommonly used for a variety of psychiatric diagnoses. Often there are several theoretical reasons for applying drugs developed for one condition to the treatment of other conditions for which new pharmacotherapy approaches are desirable. Sometimes this proves successful, and sometimes not. The pattern holds true for BED in that several previously available agents have been tried, with generally encouraging results. In particular the serotonin reuptake inhibitors may impact substantially on binge eating behavior, although their benefits for weight loss are modest at best. There also has been a great deal of interest in drugs that target not only on binge eating but also weight. These include topiramate and zonisamide which are not currently and never will be approved by the Food and Drug Administration in the United States for BED because they are available as generic agents. Nonetheless they have significant effect on binge eating frequency and on weight. Several other drug classes, reflecting other theoretical mechanisms, have been studied, and some appear promising. These include GABA agonists, agents that antagonize the endogenous opioid system such as naloxone and naltrexone, and combinations of drugs targeting obesity that may also suppress binge eating, several of which are in the pipeline. However, a major problem remains: drugs that suppress binge eating for the most part have minimal effects on weight and vice versa. The exceptions to this rule, i.e. the weight-reducing drugs that also suppress binge eating, are at times difficult to use and can result in significant side effects and toxicity.

So how does one achieve substantial and prolonged weight loss and at the same time suppress or eliminate binge eating behavior? One avenue of investigation stems from our growing knowledge of the psychobiology of the control of eating and appetite, including overeating and binge eating. We have learned much the past ten years about both the central and peripheral mechanisms of appetite and weight regulation. We know now that there are separate but interconnected systems in the central nervous system, the peripheral nervous system, and the gut, and the number of chemical transmitters involved, in particular peptidergic substances which have been found to play important roles, continues to multiply. Our knowledge of these factors and how to manipulate them will contribute to effective and, ideally, specific pharmacological approaches to the treatment of binge eating disorder and obesity. Additionally, there has been a growing interest in the genetics of obesity and of binge eating and, despite the complexity, progress is being made.

Ultimately, the development of treatments for BED will rely on the confluence of scientific knowledge and clinical experience. This spans our psychosocial understanding of the disorder and the ways in which we can help patients achieve healthy change in their attitudes and behaviors, along with our biological knowledge of BED and its strong genetic and psychobiological components, perhaps modifiable through pharmacologicalor other means. The end result may be a combination of approaches. Despite the complexities involves this is an exciting time with potentially rewarding opportunities for more concerted and aggressive development of new treatment approaches.

The community response to BED

As reviewed above, we have witnessed, in a relatively short time, impressive progress in our understanding of BED, including its pathophysiology, diagnosis, and treatment, and we look forward to major advances, perhaps even significant reappraisals of our current understanding, in the years ahead. Yet, regardless of advances in our understanding, those affected by BED, including patients, carers, and clinicians, will only be served to the degree to which we as a community embrace the challenge of eradicating BED and promoting both healthy lifestyles and healthy attitudes toward our bodies. The phenomenal efforts in this direction by and on behalf of those affected by BED have been well described in this volume. In closing, we wish to highlight a few hallmarks of advocacy that serve both as indicators of how far we have come and as reminders of how far we still need to go.

Advocacy is recognizing need

A real advance in the past two decades has been the sophistication with which we are able to recognize the suffering of those who seek help for binge eating. Recognition goes beyond mere acknowledgement. As reflected in the opening dialogue in the Foreword, well-meaning acknowledgement falls short of the informed empathic understanding that we as clinicians must provide in order to be most effective in helping those in need. Even prior to treatment *per se*, recognition and expert diagnosis can be extremely therapeutic in its own right. The challenge for us in the years ahead, as clinicians and as a society, is to provide more refined and accurate recognition for those suffering with BED as a first step toward helping. While this may sound rather abstract, it is a capability that is based on extensive and in-depth communication among patients, clinicians, researchers, and the public, and the infrastructure for this is still in its early stages of development.

Advocacy is speaking with courage and listening with humility

We tend to think of advocacy as speaking – loudly and to whoever will listen. Indeed, the courage of our convictions is essential to effective advocacy, and much has been achieved by remaining on message with regard to the central principles reflected in the preceding chapters: that BED is a serious eating disorder that deserves recognition and treatment, that BED and obesity must not be conflated, that weight stigmatization cannot be tolerated. At the same time, a willingness to question our assumptions and to listen carefully is equally essential. As suggested in the dialogues that open and close this volume, it has only been through careful listening to one another on the part of researchers, patients, and clinicians that the BED diagnosis has been recognized and codified.

We are at a point at which our community is faced with a large and rising burden of illness resulting from unhealthy weight gain-promoting lifestyles, and at the same time tremendous distress and dysfunction stemming from weight stigmatization. The eating disorders community is sensitized to the adverse effects of naming obesity as the problem, of assuming that body size or shape necessarily reflects lifestyle, and of conflating disordered eating with body type. Along with conveying this understanding to our colleagues engaged in battling what has come to be known as the obesity epidemic, we are also challenged to listen carefully to their experience and their concerns, and to embrace them as ours. We have made progress in the past two decades in bringing the eating disorders and obesity communities together and, as reviewed in Chapter 7, in developing approaches to prevention that promote both psychological and physiological health; indeed, the two are undoubtedly synergistic. Much remains to be accomplished and the well-coordinated efforts of all concerned are required to substantially elevate the level well-being in our community, recognizing that medical and psychological dimensions are inextricably intertwined.

Advocacy is sharing knowledge and skills

Words are important. As well reviewed in the Introduction to Section 2, seemingly straightforward efforts such as "dissemination" of empirically-based treatments may be undercut by the implication, intended or not, of top-down uni-directional knowledge flow. Just as motivational interviewing has taught us that motivation exists in the dyad, so our efforts at fostering expertise must be based on not simply the appearance of sharing but rather the genuine sharing of knowledge and skills, recognizing that expertise comes in many forms and, in its most highly developed form, exists in the space between researcher, clinician, patient and carers. The "virtuous cycle" model introduced herein provides a valuable framework, and its application to all areas of endeavor, including etiology, diagnosis, treatment, and prevention, will be a major challenge in the years ahead.

Advocacy is engendering the collective will to change

Ultimately, what is true for the individual is true for the community: motivation is essential for change. Unfortunately, change is expensive, consuming time, energy and money. And, of course, attempts at unilateral motivation are no more successful in the community than at the individual level. Effective motivation requires engagement and, while many strides have been made toward community engagement, much greater unity and broader involvement is possible. It is our hope that this volume represents a step in the direction of engagement of clinicians, researchers, patients, carers, policy makers, and members of the community in a joint endeavor to eliminate BED. To the degree that it promotes conversation among all of us whose lives are touched by BED, its purpose will have been well served.

Index